Devotional Refrains in Medieval Latin Song

Throughout medieval Europe, male and female religious communities attached to churches, abbeys, and schools participated in devotional music making outside of the chanted liturgy. Newly collating over 400 songs from primary sources, this book reveals the role of Latin refrains and refrain songs in the musical lives of religious communities by employing novel interdisciplinary and analytical approaches to the study of medieval song. Through interpretive frameworks focused on time and temporality, performance, memory, inscription, and language, each chapter offers an original perspective on how refrains were created, transmitted, and performed. Arguing for its significance as a marker of form and meaning, this book identifies the Latin refrain as a tool that communities used to negotiate their lived experiences of liturgical and calendrical time; to confirm their communal identity and belonging to song communities; and to navigate relationships between Latin and vernacular song and dance that emerge within their multilingual contexts.

MARY CHANNEN CALDWELL'S research focusing on medieval song, liturgy, pedagogy, and intertextuality has been published in the *Journal of the American Musicological Society, Music & Letters*, the *Journal of the Royal Musical Association, Plainsong & Medieval Music*, and *Early Music History*. She is an Assistant Professor of Music at the University of Pennsylvania.

T0381887

Devotional Refrains in Medieval Latin Song

———

MARY CHANNEN CALDWELL

University of Pennsylvania

CAMBRIDGE
UNIVERSITY PRESS

Shaftesbury Road, Cambridge CB2 8EA, United Kingdom

One Liberty Plaza, 20th Floor, New York, NY 10006, USA

477 Williamstown Road, Port Melbourne, VIC 3207, Australia

314–321, 3rd Floor, Plot 3, Splendor Forum, Jasola District Centre, New Delhi – 110025, India

103 Penang Road, #05–06/07, Visioncrest Commercial, Singapore 238467

Cambridge University Press is part of Cambridge University Press & Assessment, a department of the University of Cambridge.

We share the University's mission to contribute to society through the pursuit of education, learning and research at the highest international levels of excellence.

www.cambridge.org
Information on this title: www.cambridge.org/9781009044004

DOI: 10.1017/9781009043298

First published 2022
First paperback edition 2024

A catalogue record for this publication is available from the British Library

Library of Congress Cataloging-in-Publication data
Names: Caldwell, Mary Channen, 1983– author.
Title: Devotional refrains in medieval Latin song / Mary Channen Caldwell.
Description: [1.] | New York : Cambridge University Press, 2022. | Includes bibliographical references and index.
Identifiers: LCCN 2021044763 (print) | LCCN 2021044764 (ebook) | ISBN 9781316517192 (hardback) | ISBN 9781009043298 (ebook)
Subjects: LCSH: Songs, Latin (Medieval and modern) – 500–1400 – History and criticism. | Sacred vocal music – 500–1400 – History and criticism. | Refrain. | BISAC: MUSIC / General
Classification: LCC ML190 .C25 2022 (print) | LCC ML190 (ebook) | DDC 782.2/0902–dc23
LC record available at https://lccn.loc.gov/2021044763
LC ebook record available at https://lccn.loc.gov/2021044764

ISBN   978-1-316-51719-2   Hardback
ISBN   978-1-009-04400-4   Paperback

Cambridge University Press & Assessment has no responsibility for the persistence or accuracy of URLs for external or third-party internet websites referred to in this publication and does not guarantee that any content on such websites is, or will remain, accurate or appropriate.

For Daniel, Ella, and Max

Contents

Figures

Tables

Music Examples

Acknowledgments

This book is the result of years of work carried out with the input and assistance of countless colleagues and institutions. I am especially indebted to the support of the many libraries and librarians who have helped me access the manuscripts and archival sources at the core of this book. Fellowships and research support from the John Anson Kittredge Fund and the University of Pennsylvania enabled research trips and the acquisition of materials that have made their way into the following pages. The Wolf Humanities Center at the University of Pennsylvania funded a Manuscript Development Workshop in 2020 which, although delayed due to COVID-19, eventually made possible the workshopping of an early draft of the entire book by Ardis Butterfield, whose generous and thoughtful input significantly shaped its final form. Material from Chapter 4 is reproduced here through the generosity of the *Journal of the Royal Musical Association*, in which it was published as Mary Channen Caldwell, "Cueing Refrains in the Medieval Conductus," *Journal of the Royal Musical Association* 143 no. 2 (2018): 273–324.

I began developing this project as a doctoral student at the University of Chicago under the advising of Anne Walters Robertson, Robert Kendrick, and Lawrence Zbikowski, and I have unending appreciation for their continued support and encouragement. Although the roots of this book are to be found in my graduate studies, the seeds of my interest in early music and dance were planted long ago. First, in my younger years, by my piano teacher, and a historian in his own right, Peter McKinnon, and my longtime dance teacher, Beverley Brown-Chislett. During my undergraduate program at Queen's University in Kingston, Ontario, Dr. Olga Malyshko inspired my interest in early music and taught me discipline in research, while Dr. Gordon Smith encouraged my work in dance studies.

I have changed affiliations several times while working on this book, with visiting positions at Williams College in Williamstown, MA and at the University of Texas at Austin, and an assistant professorship at Wichita State University, before taking up my current position as assistant professor of music at the University of Pennsylvania. I am deeply thankful for the support of my colleagues and departments at each of these institutions. In the Music Department at the University of Pennsylvania, the always-vital staff – Maryellen Malek, Margaret Smith Deeney, Alfreda Frazier, Jacquelyn Jordan, and Madeleine Hewitt – have made all things possible in the realm of academics and teaching and have also been my companions during long days of work in the department. My colleagues past and present, Mauro Calcagno, Glenda Goodman, Jeffrey Kallberg, Jairo Moreno, Carol Muller, Guthrie Ramsey, Timothy Rommen, Jim Sykes, Anna Weesner, Eugene Lew, Michael Ketner, Jamuna Samuel, Natacha Diels, Tyshawn Sorey, Naomi Waltham-Smith, and Jay Reise, have variously mentored, encouraged, and assisted me in manifold ways during my time at Penn; I'm grateful to be part of this generous and warm intellectual community. My colleague, pianist and composer James Primosch, passed away during the final stages of this book, and he will be dearly missed by all. Over the years I've also been fortunate to lead and participate in seminars with graduate students at Penn across disciplines who have added to and challenged my way of thinking about early music; their insights and contributions are unquestionably reflected in these pages.

I have been privileged at Penn to work alongside and benefit from the knowledge and expertise of our music librarian Liza Vick and the special crew, past and present, of the sixth floor of Van Pelt library – Will Noel, Richard Griscom, Lynn Ransom, John Pollack, Lynn Farrington, Nick Herman, Mitch Fraas, and Elizabeth Bates, among others, all of whom are part of the vibrant Kislak Center for Special Collections, Rare Books and Manuscripts and the Schoenberg Institute for Manuscript Studies. Within the University more broadly, I am happily part of the ever-expanding Global Medieval and Renaissance Studies group, and I have benefited enormously from the collegiality of many colleagues working on premodern areas, most especially Julia Verkholantsev, Emily Steiner, Rita Copeland, and Kevin Brownlee. Finally, Penn's Medieval-Renaissance Seminar in the English Department kindly workshopped my book prospectus, and the Workshop in the History of Material Texts generously hosted me for a discussion of work that appears in Chapter 4.

I have also been extremely lucky in my cohort here at Penn. Not only did I begin in the Music Department the same year as Glenda Goodman, now my friend and colleague, but I also began within a year of medievalists Ada Kuskowksi and Sarah Guérin. In addition to organizing a conference together on the "Gothic Arts" (2018), the three of us have shared writing over the years and had many a lively lunch together; as well as being brilliant colleagues and friends, insights from their respective disciplines (history and art) have been invaluable in shaping my work in this book and on other projects. Although only indirectly connected to this book, working with Mauro Calcagno and the staff of the Kislak Center at Penn's library on the Music in the Pavilion concert series has been a real joy, and a way that our shared love of early music and material culture has found a public-facing outlet through the years.

Numerous colleagues have generously shared their knowledge with me over the years. Special thanks are owed to Martha Sprigge, Michelle Urberg, Glenda Goodman, Emma Dillon, Kate van Orden, Mark Everist, and Anne Walters Robertson for reading drafts of my prospectus; Meghan Quinlan, Sarah Guérin, and Ada Kuskowski for reading chapter drafts; and Cesar Favila for continued support and for enabling a fruitful and stimulating visit to UCLA in winter 2019, where I presented material from Chapter 5. Emma Dillon, Rebecca Maloy, Anne Walters Robertson, and Timothy Rommen have been diligent supporters and readers of my writing over the years, and I appreciate their efforts on my behalf and their input on my work and career. I owe a huge debt and my most sincere thanks to Jennifer Saltzstein and Mark Everist, each of whom read a draft of the manuscript in its entirety and improved it enormously. JoAnn Taricani graciously invited me to participate in a symposium on lyric cultures at the University of Washington (2019), where I shared work that appears in Chapter 5, and Martha Sprigge kindly invited me to present work appearing in Chapter 4 at the University of California, Santa Barbara (2018). At a late-stage Wulf Arlt also offered feedback and generously assisted in tracking down much-needed citations. Conference papers at the Medieval and Renaissance Music Conference (2017), AMS Annual Meeting (2017), Renaissance Society of America Annual Meeting (2017), and AMS-Southwest Spring Chapter Meeting (2014) all led to useful discussions around material that appears throughout this book.

The process of publishing a first book is long and full of unknowns, but Dr. Katharina Brett and Hal Churchman at Cambridge University Press supported this book through the review and publication process with consistent feedback, support, and encouragement. Nigel Graves and Raghavi Govindane then guided the book through the production process, and Frances Tye's copy editing was crucial; I thank them all for making this process both possible and enjoyable. Bonnie Blackburn copy-edited the entire manuscript at an earlier stage and made sure that embarrassing errors were eliminated, and Jennifer Ottman polished many of the translations; whatever errors remain are mine alone.

It takes a village to write a book and raise a family, and I've been lucky to have villages to help with both. Here in Philadelphia, our neighborhood community, and especially the Neukrugs, have been touchstones for us as well as an extended family. The childcare providers at the Parent Infant Center have cared for and loved both of my children over the years, a privilege for which I remain eternally thankful, and Jesse Schuschu, Debbie Larson, and Susana Fattorini have been beloved caregivers, enabling me to have time for research and writing. Many people have witnessed, and contributed to, the efforts of the past decade, including James Blasina, Marcelle Pierson, Trent Leipert, Michelle Urberg, Rob Walsh, Dawn Teele, Barrett Bridenhagen and Marc Meredith, Theodore van Loan, Jeffrey Wayno, Yossi Maurey, Catherine Saucier, Andrew Cashner, Thomas Payne, Melanie Shaffer, Anne-Zoé Rillon-Marne, Christopher Chaguinian, Catherine Bradley, Flannery Cunningham, Erika Honisch, Amy Williamson, Gregorio Bevilacqua, Océane Boudeau, and many others who have served as friends, colleagues, and interlocuters over the years in different ways – thank you for the conversation and support. I'm especially grateful for Martha Sprigge and Mariusz Kozak, and their respective spouses Ben Levy and Johanna Kozak: friends in academia as well as real life, and I wouldn't want it any other way. Closer to family than friends, Samantha Shaw, Meghan Leadbeater, and Sarah Bennett have been constants for so many years; I adore growing up with you.

I would not have pursued music or a graduate degree without the support of my family, and especially my parents, Esther Dawn Caldwell (née Skidmore) (1946–2007) and William Brian Caldwell (1950–2018), who are dearly missed. My brothers, Ian Caldwell and David Caldwell, have been longtime friends and teasing companions, and I am grateful through them to have gained Natasha Caldwell and Julie Williams as sisters as well as my two nieces, Viola and Liesl Caldwell. To my aunt, Dakshina Clark, you continue to be the person that knows me best; thank you for always being there. I feel privileged to have, and have had, special grandparents who offered unconditional love: my paternal grandparents Ellard Stitt and Frances Stitt (née O'Shaughnessy) and my maternal grandparents Ethel Ball (née Gillespie) and Esmond Skidmore, the last encouraging my pursuit of music. Through my husband Daniel Steinberg, I also gained another family: my mother-in-law Carol Warshawsky, who has been like a mother to me; my parents-in-law Michael Steinberg and Katharina Galor, who have provided wisdom and love in career and life; and my siblings-in-law Andrew, James, and Anna, who have been patient, caring, and supportive. My two grandmothers-in-law, Suzanne Steinberg and Sarita Warshawsky, were and are special role models for me as strong, intellectual women and mothers. Both my own extended family and Daniel's – cousins, aunts, uncles, and beyond – have been an integral part of our support system over the years, enabling us to live our hectic life, pursue careers, and raise our children.

This book is dedicated to my husband, Daniel, and our children, Isabel and Maxwell (and to our ever-patient dog Mal). It is thanks to the support and love of my family that this book came into being, and I am forever grateful to Daniel for creating the time and space to make not just this book, but my career as a whole possible.

Abbreviations

Manuscript Sigla

Antiphonarium Lausannense III.3.1	Freiburg, Kapitelsarchiv St. Niklaus, CSN III.3.1
Antiphonarium Lausannense III.3.2	Freiburg, Kapitelsarchiv St. Niklaus, CSN III.3.2
Antiphonarium Lausannense vol. 1	Estavayer-le-Lac, Paroisse catholique Saint-Laurent, vol. I
Aosta Cod. 11	Aosta, Seminario Maggiore, Biblioteca, Cod. 11
Aosta Cod. 13	Aosta, Seminario Maggiore, Biblioteca, Cod. 13
Apt 6	Apt, Basilique Sainte-Anne, Trésor, MS 6
Arundel 248	London, British Library, MS Arundel 248
Autun S 175^{10}	Autun, Bibliothèque municipale, S 175^{10}
Basel B.XI.8	Basel, Universitätsbibliothek, Musiksammlung, B.XI.8
Bekynton Anthology	Oxford, Bodleian Library, MS Add. A.44
Berlin 1996	Berlin, Staatsbibliothek zu Berlin Preußischer Kulturbesitz, MS Phillips 1996
Bobbio	Turin, Biblioteca nazionale, MS F.I.4
Bord 283	Bordeaux, Bibliothèque municipale, MS 283
Brugge 111/178	Brugge, Grootseminarie, 111/178

Brussels 5649–5667	Brussels, Koninklijke Bibliotheek België (Bibliothèque royale de Belgique), MS 5649–5667
Cambridge R.9.11	Cambridge, Trinity College, MS R.9.11
Cambridge Songs	Cambridge, University Library, MS Gg.V.35
Cantigas de Santa María	El Escorial, Real Monasterio de El Escorial, MS b.1.2
Carmina Burana	Munich, Bayerische Staatsbibliothek, clm 4660–4660a
Chansonnier de Clairambault	Paris, Bibliothèque nationale de France, n.a.f. 1050
Chansonnier de Noailles	Paris, Bibliothèque nationale de France, fr. 12615
Charleville 190	Charleville, Bibliothèque municipale, MS 190
Codex Calixtinus	Santiago de Compostela, Archivo-Biblioteca de la Catedral, MS s.s.
Codex Sangallensis	Sankt Gallen, Stiftsbibliothek, MS 546
Colmar 187	Colmar, Bibliothèque municipale, MS 187
Cologne 196	Cologne, Erzbischöfliche Diözesan- und Dombibliothek, Cod. 196
Douce 308	Oxford, Bodleian Library, Douce 308
Engelberg 102	Engelberg, Stiftsbibliothek, MS 102
Engelberg 1003	Engelberg, Stiftsbibliothek, MS 1003
Engelberg Codex	Engelberg, Stiftsbibliothek, MS 314
Erfurt Codex	Erfurt, Stadtarchiv, Ampl. quart MS 332
F	Florence, Biblioteca Medicea Laurenziana, Pluteus 29.1
Fauvel	Paris, Bibliothèque nationale de France, fr. 146
Graz 258	Graz, Universitätsbibliothek, MS 258
Graz 409	Graz, Universitätsbibliothek, MS 409
Harley 978	London, British Library, Harley 978
Harley 1010	London, British Library, Harley 1010

Hortus Deliciarum	Hortus Deliciarum (destroyed; folios follow Green, ed., *Herrad of Hohenbourg*)
Hu	Burgos, Monasterio de Las Huelgas, MS 9
Klagenfurt Perg. 7	Klagenfurt, Studienbibliothek, Perg. 7
Laon 263	Laon, Bibliothèque municipale, MS 263
Later Cambridge Songbook	Cambridge, University Library, Ff. I.17
Le Puy A	Grenoble, Bibliothèque municipale, MS 4413
Le Puy B	Le Puy-en-Velay, Bibliothèque du Grand Séminaire, s.n.
Leipzig 225	Leipzig, Universitätsbibliothek, MS 225
Llibre Vermell	Montserrat, Monasterio de Santa Maria, MS 1
LoA	London, British Library, Egerton 2615
LoB	London, British Library, Egerton 274
Ludus super Anticlaudianum	Lille, Bibliothèque municipale Jean Levy, MS 316
Luxembourg 27	Luxembourg, Bibliothèque nationale de Luxembourg, MS 27
Ma	Madrid, Biblioteca Nacional de España, MS 20486
Mad 288	Madrid, Biblioteca Nacional de España, MS 288
Mad 289	Madrid, Biblioteca Nacional de España, MS 289
Mad 19421	Madrid, Biblioteca Nacional de España, MS 19421
Metz 535	Metz, Bibliothèque municipale, MS 535
Mo	Montpellier, Bibliothèque Inter-Universitaire, Section Médecine, H196

Moosburger Graduale	Munich, Universitätsbibliothek, Cim. 100
MüC	Munich, Bayerische Staatsbibliothek, clm 5539
Munich 16444	Munich, Bayerische Staatsbibliothek, clm 16444
Munich 21053	Munich, Bayerische Staatsbibliothek, clm 21053
Munich Cg. 42	Munich, Bayerische Staatsbibliothek, Cg. 42
Munich cgm. 1113	Munich, Bayerische Staatsbibliothek, cgm. 1113
OBod 937	Oxford, Bodleian Library, Bodley 937
OCCC 2*	Oxford, Corpus Christi College, MS 2*
ORawl	Oxford, Bodleian Library, Rawlinson C.510
Paris fr. 372	Paris, Bibliothèque nationale de France, fr. 372
Paris fr. 1581	Paris, Bibliothèque nationale de France, fr. 1581
Paris fr. 1593	Paris, Bibliothèque nationale de France, fr. 1593
Paris fr. 2090–2092	Paris, Bibliothèque nationale de France, fr. 2090–2092
Paris fr. 23111	Paris, Bibliothèque nationale de France, fr. 23111
Paris lat. 1112	Paris, Bibliothèque nationale de France, lat. 1112
Paris lat. 1154	Paris, Bibliothèque nationale de France, lat. 1154
Paris lat. 4880	Paris, Bibliothèque nationale de France, lat. 4880
Paris lat. 11331	Paris, Bibliothèque nationale de France, lat. 11331
Paris lat. 13091	Paris, Bibliothèque nationale de France, lat. 13091
Paris lat. 15181	Paris, Bibliothèque nationale de France, lat. 15181

Paris lat. 16663	Paris, Bibliothèque nationale de France, lat. 16663
Paris n.a.l. 426	Paris, Bibliothèque nationale de France, n.a.l. 426
Prague XIII.H.3 c	Prague, Univerzitní Knihovna, MS XIII.H.3c
Red Book of Ossory	Dublin, Representative Church Body Library, D11/1.2
Royal 7.A.VI	London, British Library, Royal 7.A.VI
Saint Omer 351	Saint Omer, Bibliothèque municipale, MS 351
Seckauer Cantionarium	Graz, Universitätsbibliothek, MS 756
Sens 46	Sens, Bibliothèque municipale, MS 46
SG 382	Sankt Gallen, Stiftsbibliothek, MS 382
SG 383	Sankt Gallen, Stiftsbibliothek, MS 383
SG 392	Sankt Gallen, Stiftsbibliothek, MS 392
SG 1397	Sankt Gallen, Stiftsbibliothek, MS 1397
Sloane 2593	London, British Library, Sloane 2593
St-M A	Paris, Bibliothèque nationale de France, lat. 1139
St-M B	Paris, Bibliothèque nationale de France, lat. 3549
St-M C	Paris, Bibliothèque nationale de France, lat. 3719
St-M D	London, British Library, Add. 36881
St. Pölten Processional	St. Pölten, Diözesanarchiv, MS 13
St-Victor Miscellany	Paris, Bibliothèque nationale de France, lat. 15131
Stuttg	Stuttgart, Württembergische Landesbibliothek, HB I Asc. 95
StV	Paris, Bibliothèque nationale de France, lat. 15139
Tort	Tortosa, Catedral, Cód. 97
Tours 927	Tours, Bibliothèque municipale, MS 927

Trouv P	Paris, Bibliothèque nationale de France, fr. 847
Trouv U	Paris, Bibliothèque nationale de France, fr. 20050
Trouv W	Paris, Bibliothèque nationale de France, fr. 25566
Vienna 4494	Vienna, Österreichische Nationalbibliothek, MS 4494
W1	Wolfenbüttel, Herzog August Bibliothek, Cod. Guelf. 628 Helmst.
W2	Wolfenbüttel, Herzog August Bibliothek, Cod. Guelf. 1099 Helmst.
Zurich C. 58	Zurich, Zentralbibliothek, Musikabteilung, C. 58

Other Abbreviations

AH	*Analecta hymnica medii aevi*, 55 vols., ed. Guido Maria Dreves and Clemens Blume (Leipzig, 1886–1922). References are from Analecta hymnica Medii Aevi Digitalia (Erwin Rauner Verlag, webserver.erwin-rauner.de)
CCSL	Corpus Christianorum Series Latina (Turnhout: Brepols, 1953–)
CPI	*Cantum pulcriorem invenire*: Thirteenth-Century Music and Poetry, directed by Mark Everist and Gregorio Bevilacqua, University of Southampton, http://catalogue.conductus.ac.uk
Glossarium	Charles Du Fresne Du Cange, *Glossarium mediæ et infimæ latinitatis* (L. Favre, 1883–7) (accessed via ducange.enc.sorbonne.fr/)
GMO	*Grove Music Online*. www.oxfordmusiconline.com
Piae Cantiones (1582)	*Piae Cantiones Ecclesiasticae et Scholasticae Veterum Episcoporum ... ex Psalmis recentioribus*, ed. Theodoric Petri (Greifswald, 1582), repr. Chiswick Press, 1910.

Piae Cantiones (1625)	*Cantiones Piae et Antiquae Veterum Episcoporum & Pastorum … Cantiones quedam nova*, ed. Theodoric Petri et al. (Rostock, 1625).
PL	Patrologiae cursus completus, series Latina, 221 vols., ed. J. P. Migne (Paris, 1844–1879) (accessed via online database, Patrologia Latina: The Full Text Database (Chadwyck-Healey, Inc., 1996), http://pld.chadwyck.co.uk)
vdB	Nico H. J. van den Boogaard, *Rondeaux et refrains du XIIIe siècle au début du XIVe*, Bibliothèque française et romane, Série D: Initiation, textes et documents, 3 (Klincksieck, 1969).

Biblical citations are from the Latin Vulgate and Douay–Rheims translation (unless otherwise indicated); cited from Douay–Rheims Bible Online: www.drbo.org.

Introduction: Latin Song and Refrain

Within medieval Latin song, the refrain is a unit of text and music that repeats regularly in the course of an individual song. The refrain represents a moment of return, repetition, and remembering, the "re-" prefix signaling its functional and structural identity: the Latin refrain always repeats. The songs in which refrains appear typically feature rhymed, rhythmic, and largely devotional, yet generally nonliturgical, Latin poetry; songs are set to music for one or more voices, copied in manuscript sources beginning in the twelfth century, and transmitted as late as the sixteenth century in printed song anthologies. Identified as *conductus, versus, cantilena, cantio, prosa, planctus,* and *rondellus,* among other labels, in the Middle Ages and contemporary scholarship, medieval Latin songs easily number over 1,000, transmitted in hundreds of manuscript sources throughout Europe.[1] Songs with refrains comprise more than a third of this extensive repertoire, making the structural return of music and text one of the most significant formal features of medieval Latin song.[2]

This book takes the refrain as a starting point in the study of medieval Latin song culture, identifying the repetition of music and poetry as a locus for generating musical, poetic, and cultural meaning. By focusing on a formal feature, I purposefully seek continuities and connections in the creation, copying, and performance of Latin song across the Middle

---

[1] A precise tally is challenging to calculate due to the problems of defining scope and accounting for the variability of genre and function. Catalogues and inventories of *conductus* and *versus* do exist. *Cantum pulcriorem invenire* (hereafter *CPI*), directed by Mark Everist and Gregorio Bevilacqua, is the most recent inventory of the *conductus*. It updates Gordon Anderson's *Opera Omnia* for the *conductus*: Anderson, ed., *Notre-Dame and Related Conductus,* catalogued in Anderson, "Notre Dame and Related Conductus." Earlier inventories of the *conductus* can be found in Gröninger, *Repertoire* and Falck, *Notre Dame Conductus.* For the *versus* and songs referred to in modern scholarship as *nova cantica,* a new edition is underway by the Corpus Monodicum research group based at the University of Würzburg (directed by Andreas Haug): www.musikwissenschaft.uni-wuerzburg.de/forschung/corpus-monodicum.

[2] See the Appendix. In constructing this archive of refrain songs – which should not be understood as exhaustive, but rather as always evolving – I am indebted to the existing catalogues, inventories, and scholarship cited in the previous note. However, my conclusions and definition of scope differ from these in many cases, and the Appendix includes sources and songs yet to be accounted for or included in modern catalogues.

Ages. This approach contrasts with previous scholarship, which has tended to privilege genre, individual manuscripts or sources, polyphonic settings, and authorship as rubrics for categorization and analysis, as a result eliding songs and sources that fall outside of these variously medieval and modern parameters. In this book, I am not interested in defining a new subgenre, or in rejecting the utility of previous scholarly paradigms. Rather, placing the refrain at the center of inquiry allows an examination of the materiality, performance, and cultural meaning of Latin song that captures both its transregional and local creation and transmission, as well as its generic fluidity.

There is no singular meaning or interpretation possible for the Latin refrain beyond its identity as a repeated unit of music and text. Like medieval Latin song more broadly, songs with refrains – for which I use the general term "refrain songs" – looked, sounded, and functioned differently depending on where and by whom they were created, copied, and sung. Yet at the same time, commonalities emerge, namely shared stylistic and poetic traits, performance rituals, or manuscript contexts that overtly acknowledge the refrain as a formal component capable of shaping and conveying a particular set of meanings. Throughout this book I move between unique or exceptional, and shared or universal examples, highlighting what each might tell us about both the Latin refrain and devotional song culture in the Middle Ages. I begin by asking what the refrain is and what it does in medieval Latin song. In other words, what distinguishes a song with a refrain from one without a refrain, and is this distinction meaningful from a medieval perspective or as an analytical tool? How do refrains alter or inflect the performance and transmission of songs? In what way do refrains signal cultural or ritual meanings that are different from those of songs without refrains? What can refrains tell us about medieval song cultures more broadly, not only encompassing Latin song alone, but also refrain forms in vernacular song? When, how, and by whom were Latin refrain songs performed?

These are questions that have rarely been asked, not only about refrain song, but in most cases about medieval Latin song more generally. Only recently has Latin song begun to receive serious analytical and interpretive attention beyond cataloguing and editing, both of which have represented central scholarly concerns and efforts for over a century. The work of musicologists Mark Everist, Thomas Payne, Anne-Zoé Rillon-Marne, Andreas Haug, Helen Deeming, and Rachel May Golden, among others, has begun moving the study of Latin song, and especially the *conductus* and *versus*, toward a deeper engagement with song's cultural work and embedment in medieval communities, whether populated by intellectuals, preachers, clerics, or students.[3]

For the refrain in medieval Latin song, Margaret Switten and Andreas Haug have offered productive models for analysis, both with a focus on the twelfth-century *versus*. Switten compares refrains in the *versus* with those in troubadour song, examining the range of ways in which refrains manifested compositionally between languages to different effects and performative ends.[4] Haug, by contrast, focuses on Latin song, with only brief references to vernacular song, and differentiates between what he terms "real" and "virtual" refrains.[5] The former consists of a ritual and responsorial component of "old" Latin liturgical song that carries over to "new" song of the twelfth century (namely, *versus*). The "virtual refrain," comprising short repeated sounds and words, or grammatical features, emerges alongside the "real refrain" as an aesthetic feature of the "new" song. While Haug and Switten offer important insights into the medieval Latin refrain, their focus on the twelfth-century *versus* leaves the majority of refrains and refrain songs unexamined and undertheorized.

The relative paucity of research on Latin song and refrain is striking in comparison with the sheer volume of work dealing with vernacular song, especially the French *chanson* and, above all, the *refrain*.[6] The French *refrain* of the thirteenth century has rightfully been a focal point in studies of medieval song, with musicologists and literary scholars alike offering a range of interpretations of the structural, aphoristic, citational, and intertextual French *refrain* located in song, romance, and the motet.[7] Although comparing the French *refrain* to the Latin refrain is, in most cases, like comparing apples to oranges, the *refrain* is inextricably linked to

---

[3] The Bibliography and notes for this book paint a more complete picture of scholarship on Latin song; however, see, for example, the recent book-length study of the *conductus* by Everist, *Discovering Medieval Song*; Payne, "Poetry, Politics, and Polyphony," "*Aurelianus civitas*," and "Chancellor *versus* Bishop"; Rillon-Marne, *Homo considera*; and Golden, *Mapping*. The collected essays in Deeming and Leach, eds., *Manuscripts and Medieval Song*, also include several manuscripts transmitting Latin song, and Deeming herself has published numerous articles dealing with Latin as well as vernacular song, employing a range of methodologies.

[4] Switten, "Versus and Troubadours."

[5] Haug, "Ritual and Repetition" and "Musikalische Lyrik."

[6] Judith Peraino's point regarding terminology around the *refrain* and its italicization is well taken, in that she avoids italicization of "refrain" when referring to its "autonomous" as opposed to structural role. See Peraino, "*Et pui conmencha a canter*," 1 n. 1. For the purposes of clarity, however, I use italics for refrains in French contexts as opposed to in Latin song; refrains in other vernaculars are identified by the specific language. Throughout, abbreviations are expanded without notice and spelling of all original texts conforms to individual manuscripts.

[7] For scholarship and bibliography on the French refrain, see Butterfield, *Poetry and Music*; Ibos-Augé, *Chanter et lire*; and Saltzstein, *Refrain*.

Latin refrains due to processes of contrafacture explicitly connecting refrains across language. Latin refrains, however, cannot be understood or interpreted using the same methodologies used for the *refrain*; the mechanisms by which the Latin refrain was employed in song, and its transmission, performance, and meaning, are vastly different from those of the *refrain*.

First and foremost, the *refrain* repeats structurally within individual songs but it also travels independently between genres, without necessitating repetition either within songs or among different contexts for its identification.[8] In this regard, the *refrain* represents a singular phenomenon in medieval music, poetry, and literature. By contrast, repetition is a *sine qua non* for the Latin refrain. Moreover, although the French *refrain* is often positioned as a vernacular touchstone for the Latin refrain, a fuller examination of the body of Latin refrain songs reveals connections among refrains and refrain songs in several languages. In this book I grapple with the complex relationship of the Latin refrain not only to the French *refrain*, but also to refrains in English and German. As extensive scholarship on the French *refrain* has usefully illustrated, however, what refrains mean and what role they play in song and culture depends on many factors, not all of which apply equally across language.

Defining the Latin Refrain

Genre is the most contentious factor in the historiography of Latin song. Although the categories of *versus*, *conductus*, and the term coined in the twentieth century, *nova cantica*, each have historiographical traditions and, in the case of the first two, medieval support in the form of theoretical discussions and scribal rubrication, Latin songs go by many different names in medieval and modern contexts, making it challenging to connect terms to specific works.[9] The limits of a single genre are also complicated by transmission patterns in which songs might be rubricated as *versus* in one source and *conductus* in another, or a *cantilena* in one and *prosa* in another. It is currently impossible to acquire complete repertorial control over genres of medieval Latin song; its edges and limits are constantly in flux

---

[8] On the role of repetition (or lack thereof) for the French *refrain*, see Saltzstein, *Refrain*; Butterfield, "Repetition and Variation"; and Doss-Quinby, *Les Refrains*.

[9] On medieval song genres and labels, and terminological challenges, see Strohm, "Late-Medieval Sacred Songs"; Stevens, *Words and Music*, 48–52; Reckow, "Conductus"; Falck, *Notre Dame Conductus*, 1–8; Gillingham, *Critical Study*, 49–55; and Deeming, "Latin Song I," 1023–1024.

and impacted by issues of source history and survival, and the status of cataloguing.

I have chosen to be inclusive in this book. The refrain songs discussed throughout this book and listed in the Appendix have most frequently been labeled by scholars, or rubricated in manuscripts, as *conductus, versus, rondellus,* and *cantilena,* and less often as *Benedicamus Domino* tropes and *prosas.* Although labels such as these will crop up at points in this book to clarify transmission history or issues of historiography, I use "song" to emphasize continuities among sources and contexts. In so doing, I do not intend to efface the particularities of specific genres, but instead focus attention on a formal aspect of Latin song that, more than other formal or stylistic features, traverses genre, time, and place. Justification for this inclusivity is found in the songs themselves and their manuscript transmission. Song concordances generate networks through-out the entire corpus of medieval Latin song and its sources, regardless of medieval and modern genre categories.

In opting for inclusivity, I have not avoided the challenges of defining an archive of Latin song. Decisions I have made beyond language (Latin) and form (refrain) include the nature of the poetry itself, namely the exclusion of the admittedly few metrical poems, and a focus instead on the more numerous *rithmi* – rhymed, rhythmical, accentual, and syllabically regular poems often set to music.[10] Less a choice and more by virtue of the repetition necessitated by refrains, nearly all the songs I consider are also strophic rather than through-composed. Most songs also survive with musical notation in at least one source, although not always; I have opted to include unnotated sources when there is either internal or external evidence suggesting the possibility of a musical rendering. In terms of temporal scope, I begin with the earliest collections of notated *rithmi* in the twelfth century, comprising manuscripts of songs commonly termed *nova cantica* and rubricated, depending on source, as *versus* and *conductus,* and conclude with the first printed sources for medieval song in the sixteenth century. This chronological scope is supported by a twelfth-century watershed in the composition of musical settings of largely devotional Latin *rithmi,* while the end date is defined by the first appearance of

---

[10] Notably, not all refrain song concordances retain the refrain, nor are all refrain songs monolingual. For definitions and overviews of the *rithmus,* see Fassler, "Accent"; Sanders, "Rithmus"; Page, *Latin Poetry,* 28–53; Norberg, *Introduction,* 81–129; and Everist, *Discovering Medieval Song,* 74–76 and *passim.* On later printed sources for medieval Latin song, see ibid., 280–281.

medieval Latin song in print, ushering in a novel – if understudied – history.[11]

The poetry of the Latin refrain song is chiefly devotional, dedicated to celebrating the liturgical and calendar year and favorite holy and saintly figures (see Chapters 1 and 2). This is a feature of medieval Latin song more broadly, and is amplified when limiting by form – nondevotional, satirical, polemical, topical, or amorous poems are in the minority when refrains are present. Consequently, although the corpus is inclusive, the following chapters deal exclusively with the more numerous devotional songs. Extraliturgical Latin songs, including those with refrains, share many formal, poetic, and contextual features beyond language with liturgical genres such as sequences, hymns, and tropes, and were also transmitted in several troped liturgies, particularly for the Feast of the Circumcision.[12]

One approach in previous scholarship has distinguished between liturgical and nonliturgical songs. This is problematic, however, given not only the inclusion of Latin songs in troped liturgies, but also the identity of many Latin songs as song-form tropes of Office versicles, most notably *Benedicamus Domino*.[13] I include, consequently, song-form tropes and reworkings as well as songs serving liturgical functions, so long as they feature a refrain and do not explicitly belong to a specific liturgical tradition other than troping; in other words, I exclude hymns or sequences while including song-form reworkings of both genres. In many cases, such works are transmitted alongside Latin refrain songs lacking specific liturgical designations, demonstrating scribal awareness of the close link between liturgical and devotional song.[14] Importantly, songs are not static. In one

---

[11] Beginning with twelfth-century song collections is complicated by the survival of earlier collections of Latin songs, such as the *versus* collection, including *rithmi* and metrical poetry, in Paris lat. 1154, or the Cambridge Songs. My rationale for excluding these from discussion rests in the patterns of transmission that link repertoires copied from the twelfth century onward, including songs copied in the Carmina Burana.

[12] On the mixture of Latin songs and tropes in troped liturgies for the Feast of the Circumcision, see Arlt, *Ein Festoffizium des Mittelalters*; "Office" and Boudeau, "La question des variantes." As Jeremy Llewellyn eloquently states with respect to the earliest twelfth- and thirteenth-century repertoires, "the *nova cantica* blossom within a context of troping: oftentimes they breathe in a performative synchrony with other, pre-existing texts," referring above all to the *Benedicamus Domino* versicle (see later in this Introduction); "Nova Cantica," 149.

[13] On the relationship between the *Benedicamus Domino* and Latin song, see Harrison, "Benedicamus, Conductus, Carol"; Arlt, *Ein Festoffizium des Mittelalters*, 1:160–206; Hiley, *Western Plainchant*, 213–215; Stevens, ed., *Later Cambridge Songs*, 27–29; and Everist, *Discovering Medieval Song*, 49–52 and 199–213.

[14] A similar choice is often made for the *versus*, and *nova cantica* more generally, supported by parallels in poetic form and musical construction between songs with and without a reference to, or citation of, the *Benedicamus Domino* versicle. See, for example, Fuller, "Aquitanian Polyphony," 1:22–27;

source, a song might conclude with the text of the *Benedicamus Domino* and in another the versicle text might be absent, exposing the permeability of genre and function within medieval Latin song (see Chapter 4).

The definition of a refrain as a unit of text and music that repeats, while simple, does not fully account for the spectrum of refrains and repetition in Latin song. As Haug's distinction between "real" and "virtual" refrains implies, the repetition of text, music, or text and music takes many forms. As a result, what constitutes a refrain in Latin song becomes another factor in demarcating boundaries. In this book I also allow the refrain to recur among songs as well as between strophes, but in these cases, it typically repeats structurally within its new context as well. I also include the structural repetition of music with a variable text in cases where it is clear that these sections functioned as a refrain based on musical and poetic form, rhetoric and scansion, or scribal cues. This does not entirely avoid thorny issues of identification and inconsistencies brought about by individual songs but, as I explore in Chapter 4, moments of inconsistency and ambiguity offer insights into the intricacies of the inscription and performance of Latin refrains and refrain forms. Finally, within single manuscripts, songs with refrains of varying lengths frequently sit side by side; the relative length of refrains is not a definitive marker of difference in terms of meaning or function.

Although texture – the number of voice parts – has frequently, and rightly, defined boundaries of study within medieval Latin song, refrain songs survive both in monophonic and polyphonic settings, with an emphasis on the former. In rare cases, songs survive in both single- and multi-voice settings, or refrain and strophes can be set in contrasting textures (see Chapter 3). Notably, texture does not necessarily correlate with the relative length or complexity of refrains. Monophonic and polyphonic settings both include examples of shorter and longer refrains of varying complexity in terms of poetry and music. The skill levels necessitated by musical settings of refrain songs are also variable, although the emphasis on monophony is paralleled by an emphasis on syllabic settings and singable melodies featuring narrow ranges and limited intervals. Only a handful of refrain songs include elaborate melismas (including *caudae*) or feature intricate musical settings, whether monophonic or polyphonic. By and large, this is a repertoire of repetitive, tuneful, and singable songs, approachable by amateurs and trained singers alike. And for all that refrain

note, however, possible stylistic distinctions discussed in Marshall, "A Late Eleventh-Century Manuscript," 71–100 and Carlson, "Devotion to the Virgin Mary," 1:26–29.

songs have been mostly overlooked by scholars, modern performers and ensembles have long recognized their musical and poetic value.[15]

In terms of meter and rhythm, musical settings of refrain songs are typically notated in nonmensural or unmeasured notation, occasionally at odds with the clear and regular rhythmic patterning of their poetry. Following the work of Christopher Page and Mark Everist in particular, I transcribe unmeasured notation in a rhythmically neutral fashion, unless the notation is either explicitly modal or mensural (for example, in polyphonic *caudae* in thirteenth-century repertoires or mensurally notated works in fourteenth- and fifteenth-century songbooks).[16] Mensural or metrical notation is an exception, however, and the rhythmic feel of the songs in performance stems from the regular rhythm and accent pattern of the *rithmus*, and not from the musical notation.[17]

Melody parallels form in the Latin refrain song, its contours shaping and following the poetry. Text–music relationships in the repertoire range from highly expressive to virtually formulaic and, for the most part, these distinctions do not align cleanly with factors such as genre, function, or transmission.[18] A central concern in analyzing the music and poetry of refrain forms, however, is the relationship between strophic material and refrain material. Since nearly all refrain songs are strophic, repetition occurs musically in both strophes and refrain; literal repetition of text typically only occurs in the refrain, although certain songs may feature various levels of repetitive wordplay in strophes, edging closer to Haug's "virtual" refrain. Although factors such as length, texture, complexity, and text setting can be helpful in classifying refrain songs, examining the structure of the refrain's repetition within individual songs points toward two main categories of refrain songs: (1) songs in which refrains are sung between individual strophes (which I term strophic+refrain) and (2) songs in which the refrain, or a part thereof, occurs both within and between individual strophes.

---

[15] As Christopher Page writes, many Latin refrain songs have "bold and ingratiating musical settings" that appeal to a range of listeners (*Voices and Instruments*, 88), an assertion backed up by the frequent recording of refrain songs by early-music ensembles.

[16] Page, *Latin Poetry*; and Everist, *Discovering Medieval Song*.

[17] On mensural notation and Latin song, see Everist, *Discovering Medieval Song*, 283–294, and for a more general overview, Strohm, "Sacred Song."

[18] Wulf Arlt in particular has explored music–text relationships in *nova cantica*; see "Nova cantica." On the *versus* alone, see Carlson, "Striking Ornaments" and "Two Paths." For the *conductus*, see especially Rillon-Marne, *Homo considera*, and Everist, *Discovering Medieval Song*, 151–180 and *passim*. See also several articles and chapters by Helen Deeming dealing precisely with the question of how music and text work together in Latin song, exemplified in Deeming, "Music and Contemplation."

The former is by far the most common form for Latin refrain songs, recognizable as a verse–chorus form that characterizes many song repertoires. The latter is a more specific formal structure that shares many similarities with the medieval French *rondeau*, taking the musical and poetic form of aAabAB or ABaABabAB, or variations thereof – the partial repetition of the refrain within individual strophes is the main marker of the *rondeau*. Many songs, for instance, take the form aAbB, which Hans Spanke refers to in his study of Latin *rondeaux* as the embryonic form of the *rondeau*; for Spanke, all permutations of the *rondeau* with its "Binnenrefrain" ("internal refrain") are related to this basic shape.[19] The presence of an internal refrain, consequently, establishes a key formal difference among Latin songs, a difference I retain here. Moreover, similarities between the French *rondeau* and some Latin refrain songs have led to the contemporary label of *rondellus* (plural *rondelli*), a Latinization of *rondeau*, a term I employ throughout this book to differentiate between song forms.[20] Following Spanke and others, I identify *rondelli* as songs in which one or more lines of the refrain are inserted within strophes as an "internal refrain," as well as occurring at the beginning and/or end of strophes.

Rondelli represent roughly 20 percent of refrain songs, with ninety-six extant works in the Appendix, although they are among the most cited and edited.[21] The formal similarity of the *rondellus* to the French *rondeau* has led to numerous theories positing a strong directionality between the two brought about, variously, by contrafacture, shared authorship, or influence. The precise directionality of the relationship between Latin *rondelli* and French *rondeaux* remains unclear and, to a degree, matters less than

---

[19] Spanke, "Das lateinische Rondeau," 131–132.

[20] Modern scholarship has labeled *rondeau*-form Latin songs *rondelli* starting with Friedrich Ludwig in his *Repertorium*; see Ludwig, *Repertorium*, 1:124–125. For its recent use, see Everist, *Discovering Medieval Song*, 22. Not all scholars adopt the Latin term; some refer to these songs as "Latin *rondeaux*"; see Spanke, "Das lateinische Rondeau" and Anderson, ed., *Notre-Dame and Related Conductus*, vol. 8. The term *rondellus* as used here should not be confused with the compositional technique of voice exchange described by music theorists; see Sanders, "Rondellus," *GMO*; Falck, "'Rondellus', Canon, and Related Types"; and Reckow, "Rondellus/ rondeau, rota."

[21] Scholars and editors often limit investigation of Latin refrain forms to *rondelli*, and even more often to the final fascicle of F, effectively limiting the repertoire to fewer than sixty songs; see, for instance, Aubry, *La Musique et les musiciens d'église*, 45–51; Spanke, "Das lateinische Rondeau"; Rokseth, "Danses clericales"; Aubrey, "The Eleventh Fascicle"; Falck, *Notre Dame Conductus*, 123–129; Stevens, *Words and Music*, 178–186; Page, *Voices and Instruments*, 88–91; Wright, *Maze and the Warrior*, 151–155; and Haines, *Medieval Song*, 67–75.

probing the complicated relationship between the two. The most striking characteristic of *rondelli* compared to strophic+refrain songs is where and how they are transmitted. *Rondelli* are transmitted in a narrow range of sources (see the following section) and, in each of these, songs tend to be clustered or otherwise organized deliberately according to form. In other words, scribes paid attention to form and, not just the presence of a refrain, but the nature of the refrain form itself. The tension between these two formal manifestations of refrains will arise throughout in this book in light of the implications of form for performance, interpretation, function, and the relationship of Latin and vernacular song.

Manuscript Sources

Manuscript and transmission history provide the best justification and support for the privileging of the refrain, as I have defined it, in medieval Latin song. Patterns of compilation and organization speak to a distinctively medieval desire to group like with like, resulting in several large collections of refrain-form songs. These are found in manuscripts copied in the thirteenth and fourteenth centuries; twelfth-century scribes showed less inclination to organize according to form. The pinnacle of the Latin refrain song in terms of individual sources is located in two manuscripts copied in thirteenth-century France: Tours 927 (copied between 1225 and 1245) and F (copied *ca.* 1240s–1250s). The former is well known for its preservation of an Easter play and the *Jeu d'Adam*, among other Latin and French texts and musical items; F is widely known among musicologists as a central source for Parisian polyphony and monophony, transmitting the *Magnus liber organi*, Latin motets, and *conducti.*[22] Notably, these two sources together transmit the greatest number of *rondelli*, as well as strophic+refrain songs. Tours 927 alone transmits thirty-one monophonic refrain songs (eighteen of which are *rondelli*) and F transmits fifty-five monophonic refrain songs in its final eleventh fascicle, fifteen of which are concordant with Tours 927 and forty-nine of which are *rondelli*. F transmits an additional twenty-two monophonic and polyphonic refrain-form works in earlier fascicles.

---

[22] The most recent reconsideration of Tours 927, including its dating, is in Chaguinian, ed., *The Jeu d'Adam*. The bibliography on F is extensive; for overviews on dating and citing pertinent scholarship, see Roesner, ed., *Antiphonarium*, 7–39; Haggh and Huglo, "Magnus liber"; and Williams, "Magnus Liber Organi." See also Bradley, "Contrafacta and Transcribed Motets" and *Polyphony in Medieval Paris.*

F and Tours 927 transmit a total of ninety-three refrain songs, the greatest number shared among the fewest sources, along with the greatest concentration of *rondelli*. Indicative of the Latin refrain song more broadly, the majority of works in Tours 927 and F are unique to one or both sources; however, when songs have concordances, they generally have several and are occasionally set both monophonically and polyphonically (see, for instance, *Luto carens et latere*, discussed in Chapter 3). F and Tours 927 are also significant for what they illustrate about scribal approaches to compiling refrain songs. In Tours 927, the songs are copied together one after the other, between the *Ludus paschalis* and *Jeu d'Adam*; in F, 55 of the refrain songs, many *rondelli*, are copied together in the final eleventh fascicle.[23] In both manuscripts, scribes noted formal parallels and deliberately gathered songs of similar forms together. This is most striking in F, in which two fascicles contain monophonic *conducti* (Fascicles X and XI), but *rondelli* are copied in Fascicle XI alone; as Everist writes, "differentiating monophonic *conducti* from *rondelli* is an interesting move by the compiler as well; it represents an attempt to subdivide genre in ways that go beyond number of voices or ... language of texts."[24]

Although F and Tours 927 together preserve the greatest number of songs, more than 100 further manuscripts from across Europe contain anywhere from 1 to over 30 refrain songs. These manuscript sources vary considerably in type, structure, and content, although commonalities emerge. First and foremost, refrain songs tend to be consciously compiled, not only in thirteenth-century sources such as F and Tours 927, but also in predominantly fourteenth-century manuscripts including processionals (St. Pölten Processional), liturgical books or tropers with added songs, some including polyphony (Moosburger Graduale, Engelberg Codex, Codex Calixtinus, Bobbio, and Graz 258 and 409), or text-only sources and miscellanies (Saint Omer 351, OBod 937, St-Victor Miscellany, and the Red Book of Ossory), among others. The number of sources in which Latin refrain songs are deliberately copied and compiled, even if geographically and chronologically diffuse, is striking and provides ample material support for considering refrain forms as distinct from other Latin songs. Especially after 1250, scribes and copyists actively participated in processes of *compilatio* and

---

[23] The contents of Tours 927 are discussed in Chaguinian, ed., *The Jeu d'Adam*, and F has most recently been inventoried in Masani Ricci, *Codice Pluteo 29.1*.

[24] Everist, *Discovering Medieval Song*, 22. See also Roesner, ed., *Antiphonarium*, 31.

ordinatio, making decisions about what – for them – logically belonged together.[25]

In the manuscripts just referenced, the refrain provides a key connective strand. In sources where refrain songs were not deliberately copied together, there are nevertheless indications of an active interest in creating and collecting refrain forms. Sources in which significant numbers of refrain songs are copied include the twelfth- and early thirteenth-century sources for *nova cantica* (the Norman-Sicilian tropers Mad 19421, Mad 288, Mad 289, Aquitanian *versaria* St-M A, St-M B, St-M C, and St-M D, and the Later Cambridge Songbook); poetic compilations like Saint Omer 351, attributed to Walter of Châtillon, and the St-Victor Miscellany; service books and theological compilations like the Moosburger Graduale and Graz 258 and 409; and even the latest sources I include, the printed Finnish/Swedish *Piae Cantiones*. Only a small number of manuscripts transmit *rondelli*, however, and in these, *rondelli* are grouped together. Scribes consciously grouped songs not solely based on the presence of the refrain, but also the presence of an internal refrain.[26]

Secondly, these songs belong to chiefly devotional, ritual, and pedagogical spheres. The majority of sources for the refrain song are service books, most often those transmitting tropes and occasionally polyphony and representational rites and dramas; troped liturgies; and song or music books. This last category includes manuscripts whose main focus – like that of F – appears to be compiling musical works, both liturgical and non-liturgical. Songs also survive as additions to miscellaneous textual sources and as fragments or in gatherings of pedagogical and theoretical materials.

As the varied manuscripts already cited suggest, refrain songs and their sources are both local and transregional. Many of the songs are unica, or survive in only two or three sources; some were well-loved and transmitted through written (and unwritten) processes throughout Europe. In certain cases, songs with transregional transmission were adapted to fit the needs

---

[25] Parkes, "Influence of the Concepts of *Ordinatio* and *Compilatio*." For song-specific discussions of organization and compilation, see Deeming, "Isolated Jottings?" The grouping of like with like is also attested to by Anonymous IV with respect to the *conductus* as well as *organum*; edited in Reckow, *Der Musiktraktat des Anonymus 4*, 1:82, and translated in Yudkin, *Music Treatise of Anonymous IV*, 73–74.

[26] The *rondellus* is related to vernacular refrains and refrain songs in several of these sources: English song in the Red Book of Ossory; German in the Engelberg and Erfurt Codices; and French in LoB, St-M D, Adam de la Bassée's Ludus super Anticlaudianum, and the St-Victor Miscellany (see Chapter 5). The other sources transmitting *rondelli* are two of the Aquitanian *versaria*, St-M A and St-M D, and OBod 937, the latter two sharing a contrafact and concordances, respectively, with F and Tours 927.

of local communities, whether by altering text, adding or subtracting voices, or adapting the melody or form. Despite their wide geographical reach, clusters of sources and concordances in thirteenth-century France and fourteenth-century Germanic areas testify to heightened interest in particular linguistic and cultural regions. Finally, some sources appear with greater frequency throughout the following chapters. The decision to highlight these sources and, as a result, elide the significant witness of many more, has to do with both patterns of transmission linking certain sources and also with scribal interventions and additions in specific manuscripts that speak to questions of performance, inscription, and interpretation. Although the evidence of a single manuscript cannot be made to speak for all Latin refrain songs, I have chosen to focus on sources that offer a greater sense of context in the hopes of providing new avenues and insights into this relatively unexamined body of works.

Theorizing the Refrain

While scribes were aware of the refrain as a defining characteristic of Latin song, music theorists are relatively silent. Akin to the French *refrain*, little theorizing was undertaken by medieval writers on refrains or refrain forms. Indeed, the modern term "refrain" for the Latin repertoire has no exact or singular parallel in medieval writings; instead, terminology for the repetition of text, music, or text and music ranges widely. For the *conductus*, the first Latin song repertoire with a significant theoretical grounding, accounts of the genre by theorists such as Johannes de Garlandia, Walter Odington, and the anonymous author of the *Discantus positio vulgaris* focus on polyphonic, rhythmically notated, and ascribed works, seldom mentioning simpler, monophonic, forms.[27]

The monophonic *conductus* is treated only in passing, as it is by Anonymous IV, who terms it *simplex conductus* and cites as an example the melismatic *Beata viscera* attributed to Perotinus, with poetry probably by Philip the Chancellor.[28] (Notably, *Beata viscera* features a refrain, which is not noted by Anonymous IV.) Johannes de Garlandia mentions monophonic *conducti* only in relation to the musical use of rhetorical

---

[27] For a recent overview of theoretical treatments of the *conductus*, see Everist, *Discovering Medieval Song*, 17–20.

[28] Edited in Reckow, *Der Musiktraktat des Anonymus 4*, 1:46, and translated in Yudkin, *Music Treatise of Anonymous IV*, 39.

colores.[29] In other words, little in the corpus of theoretical writings indicates that largely monophonic, anonymous, melodically and poetically simple, and syllabic refrain songs were considered in the same vein as more elaborate polyphonic *conductus*. Although the term "rondellus" occurs, it is in reference to voice-exchange techniques and not *rondeau*-form Latin songs.[30] While there is something markedly different about how a song looks and functions when it has a refrain, medieval music theorists seemed largely unconcerned with the structural distinction.

Albeit not in reference to Latin song, one exception comes via the unwieldly witness of Johannes de Grocheio's *ca.* 1300 treatise, *Ars musice*, in which he constructs a typology of secular vocal and instrumental music.[31] Within the category of music made with the human voice (*voce humana*), Grocheio offers two categories, *cantus* and *cantilena*, each subdivided into further categories. The *cantus* is characterized by Grocheio as lofty, fit for nobles, and "sung before kings and princes," while *cantilenae* are best suited to "young men and girls," especially at "great feasts" or to lead them away from unsavory diversions.[32] The latter songs, *cantilenae*, are of interest in the context of the Latin refrain song since all types are characterized by a refrain identified by Grocheio as either a "responsorium" (response) or "refractus" (from *refringere*, to break open). Grocheio thus defines the genre of the *cantilena* not solely by means of its function and intended performers and audience, but also by its shared formal feature, the refrain.

Aside from Grocheio with his focus on vernacular song and refrain, the relative silence from music theorists would leave the Latin refrain with little music-theoretical grounding were it not for an ambiguous passage in the final (and probably added) chapters of Garlandia's thirteenth-century treatise *De mensurabili musica.*[33] These chapters lay out a number of

---

[29] Ibid.   [30] See n. 20 above.

[31] Edited and translated most recently in Grocheio, *Ars musice*. For an overview of similar typologies in vernacular song in Dante's *De vulgari eloquentia* and Guillem Molinier's *Las Leys d'amor*, as well as Grocheio's *Ars musice*, see Peraino, "New Music," 26–72. Peraino notes that all three texts divide song into two broad categories based on the presence or absence of a refrain, with implications for style and function. On questions of style and register in typologies and theories of medieval song, with reference to the refrain as a marker of a "Lower" style, see Aubrey, "Reconsidering 'High Style' and 'Low Style.'"

[32] Grocheio, *Ars musice*, 68–71.

[33] These chapters are found only in Jerome of Moravia's revised version of Garlandia's *De mensurabili musica* in Paris lat. 16663, fol. 66ʳ–76ᵛ. On the revised version of the treatise, see Garlandia, *De mensurabili musica*, 44; and Larkowski, "The 'De musica mensurabili positio' of Johannes de Garlandia," Larkowski edited and translated this version in its entirety.

additional theories concerning a variety of topics, including ornamentation (*colores*), the avenue through which Garlandia engages with the rhetorical organization of sound (*sono ordinato*).[34] He draws specifically on rhetorical figures to describe melodic gestures that enhance the beauty of what is heard in the same way that rhetorical figures in writing lead to greater pleasure, describing three *colores*, or figures: *sono ordinates*, *florificatio vocis*, and *repetitio*.[35] This last figure is the most interesting for its potential to describe the musical counterpart to rhetorical figures of repetition. *Repetitio* in this context, however, does not align with its use in contemporary poetic treatises; rather, it is interpreted by Garlandia as melodic repetition:[36]

Repetitio of the same voice is color: which makes unknown sound known, through which recognition the sense of hearing receives pleasure. And in this manner [repetition] is used in *rondelli* and vernacular songs. Repetition of different voices is the same sound repeated at a different time in different voices. And this manner is found in *tripla*, *quadrupla*, and conductus and in many others.[37]

Specifying voice-exchange works (*rondelli*) and "cantilenis vulgaribus," as opposed to the Latin *conductus*, grouped instead with polyphonic genres, Garlandia's use of *repetitio* is suggestive of refrains and other forms of musico-poetic repetition not confined to a single genre. The relationship of *repetitio* to the repetition of a refrain-like unit of music and poetry is cited once again when Garlandia describes the modularity of *colores* and suggests they can be replaced with other "known songs," including clauses of *lai* (*clausulam lay*): "Put *colores* in the place of unknown, proportioned

---

[34] Chapters 15 and 16 are edited in Reimer, ed., *Johannes de Garlandia*, 1:94–97, and translated in Garlandia, *De mensurabili musica*, 51–57.

[35] "Color est: pulcritudo soni: uel obiectum auditus: per quod auditus suscipit placenciam." "Color is the beauty of a sound or that which is heard, through which the sense of hearing is pleased." Paris lat. 16663, fol. 75ᵛ, edited in the *Thesaurus Musicarum Latinarum* at https://chmtl .indiana.edu/tml/13th/GARDMP_MPBN1666, translated in *De mensurabili musica*, 53. For an investigation of Garlandia's musical rhetoric as it manifests in Notre Dame polyphony, see Voogt, "Repetition and Structure"; Gross, "Organum at Notre Dame," *Chanter en polyphonie*, and "L'Organum."

[36] Geoffrey de Vinsauf's *Poetria nova* defines *repetitio* as the repetition of a word at the beginning of several lines of verses or clauses; this not precisely what the refrain does in strophic song or *rondelli*. Vinsauf, *Poetria nova: Revised Edition*, 49, 51. Definitions of *repetitio* are relatively consistent across treatises on poetry and rhetoric.

[37] "Repetitio eiusdem vocis est color: faciens ignotum sonum: esse notum: per quam noticiam: auditus suscipit placenciam. Et isto modo: utimur: in rondellis et cantilenis vulgaribus. Repetitio diverse vocis est idem sonus reppetitus in tempore diverso a diversis vocibus. Et iste modus reperitur in triplicibus quadruplicibus et conductis: et multis aliis." Paris lat. 16663, fol. 75ᵛ. Translation adapted from Voogt, "Repetition and Structure," 45–46, and Garlandia, *De mensurabili musica*, 54.

sounds; the more *colores* there are, the more a sound will be known, and if it is known, it will be pleasing."[38] In both contexts, Garlandia emphasizes the function of *repetitio* as a rhetorical figure that aims at pleasing the listener – repetition increases familiarity, which in turn increases pleasure.

As Garlandia's use of rhetorical terms suggests, rhetoric and the *ars poetriae* more generally are useful avenues for interrogating the identity and function of the Latin refrain in poetry, if not song.[39] In particular, rhetorical *figurae*, referring to the techniques of stylistically ornamenting an argument, offer a possible vocabulary for the refrain and its poetic function. Figures of repetition are among the most common and numerous in terms of rhetorical texts and involve repetition at the level of letters, words, and up to entire phrases; such figures are commonly employed by poets and songwriters.[40] Closest to the refrain is *epimone*, described by Eberhard of Béthune in *Graecismus* (*ca.* 1212) as "a sentence which is repeated often, [as] is clear in verses with a refrain" ("epimone sententia fit crebro repetita, interscalares uersus istud manifestant").[41] While the rhetorical figure is identified as *epimone*, Eberhard labels the repeating unit of the refrain as "interscalares uersus," or interpolated verse – the result of repeating a sentence in verse.[42] In rhetorical terms, figures of repetition serve several functions, whether to emphasize, to create breaks in structure, to introduce a certain ethos, or to affect the temporal experience of song's meaning and performance. While commentary on refrains from the perspective of rhetoric offers additional terminology and some insight into the affective qualities of the refrain, the inconsistency of labels is noteworthy.

---

[38] "Pone colores loco sonorum proporcionator ignotorum et quanto magis colores: tanto sonus erit magis notus Et si fuerit notus. erit plicens [*sic* placens]: Item loco coloris in regione cuiuslibet: ponne cantilenam notam copulam. uel punctu: uel descensum uel ascensum alicuius instrumenti: uel clausam: lay." Paris lat. 16663, fol. 76ᵛ. Translation adapted from Butterfield, *Poetry and Music*, 289, and Garlandia, *De mensurabili musica*, 57. Previous scholars have noted the parallel here between the *colores* and refrains; see Butterfield, *Poetry and Music*, 288–289; and Doss-Quinby, *Les Refrains*, 116.

[39] There are numerous ways in which rhetorical figures could be drawn on to describe the role of repetition in Latin song, including the refrain; see Poteat, "Functions" and "Functions of Repetition"; and Caldwell, "Singing, Dancing, and Rejoicing," 86–96. For the application of rhetorical analysis to medieval Latin song, see, for example, Carlson, "Striking Ornaments" and "Two Paths"; and Rillon-Marne, *Homo considera*.

[40] Poteat, "Functions" and "Functions of Repetition"; and Smith, *Figures of Repetition*. For a general list of figures of repetition, see Lanham, *Handlist*, 189–191.

[41] *Graecismus*, 5, edited by Wrobel, and translated in Copeland and Sluiter, eds., *Medieval Grammar and Rhetoric*, 589.

[42] "Interscalares uersus" or more commonly "versus intercalaris" is used to describe the repetition of verses as a refrain, but in a descriptive sense only.

Manuscript evidence offers support for the use of certain terms to refer to Latin refrains in the context of song and performance. Several sources, all liturgical, use "repetitio," or abbreviations thereof, to signal refrains.[43] In each source, textual cues unambiguously point to the literal repetition of the refrain; in some sources, an additional cue is employed, derived from "respondere," which shares the same connotation as one of the two terms used by Grocheio in his discussion of vernacular refrains (*responsorium*).[44] A scribe in the twelfth-century Carmina Burana, on the other hand, uses the abbreviation "refl." several times to cue refrains, probably derived from *reflecto, reflectere*, to convey a sense of turning or bending back around.[45] Although sharing the same idea of return (with the emphasis on the prefix "re-"), the rubrics and performance directions "repetitio," "responde," and "reflecto" all have slightly different connotations. "Repetitio" refers to the repetition of the same word or phrase, "responde" to an answer or response, and "reflecto" to a return or turning back.[46] The second of two terms employed by Grocheio to refer to refrains in *cantilenae*, "refractus" (from *refringere*, to break open or into, or to refract), is similar but not identical in meaning to these terms, sharing the "re-" prefix.[47] These terms and their implications for questions of performance, inscription, and memory will arise at various points in the following chapters.

The greatest number of identifiers for the Latin refrain, and those closest to the songs themselves in manuscript sources, focus on the aspect of return signaled by the prefix "re-." Since the identity of the Latin refrain involves a structural return, scribal cues and abbreviations typically reflect this condition. The question, however, is whether there is anything substantially different about a repeated Latin refrain that "breaks into" song (*refractus*), as opposed to one that bends the song back on itself (*reflecto*), one that repeats (*repetitio*), or one that serves as a response (*responsorium*), or whether theorists and scribes were experimenting with methods of describing this newly widespread formal aspect of song. Vacillation between terms on the part of writers and scribes supports the latter conclusion. Not only does Grocheio offer "responsorii vel refractus," but other writers oscillate between terms too, including Gerald of Wales in

---

[43] These are the Moosburger Graduale, Graz 258, SG 392, the Engelberg Codex, and the St. Pölten Processional.

[44] See, for example, SG 382, p. 89; see Chapter 4, Figure 4.3.

[45] For a more thorough overview, see Caldwell, "Cueing Refrains."

[46] "Repetitio" implies both the general definition of repetition and more specific uses in rhetoric and, as above, in music theory.

[47] On the refrain as a break, drawing on this term, see Hollander, "Breaking into Song."

a twelfth-century anecdote on the penetration of a vernacular refrain into the mind of a preacher: "refectorium seu refractoriam vocant."[48] As prevalent as the Latin refrain was in the poetry and song of the high Middle Ages, the lack of a coherent technical vocabulary left its terminological identity in the hands of composers, poets, and scribes.

Creating and Performing the Latin Refrain Song

Who were the composers, performers, scribes, and audiences of this repertoire? Medieval Latin song is often frustratingly silent on this question. Although certain works – including refrain songs – have acquired authorial attributions via rubrics and references in textual and theoretical sources, including well-known figures such as Philip the Chancellor, Peter of Blois, Walter of Châtillon, and Alan of Lille, most songs lack a connection to an author, verifiable or not.[49] By combining the few names we do have along with evidence offered by the music and its contexts, however, an outline of the types of communities responsible for devotional Latin song emerges. These are songs created, compiled, transmitted, and performed by literate people who resided, worshipped, and studied within monastic, clerical, and scholarly milieus.[50] Individuals within these largely anonymous communities – composers, poets, compilers, scribes – were evidently fluent in the language of liturgy, deeply engrained in church rites and customs, and well-versed in literature ranging from the classic to the contemporary.[51] Considering the predominantly devotional and at times liturgical slant of the poetry across centuries, religious and scholarly communities, clerical and monastic alike, stand as the most logical spheres of cultivation for this Latin song tradition.

---

[48] Latin edited in Giraldus, *Giraldi Cambrensis Opera*, 2:120. On this passage including a translation, see Weller, "*Vox – littera – cantus*," 244.

[49] On *conducti* with names associated with either poetic or musical composition in Latin song (limited to the *conductus*), see Dronke, "Lyrical Compositions"; Payne, "Poetry, Politics, and Polyphony"; "*Aurelianus civitas*"; Traill, "More Poems"; Payne, ed., *Motets and Prosulas*; Rillon-Marne, *Homo considera*, 33–76; Mazzeo, "Two-Part Conductus," 25–69; and Everist, *Discovering Medieval Song.*

[50] Although women have been sidelined in the historiography of Latin song, they did sing monophonic and polyphonic Latin songs, as evidenced by the Las Huelgas Codex, Hortus Deliciarum, Stuttg, and Wienhäuser Liederbuch, among other manuscripts associated with female religious institutions.

[51] For a recent consideration of clerical communities around the *conductus* in particular, see Woodward, "Blinded by the Desire of Riches" and Caldwell, "Singing Cato."

Two unique manuscripts from the fourteenth century are at odds with the relative anonymity of the repertoire by including indications of authorial control and intent that sketch the contours of the local communities for which the songs were composed and compiled. These are the musical and poetic collections of the Moosburger Graduale and the Red Book of Ossory, copied in Germany and Ireland, respectively.[52] Beyond transmitting refrain-form works, the two geographically disparate sources are linked by prefaces that situate the songs they transmit within the lives and musical practices of each clerical community, penned by, or naming, authority figures within each community.[53] In the Moosburger Graduale, the preface is attributed to the dean of the song school, Johannes de Perchausen, and in the Red Book of Ossory the collection of unnotated poems contains a preface attributed to the diocesan bishop, Richard Ledrede.

These examples are invaluable for the insight they might provide concerning the cultural roles and perceptions of Latin song, offering extended points of contact mediating between the reader (singer?) and the songs that follow. First and foremost, in the prefaces the scribes attempt to establish authorial control over the lyrics while also asserting their intent. The prefaces instruct the reader/performer as to why and by whom these songs have been copied, and how they ought to be received and sung, namely by "new little clerks" ("novellis clericulis" in the Moosburger Graduale) and vicars, priests, and clerks of the cathedral church ("vicariis Ecclesie Cathedralis sacerdotibus et clericis" in the Red Book of Ossory), explicitly placing the performance of song in the hands of these clerical ranks. The prefaces and song collections of these two unusual manuscript sources speak to both the local nature of many Latinate song practices and the more broadly clerical nature of many sources.

The poetry of the refrain song provides further insight into the communities implicated in processes of transmission and performance, with clear ties to types of communities signaled in the prefaces just discussed. While

---

[52] On the Moosburger Graduale, see Spanke, "Das Mosburger Graduale"; Stein, "Das Moosburger Graduale"; and Hiley, *Moosburger Graduale*. On the Red Book of Ossory, see Colledge, *Latin Poems*; Greene, *Lyrics*; Stemmler, *Latin Hymns* and "Vernacular Snatches"; and Rigg, "Red Book." The preface in the Red Book of Ossory is discussed further in Chapters 1 and 5; the preface in the Moosburger Graduale is edited and discussed in Brewer, "Songs," 33–35, and Chapter 1 below.

[53] Although prefaces are rare, the late fourteenth-century *Llibre Vermell* also includes an explanatory note, or preface, in its *cantionale* section; although the text indicates the function of the Latin and Catalonian songs in the *cantionale* as songs for the pilgrims at the monastery of Montserrat, no mention is made of authorship. See Anglés, "El 'Llibre Vermell' de Montserrat," 47–48.

in Chapter 3 I explore questions of vocal performance and the refrain's associations with dance, the poetic texts more generally construct an anonymous body of performers and audiences. References are nearly always collective in spirit, referring to groups of singers or audience members defined by rank, position, or age. *Clerici* (clerics), *cantores* (cantors), *clericuli* and *pueri* (young clerics/choirboys and boys), *lectores* (lectors), and *presuli* (bishops) all appear in the poetic language of song and refrain as well as in rubrics to various degrees, identified as addressees or, in some cases, presumptive performers.[54] The laity make occasional appearances too, although typically framed rhetorically within poetic calls to "both clerics and laity" rather than situated as possible performers. Poetic references are paralleled to a smaller degree by rubrication in certain manuscripts (usually service books), clarifying the performance of individual songs by various clerical or monastic ranks akin to those identified in the prefaces of the Moosburger Graduale and Red Book of Ossory. While the value of poetic references as evidence of actual performance practice is debatable, the repeated invocation of devout, ordained, and scholastic singers and listeners is difficult to overlook.

Although medieval Latin song more broadly shares a similar base of creators, performers, and singers, the repeated invocation of *pueri* and *clericuli* across refrain songs evinces a decided slant toward younger members of religious institutions and schools.[55] *Clericuli* in particular are connected to songs for, among other feasts, St. Nicholas, the boy bishop, Nativity, the Holy Innocents, and the Circumcision – a decidedly youthful selection of feast days (Chapter 1). Counterparts to the *clericuli*, boys under twelve, *pueri*, are frequently commanded to rejoice in Latin songs, most often in connection with feast days such as the Holy Innocents (December 28), traditionally celebrated by children due to their identification with the biblical innocents.[56] The *presuli*, bishops, that populate refrain songs vary in identity, referring not only to historical bishops and St. Nicholas, a favored patron saint of clerics and schoolboys, but also to so-called boy bishops, choristers elected during Advent to the temporary

---

[54] I have yet to locate rubrics that specify performance by women, even in sources associated with female institutions.

[55] Although the word for boy (*puer*) was fairly common, the term *clericulus* is less so; see "clericulus" in *Glossarium*. See, however, references to *clericuli* in a Laon ordinal cited in Boynton, "Boy Singers," ordinal edited in Chevalier, *Ordinaires*.

[56] See, for example, the repeated invocation of *pueri* in the Holy Innocents song in the Later Cambridge Songs, *Magno gaudens gaudio*, fol. 4ᵛ (297ᵛ); edited and translated in Stevens, ed., *Later Cambridge Songs*, 95–98.

position of bishop (often on the Feast of St. Nicholas).[57] The prominence of the boy bishop and his associated rituals in the Latin refrain song speaks volumes as to its intended singers and auditors. By citing *clericuli*, *pueri*, and the boy bishops, a significant proportion of refrain songs becomes oriented around rituals and festivities – not always liturgical – linked to younger members of church and school, as well as junior ranks. Although few names can be concretely attached to the composition of the refrain song, these works nevertheless permit occasional glimpses into their production and probable, if poetically constructed, performance forces and audiences. Developing from the poetry of the refrain song is an outline of intended performers and audiences that will be fleshed out in the following chapters, bringing the refrain in devotional Latin song into sharper focus.

Lastly, throughout nearly a century of scholarship, the performance of Latin refrain songs has been principally and, at times, exclusively linked to dance. The refrain song has been imagined to be vocal music intended to accompany religious men and women in spontaneous or planned choreographies taking place in church naves and choirs, on pilgrimage routes, during processions, and in city streets. Evoked in nearly all published work on devotional dance in the Middle Ages as an example par excellence of the survival of notated dance songs, the Latin refrain song's choreographic identity became cemented in Yvonne Rokseth's oft-cited 1947 article "Danses cléricales du XIIIe siecle," in which the songs in Fascicle XI of F are identified as the accompaniment of dancing clerics and choirboys at Notre Dame Cathedral in thirteenth-century Paris.[58] In 1986, John E. Stevens reworked Rokseth's central point in English by labeling the *rondellus* a "clerical dance-song," further extending the scope to include not solely F, but many of the other songs and sources discussed in this book.[59] This appellation has persisted into the twenty-first century. In July 2020, a workshop held in Besalú, Spain was titled "The Clerical Dance-Song of the Ms. Pluteo 29," while in December 2020 Ensemble Labyrinthus released an album entitled *Carmina Tripudiorum: XII–XIV cc. Clerical Dance Music*, featuring primarily Latin refrain songs from F, the Moosburger Graduale, and elsewhere.[60]

---

[57] A list of "Bishop" songs (*conducti* and related works), that is, works referring to identified or unidentified bishops, in just one manuscript, F, is included in Payne, "Chancellor *versus* Bishop," 278–279, table 1. On the boy bishop, see Chapter 1.

[58] Rokseth, "Danses clericales."   [59] Stevens, *Words and Music*, 178–186.

[60] The workshop in Besalú was led by Dr. Mauricio Molina, online.medievalmusicbesalu.com/ site/workshop-the-rondelli-of-the-pluteo-29. Ensemble Labyrinthus's album was released on the Artes Mirabiles label as a DXD recording available here: www.nativedsd.com/product/ am200009-carmina-tripudiorum-xiixiv-cc-clerical-dance-music/.

The perceived relationship of Latin refrains to dance is closely related to the one envisioned for its vernacular counterparts; for the French *refrain* in particular, the narrative of its origin in the *rondeau*, and in dance song more generally, has only in recent decades been questioned and overturned.[61] For musicologists and literary scholars alike, the refrain, regardless of language, seems to be a musico-poetic marker of bodies in motion, whether in the context of choreographed aristocratic dances or popular social dances.[62] However, the refrain is only a marker of identity for dance music insofar as scholars have agreed it is one – the medieval "dance song" is ambiguous, its identification driven by context and local-ized within specific genres, song communities, and regions. Throughout the book I avoid identifying dance as a referent and interpretive tool, choosing instead to resituate the Latin refrain within a wider landscape of medieval musical and devotional practices.

The sheer amount of scholarship citing dance and movement as a chief performance and ritual context for the Latin refrain song demands consideration, however, and in Chapter 3 I reflect on the evidence that identifies refrain songs as clerical or monastic dance music, with a focus on F's Fascicle XI. I suggest that the connection of the Latin refrain song to devotional dance rests on uncertain ground, and that the prominent witness of F more productively suggests a metaphorical rather than literal relationship. Uncoupling the Latin refrain from dance in the course of this book ultimately allows for a plurality of perspectives and interpretations beyond dance to emerge around the function and performance of Latin refrains and refrain songs.

✶✶✶✶✶

Certain themes run throughout the following six chapters, all motivated by the poetry, material sources, and performance contexts of the Latin refrain song. These include performance, broadly conceived; inscription and materiality; time and temporality; community; memory and modes of transmission; contrafacture; and language.

Chapter 1 contextualizes the performance of the refrain song within the feasts and seasons of the church and calendar year, situating the repertoire

---

[61] See especially Saltzstein, *Refrain*, 8–16.

[62] Dorothea Klein, Brigitte Burrichter and Andreas Haug employ the term "Ausweis" to refer to the refrain as a "marker of identity" of dance in music and poetry. *Das mittelalterliche Tanzlied,* viii.

within a pluralistic temporal framework. I identify the Latin refrain and its songs as inherently seasonal and calendrical forms of musical expression, emerging out of a broader liturgical and popular interest in musically amplifying periods of the year characterized by the interplay of calendrical and liturgical time. Chapter 2 is concerned with how this calendrical repertoire plays out for singers in the moment of performance, how they might have understood the songs as a form of religious narrative, and how the refrain interacts with the experience of narrative time in poetry and performance.

Chapter 3 focuses on the implications of the refrain for performance, reappraising its role as a marker of responsorial song. I argue that the refrain in devotional Latin song brought individuals and communities together in the moment of performance through the act of remembering together, responding collectively and worshipping communally. Chapter 3 also includes a discussion of the role of dance in relation to the performance of the refrain song, suggesting a relationship between its implicit choreographic identity and the discourses of community conveyed by the refrain. Chapter 4 explores the memorial aspects of the Latin refrain and its circulation between genres and among works. The chapter concludes with a case study of two fourteenth-century sources from an Austrian abbey, considering how the inscription of refrains in these manuscripts evidences an evolving, living practice of remembering, singing, and copying Latin refrains.

Lastly, in Chapter 5 I interrogate the relationship between vernacular and Latin refrains through the witness of three unique sources, the St-Victor Miscellany, the Engelberg Codex, and the Red Book of Ossory. Songs in these three notated and unnotated sources feature parallel forms of scribal evidence that illustrate the interaction between Latin and vernacular refrains through contrafacture and offer insight into the multilingual communities behind this song repertoire.

1 | Latin Song and Refrain in the Medieval Year

Thus, there were two dancing seasons, that of Christmas for the winter, that of Easter for the springtime. The first often began on the Feast of St. Nicholas and did not conclude until Epiphany, and the second extended until the Feast of St. John the Baptist, feast of superstitious observance par excellence. Now these two seasons, based on the ecclesiastical calendar, corresponded precisely to two periods of pagan revelry, the first having as its culminating point the Kalends of January, the second the Kalends of May.

–Gougaud, "La Danse dans les églises"

Writing in the early part of the twentieth century, Louis Gougaud provides the epigraph to this chapter by concluding his study of medieval church dance with the observation that there were two seasons in the year appropriate for dancing and rejoicing in song: Christmas and Easter.[1] The former began in early winter on the Feast of St. Nicholas (December 6), and the latter ended in midsummer on the Feast of St. John the Baptist (June 24).[2] Although Gougaud was concerned primarily with the role of dance and its accompanying music in religious contexts, abundant evidence throughout medieval Europe attests to the fact that certain times and seasons were marked by an efflorescence of song. Perhaps the most familiar of these seasons of song in Latin and vernacular contexts is springtime, as evoked in the *exordium* of a *rondellus* in thirteenth-century Parisian manuscript F: "The beginning of spring ... gives us joy, [so] let us sing, eia!"[3] Medieval song across genre and language offers countless examples in this vein, interlacing song and season in ways that reflect not only the natural

---

[1] Gougaud, "La Danse dans les églises," 19: "Il y avait ainsi comme deux saisons dansantes, celle de Noël pour l'hiver, celle de Pâques au printemps. La première commençait souvent dès la Saint-Nicolas pour ne se clore qu'à l'Épiphanie, et la seconde se prolongeait jusqu'à la Saint-Jean-Baptiste, fête à observances superstitieuses par excellence. Or ces deux saisons, basées sur le calendrier ecclésiastique, correspondaient précisément à deux périodes de réjouissances païennes, la première ayant pour point culminant les calendes de janvier, la seconde les calendes de mai."

[2] Ecclesiastes 3:1–4 provides biblical grounding for Gougaud's observation that "all things have their season," including dance: "omnia tempus habent."

[3] F, fol. 468ʳ: "Veris principium ... dat nobis gaudium | cantemus eia."

world and its seasons, but an awareness and marking of the pluralistic medieval calendar and the communities who lived according to its rhythms.[4]

Calendar and seasonal time represent a key to interpreting the performance contexts and cultural functions of the Latin refrain song. With chiefly devotional texts and frequent links to the liturgy through troping, it is no surprise that Latin song plays a role in the musical landscape of the liturgical year as well as in extraliturgical devotional and festive rituals; indeed, medieval Latin song has long been envisioned as a form of religious and festive recreation.[5] In this chapter I suggest that the refrain song reflects a unique and heightened relationship with the medieval year in ways that are constructed and expressed through poetry and rhetoric, patterns of creation and transmission, and implicit as well as explicit performance contexts. Throughout this chapter the refrain song emerges as a nexus for the musical and poetic expression of time and temporality, rooted in its harmonization with the calendar year; the thematic, topical, and material contours of the refrain song are shaped around calendar and seasonal time in remarkably consistent ways over several centuries of cultivation and transmission.

In addition to aligning with the calendar year, the poetry of the refrain song repeatedly dictates how time, and especially festive time, should be experienced. Rather than passively reflecting notions of time, the refrain song could influence or change the way time was experienced. This develops out of a poetic vocabulary of sobriety and moderation that signals the inherent temporal plurality of the medieval calendar as both a record of solemn and devout feasts and a framework for seasonal and festive celebration. As Gougaud's description of two dancing seasons suggests, the medieval year could be defined according to season (spring and winter), feast days (Christmas and Easter, the feasts of Sts. Nicholas and John the Baptist), or dates associated with so-called "pagan revelries" (New Year's

---

[4] For the standard overview of nature *exordia* and the *locus amoenus* in Latin poetry, see Curtius, *European Literature*, 183–202. See also Diehl, *The Medieval European Religious Lyric*, 152–156 on references to time and seasons in religious poetry. The ubiquity of opening gestures, or *exordia*, in medieval song to seasons and calendar feasts or days has only recently been examined as more than a literary motif or genre characteristic; see Rothenberg, "Marian Symbolism of Spring" and *Flower of Paradise*; Anderson, "Fire, Foliage and Fury"; Plumley, "French Lyrics"; and Saltzstein, "Songs of Nature."

[5] See, for example, Gröninger's statement that the *conductus* should be understood as a repertoire created for a "living circle of clergy" ("Lebenskreis des Klerus") principally for feasts of the liturgical year. *Repertoire*, 13. See also Spanke, "Tanzmusik," 110, and Haines, *Medieval Song*, 68–72.

and May Day).[6] Within the medieval calendar, certain moments occasioned greater temporal plurality than others; these were moments when song, as Gougaud observed, became a preferred, if occasionally contested, mode of expression. The Latin refrain song closely traced these periods of heightened temporal plurality, its music, poetry, and performance fostering a figurative and literal reframing of how time was experienced.

Calendrical Song: Thematic Distribution and Manuscript Ordering

Patterns of manuscript transmission and the ordering of the refrain song beginning in the thirteenth century, along with the framing of refrain songs by means of rubrics and prefaces in the fourteenth century, signal an awareness of the refrain song as ritually and poetically tethered to the liturgical year. The poetry of the devotional refrain song is highly calendrical, coalescing chiefly around the liturgical seasons of Christmas and Easter, with songs also dedicated to the Virgin Mary and Christ.[7] The seasonal year is also emphasized with songs celebrating springtime or the transition from winter to spring; in many cases these are not secular songs, but instead, as discussed later in this chapter, allegorically frame the seasons. Figure 1.1 offers a synoptic view of the major liturgical and festive themes and topics explored in the poetry of the refrain song, with liturgical period or feast paired with season.[8] The thematic grouping of refrain songs aligns with liturgical and seasonal periods spanning from early winter, signaled by the Feast of St. Nicholas (December 6), to the New Year (January 1) and its octave, and then springtime, from Easter to Pentecost and its octave – a reflection, in other words, of Gougaud's "dancing seasons."

---

[6] Medieval dating practices attest to the deeply plural nature of the early calendar; see, for instance, the example cited in Mondschein and Casey, "Time and Timekeeping," 1665.

[7] On the typology of poetry in the *conductus* specifically and its devotional orientation, see Everist, *Discovering Medieval Song*, 62–74. *Versus*, and *nova cantica* more broadly, are similarly devotional in scope, with an emphasis on Christmas; for observations on the topical distribution of songs in *versaria*, see Grier, "Some Codicological Observations." On Marian refrain songs, see Caldwell, "Litanic Songs."

[8] The use of visuals rather than numbers acknowledges the difficulty of assigning exact numbers to the repertoire. This graph reflects the songs in the Appendix while excluding Marian songs unconnected with Christ's Nativity or Resurrection, and secular or moralizing poems, which comprise approximately 11 percent of the total number of Latin refrain songs; the majority of these are transmitted in the Carmina Burana.

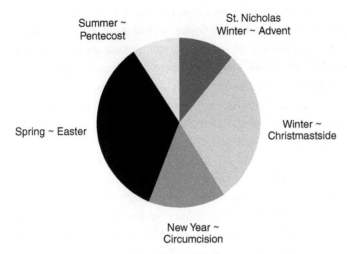

Figure 1.1 Calendrical and seasonal distribution of refrain songs

The thematic distribution of the refrain song is compelling since it does not mirror that of Latin song more broadly. Although Latin songs survive in all poetic forms and musical structures for the feasts and seasons listed in Figure 1.1, refrain songs survive more often, in greater quantity, and across more sources, for these specific feasts and temporal periods. St. Nicholas, for instance, appears in medieval Latin song more frequently than any other saint, and more than two thirds of these songs have refrains.[9] Similar ratios obtain for the other temporal periods indicated in Figure 1.1, with noteworthy numbers of refrain songs for Easter and springtime in particular. Easter is generally not well represented in the *versus* of the twelfth century, and although it appears as a topical focus in later *conducti* and *cantilenae*, Christ's Resurrection is most numerously and explicitly celebrated in refrain songs, and especially *rondelli*. I examine this link later in this chapter in relation to the springtime topos; here, however, it reflects a correspondence between form and poetic content. Finally, although the feasts of the Nativity and the Circumcision are amply represented in Latin song, refrain songs for the latter are unusually well represented and, as detailed later in this chapter, present a special case study within the history of medieval Latin song.

---

[9] On hagiographical *conducti*, see Everist, *Discovering Medieval Song*, 65. Aside from St. Nicholas, most saints are represented by only one or a small handful of songs, tending to reflect the motivations of local cults. On hagiographical *versus*, see Grier, "Some Codicological Observations," 53–56.

Individual manuscripts reveal further how the transmission of the refrain song shapes and underscores its calendrical orientation. Form provides a primary organizing principle in sources for the refrain song, evidenced best by F, in which monophonic songs are copied in Fascicles X and XI, yet the majority of refrain songs, and all *rondelli*, are found in Fascicle XI. In manuscripts where refrain forms are deliberately clustered, another layer of internal organization is also typically employed. For smaller collections of songs, thematic homogeneity tends to be the convention. This is the case for the three Easter *rondelli* copied in the final folios of OBod 937, fol. 446^v–447^r, a manuscript otherwise transmitting texts pertaining to Thomas Becket; a series of Christmastide refrain songs, with rubrics indicating performance in relation to the Office Hours in the Austrian St. Pölten Processional; and a collection of Christmas and Marian refrain songs copied in the fourteenth-century Italian antiphoner, Bobbio.[10]

In larger manuscript collections of refrain songs, calendrical ordering is used as an organizational tool. F is once again a central example, its sixty songs beginning with Easter (the first half of the collection), then moving to a mixture of Christmas songs, including groups of songs for Easter, the Virgin Mary, and St. Nicholas, as well as Christological songs and a single secular song (see Table 1.1). By contrast, the monophonic *conducti* in Fascicle X of F are not arranged calendrically or by any apparent logic beyond texture.[11]

Ordering according to form and subject matter is taken further internally; namely, the initial twenty-eight Easter songs in Fascicle XI are all *rondelli*, except for *Passionis emuli*. Following the main gathering of chiefly Easter and Christmastide *rondelli* up to folio 469^r, the scribe then copied a greater assortment of works and forms, including strophic and through-composed songs and one troped hymn.[12] The ruled but empty folios following a tetrad of Nicholas songs also suggest the possibility that further songs for saints may have been planned. This is especially intriguing considering the position of St. Nicholas's feast day at the beginning of the liturgical year in Advent; if further songs were planned for saints, their

---

[10] The *rondelli* in OBod 937 are edited in Deeming, *Songs*, 141–143. For inventories of the St. Pölten Processional and Bobbio, see Huglo, *Les Manuscrits*, 2:30–31 and Damilano, "Laudi latine," respectively.

[11] Caldwell, "Singing, Dancing, and Rejoicing," 18–19; and Haines, *Medieval Song*, 68–72. The organization in the eleventh fascicle echoes that of both *organum* and motet fascicles earlier in F, which tend to follow a liturgical order; see Bradley, "Ordering."

[12] Of these sixty songs, *In rerum principio*, *In hoc statu gratie*, *Leto leta concio*, *O quanto consilio*, and *O summi regis mater inclita* are not refrain forms; *Iam lucis orto sidere* is a hymn troped with a refrain (see Caldwell, "Troping Time").

Table 1.1 The contents and thematic organization of F, fol. 463ʳ–476ᵛ (Fascicle XI) (for folio numbers see the Appendix)

No.	Incipit	Form	Occasion
1	*De patre principio*	*rondellus*	Easter
2	*Felix dies et grata*		
3	*Decet vox letitie*		
4	*In hac die Dei*		
5	*Filii calvarie*		
6	*Luto carens et latere*		
7	*Vivere que tribuit*		
8	*A solis ortus cardine*		
9	*Mors vite propitia*		
10	*In domino confidite*		
11	*Rex omnipotentie*		
12	*Mundi princeps ejicitur*		
13	*Exultet plebs fidelium*		
14	*Christo psallat eccelsia*		
15	*Vetus purgans facinus*		
16	*Omnes gentes plaudite*		
17	*Fidelium sonet vox sobria*		
18	*Christus patris gratie*		
19	*A sinu patris mittitur*		
20	*Vocis tripudio*		
21	*Processit in capite*		
22	*Culpe purgator veteris*		
23	*Dies salutis oritur*		
24	*Vineam meam plantavi*		
25	*Passionis emuli*	strophic+refrain	
26	*Gaudeat hec concio*	*rondellus*	
27	*Transite Sion filie*		
28	*Qui pro nobis mori non respuit*		
29	*Pater creator omnium*		Christmastide
30	*Offerat ecclesia*		Easter
31	*Descende celitus*		Pentecost
32	*Procedenti puero*		Christmas/New Year
33	*Ut iam cesset calamitas*		Christmas
34	*Annus renascitur*		Christmas/New Year
35	*Illuxit lux celestis gratie*		Easter
36	*Exultemus sobrie*		
37	*Veris principium*		
38	*Christo sit laus in celestibus*		
39	*Veterum memorem pellite*		
40	*Ecce tempus gaudii*		
41	*Novum ver oritur*		
42	*Iam ver aperit terre gremium*		
43	*Psallite regi glorie*		
44	*Breves dies hominis*		secular

Table 1.1 (*cont.*)

No.	Incipit	Form	Occasion
45	*In rerum principio*	strophic	Dedication
46	*Gaude Syon, devoto gaudio*	*rondellus*	Christmas
47	*Salve virgo virginum*	*rondellus*	Marian
48	*Ave Maria virgo virginum*	*rondellus*	Marian
49	*Ecce mundi gaudium*	strophic+refrain	Christmas
50	*In hoc statu gratie*	strophic	Christmas
51	*Tempus adest gratie*	*rondellus*	Christological
52	*Salva nos stella maris*	*rondellus*	Marian
53	*Leto leta concio*	through-composed	Christmas
54	*O quanto consilio*	through-composed	Christological
55	*Iam lucis orto sidere*	troped hymn	Prime hymn
56	*O summi regis mater inclita*	strophic	Marian
57	*Nicholae presulum*	strophic+refrain	St. Nicholas
58	*Gaudeat ecclesia*		
59	*Nicholaus pontifex*		
60	*Exultet hec concio*	*rondellus*	

calendrical ordering in the Sanctorale may have mirrored the calendrical organization of the Temporale portion (Easter to Christmas) of the fascicle.

Only with F, in the middle of the thirteenth century, do examples of calendrical ordering appear, in addition to ordering Latin song by form, voice number, or subject matter. Earlier manuscripts, including a source with many concordances in F, Tours 927, are frequently organized thematically and according to form or genre, but not calendrically.[13] In the fourteenth century and beyond, several manuscripts organize refrain songs by form as well as calendrically; among these, the Moosburger Graduale is most explicit due to rubrication.[14] The grouping of Latin songs into a discrete "cantionale" already sets the songs apart from the liturgical contents of the gradual; an introductory preface (translated and discussed later in this chapter) and rubrics, moreover, ensure that the songs are read as proper to certain feasts and rituals of the calendar year.[15] Attributed to the dean of the song school Johannes de Perchausen, the preface also specifies *clericuli*, young choirboys, as the intended audience, a community that makes sense given that the songs

---

[13] On the compilation of refrain songs in Tours 927 and their internal logic, see Caldwell, "*Pax Gallie.*"

[14] This becomes the norm for later *cantionales*, or song collections; see Strohm, "Sacred Song."

[15] For internal divisions of the song repertoire in the Moosburger Graduale, see Brewer, "Songs," 36–37. On the role of the song school dean Johannes de Perchausen in the creation and compilation of the *cantionale*, see ibid. and discussion later in this chapter.

Table 1.2 Liturgical organization of the *cantionale* in the Moosburger Graduale, fol. 231ʳ–246ʳ (for folio numbers see the Appendix)

Rubric	Incipit	Feast
Cum episcopus eligitur	*Castis psallamus mentibus*	Boy Bishop
Cum itur extra ecclesiam ad choream	*Mos florentis venustatis*	
Item alia	*Gregis pastor Tytirus*	
Cum infulatus et vestitus presul intronisatur	*Anni novi novitas*	
In die S. Nicolai episcopi cantio	*Intonent hodie*	St. Nicholas
De nativitate Domini cantio prima	*Gaudeat ecclesia*	Nativity
De nat. Domini	*Nove geniture*	
De nat. Dom.	*Ecce venit de Syon*	
De nativitate Dom.	*De Syon exivit tenor legis* (*no refrain)	
De nat. Dom.	*Ecce nomen domini*	
De nat. Dom.	*Fulget dies hec pre ceteris*	
De nat. Dom.	*Resultet plebs fidelis*	
De nat. Dom.	*Nunc angelorum gloria*	
De nat. Dom.	*Dies ista colitur*	
De nat. Dom.	*De supernis sedibus*	
De nat. Dom. cantio	*Verbum patris humanatur*	
De nat. Dom. cantio	*Deinceps ex nulla*	
Item de nat. Dom.	*In natali summi regis*	
De beata Virgine cantio	*Mater summi domini*	Virgin (with a
De beata Virg.	*Nove lucis hodie*	focus on the
De beata Virg.	*Ave virgo mater Jesu Christi*	Nativity)
Item de beata Virg.	*Ave virgo mater intemerata*	
Item de beata Virg.	*Flos campi profert lilium*	
De beata Virgine	*Ad cultum tue laudis*	
De S. Stephano prothomartyre	*Dulces laudes tympano*	St. Stephen
Johannis Evangeliste	*Christi sit nativitas*	John the Evangelist
In die Ss. Innocentium	*Ecce iam celebria*	Holy Innocents
Generalis ad predictas festivitates	*Evangelizo gaudium*	General feasts
De nativitate et beata virgine	*Letatur turba puerorum*	Nativity and the Virgin Mary
In circumcisione Domini	*Nostri festi gaudium*	Circumcision
Ad novum annum	*Ecce novus annus est*	New Year
In die sancto et in octava Epiphanie cantio	*Tribus signis deo dignis*	Epiphany
In Epiph. Domini et in octava eius cantio	*Stella nova radiat*	

begin with the Feast of the Boy Bishop, a liminal ritual for choirboys that formed an accretion to the Advent and Christmastide liturgy (see Table 1.2).[16]

---

[16] On the boy bishop, see Chambers, *The Mediaeval Stage*, 1:336–371; Shahar, "Boy Bishop's Feast"; Davidson, *Festivals and Plays*, 5–12; Dahhaoui, "Enfant–évêque," "Voyages," and "Le Pape de Saint-Étienne"; Milway, "Boy Bishops"; and Harris, *Sacred Folly, passim.*

The songs begin with the choirboys' special festivities surrounding the election of the boy bishop, evidencing an alignment with the preface, in which choirboys are specified as the audience for, and performers of, these songs. The chorister-turned-bishop was typically elected on the Feast of St. Nicholas (a proto-bishop and patron saint of choirboys) in early Advent and presided during the weeks leading up to Christmas and, on occasion, through Epiphany. Logically, a song for St. Nicholas thus directly follows those for the boy bishop's rites. In the *cantionale*, two Epiphany songs close out the collection, *Tribus signis deo dignis* and *Stella nova radiat*, and signal the end of the boy bishop's seasonal reign. Between these two moments – the election of the boy bishop and Epiphany – the entire breadth of the Advent and Christmas season, including its saints, is adumbrated in devotional song, refrain, and rubric.[17]

In a parallel example from fourteenth-century Ireland, the sixty unnotated poems, including thirty-nine refrain-form poems, of the Red Book of Ossory are accompanied by an introductory preface and, for the initial four songs, rubrication. For performance contexts, the preface attributed to the Bishop of Ossory, Richard Ledrede, indicates only that the songs were to be sung on "important holidays and at celebrations" ("in magnis festis et solaciis"); the rubrics on the initial folio of the collation are more specific, singling out the Nativity.[18] The first, "Cantilena de Nativitate Domini," is followed by three more that indicate the same feast (e.g. "Alia cantilena de eodem festo"). Despite the lack of similar rubrics indicating the occasion throughout the remaining folios, which transmit fifty-six poems, Christmas or related poems (such as ones for Epiphany) are largely grouped near the beginning, while Easter poems appear in a cluster toward the middle of the collection. Significantly, unlike the preceding works, the final thirteen poems are not unique but instead incorporate borrowed material and exploit different poetic forms and styles.[19] The majority of the poems are for Christmastide and Eastertide; the remainder are either Marian, including one appropriate for the Feast of the Annunciation, or explore a small range of devotional subjects. The "magnis festis et solaciis" presumably refers chiefly to the feasts of the Christmas and Easter seasons,

---

[17] The ordering of the *Benedicamus Domino* song-tropes that follow on fol. 246ʳ–250ᵛ repeats the liturgical cycle, with Easter figuring more prominently. With respect to the integration of feasts of the Temporale and Sanctorale in the ordering, this is the norm in early chant books for the saints' days between Christmas and Epiphany; see Hughes, *Medieval Manuscripts*, 8–9.

[18] Red Book of Ossory, fol. 70ʳ. See Chapter 5 for the complete text and translation of the preface.

[19] On the poems and their topical distribution, see Colledge, *Latin Poems*, xli; Greene, *Lyrics*, v–vi; and Stemmler, *Latin Hymns*, xxii.

in addition to Marian feasts or devotions. The scribe thus consciously tried, even if not always precisely, to organize the poems along the lines of the great feasts cited, as performance context.

Between thematic and formal homogeneity and calendrical organization, sources for the refrain song show a tendency toward grouping by several parameters. While collating songs according to the presence of a refrain suggests an interest in formal typologies, the calendrical clustering and ordering apparent in several sources point to the close alignment of the refrain song with the calendar year and church seasons. In this, the transmission of the medieval Latin refrain song has much in common with liturgical Latin songs such as hymns or sequences, as well as later collections of sacred Latin and vernacular songs.[20] Latin song, and the refrain song most of all, cannot be easily untangled from the church year and its musical expression. Although this is hinted at in the language, devotional register, and, in some cases, liturgical function of many Latin songs, the *compilatio* and *ordinatio* of sources for the refrain song underscore its calendrical embeddedness.

The Plurality of Time: Easter and Springtime

The refrain song engages in discourses around time not solely by reflecting the liturgical calendar through manuscript ordering, but also poetically by commenting on and intervening in the experience of time and its plurality of overlapping feasts and seasons. Refrain songs frequently offer implicit commentaries on the plurality of time, and specifically the calendar year; for instance, the widely transmitted song *Dies ista colitur* is rubricated in four sources, two referring to its performance in troped liturgies for the Feast of the Circumcision, and two others indicating Christ's Nativity and the Virgin Mary as topics.[21] *Dies ista colitur* is meaningful in any of these contexts; the changing rubrics reflect theological parallels that enable the same song to praise the Virgin, while also celebrating Christ's Nativity, and honoring his Circumcision. *Rondelli* in final fascicle of F offer special insight into how poetry and music participate in discourses of temporal plurality during Eastertide in particular. Specifically, within the large-scale calendrical ordering of Fascicle XI of F, the internal grouping of *rondelli*

---

[20] Strohm, "Late-Medieval Sacred Songs." On later Christmas songs and motets in particular, many with ties to earlier repertoires, see Schmidt-Beste, "Psallite noe!"

[21] These latter two rubrics read, respectively, "de nativitate domini" in the Moosburger Graduale and "de sancta maria" in Stuttg.

according to calendar and seasonal time, along with an unusually consistent poetic and thematic vocabulary, showcase an interest in promoting and tempering the celebration of feasts while symbolically fusing seasonal and liturgical cycles of time.

Latin refrain songs, and especially those in Fascicle XI of F, have frequently been described as lighthearted, ingratiating, festive, and energetic, in part due to long-standing associations with dance.[22] Certainly, the poems in Fascicle XI, along with their refrain forms and liturgical ordering, convey an entirely different mood than the *conducti* in earlier fascicles of F. *De patre principio* on the initial folio of the fascicle, with the refrain "Let us rejoice, eia" ("Gaudeamus eȳa"), sets the scene for similar invocations of praise and rejoicing.[23] Yet the fascicle also includes songs and refrains featuring a more somber tone, as in the refrain of *Mundi princeps eicitur* for the Resurrection: "For life dies on the Cross ... The victim who suffered for us | opens the gate of salvation."[24] Throughout the final fascicle of F, the poetry fosters festive celebration on one hand, and devotional contemplation and prayer on the other.

The vocabulary of temperance and moderation in the refrain songs of F offers a strategic framing of the liturgical feasts cued in the poetry, constructing a repertoire of festive and celebrative yet sober songs. Indicative of this duality of tone is the frequency of the adjective *sobrius* (literally meaning "not drunk," or "sober") throughout the songs, and accompanying turns of phrase that convert joyous outpourings into temperate expressions.[25] Although the adjective is not uncommon in Latin poetry, it appears with conspicuous regularity in the Easter *rondelli* of F (see Table 1.3).[26] These five Easter songs each employ *sobrius* as a way to inflect expressions of praise or to moderate the voicing of joy. This is especially noteworthy in the context of songs for major feasts and holidays of the church year; song and voice are constant themes throughout the fascicle, yet always referred to in ways that suggest these utterances are carefully controlled and never excessive.

The refrain forms and musical settings are also noteworthy in light of this rhetoric of restraint. The *rondelli* in F present particularly careful and

---

[22] Haines has most recently noted the "energetic, sensuous joy of the ring dance" of the songs in Fascicle XI of F; see Haines, *Medieval Song*, 70–71; see also Chapter 3.

[23] F, fol. 463ʳ.

[24] F, fol. 464ᵛ, "In ligno vita moritur ... Salutis pandit ostia | Passa pro nobis hostia."

[25] See "sobrius" in *Glossarium*.

[26] The first three have concordances, while the final two (*Exultemus sobrie* and *Psallite glorie*) are unique to F; see the Appendix.

Table 1.3 "Sober" songs in Fascicle XI of F

Incipit	Fol.	Strophe /Refrain	Phrase	Translation
Fidelium sonet vox sobria	465ʳ	1	Fidelium sonet vox sobria	Let the sober voice of the faithful sound
Vocis tripudio	465ᵛ	1	Vocis tripudio | sed mente sobria.	With joyful leaps of the voice, but with a sober mind.
Processit in capite	466ʳ	2	Regi nostro psallite | sensu tamen sobrio.	Sing psalms to our king, yet with sober feeling.
Exultemus sobrie	468ʳ	1/Ref.	Exultemus sobrie | Christo regi glorie	Let us soberly exult *in Christ the King of Glory*
Psallite regi glorie	469ʳ	3	Christo laus sonet sobrie	Let praise be sung soberly to Christ

Example 1.1 F, fol. 465ᵛ–466ʳ, *Vocis tripudio*, first strophe and refrain

controlled forms; their largely syllabic, narrow-ranged, and strophic musical settings are far from excessive, as in *Vocis tripudio* (see Example 1.1). Lacking melismas, large leaps, and ligated pitches, the musical setting proceeds largely stepwise; the two musical phrases, more-over, are nearly identical, resulting in an economy of musical material. Not all refrain songs are as unassuming and sparse as *Vocis tripudio* in F; indeed, in Tours 927, the musical setting of the same poem is more adventurous melodically and formally.[27] In keeping with the rhetorical tone throughout the songs in Fascicle XI of F, however, musical settings often convey a sense of moderation and restraint by avoiding melismas and leaps. Individual songs may be lighthearted or energetic, keeping the theme of rejoicing front and center, but the fascicle on the whole advocates for the "sober" musical commemoration of liturgical time.

Exultemus sobrie and *Psallite regi glorie* in Table 1.3 are, moreover, part of an internal cluster of songs that reflect a different temporal duality. In

[27] For a comparison of the two versions, see Caldwell, "*Pax Gallie*," 116–117. Melismatic *rondelli* in the Engelberg Codex are discussed in Chapter 5.

Table 1.4 Easter/springtime *rondelli* in F

Incipit		Fol.
Illuxit lux celestis gratie	The light of heavenly grace shines	468ʳ
Exultemus sobrie	Let us temperately exult	
Veris principium	The beginning of spring	
Christo sit laus in celestibus	Let there be praise to Christ in the heavens	
Veterum memorem pellite	Drive away ancient sadness	468ᵛ
Ecce tempus gaudii	Behold, the time of joy	
Novum ver oritur	A new spring arises	
Iam ver aperit terre gremium	Now spring opens the bosom of the earth	469ʳ
Psallite regi glorie	Sing psalms to the King of Glory	

addition to balancing rejoicing with moderation, a series of nine *rondelli* plays with the poetic plurality around Christ's Resurrection and spring-time, while also gesturing toward Christ's Nativity, the earthly birth preceding his divine rebirth (see Table 1.4).[28] All nine songs are steeped in vernal symbolism, referencing flowers, springtime, and, in many cases, the transition from winter to spring; each also identifies the "flower" in question as Christ, the "King of Glory" and "King of Heaven." The word "flower" ("flos") and its various forms alone occurs more than forty-three times over the course of these nine songs (including repetition due to refrains), unremittingly relating spring's vernality to Jesus as the ultimate flower of Christianity.[29]

Notably, these nine songs have been linked to Christ's Nativity in previous catalogues and inventories, with the arrival of springtime and Christ as flower understood as allegorical references to his birth.[30] The refrain of *Novum ver oritur*, for instance, includes the word "epȳphania," although in this context it appears less likely to refer to the Feast of Epiphany, as has been assumed, and instead to a more general idea of manifestation or appearance. This is supported in the fifth strophe by a reference to the trope of the dragon (Satan or sin) being crushed by Christ as he steps from the tomb on Easter morning, although this strophe is solely transmitted in Tours 927:[31]

---

[28] Songs edited and translated in Anderson, *Notre-Dame and Related Conductus*, 8:xxviii–xxx.
[29] Compared to the continual repetition of "flos" and its various forms in these songs, the "flower" only appears a handful of times elsewhere in Fascicle XI of F.
[30] See, for example, Haines, *Medieval Song*, 69–70.
[31] On the symbolism of the dragon, or the *caput draconis* theology, see Robertson, "The Savior, the Woman, and the Head of the Dragon."

1. Novum ver oritur	1. A new spring begins,
Letemur igitur	*therefore, let us be glad,*
Iam flos egreditur.	for now, the flower is budding.
Cesset tristitia	*Let sorrow cease,*
Floralis gaudia	*epiphany gives way to*
Dat epȳphania.	*the joys of Flora.*
. . .	. . .
5. Draco conteritur	5. The dragon is crushed,
Letemur igitur	*therefore, let us be glad,*
Pax nobis redditur.	and peace is restored to us.
Cesset tristitia	*Let sorrow cease,*
Floralis gaudia	*epiphany gives way to*
Dat epȳphania.	*the joys of Flora.*

Nowhere in any of the poems is Christ's Nativity explicitly named (as it is in other Christmas songs in F); neither, however, is his Resurrection. Instead, the poems refer most often to the passing of winter and arrival of spring and all that the new season encompasses and signals. The beginning of spring ("veris principium"), which melts wintery ice ("glacie sepulta" and "victa glacie") as winter departs and a new season begins ("hiemis extinguitur estas reducitur"), reverberates across the songs, resulting in a richly allegorical outpouring of springtime symbolism that links these nine *rondelli* and sets them apart from other Easter songs in Fascicle XI.[32]

Clear parallels emerge in these songs with the springtime topos in vernacular song and the *Natureingang*. Three songs begin with rhetorical gestures of season and time – *Veris principium, Novum ver oritur,* and *Iam ver aperit terre gremium* – while the remainder invoke springtime throughout strophes and refrains. One of the most striking moments in the nine songs is in the third and final strophe of *Veterem merorem pellite* in which a bird – a sonic marker of springtime – makes an appearance, replete with direct speech:[33]

---

[32] Quotations from, respectively, *Veris principium, Exultemus sobrie, Psallite regi glorie,* and *Novum ver oritur.* See also the similar themes in vernacular song discussed most recently in Saltzstein, "Songs of Nature."

[33] On birdsong in the Middle Ages, see Leach, *Sung Birds,* and for the connection with the springtime topos, Saltzstein, "Songs of Nature."

3. Veterem [habitum] ponite
  Domino gratias agite
Clamitat avis exuite
Hiberna pallial.
  Domino gratias agite
  Qui fecit omnia.

3. "Put off the old mantle,"
  give thanks unto the Lord,
clamors the bird, "cast aside
winter coverings!"
  Give thanks unto the Lord,
  who has made all things.

The clamoring of the bird in this strophe reflects the broader trope of bird songs and sounds in medieval music; its message here is one of renewal, casting off the old (i.e. sin) in order to welcome the new (i.e. Christ).[34] Evoking the topos of springtime and birds employed countless times in medieval song across register and language, *Veterem merorum pellite* features the allegorical reframing and repurposing of nature imagery in the context of Easter. Although neither new nor unique to F, the poets and compilers of the fascicle deliberately grouped songs engaging in the same allegorical mode that links liturgical and seasonal time.

The songs in the final fascicle of F shape the experience of festive time and the medieval calendar by highlighting tensions between different ways of experiencing time. In some cases, songs focus on the balance between rejoicing and restraint, advocating for the kind of lighthearted celebration frequently associated with Latin refrain songs, yet tempered rhetorically by moderation and sobriety. The series of Easter *rondelli* characterized by springtime topoi, on the other hand, acknowledge the intersection of liturgical and natural time, bringing Christ's Resurrection together with the imagery of springtime. The emphasis on moderation and sobriety, moreover, is a marked feature of the fascicle that signals the broader cultural context of the refrain song beyond F. Although Eastertide is a specific focal point in F, the calendrical distribution of the refrain song includes the other major season of the liturgical year, Christmastide, bringing different concerns into play around the regulation of how the medieval year was experienced through song.

---

[34] A well-known example of the avian symbolism of springtime and the Resurrection is the contrafact pair in Harley 978, fol. 11ᵛ, *Sumer is icumen in* and *Perspice christicola*. See the recent discussion of this song, and Harley 978, in Deeming, "English Monastic Miscellany"; see also Colton, *Angel Song*, 13–38.

Reforming Festivity: Disciplining Time Through Song and Refrain

As the Easter *rondelli* in Fascicle XI of F illustrate, the refrain song intervenes most markedly at moments of temporal plurality in the medieval calendar. While the *rondelli* of F are concerned with Easter, springtime, and their "sober" celebration, the late fall and early winter season from the Feast of St. Nicholas through Epiphany on January 6 presents further tensions between liturgical, calendrical, and seasonal temporalities mediated in and through song. Within the span of early winter and Christmastide feasts and festivities, the refrain song and its material contexts highlight moments singled out for regulation and reform by church authorities, motivated by musical, choreographic, and ludic activities that stemmed from competing ways of celebrating feasts, holidays, and seasons.

The refrain song's emphasis on the Feast of St. Nicholas and rituals of the Advent season and Christmastide, including the Feast of the Circumcision (January 1), is significant since these seasons and feasts frequently coincided, like Easter and springtime rites, with extraliturgical, seasonal, and so-called "pagan" festivities. For Advent, the Feast of St. Nicholas initiated clerical and lay festivities, ushering in school holidays and secular early winter rituals and, in the church, marking the election of the boy bishop (as in the Moosburger Graduale, above). Within the liturgy of the church, the festive Christmas season also invoked significant excess and widespread celebration, including the clerical celebration of the feasts following Christmas (referred to as the *Libertas Decembrica*). Within and outside of the church, the Christmas season was additionally inflected by celebrations of the solstice and of the Kalends of January, reflecting ritual holdovers from antiquity as well as medieval New Year's traditions. This varied cycle of winter festivities, which incorporated condoned and condemned, secular and liturgical, rites and rituals, has most often been termed a part of the "festive," "merry," or "ritual" year celebrated throughout the Middle Ages in church and town.[35]

Celebration of the festive year attracted near constant criticism from the church throughout the Middle Ages, which focused on varied practices

---

[35] On festive years and calendars, see Hutton, *Rise and Fall*, 5–48 and *Stations of the Sun*; Delale and Delle Luche, "Le temps," 11–23; Davidson, *Festivals and Plays*, 3–47; Duffy, *Stripping of the Altars*, 11–52; Humphrey, *Politics of Carnival, passim*; Muir, *Ritual in Early Modern Europe*, 62–88; Phythian-Adams, "Ceremony and the Citizen"; Cressy, *Bonfires and Bells, passim*; and Davis, *Society and Culture*, 97–123. The word "festivity" has no medieval equivalent, although its origins in the noun "feast" predate the Middle Ages. See also n. 39 below.

ranging from mummery, games, and drunkenness to singing and dancing. Descriptions of singing and dancing in particular follow certain patterns – vulgar, lewd, pagan, diabolical, scurrilous, bawdy, and indecent are but a sample of the negative epithets applied to music and movement accompanying secular, seasonal, and liturgical festivities. Notably, the calendrical distribution of the Latin refrain song traces similar contours to these festive seasons and their "scurrilous" songs. Latin refrain songs are not, however, the scurrilous, bawdy, or diabolical songs decried by preachers, nor are Latin songs more broadly. Instead, the refrain song appears, in several instances, to be a strategic response to secular musical practices enacted in the celebration of the festive year. Evidence from condemnatory writings, manuscript contexts and paratexts, and the poetry of songs themselves identifies portions of the Latin refrain song repertoire as musical responses to the contested celebration of the festive year. This is already hinted at in the Easter *rondelli* of F; a broader perspective shows the way in which the Latin refrain song balances the simultaneous festive and solemn commemoration of other feasts and seasons.

Condemnations, typically ecclesiastical, of song and dance almost have the status of clichés in medieval texts, with a focus on vernacular song and the dances of women. Condemnations exist in the hundreds, mostly concerned with the body (especially women's bodies), inappropriate performance spaces (such as cemeteries), and poetic register (lewd, sexual, etc.).[36] Throughout legal texts, penitentials, sermons, chronicles, registers, and even exegetical writings, complaints are frequently recycled, with language and phrasing verging on the repetitive. Similarly, the occasions at the center of critique and admonishment form a relatively limited cycle of liturgical feasts, saints' vigils and feast days, seasonal markers (equinoxes and solstices), and calendrical transitions, with the New Year featuring prominently.[37] While liturgical feasts are singled out, complaints are most often framed around associated "pagan" celebrations and the desire to rid Christian rituals of non-Christian elements.[38] Since many of these same feast days were obligatory holidays (*festa ferianda*), there was added incentive to maintain a degree of solemnity within and outside of the church, since communities were otherwise free from daily labors and therefore quite literally had time to fill with potentially unsavory activities.[39]

---

[36] See, for instance, the condemnations cited in Dronke, *The Medieval Lyric*, 15–16; Page, *Owl and the Nightingale*, 110–133; and Haines, *Medieval Song*, 55–67 and 162–171.

[37] Haines, *Medieval Song*, 60.   [38] Filotas, *Pagan Survivals*, 153–192.

[39] *Festa ferianda* required cessation of all activities, including manual labor and study, and they included major feast days like Christmas and Easter, and a flexible list of other feasts depending

The surviving register of the thirteenth-century archbishop of Rouen Eudes Rigaud exemplifies the spirit of musical and poetic reform around certain feast days, at least in Normandy.[40] Providing accounts of Rigaud's archdiocesan travels between the years 1248 and 1269, the *Regestrum* offers insight into the activities of a range of institutions (male and female, secular and monastic), with a focus on recording and disciplining inappropriate behaviors. Throughout the years covered in the *Regestrum*, several feasts occasioned repeated musical, poetic, choreographic, and ludic offenses at a handful of female and male institutions: the Feast of the Holy Innocents receives seven mentions, and there are two for St. Nicholas, and one each for the feasts of Sts. John, Stephen, Katherine, Hildevert, and Mary Magdalene (see Table 1.5).[41] Prohibited activities in Rigaud's entries vary from general to specific. Dance (*choreas*) is referenced on several occasions, and games make appearances too, while songs range from those described as "scurrilous" to the generic descriptor *cantilenas*. Significantly, Rigaud identifies several genres, namely *virelais*, *conducti*, and motets in the case of the entry from January 12, 1260, and also gestures toward the musical practices of women (specifically nuns) as well as men. In all cases, Rigaud attempts (and seemingly fails) to reform the celebration of certain feasts across his archdiocese and, more specifically, to abolish the nonliturgical songs, verses, and dances that detracted from otherwise sanctioned feasts.

Although the precise musical works cited by Rigaud remain unknown (and the level of exaggeration and embellishment in his account is unclear), extra-liturgical Latin songs survive for the feasts he singles out in compelling numbers. This is especially the case for the Feasts of Nicholas and the Holy Innocents. Specifically, Rigaud's reference to the singing of *virelais* on the Feast of St. Nicholas resonates with the existence of a significant corpus of Latin refrain songs venerating the saint from across Europe between the twelfth and fourteenth centuries (see Table 1.6). Significantly, Nicholas is not only the saint most substantially represented in the poetry of *nova cantica*, *conducti*, and *cantiones*, outstripped in popularity only by the Virgin Mary

---

on place. While *festa ferianda* had a greater impact on the laity, since the mandatory feast days required laity to attend church (thus enforcing the regular experience of "sacred" time), labor was also lessened for clergy and others affiliated with churches and schools, including universities. See Rodgers, *Discussion of Holidays*; Cheney, "Rules"; Harvey, "Work and *Festa Ferianda*"; and Bartlett, *Why Can the Dead Do Such Great Things?*, 133–136.

[40] Edited and translated in Bonnin, *Regestrum*; O'Sullivan, *Register*. More generally, see Davis, *Holy Bureaucrat*.

[41] Latin texts in Bonnin, *Regestrum*, 44, 166, 197, 261, 384, 431, 466, 471, and 517. Translations adapted from O'Sullivan, *Register*, 50, 182, 212, 293, 436, 490, 530–531, 536, 554, and 591.

Table 1.5 References to music, dance, and games on feast days in Rigaud's *Regestrum, ca.* 1249–1265

Date	Place	Reference
July 9, 1249	Priory of Villarceaux	Item, we forbid you to continue the farcical performances which have been your practice at the **Feast of the Innocents** and of the **Blessed Mary Magdalene**, to dress up in worldly costumes, or to lead dances with each other or with laity [*cum secularibus choreas ducendo*].
Sept. 12, 1253	Priory of Villarceaux	They sing songs [*cantilenas*] on the **Feast of the Innocents**.
Jan. 5, 1254	Abbey of St-Léger-des-Préaux	We forbade them to celebrate the **Feast of the Innocents** because of the customs contrary to the Rule.
Oct. 23, 1256	Abbey of La-Trinité-de-Caen	The young nuns … at the **Feast of the Innocents** sing the Office with farses [*cum farsis*]; we forbade this.
Jan. 12, 1260	Abbey of Montivilliers	Item, at the **Feasts of St. John, St. Stephen, and the Holy Innocents** they conducted themselves with too much hilarity and sang scurrilous songs such as drunken farses, *conducti*, and motets [*nimia iocositate et scurrilibus cantibus utebantur, ut pote farsis, conductis, motulis*]; we ordered them to behave more decorously and with more devotion in the future.
May 22, 1262	Abbey of Montivilliers	They said that they had entirely abandoned the farses [*facere*] which they used to act at the **Feast of the Innocents**; item, we ordered them to abstain from all such things entirely.
Aug. 22, 1263	Church of St-Hildevert-de-Gournay	Item, on some of the feast days, particularly that of **St. Nicholas**, the clerks, vicars, and even the chaplains [*clerici, vicarii, ac etiam capellani*] conducted themselves in a dissolute and scurrilous manner, dancing through the town and singing *virelais* [*ducendo choreas per vicos et faciendo le vireli*].
Oct. 1, 1263	Church of St-Hildevert-de-Gournay	Item, we issued a general prohibition against dancing [*choreas ducerent*] on the **Feasts of St. Nicholas, St. Katherine, St. Hildevert**, or any other.
May 9, 1265	Abbey of Montivilliers	Item, we ordered them to refrain altogether from games [*ludis*] on the **Feast of the Innocents**.

and Christ; he is also honored most often in refrain-form songs.[42] Although these Latin refrain songs are not *virelais*, the French *forme fixe* is similarly characterized by a structural refrain; the songs in Table 1.6 are, however, far from "dissolute" or "scurrilous." Each poem comprises a doctrinally sound prayer to Nicholas, drawing in most cases on his *vita* and miracles and directing attention toward the theme of pious song, as in *Laudibus Nicholai* from the St-Victor Miscellany: "Let us devote ourselves to sweet songs and praises of Nicholas."[43]

---

[42] See n. 9 above.   [43] "Laudibus Nicholai dulcibus vacemus cum cantibus."

Table 1.6 Refrain songs for St. Nicholas

Incipit	Source	Provenance	Date
Incomparabiliter cum iucunditate	St-M A, 46^v	Aquitaine	12th c.
Exultemus et letemur	Later Cambridge Songbook, 4^r	England	late 12th c.
Nicholaus inclitus	Tours 927, 11^v	northern France	*ca.* 1225
Gaudeat ecclesia	F, 471^r	Paris, France	*ca.* 1240s–
Nicholae presulum	F, 471^r		1250s
Nicholaus pontifex	F, 471^r		
Exultet hec concio	F, 471^v		
Sancti Nicholai	St-Victor Miscellany, 178^v	northern France	late 13th c.
Nicolai laudibus	St-Victor Miscellany, 182^r		
Nicolai sollempnio	St-Victor Miscellany, 186^v		
Laudibus Nicholai	St-Victor Miscellany, 189^r		
Intonent hodie	Moosburger Graduale, 232^v	Moosburg, Germany	late 14th c.

While it would be misleading to see these songs for St. Nicholas as pious substitutes for the *virelais* disdained by Rigaud, the existence of this complex of hagiographical songs speaks to an impulse to reframe festivities that expanded beyond boundaries set by the church.[44] It is striking to note the resonance of Rigaud's "clerks, vicars, and chaplains" with the communities and contexts of the sources in Table 1.6. For the most part, the manuscripts in this table reflect clerical milieus, although St-M A is closely linked with the Abbey of St-Martial in Limoges, and the origins of the Later Cambridge Songbook remain elusive.[45] For Tours 927, F, the St-Victor Miscellany, and the Moosburger Graduale, clerical, pedagogical, or scholastic origins are likely. The St-Victor Miscellany emanates from the environs of a northern French university (see Chapter 5) and the songs of the Moosburger Graduale were compiled and in some cases composed by the dean of the song school in Moosburg, Johannes de Perchausen; while F and Tours 927 betray clerical origins, the former connected to the Notre Dame

---

[44] Caldwell, "Singing, Dancing, and Rejoicing," 451–477. Aubry likewise sees a parallel between Rigaud's mention of *virelais* and the Nicholas songs in F, suggesting these could have been the songs Rigaud witnessed, which is unlikely; *La Musique et les musiciens d'église*, 45. See also Page, *Voices and Instruments*, 90.

[45] On the origins of St-M A, see Grier, "Some Codicological Observations," which builds on Fuller, "Aquitanian Polyphony." On the Later Cambridge Song Book, which was used, if not also copied, in England, see Stevens, ed., *Later Cambridge Songs*, 35–39. Stevens (p. 32) describes many of the songs in the manuscript as "linked together by what may be called, in broad terms, purposes of festivity, social celebration, and entertainment," with the church and "churchmen" the creators and intended audience, a description that fits with the framework offered in this chapter.

Cathedral in Paris and the latter showing several signs of clerical compilation and use.[46]

These sources and songs, in other words, transmit repertoires composed by, or accessible to, a wide range of clerical ranks and students. Moreover, although Rigaud's *Regestrum* only accounts for the archdiocese of Rouen, the northern French emphasis in the refrain songs for St. Nicholas is notable. Nicholas's feast day was highly ranked across France by the twelfth century, and pockets of heightened devotion developed in Paris and northern France around his cult, including among clerics and students, as well as vernacular poets and playwrights.[47] In Paris, for instance, Nicholas's feast day at both the University of Paris and Notre Dame Cathedral was a day marked for festivity, yet was also frequently an occasion for excess and wrongdoing – like Rigaud, authorities in Paris lamented the way clerics and students celebrated a favored saint's feast day (Nicholas was a patron saint of clerics and students, as well as the University of Paris).[48] Across northern France, consequently, Nicholas's feast day was an occasion for musical, ludic, and ritual excess. The survival of Latin songs, many with refrains, in honor of the saint attests to a desire to magnify the feast day with nonliturgical music at a far remove from the bawdy and scurrilous ditties sung and danced in village streets in Normandy and elsewhere. The refrain is a key pivot between secular excess and devotional exuberance; Rigaud's *virelais* for Nicholas have their counterpart, albeit unstated, in the Latin refrain song.

While parallels between the Latin refrain song and Rigaud's records are difficult to establish, his register offers an important perspective on the musical disciplining of feast days. Texts like Rigaud's witness how song, accretion, and festivity were linked in the context of the calendar year, highlighting the "noisiest" moments and, consequently, the ones most in need of reform and regulation. Feasts and holidays had a particular soundscape throughout medieval Europe, with quotidian labors ceasing and the devotional labors of the daily Mass and Office increasing by means of tropes and polyphony, along with the bells that pealed according to the rank of the feast and mood of the season.[49] Song played a role in this soundscape too, at times adjacent to the liturgy (as in tropes or in the context of dramas and plays) and other times at ambiguous moments involving both devotional and secular forms of recreation.

---

[46] On the clerical context of Tours 927, see Chaguinian, ed., *The Jeu d'Adam*.

[47] On St. Nicholas in Arras, see Symes, *A Common Stage*, 32–68. On the Norman cult of St. Nicholas, see Jones, "Norman Cult," and Gazeau and Le Maho, "Les Origines."

[48] Caldwell, "Singing, Dancing, and Rejoicing," 454–459.

[49] See, for example, Symes, *A Common Stage*, 141.

Pious Substitutes in the Moosburger Graduale and Red Book of Ossory

Manuscript sources for the refrain song provide further textual and repertorial insights into how composers, poets, and scribes conceived of the relationship between song and the festive year. The inclusion of Latin song in troped liturgies and the existence of unique paratexts such as prefaces or descriptive rubrics allow for a cautious understanding of Latin song, and especially the refrain song, as reflecting the church's attempts to control the experience of the festive year within local communities and song cultures. In addition to troped liturgies of the late twelfth and thirteenth centuries, two main witnesses are fourteenth-century manuscripts in which textual prefaces contextualize collections of songs and poems: the Moosburger Graduale and Red Book of Ossory together frame calendrically ordered song collections as repertoires intended as festive yet pious substitutes for the lewd songs frequently embraced by named communities of choirboys and clerics.

The preface in the fourteenth-century Moosburger Graduale, self-consciously written by the former dean of the song school Johannes de Perchausen, is the longer of the two and rehearses many of the age-old complaints of church authorities around the song and singing:

O gracious mother church! "For holiness befits the house of the Lord; and it is fitting that He whose abode has been established in peace should be worshipped in peace and with due reverence."[50] In the council of Lyon, as is found in the Sixth Book of the Decretals concerning the immunities of churches and cemeteries, it forbids songs and public colloquies to be performed in churches. Therefore let not worldly colloquies nor the din and clamor and cackling of worldly songs prevail in our choir on account of the schoolboys' bishop, with whom there is customarily dancing in many churches by the younger clergy, for the particular praise and adornment of the birth of the Lord. On account of which [colloquies and songs] the priest celebrating the divine services at the altar is quite frequently distracted, the discipline of the choir is disturbed, and the devotion of the people stirred into laughter and lasciviousness . . . . I have collected into one document and annexed to the present book the following songs, formerly from antiquity and often sung with the schoolboys' bishop even in major churches, along with a few modern [songs] and also a few of my own that I composed in praise of the Nativity of the Lord and of the Blessed Virgin when I was formerly rector of the schoolboys, for the special reverence of the Savior's infancy, so that at the time of His Nativity, with these

[50] This is a quote from a conciliar decretal, edited and translated in Tanner, ed., *Decrees*, 1:328–329, cited in Brewer, "Songs," 34, n. 12.

songs by the new little clerks, as if from the mouth of infants and suckling children, praise and hymnic devotion might be displayed both decently and reverently, neglecting the lasciviousness of the common people.[51]

Citing a conciliar decretal, Johannes denounces the singing of "worldly" songs and colloquies in the church, since they disrupt the priest at the altar and promote "laughter and lasciviousness." He offers as a replacement a collection of songs, all but one with refrains, to be sung by *pueri*, choirboys, at the time of the Nativity and the ritual of the boy bishop, whose election occurred on the Feast of St. Nicholas.

Unfortunately, Johannes never clarifies whether the songs were to be sung during a church service or at some other moment, although one clue survives in the rubrication of the songs that accompany the boy bishop's rituals (see Table 1.2). The first rubric ("cum episcopus eligitur") refers to the election of the boy bishop, while the second and third ("cum itur extra ecclesiam ad choream" followed by "item alia") pointedly invite the boy bishop, and his choirboy entourage, "to the dance" outside of the church. The installation of the boy bishop then follows ("cum infulatus et vestitus presul intronisatur"), presumably now back in the church.[52] The remaining rubrics solely refer to the feast days and do not offer further glimpses into the choreography or performance of the songs. Yet Johannes's framing of these works as a response to "lascivious" and "worldly" songs, along with the clear festal orientation, first around the boy bishop's feast and then subsequently the major feasts of Christmastide, offers a strong statement on the refrain song as a musical pivot from secular excess to devotional recreation.

---

[51] "Alma mater ecclesia. 'Nam decet domum domini sanctitudo, et decet ut cuius in pace factus est locus, eius cultus sit cum debita veneracione pacificus.' In concilio Lugudunensi ut habetur Sexto libro decretalium, de emunitatibus ecclesiarum et cimiteriorum, prohibuit in ecclesiis fieri canciones et publica parlamenta. Ne igitur propter scolarium Episcopum cum quo in multis ecclesiis, a iuniori clero, ad specialem laudem et decorem natalis domini solet tripudiari, secularia parlamenta, nec non strepitus, clamorque, et cachitus mundanarum cancionum in nostro choro invalescant. Ex quibus sacerdos in altari divina celebrans, frequentius abstrahitur, disciplina choralis confunditur, necnon popularis devotio in risum et lasciviam provocateur ... Infra scriptas canciones, olim ab antiquiis eciam in maioribus ecclesiis cum scolarium Episcopo decantatas, paucis modernis, eciam aliquibus propriis, quas olim, cum Rector fuissem Scolarium, pro laude nativitatis domini, et beate virginis composui adiunctis, cepi in unum scriptum colligere, et presenti libro annectere, pro speciali reverencia infancie salvatoris, ut sibi tempore sue nativitatis, hiis cancionibus a novellis clericulis, quasi ex ore infancium et lactencium laus et ympnizans devocio, postposita vulgarium lascivia, possit tam decenter quam reverenter exhiberi." Moosburger Graduale, fol. 230ᵛ. Text and translation, the former emended from the manuscript and the latter by Jennifer Ottman, from Brewer, "Songs," 33–35.

[52] Moosburger Graduale, fol. 231ʳ–232ʳ.

The brief preface attributed to the Bishop of Ossory, Richard Ledrede, in the Red Book of Ossory resonates rhetorically with Johannes's in the Moosburger Graduale. In what is described by Ardis Butterfield as a "belligerent instruction" by a "thin-lipped bishop," the preface notes that the Bishop made the songs for the vicars, priests, and clerks of the cathedral for important holidays and celebrations so that "their throats and mouths, consecrated to God, may not be polluted by songs which are lewd, secular, and associated with revelry."[53] In the broader context of condemnations against song, Ledrede's introductory remarks seem less belligerent than part of a longer history of crackdowns on musical outpourings of festivity. Although the rubrication that follows is less informative than that in the Moosburger Graduale, the context of the songs within the festive calendar of "great feasts" is readily apparent, and their performance by clergy made explicit by Ledrede. Latin songs for liturgical feasts are once again framed as pious substitutes, although I examine further in Chapter 5 how music as opposed to poetry fits into Ledrede's conception of "lewd" versus devotional.

The picture emerging from these prefaces is one of church authorities reframing the sonic experience of time. By determining the sounds by which the highest feasts were commemorated outside of or adjacent to the liturgy, authority figures in religious communities refocused attention on the year as defined by the church in devotional song, rather than as expressed through secular music making.

A spirit of reform similarly emerges in the context of elaborately troped liturgies for the Feast of the Circumcision on January 1.[54] The troped Circumcision liturgy is especially notable for its connection with the clerical Feast of Fools, also known as the Feast of the Staff, a special yet often raucous feast day celebrated by subdeacons during the *Libertas Decembrica*, a cycle of feast days following Christmas particularly celebrated by different clerical ranks.[55] Max Harris has most recently argued

---

[53] Butterfield, "Poems without Form?," 182–183. See the Introduction and full citation in Chapter 5: "ne guttura eorum et ora Deo santificata polluantur cantilenis teatralibus, turpibus et secularibus."

[54] For example, a quatrain in Sens 46 on the front flyleaf names the Feast of Fools while reiterating a focus on the Circumcision: "The Feast of Fools, by ancient custom celebrated every year in the noble city of Sens, delights the cantor: but all honor's due to Christ the circumcised, now and forever kind." ("Festum stultorum de consuetudine morum | Omnibus urbs Senonis festivat nobilis annis, | Quo gaudet precentor; sed tamen omnis honor | Sit Christo circumciso nunc semper et almo.")

[55] On the Feast of Fools, see Chambers, *The Mediaeval Stage*, 1:274–335; Prévot, "*Festum baculi*"; Gilhus, "Carnival"; Fassler, "Feast of Fools"; Harris, "Rough and Holy" and *Sacred Folly*. On the efforts of theologians to Christianize so-called pagan festivities, notably dance, around the *Libertas Decembrica*, see Mews, "Liturgists and Dance."

that the orthodoxy of the often-critiqued "Feast of Fools" was reinscribed
within the context of the troped liturgy of the Feast of the Circumcision,
sources for which include significant numbers of Latin songs.[56] Harris's
arguments align with views outlined by Susan Boynton and Margot Fassler
concerning clerical festivities around Christmas and the Daniel Play,
respectively, identified in each case as resulting from a desire for greater
order and reform.[57] Within the context of troped Circumcision liturgies,
Latin song thus plays a role in this process of reform; even the well-known
conductus Orientis partibus, often interpreted as bawdy and earthy due to
its "braying" vernacular refrain, "Hez hez sire asnes hez," ultimately participates in affirming the theology of the Feast of the Circumcision.[58]
Beyond the Feast of Fools, the Feast of the Circumcision overlaps calendrically with the New Year – the tensions and reconciliations that occur
musically and poetically between the feast and popular holiday are found
not only in troped liturgies but throughout Latin song.

To close this chapter, I offer a case study on how the Latin refrain
and refrain song – at times transmitted in sources for the troped
Circumcision liturgy – navigate between the calendrical and popular
celebration of January 1 as the Feast of the Circumcision and the
medieval New Year. Significantly, examination of songs for the New
Year enables a new perspective on how the Latin song and refrain
mediates between competing and complementary temporalities beyond
the witness of individual manuscripts. In the examples and manuscripts discussed so far, the contexts have been, for the most part,
highly localized and attached to particular communities; considering
songs from across time and place better demonstrates the cultural
function of the Latin refrain song within discourses around the
medieval year and its sounding.

New Songs and Refrains for the New Year

The first of January was one of the most pluralistic and noisiest days in the
medieval calendar, celebrated simultaneously as the Feast of the
Circumcision, Octave of Nativity, and the New Year, as well as being linked
to clerical festivities such as the Feast of Fools or Feast of the Staff, and Feast

---

[56] Harris, *Sacred Folly*, 98–112. See also Ahn, "Exegetical Function."
[57] Boynton, "Work and Play" and Fassler, "Feast of Fools."
[58] Ahn, "Beastly yet Lofty Burdens."

of the Ass. It was a temporally unruly day, whose identification as the beginning of the New Year was, in fact, contested, with the church making attempts throughout the Middle Ages to shift the celebration of January 1 away from unsanctioned customs and rituals by refocusing attention on the Feast of the Circumcision.[59] Frequently linked to illicit New Year's rituals, song provided one way in which a process of festal reform could be enacted within religious communities. Beginning in the twelfth century, the New Year began receiving increased musical and poetic treatment in the context of devotional Latin song as well as in troped liturgies for the Feast of the Circumcision.[60] These songs did not ignore the popularized identity of January 1 as the New Year, but instead strategically fused nonliturgical commemorations of the New Year with theological themes drawn from the liturgical feast in the church calendar in an effort to reform and control the celebrations of this pluralistic day. Within and across songs, the New Year and its associated novelties instead became "virtual" refrains, opening a window into the associations formed between calendrical customs, theological ideas, and liturgical practices.[61] Latin song and refrain serve as pivots between temporalities beyond the witness of individual manuscripts, emerging as expressive linchpins in the pluralistic celebration of the New Year across medieval Europe.

The festal and calendrical pluralism of January 1 and its ensuing popular and clerical rituals presented a long-standing problem for the medieval church. Vitriolic language around the New Year includes New Year's sermons by Augustine in which he laments the abuses occurring on the "Kalends of January."[62] Included on his list of abuses are elements familiar from condemnations of other seasonal and calendrical celebrations, such as

---

[59] On the dating of the New Year, see the overviews in Blackburn and Holford-Strevens, *Oxford Companion to the Year*, 784–786, and Ware, "Medieval Chronology," 259–260. On the contested commemoration of January 1, see, for instance, the discussion in Filotas, *Pagan Survivals*, 155–172.

[60] The New Year's song has a long history, with songs and verses pivotal to the celebration of January 1 reaching back to antiquity and the rituals around the *saturnalia*, Roman Kalends, and the cultic "birthday of the invincible sun" on December 25 (*Dies Natalis solis invicti*). Wright and Lones, *British Calendar Customs*, 2:18–21. On Kalends, see Harris, "Claiming Pagan Origins" and *Sacred Folly*, 11–24. On the *sol invictus* and its cult, see Halsberghe, *Cult*, especially 174–175.

[61] See the Introduction and Haug, "Ritual and Repetition."

[62] The *Patrologia Latina* includes four sermons for the Kalends of January – two uncertain and two attributed to Augustine. On the reinterpretation of Kalends and Saturnalia in later medieval practices, see Chambers, *The Mediaeval Stage*, vol. 1, especially 235–45 and *passim*, and Mews, "Liturgists and Dance." See, however, the rejection of theories that related medieval feasts, especially those falling in December and at the New Year, to Roman feasts in Harris, "Claiming Pagan Origins."

dancing, singing, masks, and gift giving.[63] A few centuries later, Isidore of Seville echoed Augustine by noting raucous activity at the New Year, citing people who make "a lot of noise in everything they do, leaping around and clapping their hands in dancing."[64] Complaints continued into the eighth century; St. Boniface wrote to Pope Zachary in 741 that "when the Kalends of January begin, people lead ring-dances, shouting after the pagan manner through the streets, singing sacrilegious songs of pagan custom and gorging themselves with festive meals day and night."[65]

Condemnations proliferated in the twelfth century, many resonating with and borrowing from earlier tirades against New Year's abuses and paralleling the flourishing of songs for the New Year. Two well-known texts attributed to Parisian Bishops Maurice and Odo of Sully are particularly significant. A vernacular sermon by Maurice of Sully (ca. 1168–1175) is not only one of the first medieval references to the Feast of Circumcision as the New Year, or, as he phrases it the *an renues*, the renewed year, but also one of the first high medieval condemnations of the pagan practices of New Year's gift giving and magic.[66] In 1198, Odo of Sully issued a decree that outlined the reform of the liturgy, promoting the singing of polyphony while forbidding "rimos, personas, luminaria herciarum" ("*rithmi*, masks, and hearse lights").[67] As late as the fifteenth century, irreverent songs were still being performed. The behavior of priests and clerics in particular is described in a 1445 letter from the theology faculty at the University of Paris in which song is referenced as "cantilenas inhonestas" ("wanton songs") and "verba impudicissima ac scurrilia" ("scurrilous and unchaste verses").[68] The complaints of theologians and church authorities are strikingly consistent, with song repeatedly underscored as central to, yet problematic within, New Year's commemorations.

Not all references to the sonic festivities of the New Year were disciplinary in tone. A fourteenth-century *Rituale* from the Church of Saint-Martin of Tours

---

[63] PL 38, col. 1024, and Augustine, *Sermons*, 55.

[64] Seville, *Isidore of Seville: De ecclesiasticis officiis*, 63. Latin edited in CCSL, vol. 113, bk. 1, ch. 41.

[65] "[Q]uando kalendae Januarii intrant, paganorum consuetudine choros ducere per plateas et acclamationes, ritu gentilium et cantationes sacrilegas celebrare, et mensas illa die vel nocte dapibus onerare." Cited and translated in Haines, *Medieval Song*, 59 and n. 43.

[66] Harris, *Sacred Folly*, 23. See also Buettner, "Past Presents," 621, nn. 25–26. Maurice's sermons are edited in Robson, *Maurice of Sully*.

[67] Odo's decree edited in Guérard, ed., *Cartulaire de l'église Notre-Dame de Paris*, 1:72–75, passage cited here on 74. I take *rimos* here to most likely refer to rhythmic song, or *rithmi*, as in Fassler, "Feast of Fools," 78.

[68] Cited widely; edited in Denifle, ed., *Chartularium Universitatis Parisiensis*, 4:652–656; translated in Chambers, *The Mediaeval Stage*, 1:94.

records traditions around the *festum anni novi* along with what appears to be an abbreviated *ordo prophetarum* and descriptions of song and dance:[69]

After the ninth reading, they lead the prophets from the chapter to the gate of the treasury, singing songs [*cantilenas*], and then into the choir, where they recite the prophecies to the cantor, and two *clericuli* singing in the pulpit call to them .... In the afternoon, they should lead dances [*choros ducere*] in the cloister in surplices until the church is opened and all the lights are kindled.[70]

The description of Saint-Martin of Tours is not dissimilar in spirit to the troped liturgies for the Feast of the Circumcision across France, within which song was regularly interpolated. Referring precisely to these festive liturgies, a 1327 endowment at Notre Dame du Puy prescribes "all-night" celebration of the New Year and the Feast of the Circumcision by means of sacred song, termed *lo Bosolari*, which is manifested in the troped Circumcision liturgies preserved in Le Puy A and B, two sixteenth-century manuscripts with contents and structure shared with earlier thirteenth-century sources such as Sens 46 and LoA.[71] While music making for the New Year frequently met with hostility, alternatives to scurrilous songs and dances made their way into the rites of medieval churches through troped liturgies.

The festive complex of January 1 also forms the central poetic discourse of dozens of Latin songs beginning in the twelfth century, some integrated into troped liturgies for the Feast of the Circumcision and others disseminated in songbooks and tropers.[72] All the songs highlight the plurality of the date and its ritual associations in one way or another. Since January 1 was also the Octave of Christmas, many of the songs were equally appropriate for the Nativity, linking the New Year with Christ's birth as well as his Circumcision. This is the case for *Procedenti puero*, whose strophes detail the Virgin Mary's giving birth to Christ while the refrain repeatedly exhorts joy in the New Year: "Eia, this is the new year! Give the glory of

---

[69] On the celebration of the Feast of the Circumcision in Tours, see Maurey, *Medieval Music*, 56–58 and 61–65.

[70] "Post nonam lectionem ducunt prophetas de capitulo ad portam Thesaurarii cantilenas cantando, et post in chorum, ubi dicunt cantori prophetias, et duo clericuli in pulpito cantando eos appellant .... Post prandium debent choros ducere in claustro in supelliciis donec Ecclesia aperiatur, et totum luminare accendatur." Edited Martène, *Tractatus*, 106–107. On the boy bishop in Tours, see Farmer, *Communities*, 253–255 and 93–94, and Maurey, *Medieval Music*, 62, 121–122, and 179–180.

[71] Arlt, "Office," 325.

[72] Among the *conductus* repertoire, Everist counts thirty-four works on the New Year and the Feast of the Circumcision; expanding both earlier and later to *versus* and *cantilenae* increases the number significantly. Everist, *Discovering Medieval Song*, 63, and Caldwell, "Singing, Dancing, and Rejoicing," 631–708.

praise; God is made both man and immortal."[73] The New Year is invoked in calendrical terms too, as in a *conductus* sung at Lauds on the Feast of the Circumcision at Beauvais and Sens, *Kalendas ianuarias*. The *conductus* begins by calling on Christ to make the first day of the year a sober occasion – probably an implied commentary on the proclivity of clerics to celebrate the Kalends in a less than solemn fashion.[74]

The symbolic staff or *baculus* associated with the boy bishop and featuring in clerical festivities, variously termed the Feast of Fools or Feast of the Staff, likewise finds ample expression in songs for the New Year, always carefully framed within the theology of the occasion. In the Latin refrain song *Annus renascitur*, for example, the "renewed year" is the occasion for worship of the staff ("baculus colitur"), couched within a series of familiar seasonal typologies involving the casting off of the old and welcoming of the new.[75] The theme of novelty serves as a key strategy for linking the popular celebrations of January 1, with the theology of the church year and its feasts, in particular the Feast of the Circumcision and the Octave of the Nativity. Repetitively focusing on newness, New Year's songs and texts meditate on the theological resonance of calendrical novelty with Christ's Birth and Circumcision. The newness of the New Song effortlessly functioned as a typology for the temporal confluence of birth of Christ, his Circumcision, and the New Year.

This relationship is made explicit in two sermons by Richard of St-Victor written around the middle of the twelfth century.[76] Not only does Richard explicate the relationship between the metaphorical New Song and the New Year, but he brings to the fore a plethora of related novelties and renewals in an effort to recontextualize the New Year within a theological framework. In a brief and little-discussed sermon designated "in novo anno," Richard employs a line from the Psalms on the New Song as his theme: "Sing ye to the Lord a new canticle: because he hath done wonderful things" ("Cantate Domino canticum novum, quia mirabilia fecit") (Psalm 97:1). Throughout the sermon, Richard elaborates on the significance of the "New Song" with

---

[73] The refrain follows F, fol. 467[v]: "*Eia, novus annus est!* | *gloria laudis,* | *deus homo factus est,* | *et immortalis.*" In Tours 927 the reference to the New Year is not included; in SG 383 and the Codex Sangallensis, the poem explicitly includes reference to the Circumcision as well as the New Year.

[74] "May you make solemn the Kalends of January, O Christ, and may you call us to your nuptials, king." "Kalendas ianuarias | solemnes Christe facias | et nos ad tuas nuptias | vocatus rex suscipias." See Ahn, "Exegetical Function," 240–268. Transmitted in Sens 46, pp. 56–57 and LoA, fol. 40[v] (text only).

[75] "The year is renewed | the old is banished, | Adam [is] newly born" ("Annus renascitur | vetus depellitur | Adam novo nato"). F, fol. 468[r].

[76] Richard of St-Victor's sermons are edited in PL 177, where they are attributed to Hugh of St-Victor; on Richard's authorship, see Longère, *La Prédication médiévale*, 66–67.

simple, repetitive language, emphasizing the typological replacement of the Old with the New, frequently in terms of song: "Song is life. New song, new life. Old song, old life. New life of justice, old life of sin" ("Canticum est vita. Canticum novum, vita nova. Canticum vetus, vita vetus. Nova vita justitia, vetus vita culpa").[77] Even more remarkable is another sermon by Richard, this time for the Feast of the Circumcision. His awareness of the duality of January 1 as the Feast of the Circumcision and the New Year is made abundantly clear in a litanic and rhetorical rumination on novelty:

> Let us, dear ones, seek both [goodness and truth], in order that we may have the strength to find Christ through both and to be renewed in him, just as the Apostle urged us, saying: "Be renewed in the spirit of your mind" (Eph. 4:23), that is, in your mind, which is a spirit or a spiritual thing. For it is fitting for us to be renewed, because the old is past, and "behold, all things have been made new" (2 Cor. 5:17, Rev. 21:5). New Mother, New Son, New Joy, New Song, New Boy, New Cradle, New Circumcision, New Name, New Sign, New Worshippers, New Gifts, New Marriage Bed, New Bridegroom, New Bride, New Nuptials, New Miracle, New Bridal Attendants, New Guests, New Citharists, New Progeny, New Chief, New Republic, New Battle, New Victory, New Peace, New Justice, New Sacrifice, New Testament, New Inheritance, New People, New Rite, New Year.[78]

With each new pairing, newness infuses the sermon text, ending with a statement of renewal based on Christ and his Circumcision and the renewal of the world with the arrival of the New Year: "We are renewed in the new man through the new circumcision, in this new year, in this world, so that in it [the New Year] we may win the right to be renewed in heaven."[79]

Richard's sermon is made more intriguing by a passage detailing descriptions of secular New Year's activities familiar from the earlier critiques. While his emphasis on novelty in the sermon has largely escaped notice, his condemnatory remarks in the same sermon have been widely cited in scholarship

---

[77] PL 177, col. 926B.

[78] "Nos, charissimi, utramque quaeramus, ut per utramque Christum invenire, et in ipso renovari valeamus, quemadmodum nos hortatur Apostolus dicens: renovamini in spiritu mentis vestrae (Ephes. IV), id est, mente vestra, quae spiritus est, vel quae res spiritualis est. Decet enim nos renovari, quia vetera transierunt, et ecce nova facta sunt omnia (II Cor. V; Apoc. XXI). nova mater, novus filius, novum gaudium, novum canticum, novus puer, nova cunabula, nova circumcisio, novum nomen, novum signum, novi adoratores, nova munera, novus thalamus, novus sponsus, nova sponsa, novae nuptiae, novum miraculum, novi paranymphi, novi convivae, novi citharoedi, nova progenies, novus princeps, nova respublica, nova pugna, nova victoria, nova pax, justitia nova, novum sacrificium, novum testamentum, nova haereditas, novus populus, novus ritus, novus annus." PL 177, col. 1035A–B.

[79] "Renovemur in novo homine per novam circumcisionem, in hoc novo anno in hoc mundo, ut in ipso renovari mereamur in coelo." PL 177, col. 1039B–C.

on New Year's abuses, in which priests and clerics are singled out, as is the performance of "vain and foolish rhythmic poetry" and even clapping.[80] Rarely mentioned in scholarship citing this condemnation is its larger textual context in a New Year's sermon. This passage lies in the midst of a longer address, which, while decrying certain types of excessive behavior, emphasizes themes and vocabulary repeatedly foregrounded in medieval Latin New Year's songs. Even while condemning foolish, unchaste, or wanton song, Richard nevertheless hints at an appreciation of "New Songs" celebrating the "New Year" – as long as the latter is understood as an allegory for Christ's Circumcision and the former are far from "vain and foolish."

Among extant "New Songs" for the New Year, some prominently feature the seasonal refrain "annus novus," which repeatedly emphasizes the New Year in a rhetorical parallel to Richard's sermon (see Table 1.7). "Annus novus" repeats both within songs in refrains and as a repeated strophic incipit, as well as among songs, forming a broad discursive and intertextual network of poems distinguished by the temporal marker. Mirroring springtime *exordia* or *Natureingangen*, the poetic topos of the "new year" functions as a signal of time, situating each song within a particular calendrical moment.[81] Within the larger corpus of songs for the New Year, this collection of *annus novus* songs more acutely refracts, navigates, and resolves tensions inherent in January 1 as a day of temporal and festive plurality. The "annus novus" refrain and *exordium* in Latin song specifically frame the New Year by acknowledging the plurality of January 1 – and, indeed, its popularized rather than official identity as the New Year – while emphasizing its liturgical identity. The repetition of the "new year" in the Latin song enables, akin to Richard's sermon, a rhetorical reclaiming of the feast day and its novelty for the church and its calendar.

While the repetition of "annus novus" within and across the songs functions as an intra- and intertextual "virtual" refrain, all but three songs additionally employ structural refrains (*Anni novi novitas, Anni novi prima die, Annus novus in gaudio, Ecce novus annus est, Novus annus dies magnus*, and both versions of *Novus annus hodie*) and in two songs "annus novus" appears within the refrain itself (*Circa canit Michael* and *Procedenti puero*). Two songs survive without notation: *Anni novi reditus*, a *rithmus* appended to a letter by Gui de

---

[80] PL 177, col. 1036C–D, and Fassler, "Feast of Fools," 73.

[81] Latin New Year's songs represent an unstudied manifestation of the temporal or seasonal topos, a hybrid of the *locus amoenus* or perhaps *locus temporis,* that foreshadows a later medieval phenomenon of French New Year's songs. Incipital phrases in later French song such as "ce jour de l'an" function similarly to "annus novus," although the cultural function of vernacular songs diverges from the earlier Latin repertoire, participating more often within economic and social rituals of gift giving. See Plumley, "French Lyrics" and Ragnard, "Les chansons."

Table 1.7 New Year's songs

Incipit	Refrain	Source	Provenance	Century
Anni novi *circulus*	n/a	Mad 289, 143^r	Norman Sicily	12th
Anni novi *novitas*	Gaudeamus et psallamus / Novo presuli / Ad honorem et decorum / Sumpti baculi	Moosburger Graduale, 232^r	Moosburg, Germany	14th
Anni novi *prima die*	Dum, dum, dum circumcidi sustinuit, / In quo non fuit dignum quod abscidi*	Hortus Deliciarum, 30^v	Alsace, France	12th
Anni novi *rediit novitas*	n/a	Carmina Burana (unnotated), 33^v	?Germany	13th
Anni novi *reditus*	n/a	Basochis, *Liber epistularum* (unnotated), p. 19	France	12th
Annus novus *in gaudio*	Ad hec sollempnia / Concurrunt omnia / Voce sonancia / Cantoris gracia / Et vite spacia / Per quem leticia / Fit in ecclesia	Le Puy A, 1^v / Le Puy B, 1^r / St-M A, 36^v	Le Puy, France / / Aquitaine	16th / / 12th
Ecce **novus annus** *est*	Exultandi tempus dies est [*Alleluya dies est* in *Le Puy A and B*] / Venit rex, / Venit lex, / Venit fons gracie	Graz 409 (unnotated), 2^v / Le Puy A, 53^r / Le Puy B, 30^r* / Moosburger Graduale, 244^r / St. Pölten Processional, 7^v	Austria / Le Puy, France / / Moosburg, Germany / Austria	14th / 16th / / 14th / 15th
Novus annus *dies magnus*	Quia sit genitor / Paradisi Adam / Protoplasma suum / Redit ad patriam / Crucis sub precio / Reparando viam	Le Puy A, 34^v / Le Puy B, 20^v / Mad 289, 147^v / St-M A, 40^v	Le Puy, France / / Norman Sicily / Aquitaine	16th / / 12th / 12th

Table 1.7 *(cont.)*

Incipit	Refrain	Source	Provenance	Century
***Novus annus* hodie [A]**	*Ha ha he* *Qui vult vere psallere* *Trino psallat munere* *Corde ore opere* *Debet laborare* *Ut sic deum colere* *Possit et placare*	F, 218^v Sens 46, 54^v	Paris, France Sens, France	13th 13th
***Novus annus* hodie [B]**	*Eya rex nos adiuva,* *Qui gubernas omnia*	Munich 21053 (unnotated), 5^v	Thierhaupten, Germany	15th
Circa canit Michael	*Eÿa eÿa* **Anni novi** *Nova novi* *Gaudia*	Tours 927, 13^v	northern France	13th
*Procedenti puero***	*Eia,* **novus annus** *est* *Gloria laudis* *Deus homo factus est* *Et immortalis*	Codex Sangallensis, IX^v F, 467^v SG 383, p. 172 Sloane 2593 (unnotated), 15^v Tours 927 (unnotated), 19^r	Switzerland Paris, France ?western Switzerland ?East Anglia, England northern France	15th 13th 13th 15th 13th

* This refrain is variable; see p. 58.

** Versions of *Procedenti puero* are also related to the widely transmitted *Verbum caro factum est*, which is sometimes a *Benedicamus Domino* song-trope; see Damilano, "Fonti musicali," 87–88 and *passim*.

Basoches, and *Anni novi rediit novitas* in the Carmina Burana, although the latter is transmitted alongside notated songs. While not widely disseminated, the songs emanate from a variety of contexts across Europe between the twelfth and sixteenth centuries. Significantly, the Moosburger Graduale and manuscripts with troped liturgies for the Feast of the Circumcision are among the sources transmitting New Year's songs, along with songbooks and tropers, including F and Tours 927, for example. Many of the songs in Table 1.7, in other words, are part of either calendrically and liturgically ordered song collections or liturgies for the January 1 feast day. Notably, five songs refer either to their position within a liturgical rite or are included in a troped Feast of the Circumcision: *Anni novi circulus, Annus novus in gaudio, Ecce novus annus est, Novus annus dies magnus,* and *Novus annus hodie.*[82] Songs like *Ecce novus annus est* in the Moosburger Graduale do not have a specific liturgical position, but rubrication (and the evidence of Johannes de Perchausen's preface) supports its performance adjacent to the liturgy – the rubric in this case is "Ad novum annum."[83]

Each song explores the pluralistic identity of the medieval New Year. At the farthest remove from the thematic core of these New Year's songs is *Anni novi rediit novitas* in the Carmina Burana. Although beginning with the same topos of renewal ("New year has brought renewing; winter's gone, short daylight lengthens …"), it becomes clear that the seasonal *exordium* serves a similar function in Latin as it does in vernacular song – to contextualize a love song.[84] The remaining songs, by contrast, trade solely in devotional themes, focusing attention on the New Year as an anchor for different forms of calendrical, theological, and liturgical exegesis. In all cases, poets set the scene temporally through "annus novus," while refocusing attention on the church, its members, and sanctioned festivities.

A significant intervention of the Latin New Year's song is its explicit linking of the New Year and the Feast of Circumcision. Although frequently associated in sermons such as Richard of St-Victor's, the earliest poetic suturing of feast and calendar day is in *Anni novi prima die.* Transmitted in the now-destroyed twelfth-century Hortus Deliciarum, an illuminated encyclopedia compiled by Abbess Herrad of Landsberg for novices at Hohenburg Abbey, Alsace, the neumed *Anni novi prima die* is

---

[82] *Anni novi circulus*, for example, includes in its final strophe a lectionary formula that asks congregants to pay attention.
[83] At the same time, *Anni novi novitas* in the Moosburger Graduale plays rhetorically with the New Year, but is rubricated for use within the rites of the boy bishop, illustrating the high degree of poetic ambiguity in Latin song and the theological interpenetration of themes throughout the Advent and Christmas seasons.
[84] Traill, ed., *Carmina Burana*, 1:326–329 and 542.

preceded by the rubric "de circumcisione Domini" and its developing refrain focuses on the rite of circumcision:[85]

1. **Anni novi** prima die,	1. On the first day of the New Year,
Filius virginis Marie	the Son of the Virgin Mary
Morem gessit natilie.	bore the custom of his birth.
Dum, dum, dum circumcidi	*When, when, when he endured to be*
sustinuit	*circumcised*
In quo non fuit dignum quid	*in whom there was nothing worthy of being*
abscidi.	*cut away.*
2. **Anni novi** die prima	2. On the first day of the New Year,
Superna moderans et ima,	governing the celestial and terrestrial,
Passus est sub petre lima.	He suffered under the sharpened stone.
Dum, dum, dum circumcidi	*When, when, when he endured to be circumcised*
sustinuit	*in whom there was nothing worthy of being*
In quo non fuit dignum quid	*cut away.*
abscidi.	
3. **Anni novi** die nova,	3. On the new day of the New Year,
Homo, cor, animaque nova,	person, heart, and new spirit,
Ad ipsius laudem ova.	rejoice in His praise.
Qui, qui, qui circumcidi	*Who, who, who endured to be*
sustinuit	*circumcised*
In quo non fuit dignum quid	*in whom there was nothing worthy of being*
abscidi.	*cut away.*
4. **Anni novi** festum cole,	4. Keep the feast of the New Year:
Qui manet sub utroque sole	He who abides throughout the seasons
Te peccati solvit mole.	releases you from the heavy burden of sin.
Qui, qui, qui circumcidi	*Who, who, who endured to be*
sustinuit	*circumcised*
In quo non fuit dignum quid	*in whom there was nothing worthy of being*
abscidi.	*cut away.*
5. **Anni novi** die festo	5. On the feast day of the New Year,
Pater et Spiritus adesto,	come, Father and [Holy] Spirit,
Et fac ut sis nobis presto.	and make yourself available to us.
Qui, qui, qui circumcidi	*Who, who, who endured to be*
sustinuit	*circumcised*
In quo non fuit dignum quid	*in whom there was nothing worthy of being*
abscidi.	*cut away.*

The refrain makes the rubric virtually unnecessary, since circumcision is the song's primary, repeated message; strophe 4 also refers directly to

---

[85] Edited in Green, ed., *Herrad of Hohenbourg*, 2:144. On the manuscript and its reconstruction, see Engelhardt, *Herrad von Landsperg*; Green, ed., *Herrad of Hohenbourg*; and Griffiths, *Garden of Delights*. On the music in the Hortus Deliciarum, see Kenneth Levy's contribution titled "The Musical Notation" (ch. 7) in Green, *Herrad of Hohenbourg*, 2:87–88.

circumcision with the "festum cole" (Feast of the Staff or penis). Moreover, the refrain itself features internal repetition, with thrice repeated words ("dum," then "qui") beginning each reiteration, first emphasizing the temporal immediacy of the ritual and then the personhood of Christ. All five strophes, by contrast to the variable refrain incipit, begin with the identical "anni novi" incipit and focus on identifying and expanding upon the "when" and "who" of the refrain. The song layers repetition in semantically meaningful ways – refrain and strophes together emphasize the temporality of the song, the ritual act of Circumcision, and themes of novelty through repetition.

The use of repetition to emphasize the New Year and novelty is a striking feature of both Richard's Circumcision sermon and Latin New Year's songs, as *Anni novi prima die* illustrates. In *Anni novi novitas* in the Moosburger Graduale, for example, the first strophe functions much like Richard's sermon with its litany of newness, employing rhetorical figures of repetition, including *annominatio* and *traductio*, to extend and amplify the theme of novelty:[86]

Anni novi novitas	The novelty of the New Year,
Nova lux splendoris	the new light of splendor,
Nova fit solempnitas	becomes the new solemnity
Novi promissoris.	of the new promiser.

The refrain of *Circa canit Michael* similarly plays with the stem "nov-," its morphemic repetition creating a tongue-twister of a refrain that situates the joys of Christ's birth in the strophes within the context of the New Year:

Eya, eya	*Eia, eia,*
Anni novi	*now we know*
Nova novi	*the new joys*
Gaudia.	*of the new year.*

Across New Year's songs, the opening rhetorical gesture to time is drawn repetitively throughout strophes and refrains, constructing a meta-refrain of novelty that resonates within and between songs.[87]

Indicative of this saturation, the incipital repetition of "annus novus" in *Anni novi prima die* finds a parallel in *Annus novus in gaudio*. An example of "successively notated polyphony" from the twelfth-century *versus*

---

[86] See Lawler, ed., *Parisiana Poetria*, 112–129 on figures of repetition, including *annominatio* and *traductio*.

[87] Although references to newness and novelty resonate especially well in songs for the New Year, similar expressions can be found being used in a self-referential way in *nova cantica*; see Llewellyn, "Nova Cantica," 148.

repertoire in St-M A, *Annus novus in gaudio* similarly includes a refrain and incipital repetition on "annus novus" in each strophe.[88] In this case, the noun–adjective pair "annus novus" is systematically declined throughout the song, each strophe grammatically distinct yet repetitive, and always beginning with a statement on the New Year.[89] An example of *annominatio*, a rhetorical figure whose numerous manifestations include the use of the same word in different inflections, the emphasis on the New Year is unmistakable:[90]

Nominative	1. **Annus novus** in gaudio,	1. Let the New Year now begin
	Agatur in principio,	with rejoicing; let there be great
	In cantoris tripudio	exultation in our cantor's solemn
	Magna sit exultacio.	processional song.
	Ad hec sollempnia	*In these solemnities*
	Concurrent omnia	*all people sounding with voice*
	Voce sonancia	*assemble by the grace*
	Cantoris gracia	*of the cantor and*
	Et vite spacia,	*through the times of life,*
	Per quem leticia	*through whom there is joy*
	Fit in ecclesia.	*in the church.*
Genitive	2. **Anni novi** principium	2. May our singers' voices resonate
	Vox resonet psallencium,	at the beginning of the New Year,
	Et cantorem egregium	and may the hymn of all extol our
	Hymnus extollat omnium.	most distinguished cantor.
	Ref.	*Ref.*
Dative	3. **Anno novo** fit titulus	3. Let honor be given to the New Year,
	Quem laudat omnis populus.	which all people praise.
	Sint in cantoris vocibus	Let fitting praise of the cantor
	Laudes quas decet omnibus.	be in all voices.
	Ref.	*Ref.*
Accusative	4. **Annum novum** novatio	4. Renovation and jubilation
	Decet et exultacio,	befit a New Year,
	In quo venit salvatio	in which salvation comes
	De virginis palacio.	from the palace of the Virgin.
	Ref.	*Ref.*

---

[88] Only the refrain is notated polyphonically; see Chapter 3.

[89] For similar examples of grammatically ordered Latin songs, see Caldwell, "Singing Cato."

[90] In his *Parisiana poetria*, Garland defines one type of *annominatio* as "mutatione unius dictionis" ("declining a single word"). Lawler, *Parisiana Poetria*, 120–121.

Vocative	5. **Anne nove** laudabilis O dies ineffabilis Et tu cantor mirabilis Esto per sec[u]la stabilis. *Ref.*	5. O praiseworthy New Year, o ineffable day, and you, wondrous cantor, may you remain forever steadfast. *Ref.*
Ablative	6. In **anno novo** cantica Recitentur organica In cantoris presencia Tota sonet ars musica. *Ref.*	6. Let us sing polyphonic songs in the midst of the New Year; let the entire art of music sound in the presence of our cantor. *Ref.*[91]

The incipital declension of *annus novus* throughout the song creates a virtual strophic refrain that mirrors the structural refrain between strophes; as with *Anni novi prima die*, repetition is layered on top of an already repetitive framework. However, *Annus novus in gaudio* avoids the topic of circumcision – the focus is on the celebration of the New Year under the cantor's leadership.

The song plays a functional role, however, in the festive liturgy for the Circumcision at Vespers in Le Puy A. Yet rather than aligning the feast and calendar day, as in *Anni novi prima die*, *Annus novus in gaudio* centers on the manner in which an unnamed community celebrates the New Year, positioning festive song for that day under the auspices of the authoritative figure of the cantor. This is especially significant in light of the role of the cantor in religious communities – they were responsible for "keeping the time," calculating the feasts of the liturgical year using the *computus*, keeping track of the liturgical calendar, its seasons, and its accompanying chant, and in some cases writing new music for feasts.[92] In *Annus novus in gaudio*, the cantor is further linked to the keeping of time by virtue of their identity as the celebrative figurehead of the New Year and the leader of its musical festivities. Although the Feast of the Circumcision is poetically side-lined, the song nevertheless takes up the task of moderating the sound world of January 1, calling on the singers to praise the cantor with

---

[91] Edited (with emendations here according to the manuscript) in Chevalier, *Prosolarium*, 6. St-M A does not include the sixth strophe and there are additional variants in earlier strophes; for a comparison, see Caldwell, "Singing Cato."

[92] See Bugyis, Kraebel, and Fassler, eds., *Medieval Cantors*, especially the overview of a cantor's responsibilities on pp. 2–3.

"tota … ars musica."[93] In other words, *Annus novus in gaudio* implicitly disciplines music for the New Year by positioning the cantor – the authority behind liturgical time and its musical expression – as the object of praise.

Like *Annus novus in gaudio*, not all New Year's songs make reference to Christ's Circumcision as the focal point of January 1. Several songs similarly elide Circumcision in favor of other aspects of January 1 festivities, coordinating the New Year with, for instance, the Feast of the Staff, or Baculus (*Anni novi novitas* and *Anni novi reditus*), albeit always with a theological overlay. Only one of the songs in Table 1.7, *Novus annus hodie*, refers to gift giving, a New Year's practice inherited from antiquity and widely decried by church authorities, although it becomes a focus in later French New Year's songs.[94] *Novus annus hodie* survives in two forms with closely related texts: in Munich 21053, it is a refrain-form *Benedicamus Domino* song-trope; in Sens 46 it is a refrain song with a related text but entirely distinct and lengthy refrain, rubricated as "Conductus ad bacularium"; finally, in F, it is a three-voice *conductus* with only a single strophe and iteration of the refrain of the version in Sens 46.[95] While the poem in Munich 21053 explicitly refers to the Circumcision ("in hac circumciditur"), the version in F and Sens 46 refers only to the "novus annus" as a "festum annuale," annual feast, involving song and celebration. Yet, the vocabulary of sobriety and moderation frequently found in the Latin refrain song appears here too in the refrain of *Novus annus hodie* in F and Sens 46, further linking song with the allegorical gifts of mouth, heart, and good works:

Ha, ha, he!	*Ha, ha, he!*
Qui vult vere psallere	*He who wishes truly to*
Trino psallat munere;	*sing should sing praises*
Corde, ore, opere	*with a triple gift: with*
Debet laborare,	*mouth, heart, and works*
Ut sic possit vivere	*he should labor, that he*
Deum et placare.	*might so live and please God.*[96]

---

[93] The final strophe, moreover, specifies "cantica … organica," which may reflect the polyphonic setting of the refrain.

[94] As Plumley argues in "French Lyrics." For a New Year's song that frames song as a gift, see Gui de Basoches's *Adest dies optata socii*, edited in Basochis, *Liber epistularum*, 88.

[95] For the most recent discussion of this song, see Boudeau, "L'Office de la Circoncision de Sens," 1:427–428 and 2:581–585. *Novus annus hodie* is also preserved in a different version in Trento, Archivio Capitolare, MS 93, fol. 374ʳ (three voices), and Trento, Castello del Buonconsiglio, Monumenti e collezioni provinciali, MS 1376, fols. 59ʳ and 142ᵛ–143ʳ (for four and three voices, respectively).

[96] Edited in full in Anderson, ed., *Notre-Dame and Related Conductus*, 2:viii, with the version in Munich 21053 on ix.

Novus annus hodie avoids describing the "horizontal" or reciprocal exchange of gifts between people, as expressed in later French *chansons*; instead, the refrain focuses on offering a "vertical" seasonal tribute, directed heavenward.[97] In Latin New Year's songs, the gift of song is thus a spiritual rather than literal offering, folding a frequently censured ritual practice for the New Year into a devotional framework.

As an *exordium* and/or refrain, *annus novus* serves as a marker of time that initiates rhetorically rich meditations on novelty while also bringing into alignment varied ways in which the calendar day was celebrated by religious and lay communities throughout Europe. More than an opening gambit or formulaic marker of genre, "annus novus" and its related expressions of novelty saturate the poetic sound world of the New Year's songs in ways that signal underlying cultural and theological discourses. What the New Year's song does particularly well is straddle the line between the festivities for 1 January often decried by church authorities and sanctioned forms of music making and entertainment that revolve around the liturgy for Circumcision. The New Year's song also survives within manuscript sources that frame and reform the musical experience of seasonal and liturgical time, including troped liturgies for the liturgical feast day and song collections of choirboys such as in the Moosburger Graduale. In the hands of poets and composers, song and refrain become expressive pivots in discourses around the New Year and its varied customs, bringing into the musical realm Richard of St-Victor's meditation on theological novelty and new songs at the turn of the year.

Conclusion: Contexts for the Latin Refrain Song

Although not all refrain songs engage in poetic and performative discourses around time, the majority of songs and sources beginning in the thirteenth century are attuned to, and aligned with, the medieval year. Attending to how the Latin refrain song was framed in relation to time poetically, and within manuscript sources by poets, composers, scribes, and compilers, permits new insights into questions of transmission, performance, and cultural function. Manuscript sources bear witness to the explicit regulation of festive time by means of the refrain song, underlining the intervention of Latin song at the calendrical moments most in need of

---

[97] Davis, *Gift*, 13.

musical disciplining. The performance of the Latin refrain and refrain song is positioned in medieval sources and in the poetry itself precisely at times of heightened tension in the ritual and musical commemoration of the calendar year. This is most acute in New Year's refrains and refrain songs, the thematically and textually linked group of works playing with the structural and inter/intratextual identity of the refrain while also poetically navigating the contested identities of January 1.

Situating the creation, transmission, and performance of the Latin refrain and refrain song within the calendar year confirms the embeddedness of the repertoire within clerical, monastic, and pedagogical institutions. The individuals and communities identifiable in sources and songs, including named figures and ranks such as Johannes de Perchausen, Bishop Richard Ledrede, anonymous cantors, and the clergy in Paris at the Cathedral of Notre Dame, are precisely those for whom the pluralistic medieval year had the greatest valency. Religious communities were tasked with not only computing time, but also navigating the year by means of chant and ritual. Rather than solely reflecting the "sacralization of time" enacted by chant and tropes, however, the refrain song enabled religious communities to reconcile calendrical, seasonal, and festive time in music, bolstering the calendar of the church while offering a way to experience and reframe time in song.[98]

---

[98] Le Goff, *In Search of Sacred Time*, 17.

2 | Refrains and the Time of Song

Singing Religious Narrative

In John Hollander's eloquent description of the poetic refrain, he suggests that refrains "time a poem" by marking the passage of time, just as bells toll the hours.[1] Hollander describes the refrain in strophic poetry as speaking in the "tongue of bells," contrasting with the sounds of daily life in the strophes. The metaphor brings the sound of lived time in contact with the sound of poetic time, with the strophic noise continuing onward day by day, strophe by strophe, and the refrain chiming in at regular intervals. The ringing of the refrain is always familiar and yet always refers to a different moment in time. It is heard and interpreted differently depending on whether it sounds at the beginning of a poem or the end, much like a bell that signals the start of a workday or brings it to its conclusion. Refrains, in other words, shape how poetic time is experienced sonically by articulating and measuring the passing of time charted in the gradual accumulation of strophic "hours."

In song, the refrain's impact on the experience of time is heightened by the addition of music, which further changes how the refrain sounds in comparison with the strophes. In strophic songs, music typically repeats for each strophe; the musical fabric of the song and the music and poetry of the refrain remain the same even while the poetic meaning of each strophe regularly changes. Consequently, strophic refrain songs offer a challenge to how time is experienced at the level of poetry and music by continually highlighting the tensions between linearity and circularity in music and text. We can not only ask what the refrain means each time it returns – as Hollander writes, "what is it to mean *this* time around?"[2] – we can also ask what music means when we hear it again with a new text.[3] In this chapter I explore how the refrain affects the meaning and performance of strophic Latin song from the perspective of time, transforming Hollander's assertion into a question – how do refrains toll time in song?

---

[1] Hollander, "Breaking into Song," 77: "Refrains can time a poem, tolling its strophic hours in the tongue of bells that may be wholly foreign to the noises of the stanzas' daily life."

[2] Ibid., 75.

[3] See, for example, the approaches to musical and textual repetition in Deeming, "Music and Contemplation" and Quinlan, "Repetition as Rebirth."

Chapter 1 connected refrains and refrain forms with the experience of calendrical and seasonal time; in this chapter, I consider the temporality of song itself and ways in which the refrain interacts with the linearity and circularity of poetic and musical time both separately and as they work together. My focus remains on devotional songs that form part of the experience of calendar and seasonal time in the Middle Ages, linking the broader cultural role of song to its temporal meanings in the moment of performance. Songs that most compellingly bring together the experience of calendrical time with the musical and poetic experience of time in song – thereby animating Hollander's sonic metaphor of the refrain as the bell-like tolling of the passing of strophic time – are narrative works that paraphrase or retell familiar biblical and hagiographic stories. Devotional songs performed within rites and festivities of the liturgical and seasonal year frequently retell the central narratives of these festal occasions in ways that stress particular ideas or offer new interpretations.

Through a series of case studies, I consider the ways in which the refrain shapes and defines the experience of narrative time in strophic Latin song. With each example, I highlight the musical and poetic mechanisms by which temporalities are expressed, layered, and negotiated at the level of individual works.[4] Anchored in familiar stories and texts of the Nativity, Resurrection, and saints' lives, the refrain operates within the devotional temporalities articulated in each song, at times interjecting or interrupting, and at other times integrating musically, poetically, and grammatically into the narrative flow. In song form, familiar and frequently rehearsed narratives from the church year are manipulated in different ways, their timescale shifted to that of a single song's performance and inflected temporally by forward-moving strophes and recursive refrains.

Song, Refrain, and Narrative Time

Narrative structures tend to be overlooked when they occur in repertoires that are not conventionally understood as story-based or, more significantly, in repertoires that feature circular, repetitive structures, such as works with refrains. For instance, in John E. Stevens's formative 1986 study on medieval song, he divides a discussion of sung narrative into two chapters under the heading "narrative melody," examining epics and

---

[4] For recent approaches to medieval song from the perspective of time, narrative, and repetition, see Drummond, "Linear Narratives" and Quinlan, "Repetition as Rebirth."

chansons de geste in the first, and considering saints' lives, liturgical narratives, and dramas in the second.[5] Within the framework of "narrative melody," Stevens identifies four different forms and melodic types: recitation tones, such as those used for liturgical readings; *laisse*-type melodies, used for singing epics; *lai*-type melodies, whose form freely parallels the liturgical sequence; and, lastly, strophic melodies, which Stevens associates solely with vernacular traditions.[6] Within this framework, certain song genres are characterized as inherently linear and narrative; others, including the Latin refrain song, are traditionally perceived as circular in form and consequently nonnarrative.[7]

What comprises narrative in the context of song, and does it align solely with linear structures? Borrowing from narratology, I understand narrative here to involve a sequence of connected, usually chronological, events (the story) conveyed by someone (a narrator) through some form (the narrative).[8] In the context of song, the music and poetry together serve as the narrative vessel through which a story is communicated by the narrator, who is signaled either explicitly in the narrative itself or embodied implicitly by the singer(s).[9] Distinctions between narrative and nonnarrative poetry have long been made in the context of popular song, folk genres, art-song traditions, and elsewhere. As in Stevens's typology, some genres are conventionally labeled nonnarrative, while others are "obviously" narrative in form; strophic forms and refrain forms are not as often considered alongside, for instance, genres such as epic poetry, *chansons de geste*, and dramas.[10]

Yet narratives materialize readily enough in the repertoire of devotional Latin refrain songs, despite a lack of fit with the musical and poetic forms described by Stevens and others as narrative. The refrain song is textually, melodically, and formally repetitive, largely distinct from the linear forms

---

[5] Stevens, *Words and Music*, 199–267. For a recent discussion of Stevens's typology and other theories of musical performance and narrative, see Zaerr, *Performance*, 44–51.

[6] Stevens, *Words and Music*, 200–203.

[7] Stevens includes the Latin refrain song (and specifically *rondelli*) under the category of dance songs (see Chapter 3). For a discussion of circularity and linearity in lyric, see Knox, "Circularity and Linearity" and Huot, *From Song to Book*, 84–85. Butterfield rethinks the categories of lyric and narrative in *Poetry and Music*.

[8] I am drawing broadly on Gérard Genette's definition of narrative in *Narrative Discourse*, especially 25–32.

[9] Frith suggests that "all songs are implied narratives," since songs "have a central character, the singer; a character with an attitude, in a situation, talking to someone (if only to herself)." Frith, *Performing Rites*, 169.

[10] I borrow the term "obviously" in this context from ibid., 170.

and trajectories of many narrative genres.[11] The relative absence of repetitive forms from considerations of narrative largely reflects the complication introduced by repetition; refrain forms are most often described as circular or cyclical, rather than linear, the latter of which is seemingly demanded by narrative.[12] Within the narrative space of a song, the repeating (aka static) refrain might seem at odds with the forward flow (aka nonstatic) of narrative strophes. Indeed, tensions between linearity and circularity in song and poetry are most acute when the songs are narrative in form yet feature an invariable, repeating refrain. The regular interjection of the refrain is interpreted as a disruption of narrative time, its cyclical reappearances producing temporal ruptures and fault lines within the linearly and chronologically constructed strophes. To return to Hollander, the repeated refrain in narrative contexts asks us to consider: What does the refrain mean this time around?[13] How does the repeated refrain as a structural component of song alter or inflect the time of the narrative as it is conveyed in the changing strophes?

In the context of strophic songs with refrains, the temporal framework of the narrative is chiefly bounded, or segmented, by its form and framed by repetition. As Brian McHale and others have observed, the nature of poetry as segmentable (whether by means of strophic structures, verse forms, rhyme, punctuation, etc.) parallels the episodic nature of time in narrative.[14] For Latin refrain songs, the underlying strophic structure affords the division of a narrative into discrete segments, or episodes. The refrain then operates as a frame around these temporal units,

---

[11] Despite being rarely considered alongside narrative genres such as *chansons de geste* or epic poetry, medieval Latin song is frequently narrative in structure, most obviously in historical and hagiographical contexts. Mark Everist's typology of the *conductus* lists fifty-six *conducti* as hagiographical and thirty-one as political/datable, both categories that include narrative structures; Everist, *Discovering Medieval Song*, 63. Thomas Payne counts approximately thirty that refer specifically to, or recount, historical events; Payne, "*Aurelianus civitas*," 589. The larger methodological issue is that attention to narrativity in poetry is lacking; see McHale, "Beginning to Think." See, however, Kinney, *Strategies of Poetic Narrative* and Smyth, *Imaginings of Time*.

[12] On the tension between linear narrative and repetitive refrain forms, see Drummond, "Linear Narratives." The repetitive identity of the Latin refrain contrasts with the citational and interpolated function of French *refrains* in narrative contexts; see Fowler, "Musical Interpolations"; Huot, *From Song to Book*; Boulton, *Song in the Story*; Peraino, "*Et pui conmencha a canter*"; Dillon, "Art of Interpolation"; Butterfield, *Poetry and Music*; Ibos-Augé, *Chanter et lire*; and Saltzstein, *Refrain*. In the context of French song, however, narrative *pastourelles à refrain* and more generally *chansons à refrain* employ repeated refrains; on the former, see Johnson, "Role of the Refrain."

[13] Hollander, "Breaking into Song," 75, drawing on the work of Rachel Blau DuPlessis.

[14] McHale, "Beginning to Think," 14–18.

articulating each moment within the story. To put it another way, refrains regulate the temporal flow of a story by marking the boundaries of each event or episode as they occur in the retelling. This structural function is not all that a refrain can accomplish within the narrative of song. Refrains can also serve as commentary; temporal or spatial cues; a moment of narration or narrative reflection; a pivot of voice, mood, or tense; or even a signal of music or musical performance within a narrative. Rather than presenting a challenge to narrative time, refrains can enhance and nuance how narrative is framed and expressed in song.

Music imparts its own form of temporal regulation through the temporality of performance; the forms and structures of the music shape how time is experienced by singers and listeners, whether by effecting a sense of slowing time down or speeding it up, pacing the delivery of poetry, or constructing a temporal beat and rhythm. The repetition of music in strophic forms also connects different parts of a song, since each narrative segment is experienced by means of the same melody. This creates a sense of return not only within the refrains, but also strophes, ensuring narrative continuity and comprehension since the strophic text is always fore-grounded as the sole element in a single song that undergoes transformation. At the same time, hearing the same music with different text also has the potential to change how we hear the music, just as our interpretation of the refrain can change over the course of a song. The tension between circularity and linearity, sameness and change, occurs at all levels of text and music in strophic refrain songs, underpinning and fostering the interplay of poetic meanings around time. Poets and composers have frequently exploited the ways in which the temporalities of melodies, strophe, refrain, and narrative can be shifted, reworked, and reoriented in relation to one another.

The devotional poetry of the Latin refrain song participates in the interplay of temporalities in another way by bringing the biblical and ritual past into the "here and now" ("hic et nunc").[15] Across the liturgy, the interplay of temporalities is a key feature of the experience of ritual, whether stemming from the macro perspectives of calendars and seasons or the context of specific feast days and the daily rites.[16] The "hic et nunc" of the liturgy brings to the fore the inherently narrative dimension of religious rituals – the reexperiencing of foundational stories of the faith

---

[15] On the poetic topos of the liturgical *hic et nunc*, see Jonsson, "Liturgical Function," 112; Kruckenberg, "Neumatizing the Sequence," 267; Jacobsson and Treitler, "Tropes," 84; and Haug, "Tropes," 281.

[16] See Fassler, "Liturgical Framework."

through chant, prayer, and recitation. Beyond the retelling of religious stories, the Latin refrain song heightens this temporal immediacy and the tension between the past event and its current commemoration through textual paraphrase, borrowing, and quotation from biblical, hagiographical, and liturgical texts. The Latin refrain song generates broader temporal networks of meanings by recalling the past events through the processes of textual reworking while simultaneously enacting devotion in the present and anticipating future reoccurrences. Considering the devotional contexts of the Latin refrain song alongside its poetry, form, and music reveals a complex interweaving of past, present, and future temporalities brought into relief in sung performance.

The Nativity Story Two Ways: *Ecce mundi gaudium* and *Congaudeat turba fidelium*

In the Latin refrain song, some of the most interesting play with time and narrative emerges in the reworking of stories relating to Christ's Nativity, Passion, and Resurrection. These pivotal and highly fêted feast days often inspired representational rites and dramas, signaling the rich narrative potential of these moments within the liturgy, not to mention their centrality to the church year. The emphasis on the timeline of Christ's Passion and Resurrection, moreover, exemplifies a concern with the experience of time, while its yearly enactment through liturgical texts showcases the ways in which time – past, present, and future – becomes a central focus.[17] As the human yet divine son of God, Christ in particular experienced and represents both the finite time of humanity and the eternal time of the heavens. Within biblical and exegetical texts pertaining to Christ and the events of his life, Resurrection, and Ascension, themes relating to time, or its absence in the form of eternity, frequently emerge.

Among the best-known and well-rehearsed narratives is the story of Christ's birth. Brought to life in church pageants worldwide into the twenty-first century, the familiar characters and scenes comprising annual Nativity plays are directly modeled on the narration of Christ's birth and the events recounted in the Gospels of Luke 2:1–20 and Matthew 1:18–2:23, as were medieval representational rites for Christmastide, including plays

---

[17] See Kiening, "Mediating."

featuring shepherds, Wise Men, and Prophets.[18] Certain moments in the Gospel narratives from Luke and Matthew attracted more attention than others, perhaps due to their greater dramatic and representational potential – the angelic visitation to the shepherds; the journey of the wise men; the manger and its braying animals; Herod's murderous agenda; and the lament of Rachel, a reference to Jeremiah 31:15. While Christ is at the center of the story, in his infancy he does not speak or act; instead, the narration focuses on the surrounding characters and their actions, with the Virgin Mary in the leading role as the mother of God's Word incarnate.

In two Latin refrain songs, *Ecce mundi gaudium* and *Congaudeat turba fidelium*, the Virgin features prominently among a cast of characters from the Gospels of Luke and Matthew. This is made clear in *Ecce mundi gaudium*, transmitted uniquely in F, by virtue of a Marian refrain that repeats at the end of each strophe, as well as the initial two strophes which, using language derived from the Gospels, establish the virgin birth of Christ (see Table 2.1).[19] After two strophes focused on Matthew's and Luke's account of Mary's virgin conception of Christ, the remaining strophes move successively through the Nativity story following the Gospels. Each strophe relates a single episode, segmenting the Nativity narrative and pacing the retelling. Although scant on details, the short poem encapsulates key narrative moments, placed in biblical sequence.

At first glance the refrain seems at odds with the episodic character of the strophes due to its meditative, prayer-like invocation of the Virgin: "Ave, virgo regia | Dei plena gratia." This two-line refrain stems directly from the narrative context of the Gospels as a paraphrase of Luke 1:28: "And the angel being come in, said unto her: Hail, full of grace, the Lord is with thee: blessed art thou among women" ("Et ingressus angelus ad eam dixit: Ave gratia plena: Dominus tecum: benedicta tu in mulieribus"). This passage, and by association the refrain of *Ecce mundi gaudium*, are both recognizable due to their relationship to liturgical texts and the later Rosary, *Ave maria gratia plena*.[20] In the initial two strophes, then, the refrain first falls within the narrative frame of the song, echoing the passage from Luke that inspires the poetry of the strophes. While the song progresses in its storytelling, however, the refrain remains unchanged, transforming from

[18] For an example of the rituals and accretions for the Christmas period, see Lagueux, "Glossing Christmas."
[19] Translation adapted from Anderson, ed., *Notre-Dame and Related Conductus*, 8:xxxvi, where *Ecce mundi gaudium* is misidentified as a contrafact of a vernacular song.
[20] With an emphasis on musical settings, see the wide-ranging examination of this prayer in Anderson, "Enhancing the *Ave Maria*."

Table 2.1 Biblical narrative in *Ecce mundi gaudium* (F, fol. 470ʳ)

1. Ecce mundi gaudium
Ecce salus gentium
Virgo parit filium
Sine violentia.
  Ave, virgo regia
  Dei plena gratia.
	1. Behold, joy of the world,
	behold, salvation of the nations,
	the Virgin has borne a son
	without violence.
	  Hail, virgin queen,
	  Full of the grace of God.
		Matthew 1:18–25
		and Luke 1:26–38

2. Natus est de virgine
Sine viri semine
Qui mundat a crimine
Rex qui regit omnia.
  Ave, virgo regia
  Dei plena gratia.
	2. He is born from the Virgin
	without the seed of man,
	He who cleanses from crime,
	the King who rules all.
	  Hail, virgin queen,
	  Full of the grace of God.	

3. Angelus pastoribus
Natus est in gentibus
Qui dat pacem omnibus
Sua providentia.
  Ave, virgo regia
  Dei plena gratia.
	3. The angel to the shepherds:
	He is born among the nations,
	He who gives peace to all
	through his foreknowledge.
	  Hail, virgin queen,
	  Full of the grace of God.
		Luke 2:8–12

4. Reges tria praemia
Offerentes varia
Stella duce praevia
Ad salutis gaudia.
  Ave, virgo regia
  Dei plena gratia.
	4. The kings are offering
	three various gifts,
	led by the star that leads the way
	to the joys of salvation.
	  Hail, virgin queen,
	  Full of the grace of God.
		Matthew 2:9–11

5. Cum nil scire potuit
De nato, rex fremuit
 	
Et tota gens tremuit
Christi natalitia.
  Ave, virgo regia
  Dei plena gratia.
	5. Since he was unable to know anything
	about the birthed boy, the king [Herod]
	  raged,
	and the whole nation trembled
	at the birth of Christ.
	  Hail, virgin queen,
	  Full of the grace of God.
		Matthew 2:16

6. Cum mori per gladios
Rachel videt proprios
Mesta plorat filios
Nulla sunt solatia.
  Ave, virgo regia
  Dei plena gratia.
	6. When Rachel sees the death
	of her own sons by swords
	she weeps with grief;
	there are no comforts.
	  Hail, virgin queen,
	  Full of the grace of God.
		Matthew 2:17–18

Example 2.1 F, fol. 470^r, *Ecce mundi gaudium*, first strophe and refrain

part of the narrative into a repeated prayer for the Virgin that timelessly reminds singer and listener alike of the Marian roots of the Nativity.

The musical setting affirms the poetic and temporal distinction between narrative and refrain. *Ecce mundi gaudium* is found in the final fascicle of F alongside many examples of *rondeau*-form songs, although this Christmas song is atypical in the fascicle due to its strophic+refrain form. *Ecce mundi gaudium* begins with a twofold statement of "Ecce" in lines 1 and 2 of the first strophe, emphasized musically by sharing the same melody and by virtue of a rising fifth that characterizes the strophic material more generally (see Example 2.1). Occupying a different melodic space, the refrain differentiates itself first by avoiding the D and instead emphasizing C, and by dipping below the final G to F on "-go" of "virgo." By contrast to the setting of the strophes, the two-line refrain includes five two-note clusters, while the previous three melodic lines of the strophe include one two-note pair per line. While these are minor details, they make a difference in a brief setting. Subtle melodic differences set the refrain apart from the strophe, highlighting its distance from the inner (narrative) workings of the song.

Although transmitted uniquely in F, *Ecce mundi gaudium* has become a popular song among early music ensembles, perhaps because of its resonance with more contemporary Christmas carols.[21] It is, by comparison with many Latin songs of the thirteenth century in particular, a simple song with

---

[21] See, for example, the recording of *Ecce mundi gaudium* by the popular ensemble Mediæval Bæbes on *Mistletoe and Wine: A Seasonal Collection* (Nettwerk Records 30329, 2003, CD).

a clear message. A rendering in song of the Gospel narratives of Christ's birth is underpinned by a Marian refrain, the meaning of which subtly changes over the course of a song. Initially rooted in the narrative, the refrain becomes a repeated, almost litanic, prayer with biblical and liturgical resonances.

The singularity of *Ecce mundi gaudium* in F is contrasted with the complex source history of the second Nativity song I discuss here, *Congaudeat turba fidelium*. Concordances for this refrain song survive from the twelfth century through to the sixteenth century, copied across Europe from Norman Sicily to Scandinavia (see Table 2.2).[22] Aside from four unnotated concordances, all but one of the settings are monophonic. Only the fourteenth-century Engelberg Codex transmits a two-voice setting, albeit for solely three strophes. Notably, the number and order of strophes and their precise content differ significantly across these concordances, with several of the earliest sources from Norman Sicily and Aquitaine transmitting the greatest number of strophes overall (Cologne 196 is an exception among the earliest sources). In nearly all contexts *Congaudeat turba fidelium* functions as a *Benedicamus Domino* song-trope, whether signaled by a rubric or through textual citation of the versicle, although it appears as a lectionary introduction in two fourteenth-century sources from Aosta. One unusual feature of the song's material history is its multiple copying in different textual and textural forms and among different scribal layers in two manuscripts, twice in Mad 19421 and three times in the Engelberg Codex, including once polyphonically in the latter. Mirroring its wide dissemination across time and place, the copying history of *Congaudeat turba fidelium* within individual sources speaks to its wide-ranging transmission as well as its poetic and musical malleability.

Each source transmits between one to eleven strophes, beginning in all cases with the same incipit ("Congaudeat turba fidelium"). The remainder of the first strophe varies between one of two lines: the Christological "Natus est rex salvator omnium" or the more popular Marian line "Virgo mater peperit filium." In instances in which the song serves as a *Benedicamus Domino* song-trope (nearly all of the versions in Table 2.2), the strophes beginning the second half of the song (the "Deo gratias" section) alternate between strophes beginning "In presepe" and another

---

[22] This song is extensively cited; for discussions referencing its transmission and analyzing the text and music, see Arlt, *Ein Festoffizium des Mittelalters*, 1:185–186; and "Das Eine und die vielen Lieder," 117–119. My thanks to Wulf Arlt for generously sharing his thoughts and work on this song at a late stage, not all of which I was able to incorporate into this discussion.

Table 2.2 Concordances for *Congaudeat turba fidelium*

Source	Provenance	Century	# of strophes	Musical notation	Notes (Rubrics)
Cologne 196, 63ʳ	?Liege	12th	2	notated (unheightened neumes)	Variable refrain
Apt 6, 115ʳ	?Apt	12th	9	notated	*Benedicamus Domino*
Mad 288, 188ʳ	Norman Sicily	12th	10	unnotated	*Benedicamus Domino*
Mad 289, 128ʳ			10	notated	*Benedicamus Domino* (rubric: "Al.")
Mad 19421, 107r			6	a1	Variable refrain
Mad 19421, 107ᵛ			10	a1	–
St-M A, 61ᵛ	Aquitaine	12th	11	a1	*Benedicamus Domino*; variable refrain (rubric "IHU")
Stuttg, 71ᵛ	Switzerland	13th	4	unnotated	*Benedicamus Domino*
Aosta Cod. 11, 85ᵛ	Aosta	14th	9	notated	Lectionary introduction
Engelberg Codex, 103ʳ	Engelberg	14th	4	unnotated	*Benedicamus Domino* (rubric: "item de nativitate domini")
Engelberg Codex, 180ʳ			3	a2	*Benedicamus Domino*
Engelberg Codex, 182ʳ			1	unnotated	–
Le Puy A, 107ʳ	Le Puy	16th	6	notated	Variable refrain; (rubric: "Benedicamus Domino" and "Gracias")
Le Puy B,* 60ʳ			–	notated	
Piae Cantiones (1582), no. 10	Finnish/Swedish [published in Germany]	16th	7	notated	–
Piae Cantiones (1625), no. 6		17th	7	notated	(no rubrics; gospel verses indicated in margins)

* I have been unable to verify the number, order of strophes, or rubric in Le Puy B.

beginning "Rege nato." This division corresponds in most cases to versions in which the refrain is variable (the latter) as opposed to a single refrain repeated between all strophes (the former).[23] Although I have termed Table 2.2 a list of concordances, no two manuscript sources present the same *Congaudeat turba fidelium*. Instead, the song is what could be termed modular in form. In each version, the order of events is modified episodically, with the variation in narrative structure corresponding with the total number of strophes. The refrain operates in a modular sense too, occurring either as an identical repeated refrain or a variable refrain, in both cases knit into the same Nativity narrative. A comparison of two renderings of the song separated by several centuries, one from the twelfth-century Norman-Sicilian troper Mad 289 and the other from the sixteenth-century song collection *Piae Cantiones*, demonstrates both the modular nature of the song's strophes and its construction around episodes from the Nativity story (shared text is bold, with the *Benedicamus Domino* versicle in uppercase letters in Mad 289):[24]

Mad 289, 128^{r–v}	*Piae Cantiones* (1582), no. 10
1. **Congaudeat turba fidelium** **Virgo mater peperit filium** *in bethleem.*	1. **Congaudeat turba fidelium** **Virgo mater peperit filium** *in Bethlehem.*
2. Laudem celi nuntiat angelus Et in terris pacem hominibus *in bethleem.*	2. Ad pastores descendit angelus, Dicens eis: natus ist Dominus *in Bethlehem.*
3. **Loquebantur pastores invicem:** **Transeamus ad novum hominem** *in bethleem.*	3. **Loquebantur pastores ad invicem** **Transeamus ad novum hominem** *in Bethlehem.*
4. Cuius magi notato sydere Donant ei mistico munere *in bethleem.*	4. **Ad præsepe stant bos et asnius,** **Cognoverunt quis esset Dominus** *in Bethlehem.*
5. Et donante munere mistico[25] BENEDICUNT celorum DOMINO *in bethleem.*	5. In octava dum circumciditur, Nomen ei Iesus imponitur *in Bethlehem.*

---

[23] Only in the case of St-M A is the refrain identical up to the statement of *Benedicamus Domino* before becoming variable in the *Deo gratias* response strophes. In all other versions the refrain is either completely identical throughout or entirely variable throughout.

[24] The "in Bethlehem" refrain is written out in full in both sources; it also appears abbreviated in several sources and, in the Engelberg Codex, fol. 130^{r–v}, the refrain is cued scribally. The biblically episodic nature of the text is emphasized in *Piae Cantiones* (1625), in which marginal references to gospel verses are provided.

[25] These words appear reversed in the manuscript.

6. **In presepe et bos et asinus**
Cognoverunt quis esset Dominus
 in bethleem.

7. In Egipto Marie filius
Is natus est quem querit impius
 in bethleem.

8. Tunc Herodes querit perimere
Quem deberet orando querere
 in bethleem.

9. Benedicta sint mater ubera
Lactancia regentem ethera
 in bethleem.

10. Carnem nostram quam DEO
 socias
Tibi matri agimus GRACIAS
 in bethleem.

6. Trini, trino, trina dant munera,
Regi regum sugenti ubera
 in Bethlehem.

7. Collyridas simul cum nectare
Benedicat Christus Rex gloriæ
 in Bethlehem.

1. **Let the company of the faithful**
rejoice, the virgin mother has
given birth to a son
 in Bethlehem.

2. The angel announces with praise of
heaven and peace to men on earth
 in Bethlehem.

3. **The shepherds were saying to one**
another: "let us go to the new man
 in Bethlehem."

4. To whom, having noted his star,
the magi give mystical offerings
 in Bethlehem.

5. And giving mystical offerings
they bless the Lord of the heavens
 in Bethlehem.

6. **In the manger both the ox and the**
ass knew who was the Lord
 in Bethlehem.

7. Mary's son is in Egypt, this newborn
whom the impious [king] seeks
 in Bethlehem.

1. **Let the company of faithful rejoice,**
the virgin mother has given birth to a son
 in Bethlehem.

2. The angel descended to the shepherds
saying to them: "God is born
 in Bethlehem."

3. **The shepherds were saying to one**
another: "let us go to the new man
 in Bethlehem."

4. **In the manger stood the ox and the ass;**
they knew who was the Lord
 in Bethlehem.

5. On the eighth day when he was circum-
cised, he was given the name of Jesus
 in Bethlehem.

6. Three gifts three times the three kings
gave to the king of kings suckling at the
breast
 in Bethlehem.

7. With cakes together with honey bless
Christ, the king of glory
 in Bethlehem.

8. Then Herod seeks to destroy the one
whom he should seek in prayer
  in Bethlehem.
9. Blessed are the breasts of the
mother, nursing the one who rules the
ether
  in Bethlehem.
10. Our flesh that you bring into fel-
lowship with God, to you, Mother, we
give thanks
  in Bethlehem.

The version in Mad 289 is one of the longest with ten strophes, while the *Piae Cantiones* (1582) transmits seven strophes and excludes the *Benedicamus Domino* versicle (albeit retaining the word "Benedicat" in the final strophe). In the former, a comprehensive narrative of Christ's nativity from the angelic announcement to Herod's hunt for the newborn is included. By virtue of fewer strophes, *Piae Cantiones* (1582) focuses on a selection of moments while adding Christ's Circumcision and naming events not appearing in earlier versions. Between the two versions, three complete strophes are shared, as well as the two-word refrain; other episodes, such as the Magi and their gifts, appear in both, albeit with different textual formulations. As Christmas songs, these two versions of *Congaudeat turba fidelium* function equally well, even if the precise Nativity narrative, its chosen episodes, and the ordering of these episodes vary.

The "in Bethlehem" refrain appearing in all versions of *Congaudeat turba fidelium* is somewhat unusual for its brevity and grammatical linkage to the preceding text of each strophe.[26] Not all versions have this same refrain throughout, however; four versions begin with the "in Bethlehem" refrain and then alter the four-syllable line to fit each new strophe (Table 2.2 indicates versions with variable refrains).[27] In all other versions, the "in Bethlehem" refrain is repeated identically,

---

[26] As Haug notes in "Ritual and Repetition," 94, "naturally, these two words do not constitute a separate afterthought but are integrated into both the stanzaic melody and also the syntax and thematic content of each strophe." See also "Musikalische Lyrik," 123–124, and Arlt, *Ein Festoffizium des Mittelalters*, 1:185–186.

[27] St-M A is an exception, as I indicate in footnote 23.

poetically and musically, throughout the song. Whether variable or identical, the intent is clearly for the refrain to be grammatically grafted onto the end of each strophe, a strategy that works smoothly most of the time. For instance, one identical strophe between the two versions above shows the aptness of the localizing refrain: "The shepherds were saying to one another: 'let us go to the new man *in Bethlehem.*'" Occasionally, the refrain's spatial dimension seems like a less obvious fit, as in the tenth strophe in Mad 289: "The flesh [Christ] united us to God, and to you, Virgin, we give thanks *in Bethlehem.*" With this closing poetic unit, the singers and listeners in the present give thanks to the Virgin in Bethlehem, momentarily conflating the temporality of then and now and situating the song's performance in the distant locale of Christ's birth.

The refrain's emphasis on place works in a particular way within the temporal framework of the song. As the poem moves sequentially through the Christmas story, the repeated interjection of the "in Bethlehem" refrain links time and place, resulting in a Nativity chronotope, to use Mikhail Bakhtin's term to describe the "intrinsic connectedness of temporal and spatial relationships."[28] As *Congaudeat turba fidelium* insists with each return of the refrain, the time and subsequent events of Christ's Nativity happened *in Bethlehem* – time, place, and event are inseparable. Even when Mary and Christ are in Egypt, Herod still seeks them *in Bethlehem* (strophes 7–8 in Mad 289). As it interacts with the strophic material, then, the refrain serves to orient the narrative spatially. By contrast to the Marian refrain of *Ecce mundi gaudium*, the refrain of *Congaudeat turba fidelium* actively participates in the creation of time and space within the song, manifesting less as an interruption than a continuation of the narrative strand.

The refrain's insistence on place within the temporality of the unfolding narrative points to the importance of Bethlehem within the reception and recreation of Christ's Nativity throughout the Middle Ages and beyond. A visual parallel to this sonic chronotope is a detail from Matthew Paris's mid-thirteenth-century map of Outremer, depicting Bethlehem as a small architectural structure, labeled with an abbreviation of Bethlehem, and, just above it, a star with light

---

[28] Bakhtin, "Forms of Time and of the Chronotope in the Novel: Notes Toward a Historical Poetics," in *Dialogic Imagination*, 84. For a consideration of the chronotope in medieval terms, see Gurevich, "Medieval Chronotope."

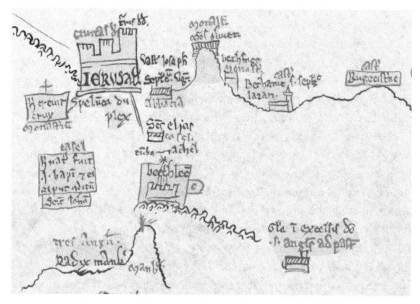

Figure 2.1 Fordham University Oxford Outremer Map Project. Image based on Oxford, CCC MS 2*, Matthew Paris, *ca.* 1250s (detail), part of the Fordham University Oxford Outremer Map Project. Image rights held by the Center for Medieval Studies at Fordham University. Creative Commons Attribution-NonCommercial 4.0 International License

streaming downward to the city (see Figure 2.1).[29] A little to the right and below the town of Bethlehem is a pair of Latin lines atop another small structure, probably a hut; the first reads "Gloria in excelsis deo" and the second, in red, reads "angelus ad pastores."

With these two lines, Matthew's signaling of place rehearses a pivotal narrative moment in Luke 2:9–14 in which the angels appear to the shepherds to announce the birth of Christ.[30] Bethlehem in Matthew's map, then, is defined not only by its geographical placement, but the most significant Christian event to take place there – Christ's Nativity. This visual chronotope is amplified on the map by the inclusion of the indeterminate field outside of Bethlehem (in Luke 2:8, "in regione eadem") identified by the reporting of the angelic announcement in the same way in which the angel's pronouncement is included in song. Music and map alike

---

[29] This detail is taken from the restored map produced as part of Fordham University's *Oxford Outremer Map* digital project: oxfordoutremer.ace.fordham.edu/neatline/fullscreen/oxford-outremer-map.

[30] On spiritual pilgrimage and Matthew's maps, see Connolly, *Maps of Matthew Paris, passim*, but especially ch. 5.

foreground the intersection of time and space in depicting and retelling the story of Christ's birth.

Musical settings of *Congaudeat turba fidelium* reflect the close-knit narrative strophes and spatially oriented refrain. However, as with the poetry, they display many variants, even while sharing a single melody centered on D. Example 2.2 compares nine extant melodies for the song in ten sources; in one case, the melody is taken from the bottom voice of the only polyphonic setting in the Engelberg Codex (see Example 2.2, line 7). While not identical, the melodies occupy the same tonal space and share key melodic markers. All but one start on D, and all versions end the refrain on D. At "turba" all but one version leap up to A, and at "peperit" or "salvator" (depending on which second line of the first strophe is used) the melody drops back down to D. In all cases, the refrain is characterized by a downward descent, although the starting pitch varies between G and F. As with the grammatical joining of refrain and strophe within the narrative framework of the song, the melody of the refrain functions as a musical close, uniformly descending to D in answer to the rising gesture that concludes each strophic line.

Among the melodies compared here, the most ornate is in the Engelberg Codex, where it serves as the bottom voice, or tenor, of a two-voice setting (melody 7 in Example 2.2). Featuring lengthy melismas, this is the outlier in Example 2.2. Comparison of the text underlay for the polyphonic version and the two unnotated versions of *Congaudeat turba fidelium* in the same manuscript, however, illustrates the potential for the same song to employ different textures. In the same hand as the polyphonic version, the copying of the text only of the initial strophe and refrain on fol. 182 reveals a similar text underlay to that on fol. 180^r, in which space is left for melismas on "ma-" of "mater" and "in," as well as possibly on "-go" of "virgo" and "-le-" of "bethleem." Conversely, on fol. 130^r, the text is copied out in a manner suggesting a predominantly syllabic setting with little to no space left for melismatic writing; in this instance, the texture seems to have been more in line with the other notated concordances in Example 2.2. The Engelberg Codex thus transmits two renderings of *Congaudeat turba fidelium*, one staying close to the core melodic trad-ition, characterized by a largely syllabic setting, and a second that features a more elaborate melody.

The varied musical treatment and modular poetic structure of *Congaudeat turba fidelium* across sources suggests the influence of oral or performance-based transmission practices. That orality underpins other narrative genres has been widely argued and studied, both within and

Example 2.2 Melodic comparison of *Congaudeat turba fidelium*

Apr 6, fol. 115r

En - gau - de - at tur - ba fi - de - li - um ma - ter vir - go pe - pe - rit fi - li - um in beth - le - em.

Mad 289, fol. 128r

Con - gau - de - at tur - ba fi - de - li - um vir - go ma - ter pe - pe - rit fi - li - um in beth - le - em.

Mad 19421, fol. 107r

Con - gau - de - at tur - ba fi - de - li - um nat - us est rex sal - va - tor om - ni - um in beth - le - em.

Mad 19421, fol. 107v

Con - gau - de - at tur - ba fi - de - li - um vir - go ma - ter pe - pe - rit fi - li - um in beth - le - em.

St-M A, fol. 61v

Con - gau - de - at tur - ba fi - de - li - um nat - us est rex sal - va - tor om - ni - um in beth - le - em.

Example 2.2 (cont.)

Aosta Cod. 11, fol. 85v and Aosta Cod. 13, fol. 62v

Con - gau - de - at tur - ba fi - de - li - um vir - go ma - ter pe - pe - rit fi - li - um in be - le - em.

Engelberg Codex, fol. 180r (bottom voice)

Con - gau - de - at tur - ba fi - de - li - um vir - go ma - ter pe - pe - rit fi-li-um in beth-le - em.

Le Puy A, fol. 107r

Con - gau - de - at tur - ba fi - de - li - um nat - us est rex sal - va - tor om - ni - um in beth - le - em.

Piae Cantiones (1582), no. 10, and Piae Cantiones (1625), no. 6 (*mensurally notated)

Con - gau - de - at tur - ba fi - de - li - um vir - go ma - ter pe - pe - rit fi - li - um in Beth - le - hem.

outside musicology, and while no consensus has been reached on the relative orality versus textuality of medieval song, a degree of orality/ aurality is impossible to deny for a repertoire dependent upon the act of performance.[31] For songs whose principal function is to convey a narrative, moreover, the comparison to the oral practices around the performance of epics and other story-based verse is inescapable.[32] In the case of *Congaudeat turba fidelium*, the episodic or modular nature of the poetry, along with its variable melodic profile, suggests a transmission history inflected by both textualization and performance, the interaction contributing to gradual changes to the song over time, even in the course of copying a single manuscript.[33] Within the poetic framework of a symmetrical text, comprising rhyming, ten-syllable-line strophic couplets, and a refrain that depends upon the strophes for its textual and grammatical meaning, it is easy to envision an extemporized performance that draws upon a series of well-known Gospel scenes of Christ's Nativity. Each version of *Congaudeat turba fidelium* realizes in performance its own unique narration of the same story, with the shared refrain anchoring singers and listeners in the place and time of Christ's birth.

Although *Ecce mundi gaudium* and *Congaudeat turba fidelium* narrate the same story, draw from the same biblical sources, and employ a refrain, the end results differ significantly, as their varying focus on the Virgin makes clear. In *Ecce mundi gaudium*, a Marian refrain begins embedded within the narrative before transforming into an unchanging prayer to the Virgin that frames, rather than participates in, episodes of the Nativity story. Conversely, the refrain in *Congaudeat turba fidelium* belongs entirely to the time and space of the narrative, its repetition enacting a quintessential chronotope of Christmas songs by locating each event in the geographical spot inseparably linked to the time of Christ's birth, *in Bethlehem*. By contrast to the unique inscription of *Ecce mundi gaudium* in F, the many witnesses for *Congaudeat turba fidelium* offer insight into the possible oral dimension of sung narratives across time due to its modular poetic construction and variable yet related musical settings.

[31] One of the most prolific proponents of orality as essential to medieval song is Leo Treitler; with reference to narrative in particular, see "Homer and Gregory."
[32] See, for example, the emphasis on orality throughout the collection of essays on performing narrative in Vitz, Regalado, and Lawrence, eds., *Performing Medieval Narrative*.
[33] Although in a far different context, Raffaele Morabito's description of modularity in oral narrative describes what might be taking place in the transmission of *Congaudeat turba fidelium*; see "Italian *Cantari*," 383.

Narrating Easter in *In hac die Dei*

The end of Christ's earthly time and the beginning of his divine existence offers rich dramatic and narrative potential similar to that of his birth, which had long been realized in the earliest liturgical dialogues and the maze dances of the medieval church on the day of Resurrection.[34] Musically, this pillar of the church year inspired great quantities of new works across liturgical and extraliturgical genres, including Latin song.[35] Many Latin refrain songs narrate the events leading up to Christ's crucifixion and subsequent Resurrection, most often by drawing on the Gospel accounts or the language of Old Testament prophecies; in some cases, Easter songs are textually inspired by, or borrow from, the liturgy, as in the Nativity songs above. In the case of the single refrain song or *rondellus* I examine here, *In hac die Dei*, its strophes lean heavily on Gospel accounts while the refrain draws on the text of a liturgical chant. Through the juxtaposition of biblical and liturgical texts, multiple temporalities emerge within the boundaries of the song, further magnified by the strategic contrast of verb tenses between strophe and refrain and an underlying temporal framework that structures the narrative of the poem. *In hac die Dei* narrates the entirety of Easter day in such a way that the lived experience of today is brought into contact with the historical yet annually reexperienced day of Christ's Resurrection.

Akin to *Congaudeat turba fidelium*, the strophes of *In hac die Dei* are variable in number and form in three manuscripts, Tours 927, fol. 11^v, OBod 937, fol. 446^v, and F, fol. 463^{r-v}.[36] Of the three versions, I focus only on the version transmitted in F, which arranges strophes in a way that unambiguously outlines the diurnal framework signaled by the incipit, "on this day of God." As Table 2.3 illustrates, the eight strophes of *In hac die Dei* in F divide thematically into two parts.[37] The first three strophes begin tracing an antisemitic path through the account of Easter in the Gospel of Matthew, introduced by "on this day of God," while a different timescale within the day is introduced in the five similarly antisemitic strophes that

---

[34] The literature on liturgical accretions for Easter is vast; for a recent overview of liturgical dramas (or representational rites), including Easter dialogues, and the surrounding scholarship, see Norton, *Liturgical Drama*. On Paschal rituals and dances involving church mazes, see Wright, *Maze and the Warrior*, 129–158.

[35] In Everist's typology of the *conductus*, for instance, Easter figures prominently, although not as significantly as the Virgin or the Christmas season.

[36] For the arrangement of strophes in each version, see Anderson, ed., *Notre-Dame and Related Conductus*, 8:51 and *CPI*.

[37] Ibid., iv, n. 1.

Table 2.3 F, fol. 463^{r–v}, *In hac die Dei*

Latin	Translation	Biblical source for strophe
PART 1: AGAINST THE JEWS		
1. **In hac die Dei**	1. **On this day of God,**	Matt. 27:64
Dicant nunc Hebrei	*let now the Hebrews sing,*	
Sepulchrum Iudei	the Jews badly	
Male servaverunt.	preserved the sepulcher.	
Quomodo Iudei	*How the Jews*	
Regem perdiderunt.	*lost their king.*	
2. Ubi corpus dei	2. Where the body of God was,	Matt. 26:66
Dicant nunc Hebrei	*let now the Hebrews sing.*	
Numquid Pharisei	Did the Pharisees	
Petram revolverunt.	roll back the stone?	
Quomodo Iudei	*How the Jews*	
Regem perdiderunt.	*lost their king.*	
3. O Scariothei	3. O Iscariots,	Various [across the Gospels]
Dicant nunc Hebrei	*let now the Hebrews sing,*	
Cum Iuda Iudei	the Jews slept badly	
Male dormierunt.	with Judas.	
Quomodo Iudei	*How the Jews*	
Regem perdiderunt.	*lost their king.*	
PART 2: DISCOVERY OF RESURRECTION		
4. **In ortu diei**	4. **At the break of day,**	Mark 16:12–19
Dicant nunc Hebrei	*let now the Hebrews sing,*	Luke 24:13–36
Viri Galilei	The men of Galilee	
Dominum viderunt.	Saw the Lord.	
Quomodo Iudei	*How the Jews*	
Regem perdiderunt.	*lost their king.*	
5. Mater Salomei	5. The mother of Salome,	John 20:2–4
Dicant nunc Hebrei	*let now the Hebrews sing,*	Mark 16:1
Nati Zebedei	The sons of Zebedee	Luke 24:1
Petrum prevenerunt.	Arrived before Peter.	
Quomodo Iudei	*How the Jews*	
Regem perdiderunt.	*lost their king.*	
6. Scribe Pharisei	6. The scribes, the Pharisees,	Matt. 23
Dicant nunc Hebrei	*let now the Hebrews sing,*	
Omnes erant rei	All were guilty,	
Omnes peccaverunt.	All sinned.	
Quomodo Iudei	*How the Jews*	
Regem perdiderunt.	*lost their king.*	

Table 2.3 (*cont.*)

Latin	Translation	Biblical source for strophe
7. Donec Nazarei	7. While the Nazarenes,–	–
Dicant nunc Hebrei	*let now the Hebrews sing,*	
Turris nostre spei	Closed the doors	
Portas recluserunt.	To the tower of our hope.	
Quomodo Iudei	*How the Jews*	
Regem perdiderunt.	*lost their king.*	
8. **Vespere diei**	8. In the evening of the day,	John 20:19–20
Dicant nunc Hebrei	*let now the Hebrews sing,*	
Diem iubilei	they returned to us	
Nobis reduxerunt.	a day of jubilee.	
Quomodo Iudei	*How the Jews*	
Regem perdiderunt.	*lost their king.*	

follow the incipital line, "at the dawn of day," bookended in the final strophe with "in the evening of the day," or "at Vespers."[38] The diurnal framing around Christ's Resurrection is the most compelling feature of this poem, and one that emerges solely through the song's arrangement in F. The succession of events that follow from daybreak ("in ortu diei") are not precisely in biblical order, although the rearrangement of events does not detract from the narrative arc around the themes of discovery and disbelief.

Throughout *In hac die Dei*, rhyme scheme and verbal tense highlight the act of narration, placing the events of the Passion and Resurrection firmly in the past by consistently employing the third-person plural of the perfect tense ending with "-runt." Thus, the disciplines "saw" the Lord, the Nazarines "closed" the gates, and so forth. The recurring tense provides the B rhyme throughout each strophe, and the opening line, "in hac die Dei," provides the A rhyme, "-ei," leading to an identical rhyme scheme through the entire *rondellus* (see Example 2.3). While Latin refrain songs are typically rhymed and symmetrically structured, *In hac die Dei* takes this interest in regularity to an extreme by maintaining the same two rhymes throughout all its strophes (-ei and -runt), providing a contrast between the static rhyme scheme and the diurnal framing of the poem. The refrain, too, participates in the rhyme scheme and narration of past events in its own

[38] Strophes 6 and 7, not to mention the refrain, are also anti-Jewish; this is rhetorically emphasized by the act of repeated naming of Jewish groups throughout the short poem (Hebrews, Jews, Pharisees, Scribes, and Nazarenes).

Example 2.3 F, fol. 463ʳ, *In hac die Dei*

fashion. The second two lines of the refrain are in the past tense, placing
blame on the Jews for "losing their king," a narration the follows the
refrain's directive to "let now the Hebrews sing." Indeed, the only present
tense in the entire song occurs in the initial line of the refrain, "dicant nunc
Hebrei," in which the present imperative to speak or sing (*dico, dicere*) is
emphasized by the adverb "nunc," now. Two temporalities are at work in *In
hac die Dei*: the underlying diurnal structure and the tension between past
and present brought about by verbal tense. The narration of biblical events
presents the story as it happened in the past, while the refrain asserts the
current moment of performance, the moment in which the story is being
retold, even as it simultaneously and repeatedly renarrates the story of
"how the Jews lost their king."

The simplicity of the music parallels the poetic economy of the text.
Only three brief musical phrases comprise the song as it survives in F, each
relatively stepwise with one key moment of intervallic action at the end of
lines 3 and 5 (see Example 2.3). At this point, a sudden descent of a fifth to
G following a fourfold repetition on D and then a jump back up to the D at
the beginning of lines 4 and 6 marks a moment of tension within the
melodic contour. Notably, this leap often accompanies descriptors of
people – Jews (*Iudei*), men of Galilei, the sons of Zebedee, and the
Pharisees. Its effect within the song is one of punctuation. This melodic
articulation of the text works especially well in the refrain, within which the
accusatory tone is inflected musically by the sudden downward motion on
"Iudei," creating a pause before the return to the central range of the song
for the final phrase.

The musical and poetic form of the song also offers possibilities for how
to interpret the temporal framework of the narrative. At three moments in
particular, the refrain blurs the past in which the story takes place and the
present "nunc" in which the singers perform. In the first strophe, the initial

line opens by placing us "on this day of God," for which the response "let now the Hebrews sing" corresponds temporally and musically by repeating the same melody; the day of God is only revealed as having happened in the past when we hear a new melody with the words "the Jews badly protected the sepulcher." At that point it becomes clear that the events are not in the here and now, but are past events being narrated. Moreover, in the framing of the day of Resurrection in strophes 4 and 8, the singing of the first line of the refrain immediately follows the temporal marking of the lines "at the break of the day" and "at Vespers." As in the first strophe, time is briefly confused, as the performance of the narrative blends with the story in the past. This is an integral conceit of the song – the temporary conflation of then and now.

The success of this temporal layering rests on the liturgical origins of the refrain text. While the strophes, as with many songs narrating Christ's Nativity and Resurrection, follow the Gospels closely, the refrain instead draws more directly from the liturgy, namely an antiphon verse from Second Vespers for Easter Sunday (it is notable that Vespers is also obliquely referenced in the final strophe of the song, where it functions as a temporal marker).[39]

Dicant nunc Iudei quomodo milites custodientes **sepulchrum perdiderunt regem** ad lapidis positionem quare non servabant petram iusticie aut sepultum reddant aut resurgentem adorent nobiscum dicentes. (Paris lat. 15181, fol. 298^(r–v))	In hac die Dei *Dicant nunc Hebrei* **Sepulchrum Iudei** Male servaverunt. *Quomodo Iudei* *Regem perdiderunt.*
Now let the Jews say how the soldiers guarding the tomb lost the king with the stone in place, why they did not preserve the stone of justice. Let them either hand over the one who was buried or venerate with us the risen one, saying.	On this day of God, *let now the Hebrews sing,* the Jews badly protected the sepulcher. *How the Jews* *lost their king.*

The refrain reworks a significant portion of the liturgical verse, changing "Iudei" to "Hebrei" in its first appearance, but using "quomodo perdiderunt regem" by rearranging it to fit the rhyme scheme. The initial strophe, too, borrows the antiphon text "sepulchrum Iudei." The resonance of the refrain with a text sung on Easter Sunday would hardly have gone

---

[39] I have yet to locate a melodic relationship between song and liturgical verse in Parisian manuscripts, although one might exist outside of the city, considering the wider dissemination of *In hac die Dei.*

unnoticed; moreover, the integration of a liturgical text into the song as a refrain enhances the experience of time within performance by bringing the liturgy of the day and its inherent *hic et nunc* into the song, connecting the narration of the Resurrection Day with the present day's liturgical rites.

The narrative framing of the three songs discussed here reflects choices on the part of the poet and/or composer to emphasize the temporality inherent to these two pivotal moments in Christ's life. In each case, the poetry derives its narrative scaffolding and even its wording directly from the Bible, closely following the chronology presented, in most cases, in the Gospels. For *In hac die Dei*, the liturgy additionally serves as an intertext, with the refrain modeled after an antiphon from the Eastertide liturgy. Although each song – *Ecce mundi gaudium*, *Congaudeat turba fidelium*, and *In hac die Dei* – similarly employs the changing strophes to tell a biblical story, the inclusion of a refrain in each differently interacts with a familiar narrative. These examples, moreover, represent only a selection of refrain songs that similarly narrate the most familiar and theologically central stories of the church. Although the interaction of strophes and refrain in terms of music, poetry, and temporality in these three works presents several unique and notable features, narrative poetry around Christ's Nativity and Resurrection can be identified across the repertoire of Latin refrain songs. Refrain songs are, in fact, frequently narrative in form, drawing in some cases on pre-existent biblical or liturgical texts, or crafting entirely new poems that recount the stories behind the major feasts of the liturgical calendar.

Saints' Time: Narrating Miracles, Singing Refrains

Many of the most thrilling stories attached to the medieval calendar of feasts involved saints. Although often formulaic for each type and subtype of saint (martyrs, virgins, confessors, et al.), lives of saints were inherently dramatic and frequently featured grisly deaths, torture, and other kinds of violence.[40] The events that comprise an individual saint's *vita* or *passio* were already structured in a narrative way, since they were designed to tell the story of the saint's life, miracles, and/or martyrdom. Throughout the Middle Ages, hagiographic texts were key sources for veneration of the saints through other media, including representational rites and vernacular

---

[40] For explorations of violence in music and drama relating to saints, see Hankeln, "Reflections" and Davidson, "Violence and the Saint Play."

dramas; pictorial narratives, whether in *libelli* or in psalters or other collections of hagiographic materials; song and verse; and the liturgy itself. Within the early medieval Gallican rite, saints' *vitae* were part of public readings during Mass and Office, while in later centuries hagiographic material was used not only as the basis of Office liturgies, but also appeared in the vernacular as farses, or textual and musical tropes, of the epistle.[41] The *novum canticum* of the twelfth century also proved to be an avenue for venerating saints, with sequences and nonliturgical song reworking hagiographies into song for performance within or adjacent to the liturgy.[42] Medieval lives of saints served as an anthology of popular stories that could be drawn on and reworked into any form in any medium, including Latin refrain songs.[43]

In his examination of "narrative melody," Stevens foregrounded saints' lives as a key form of musical storytelling, relating musical projections of saints' lives, including farsed epistles, to the performance of epic, and especially the vernacular *chanson de geste*.[44] More recently, John Haines has considered the parallels between epic and saints' lives with an eye toward recovering the music of the medieval epic, which he locates in Old French farsed epistles for St. Stephen.[45] The key witness for Haines, Stevens, and others, is Johannes de Grocheio, who brings together the *chanson de geste* and saints' lives in his treatise *Ars musice*:

We call *cantus gestualis* [*chanson de geste*] that in which the deeds of heroes and the achievements of our ancient fathers are recited, such as the life and martyrdom of saints, and the struggles and adversities that men of old suffered for faith and truth, such as the *vita beati Stephani prothomartyris* and the *hystoria regis Karoli*.[46]

---

[41] On the public reading of saints' lives, see Dunn, *Gallican Saint's Life*. On the troped epistle, see Le Vot, "La Tradition musicale"; Stevens, *Words and Music*, 239–249; Haines, *Medieval Song*, 103–115 and "Le Chant vulgaire"; Dunn, "Farced Epistle"; Hiley, *Western Plainchant*, 233–238; and Cazal, *Les Voix du peuple*, chs. 2–3.

[42] See, for example, Szövérffy, "Legends of St. Peter." The troped liturgy for St. James in the *Codex Calixtinus* notably highlights the interweaving of liturgy and new song in honor of a specific saint; see Corrigan, "Codex Calixtinus" and the essays collected in Asensio Palacios, ed., *Symposium El Codex Calixtinus*.

[43] For an overview of the importance of Voragine's anthology of saints' lives in particular, see Le Goff, *In Search of Sacred Time*, ix–xiii. Saints' plays were also vehicles for popular devotion and entertainment; see Murphy, *Medieval Mystery Plays*.

[44] Stevens, *Words and Music*, 235–249. Stevens is not the first to note the similarities between epic poetry and saints' lives; see the literature cited and summarized in Haines, *Medieval Song*, 96–97. See also Leverage, *Reception and Memory*, 23–67.

[45] Haines, *Medieval Song*, 96–115.

[46] "Cantum vero gestualem dicimus in quo gesta heroum et antiquorum patrum opera recitantur. Sicuti vita et martyria sanctorum et prelia et adversitates quas antiqui viri pro fide et veritate passi sunt. Sicuti vita beati stephani protomartyris. Et historia regis Karoli." Edited and

Grocheio unambiguously links the deeds, lives, and martyrdoms of saints with the historical figures who served as the subjects of the vernacular *chanson de geste*. Since Grocheio's discussion here refers to vernacular musical practices, this passage has rightly been seen as reflecting the practice of singing saints' lives found in early romance song, such as the partially notated tenth-century Legend of St. Léger.[47] More substantial than early fragments of sung saints' lives, though, are the extant farsed epistles in which vernacular tropes interject within Latin lections for certain saints' feast days, most often St. Stephen.[48]

While the farsed epistle may afford insight, as Haines argues, into the musical declamation of epic poetry, the survival of these notated narratives of saints also offers some picture of the music employed to tell hagiographic tales. Grocheio briefly describes the musical form of the *cantus gestualis*, or *chanson de geste*, stating that the verses of a *cantus gestualis* are comprised of several rhymed, or consonant, versicles, and that the total number of verses is not fixed but rather should fit the needs of the material and the composer's desire; the verses should also be sung to the same music.[49] Extant farsed epistles for St. Stephen in particular fit the model that Grocheio outlines for the *chanson de geste*, featuring melodic settings, which Haines suggests evoke, in some instances, the "courtly song" of the trouvères.[50] They do so by virtue of limited melodic ranges, predictable melodic phrasing, repetitive structures, and quasi-strophic forms, all features in common with twelfth- and thirteenth-century vernacular song repertoires.

The formal characteristics of the *chanson de geste* in Grocheio's formulation and its similarities to the song-like vernacular farses are significant for thinking about how the Latin refrain song of the same period could also convey saintly narratives. Few saints are venerated in medieval Latin song

---

translated in Grocheio, *Ars musice*, 66–67. Cited in Stevens, *Words and Music*, 236; Haines, *Medieval Song*, 101–102; and Zaerr, *Performance*, 43–44.

[47] Edited in Linskill, *Saint-Léger*. See also Stevens, *Words and Music*, 238 and Haines, *Medieval Song*, 25–30, 98–99, and 200–203 for an edition of the notated portions.

[48] See n. 41 above.

[49] "Versus autem in cantu gestuali est, qui ex pluribus versiculis efficitur versiculi in eadem consonantia dictaminis cadunt. In aliquo tamen cantu clauditur per versiculum ab aliis consonantia discordantem. Sicut in gesta, quae dicitur de Girardo de Viana. Numerus autem versuum in cantu gestuali non est determinatus sed secundum copiam materiae et voluntatem compositoris ampliatur. Idem etiam cantus debet in omnibus versiculis reiterari." Edited and translated in Grocheio, *Ars musice*, 70–71. For a discussion of the musical style of the farsed epistle, including its relation to Grocheio's description, see Stevens, *Words and Music*, 239–249 and Haines, *Medieval Song*, 108–114.

[50] Haines, *Medieval Song*, 109–110.

writ large. Most medieval Latin songs dedicated to saints are, moreover, nonnarrative, better resembling prayers or petitions for intercession that focus on a select number of attributes or that develop and meditate on key metaphors. In some cases, and clustered into a small of number of manuscript sources, the lives, deeds, and martyrdoms of a small number of saints are conveyed narratively in song. These are poems for Sts. Denis, John the Baptist, Katherine, Nicholas, and Stephen, all transmitted in just a handful of manuscripts from the twelfth through the fourteenth centuries (see Table 2.4).[51] A significant proportion of those poems listed here feature refrains (fifteen of the twenty); the remaining songs are strophic or through-composed. What this suggests is that, within medieval Latin song, refrain forms were employed more consistently than any other form to convey hagiographic narratives, suggesting that repetitive structures were not considered inhospitable to narrative by certain poets and composers.

My parameters for distinguishing between narrative and nonnarrative poems revolve around the retelling in poetic form events found in the lives of a saint. In other words, rather than a prayer to the saint or an extended meditation on a saints' virtues or symbols, the song narrates moments from a saint's life and martyrdom, usually originating in widely known hagiographic texts and presented in a roughly chronological sequence. Although all the poems in Table 2.4 were newly written, each song retells, or recounts, precirculating stories and employs conventional turns of phrases and vocabulary.

Singing Saints' Lives in a Parisian Miscellany

Of the thirty-two strophic and refrain-form poems in the St-Victor Miscellany, a full eighteen concern the Virgin Mary, All Saints, and Sts. Denis, Katherine, and Nicholas.[52] Of these, the eight poems for the Virgin and All Saints focus on themes related to specific feast days; only the ten distributed between Sts. Denis, Katherine, and Nicholas proceed narratively. This is by far the greatest number of Latin songs (albeit unnotated) transmitted together in honor of saints; as Mark Everist observes, despite

---

[51] This does not include songs for saints formally and structurally more akin to sequences, as is the case of the sequence *Psallat concors symphonia* for John the Baptist (despite the rubric "cantilena" in MüC, fol. 114ᵛ). On the unusual form of this "song," see Göllner, ed., *The Manuscript Cod. lat. 5539*, 210–212.

[52] See Chapter 5 on the refrain songs of the St-Victor Miscellany.

Table 2.4 Narrative songs for saints

Saint	Incipit	Source and Fol.	Form
St. Denis	*Francigene radii*	St-Victor Miscellany, 177ᵛ	strophic
	Gallia cum letitia	St-Victor Miscellany, 181ʳ	strophic+refrain
	Iucundare Gallia	St-Victor Miscellany, 185ᵛ	strophic
St. John the Baptist	*Cleri universitas*	Paris n.a.l. 426, 5ᵛ	strophic
St. Katherine	*Ad sancta Katherine*	St-Victor Miscellany, 178ʳ⁻ᵛ	strophic+refrain
	Letare mater ecclesia	St-Victor Miscellany, 181ᵛ	strophic+refrain
	Militans ecclesia	St-Victor Miscellany, 186ʳ⁻ᵛ	rondellus
	Quasi stella matutina	StV, 163ᵛ	through-composed
St. Nicholas	*Cantu miro summa laude*	St-M C, 24ʳ	through-composed
		Later Cambridge Songbook, 7ᵛ (300ᵛ)	
		St-M D, 12ᵛ	
	Sancto dei Nicholao	St-M C, 23ᵛ	?strophic
	Incomparabiliter cum jocunditate	St-M A, 46ᵛ	strophic+refrain
	Exultet hec contio	F, 471ᵛ	strophic+refrain
	Gaudeat ecclesia	F, 471ʳ	strophic+refrain
	Nicholaus pontifex	F, 471ʳ	strophic+refrain
	Intonent hodie	Moosburger Graduale, 232ᵛ	strophic+refrain
	Sancti Nicholai	St-Victor Miscellany, 178ᵛ	strophic+refrain
	Nicholai laudibus	St-Victor Miscellany, 182ʳ	strophic+refrain
	Nicholai sollempnio	St-Victor Miscellany, 186ᵛ	strophic+refrain
	Laudibus Nicholai	St-Victor Miscellany, 189ʳ	strophic+refrain
St. Stephen	*Dulces laudes [Dulcis laudis] tympano*[*]	Moosburger Graduale, 241ᵛ	strophic+refrain
		Engelberg Codex, 128ᵛ	strophic+refrain
		Antiphonarium Lausannense III.3.1, p. 103	strophic+refrain
		Antiphonarium Lausannense III.3.2, 55ʳ	strophic+refrain
		SG 392, p. 90	strophic+refrain

[*] Engelberg Codex and SG 392 employ the incipit *Martyr fuit Stephanus*.

the widespread popularity of all three saints, the emphasis on the trio appears to be a local phenomenon, since saints feature so rarely in extra-liturgical Latin song.[53] Setting the poetic collection apart further is its pedagogical slant, which, along with its Parisian origins, offers a particular perspective on the density of saint's lives narrated in poetry.[54] As patron

---

[53] Everist, *Discovering Medieval Song*, 64.
[54] See also Chapter 5, Haskins, "Life of Medieval Students" and Hauréau, *Notice*.

saints of students and the University of Paris, the foregrounding of Nicholas and Katherine among the poems accords with the manuscript's origins within a didactic institution,[55] while the presence of St. Denis – Bishop of Paris and patron saint of France – makes obvious sense in a Parisian source. When contextualized within the broader pedagogical agenda of the St-Victor Miscellany, the sheer number of works for a small number of saints might also have some clear rationale. It was not unheard of for students to be assigned a theme (often a story, sometimes drawn from classical sources but also religious texts) upon which they would compose a new poem as a rhetorical exercise. It is possible we might see examples in the St-Victor Miscellany of such thematically inspired poetry centered on the lives of saints.[56]

Looking closely at the ten narrative poems for these three saints, similarities readily emerge. All but two (*Francigene radii* and *Iucundare Gallia* for St. Denis) feature refrains, and each rehearses within the poetry's strophic structures events drawn from well-known and widely disseminated *vitae*.[57] Structurally each poem follows the same formulaic patterning of material. The first strophe, whether or not it is preceded by a refrain, typically introduces the saint by name and alludes to their biography (as in *Militans ecclesia* for St. Katherine, the first strophe of which begins "virgo Costi filia," "the virgin daughter of Costus"). Each poem concludes in its final strophe with a supplication, signaled explicitly by imperative verbs such as "exoremus," "oremus," or "rogamus," or implicitly by seeking intercession through prayer.[58] Beginning either in the initial strophe or in the following strophe, the poems narrate the life and miracles of the saints episodically, summarizing in an often-sparse manner longer prose passages found in contemporary *vitae*. For comparison, the martyrdom of St. Katherine by beheading and her subsequent heavenly transport to Mount Sinai feature logically as a central image among the three poems

---

[55] Jones, *Saint Nicholas*, 144.

[56] See below and the exercises described in Woods, "Poetic Composition," especially 134–138.

[57] *Vitae* of all three saints are included in Voragine, *Golden Legend*: St. Nicholas on 21–27, St. Denis on 622–627, and St. Katherine on 720–727. All three saints' lives were also translated in vernaculars, and in the case of Sts. Nicholas and Katherine, celebrated in numerous Latin and vernacular plays.

[58] See, for instance, the final strophe of *Ad sancte Katerine*: "Rex et pater omnium | Per eius suffragium | Nos Olympi civium | Collocet in agmine." ("May the King and Father of all through her prayers place us in the company of the heavenly citizens.") Edited and translated in Anderson, ed., *Notre-Dame and Related Conductus*, 8:lx.

in the St-Victor Miscellany. In Jacobus de Voragine's *Legenda aurea*, this key moment calls for extended textual treatment that includes direct speech between Katherine and Christ, her mystical spouse.[59] In the St-Victor Miscellany, brief strophes convey the same scene in succinct fashion across the three poems:

(fol. 178ᵛ)	(fol. 181ᵛ)	(fol. 186ᵛ)

Virgo post multa mala
Migravit acephala
Quam sepelivit ala
Christi Sȳna culmine.
	Hec tandem acephala pro
	    sanguine
	Lac fundens collocata in
	    culmine
	Sȳnaȳ fuit manu di[v]a.
		Tandem virgo regia
		Cum iugi victoria
		Capitis privamine
		Migravit in medio.

After suffering many evils, the virgin departed headless, and Christ's wings buried her on the peak of Mount Sinai.	Finally, headless, streaming milk in place of blood, she was placed by divine hands on the peak of Mount Sinai.	Finally, the royal virgin in triumphant victory with her head severed moved around in their midst.

In a similar fashion, a favored scene from the life of St. Nicholas, his rescue of sailors in a storm, receives pithy treatment across all four songs in the Miscellany, employing synonymous vocabulary:[60]

(fol. 178ᵛ)	(fol. 182ʳ)	(fol. 186ᵛ)	(fol. 189ʳ)

Ac in periculo
Nautis conquerulis
Pre mortis angustia
Donavit suffragia.
	Ac nautis
	    clamantibus
	In obvio
	    naufragio
	Subvenit sedans
	    mare.
		Nautis eius
		    clemencia
		Subvenit in
		    naufragio.
			Plebi fuit opifex . . .
			Ac in maris turbine
			Nautis conquerentibus.

And for the sailors in danger, lamenting on account of the anguish of death, he made intercession.	And by calming the seas he came to the aid of the shouting sailors amid the hostile shipwreck.	In his clemency he came to the aid of the sailors amid the shipwreck.	He was the [miracle] worker of the common people . . . and of sailors lamenting amid the turbulence of the sea.

[59] Voragine, *Golden Legend*, 725.   [60] Ibid., 22.

All ten poems operate in this fashion by distilling the most popular events in each saints' life down to poetic morsels that are stacked together into strophic settings. Enriching the sense of temporal scope, moreover, textual markers of time tend to appear in initial positions within individual strophes to demarcate the progression of the story over time, most often taking the adverbial form of "tandem," "inde," "post," and "hinc."

The poems resulting from this modular and formulaic construction treat their hagiographic source material in an episodic manner akin to the treatment of the Nativity story in *Ecce mundi gaudium* and *Congaudeat turba fidelium*. Although wording, rhyme scheme, syllable count, and number of lines per strophe differ among songs, the consistency of how each *vita* is treated is striking, as the comparison of strophes above concerning St. Katherine's beheading and St. Nicholas's marine rescue, above, illustrates. To take St. Katherine as a further example, her life and miracles are divided into nine discrete themes in the three poems in the St-Victor Miscellany:

1. Virginity and Purity
2. Learnedness
3. Disputation
4. Torture
5. Imprisonment
6. Conversion of bystanders
7. Breaking of wheel
8. Beheading
9. Angelic transport of body to Mount Sinai

Each of the three poems employs at least six of these themes, with all three emphasizing the scene of St. Katherine's debate, or disputation, with the pagan scholars (an iconic symbol of her learnedness), her torture, including the famous wheel, and her martyrdom by beheading and subsequent removal. The three poems narrate the same general sequence of events, adding and subtracting episodes as desired while maintaining the core of Katherine's saintly identity.

A parallel can be found here once again with pictorial narratives, this time with the illustration of saints' lives, whether in independent *libelli*, books of hours, in other devotional books, or on altarpieces and other devotional objects.[61] Many saints were subject to visual treatments, but the dramatic lives of popular saints such as Nicholas, Katherine, and Denis provided ample visual fodder for artists to depict, just as they provided dramatic material for playwrights and poets.[62] In Figure 2.2, a fourteenth-century

---

[61] On pictorial narratives of saints, see Pächt, *Rise of Pictorial Narrative*; Ross, *Text, Image, Message*; and Hahn, *Portrayed on the Heart*.

[62] Most famously, the life of St. Denis receives extensive visual treatment in the Vie de St. Denis manuscript (Paris fr. 2090–2092); see Lacaze, *The "Vie de St. Denis" Manuscript*.

Figure 2.2 Altarpiece, *Saint Catherine of Alexandria and Twelve Scenes from Her Life*, Getty Museum, object number 73.PB.69 (tempera and gold leaf on panel), Donato d'Arezzo and Gregorio d'Arezzo, Italy, *ca.* 1330. Image courtesy of the Getty's Open Content Program. *Centre:* St. Katherine with book and martyr's palm. *Left panel, l-r from top left:* Katherine with mother visiting hermit with image of Virgin and Christ; Vision of Virgin and Child; Baptism; Mystical marriage to Christ; Disputation with scholars; Martyrdom of converted scholars. *Right panel, l-r from top left:* Imprisonment; Empress's visit; Empress's conversion; Torture by wheel; Decapitation of soldier converts; Beheading

altarpiece from Italy depicts twelve scenes from the life of St. Katherine, visually reflecting the ordered structuring of her life featured in poems of the St-Victor Miscellany.[63]

Pictorial narratives such as this, alongside the poetic retellings collated in the St-Victor Miscellany, highlight the narrative interest inherent in saints' lives. In material and poetic form, the life of St. Katherine can be broken into its most compelling episodes and framed spatially and temporally by means of physical borders in the altarpiece and the strophic forms of the poetry – not to mention the refrains that characterize the majority of the poems for saints in the St-Victor

---

[63] On this altarpiece, and its broader contexts within devotion to St. Katherine, see Schmidt, "Painting and Individual Devotion," 25–26 and 31. See also www.getty.edu/art/collection/ objects/632/donato-d'arezzo-gregorio-d'arezzo-saint-catherine-of-alexandria-and-twelve-scenes-from-her-life-italian-aretine-about-1330.

Miscellany, segmenting song in a way that mirrors the segmentation created visually by borders.

Eight of the ten narrative saints' poems in the Miscellany feature refrains recurring between strophes, with the exception of two *rondelli*, *Militans ecclesia* and *Pange cum leticia*. Regularly interjected into and between the narrative-focused strophes, the refrains bring singer and audience back from the past in which the stories of these saints take place and into the present, by means of verbal tenses and language that stresses the collective veneration undertaken in the performance of the songs (see Table 2.5). Imperative verbs are by far the norm, with the community ("concio"), church ("ecclesia"), and even France itself ("Gallia") implored to rejoice, praise, and glory in the solemnities of these three saints. The emphasis on verbal expressions of joy and veneration is clear – the singers are to "shout" ("pangat") Alleluia, and sing "sweet songs" ("dulcibus cantibus"). The refrains do not participate explicitly in the narrative of the strophes, existing instead outside of the temporality of the story. In their musicality, the refrains of these narrative saints' songs function in a manner akin to the French *refrain* in narrative contexts in which the *refrain* often functions as a signal of music, whether or not notation is present.[64]

Yet it would be misleading to ignore the temporal interplay of these musical refrains with the narrative strophes. By means of the present tense employed in refrains, the primary intent of each poem is situated in the present: the concluding prayers of singers in the final strophes seek intercession for the present and future. Since refrains also begin each poem (as the manuscript layout in the St-Victor Miscellany suggests), the intercessory tone is made clear before the narration of each life begins, itself signaled by a move from the present to perfect tense and other textual markers of time (e.g. "ille"). Over the course of each poem, singers and listeners move between two temporalities – the "then" of the saint's life, and the "now" of performance, in which the singer(s) serve as implicit narrators. The self-reflexive emphasis on song and singing in the refrains also articulates a particular kind of narrative voice. If the collective voice of the refrains spills over into the performance of the strophes, then "we" are positioned as singers of

---

[64] See especially Peraino, "*Et pui conmencha a canter.*" Although refrains are not framed as signals of music necessarily, Drummond's consideration of linear narratives and cyclical refrain structures in the Cantigas de Santa María has resonance here, since the Cantiga's refrains are often presented as moments of prayer; "Linear Narratives."

Table 2.5 Refrains for Sts. Nicholas, Katherine, and Denis in the St-Victor Miscellany

St. Denis	*Gallia cum leticia Eximia Ana pangat alleluia.*	*Let France, with extraordinary joy shout "Alleluia" to the heights.*
St. Katherine	*Ad sancte Katerine Decus Sÿon concine. Letare mater ecclesia!*	*To the glory of St. Katherine sing, O Syon. Rejoice, Mother Church!*
	Militans ecclesia Beate Katerine Gaudeat sollempnio	*Let the militant church rejoice in the solemnity of Blessed Katherine.*
St. Nicholas	*Laudibus Nicholai dulcibus Vacemus cantibus.*	*Let us devote ourselves to sweet songs and praises of Nicholas.*
	Nicholai laudibus Cum gaudio Eximio Nos decet convacare.	*It is fitting for us to greatly devote ourselves to the praises of Nicholas, with extraordinary joy.*
	Nicholai sollempnio Letetur cleri contio.	*Let the company of clergy rejoice in the solemnity of Nicholas.*
	Sancti Nicholai Vacemus titulis, Cum summa leticia Pangentes Alleluia.	*Let us devote ourselves to the honors of St. Nicholas, shouting "Alleluia" with the highest joy.*

praise to St. Nicholas on account of the miracles that "we" recount in song.

Given the performative vocabulary of the refrains, the question of musical performance remains significant. The poems, and especially the refrains, are so rich in musical vocabulary, in fact, that performance seems to be taken for granted, even in the absence of notation. The inclusion of the French *refrain* rubrics as melodic cues for the refrain-form poems (see Chapter 5) evinces the underlying musicality of the collection. The question of how these hagiographic poems would have been performed also relates to their expression of narrative time – storytelling, whether recited or sung, takes place over time. As it happens, saints' lives were among the most popular stories performed in the Middle Ages, including (and perhaps most importantly) in the vernacular, but also in Latin and, of course, integrated into the liturgy.[65] The popularity of saints' plays, too, attests to the attention paid to the performative value of saints' lives both in Latin and in vernacular languages. Most tellingly, the performance of saints' lives was often framed as a moralizing or didactic act, regardless of language.

Notably, the performance of saints' lives in diverse contexts and languages was sanctioned by church authorities and considered to be morally uplifting. As detailed in Thomas Chobham's thirteenth-century penitential, jongleurs were to be generally condemned for their inappropriate behaviors and singing, except when singing "gesta principum et vitas sanctorum" ("deeds of princes and lives of saints").[66] In Grocheio's account of the *cantus gestualis*, or *chanson de geste*, moreover, the moral and civic rectitude of performing saints' songs is also made clear:

That *cantus* ought to be provided for the aged and working citizens and ordinary people while they rest from their usual labor, so that, having heard about the miseries and disasters of others, they may more easily bear their own, and each one may approach his work more eagerly. And therefore this *cantus* is beneficial for the preservation of the whole city.[67]

These citations, however, refer chiefly to vernacular narratives of saints and princes, and not to the kind of Latin poems found in the St-Victor Miscellany. Of the performance of hagiographic Latin song, fewer traces survive, especially for works lacking liturgical associations. Following Mark Everist's suggestion that the *conductus* may have been part of the practice of public reading, *lectio publica*, in the refectory of monasteries or in chapter houses attached to churches, songs recounting saints' lives may have been suitable material for such occasions, mirroring in performance readings already drawn from hagiographic materials.[68] Saints' songs also may have

---

[65] Leverage, *Reception and Memory*, 28–45.

[66] This passage from Thomas Chobham is widely cited; see, for instance, ibid., 29–30; Stevens, *Words and Music*, 235–236; Page, *Owl and the Nightingale*, 23–24; Baldwin, "Image," 642–643; and Haines, *Medieval Song*, 101.

[67] "Cantus autem iste debet antiquis et civibus laborantibus et mediocribus ministrari, dum requiescunt ab opere consueto. Ut auditis miseriis et calamitatibus aliorum suas facilius sustineant. Et quilibet opus suum alacrius aggrediatur. Et ideo iste cantus valet ad conservationem totius civitatis." Edited and translated in Grocheio, *Ars musice*, 66–67. Discussed in Leverage, *Reception and Memory*, 28–45; Haines, *Medieval Song*, 101–102; Zaerr, *Performance*, 43–44.

[68] Everist, *Discovering Medieval Song*, 58.

contributed to extraliturgical feast-day celebrations of the kind discussed in Chapter 1, with the specific saints venerated in the St-Victor Miscellany subjects of intense celebration both within and outside of the confines of the church and monastery.[69]

Saints' lives were rich narrative resources for medieval poets and composers, exemplified in the numerous anthologies and rewritings of saints' lives across language and genre. Saints are less often a focus in Latin song – genres driven by narrative, including dramas and troped epistles, supply a greater number of musical and poetic works, rehearsing the episodes of each saint's life and miracles. Strophic refrain forms prevail among the narratively structured songs for saints, providing insight into how repetitive structures could be employed meaningfully in the narration of hagiographical stories. For the poems in the St-Victor Miscellany, the strophic structures foster a modular approach to constructing song that we also saw in songs for Christ's Nativity and Resurrection. As a comparison of individual episodes across songs illustrates, strophic structures are used to order, reorder, and poetically retell many of the same moments in the lives of Sts. Nicholas, Katherine, and Denis. Refrains, by contrast, sit outside of the main narrative thread, representing moments of collective commentary and a way for the narrative to be musicalized even in the absence of notation. Yet refrains are also situated temporally in relation to the narrative strophes, their present tense creating cyclical movement between the historical past of the saint's lives and miracles and their present and future ability to provide divine intercession.

Conclusion: Repeating *sine termino*

A focus on narrative in the Latin refrain song enables a shift from the macro temporality of the festive year in Chapter 1 to the micro temporalities of song itself and its performance. In a range of songs narrating moments in Christ's time (his Nativity and Resurrection) and the time of saints, refrains participate in upholding, constructing, and complementing the narrativity of song. Whether a refrain functions as a prayer that regularly frames a narrative, a chronotope that locates the story in a specific time and place, or an invocation to vocal praise, refrain forms offer a

---

[69] For example, folkloric and musical activities for John the Baptist were extremely important in the Middle Ages; see Anderson, "Fire, Foliage and Fury." See also Chapter 1.

malleable expressive vehicle for narrating the familiar and well-trod stories pertaining to Christ and the family of saints.

As the songs considered in this chapter make clear, the medieval Latin refrain, as Hollander suggests, does something to the time of song. The refrains of sung narratives "toll" the strophes by marking their beginnings, endings, and occasionally their middles as in *rondelli*. In this most basic sense, the repetition of refrains paces a song's progression by returning to familiar, even memorable, material before proceeding to the exposition of new narrative information. In so doing, the repetition of refrains has an immediate impact on the temporality of song in performance by persistently bringing the past into the present and allowing us to see into the future in anticipation and expectation of a refrain's repetition *sine termino*. In many cases, the grammar and language of refrain takes this further, juxtaposing the generally historical time of the strophes with the present and future-looking time of the refrain. The perpetual return to a refrain can produce a sense of boundlessness, a sense of out of time, that contrasts with the bounded identity of song's performance that has a beginning, middle, and end. Chapters 4 and 5 consider further the "timelessness" and mobility of refrains as they move between song and language, creating additional layers of temporal meaning in the performance of the Latin refrain across time and space.

3 | Singing the Refrain

Shaping Performance and Community Through Form

What did it mean to sing a song with a refrain in the Middle Ages? The refrain was an explicit marker of form and, to a degree, function for poets, composers, scribes, and singers. Refrain forms were consciously adopted for certain subjects, gathered together, and ordered in specific ways in manuscript sources. The refrain song was created, performed, and transmitted within and among communities for whom forms of musical and poetic expression rooted in the calendar year and religious narratives were meaningful – communities for whom retelling saints' miracles in song or celebrating the Feast of the Circumcision as the New Year, for example, contributed to a vibrant and communal devotional and musical life adjacent to the liturgy. The refrain was also a formal axis linking Latin and vernacular song, a flexible and mobile unit of text and music across songs, and a possible signal for movement.

All of these aspects related to the performance, textualization, and function of the refrain testify to its currency within medieval song culture, but do not necessarily address the question of why the repetition of text and music in performance – sometimes of content as brief as a single word – carried so much cultural, musical, and poetic weight.[1] Why the refrain? How did the performance of refrains in Latin song foster and maintain certain sets of cultural and ritual associations within and across clerical, monastic, and pedagogically oriented religious communities?

The evidence of the songs themselves, their poetry, musical settings, and contexts of manuscript transmission, reveals one way in which the refrain operates in medieval Latin song that embraces and even fosters its cultural impact in performance. The refrain is powerful not solely due to the rhetorical potential of repetition – although that is significant – but also by means of the refrain's relationship to poetic, musical, and liturgical performance practices. Evinced in poetic language and grammar, form, musical settings, and scribal cues, the refrain in devotional Latin song brings individuals together in the moment of performance through the

---

[1] For a comparable question and discussion with different outcomes around the French *refrain*, see Butterfield, *Poetry and Music*, 75–121, and Saltzstein, *Refrain*.

act of remembering together, responding collectively, and worshipping communally. With roots in the responsorial, litaneutical, and ejaculatory refrains and repeated prayers of the liturgy, the refrain evokes both real and imagined performance practices around Latin song that contribute to its agency within the devotional and musical lives of medieval communities. The refrain carries cultural, musical, and poetic weight precisely because it rarely reflects the utterance of an individual, but instead expresses the voice of the community, whether defined as narrowly as a choir in a local church, or as broadly as the clergy, or even the entire church.

This chapter explores the meaning of the refrain in and for communal performance. For the communities who created, sang, and transmitted devotional Latin song, the refrain afforded a moment for the collective, shared experience of remembering and responding. It has long been assumed by scholars and performers that refrain forms in medieval song initiated, on a practical level, a call-and-response format, with strophic material performed by soloists and the refrain by a choir.[2] While there is an attractive simplicity in the equivalence of performance practice to form, the reality is more complex. Scholarship by Ardis Butterfield, Jennifer Saltzstein, and others has shown that this is not the case for the French *refrain*, for example; instead, the *refrain* evokes variable ideas of performance through its dissemination and interpolation into other genres, including narratives and the polyphonic motet. The relationship between form and performance has yet to be similarly questioned for the Latin refrain, in part because its structural, rather than intertextual and citational, identity seems to discourage deeper examination. Moreover, responsorial and refrain forms in the liturgy, most significantly processional hymns with refrains, have offered appealing and convincing touchstones for the performance of devotional Latin songs.[3]

Rather than taking responsorial – solo and choral – performance for granted, in this chapter I reexamine the ways in which the refrain functions as a moment of literal or figurative coming together in song. Drawing on the Latin refrain song's self-theorization of refrains and refrain forms through rhetoric, grammar, form, and musical texture, I illustrate how poets and composers embedded ideas about performance, community, and communal participation in their compositions. Crucially, the songs themselves define communities rooted in the structures of the church; singers

---

[2] See, for examples, Aubrey, "French Monophony"; Norberg, *Introduction*, 179; and Silen, "Dance in Late Thirteenth-Century Paris," 72.

[3] Messenger, "Medieval Processional Hymns" and "Processional Hymnody"; Hiley, *Western Plainchant*, 146–148; and Bailey, *Processions*, 174–175.

and songs belong to nested and hierarchical communities of clergy, choir, rank, and in some cases age. Working within these communities, the efforts of scribes and compilers contribute additional layers of information to the meaning and performance of refrains, with rubrication and textual cues offering rare insight into specific and relatively demarcated contexts for the refrain song's responsorial performance.

A reevaluation of assumptions around the vocal and choreographic performance of the Latin refrain song reveals the nuance of performance practices around refrain forms. Most significantly, refrains and refrain forms did not have to be sung responsorially in order to invoke the voice of the community, nor was dance inherent in their meaning and realization, by contrast to the frequently applied label of "clerical dance songs." Whether sung by soloists or a choir, standing still or moving, the Latin refrain cultivated a sense of community and belonging that buttressed its multivalent cultural, theological, musical, and poetic functions and made it possible for the structural repetition of a unit of text and music to accrue a range of meanings in performance and interpretation.

Song, Refrain, and Singing with One Voice

The fifteenth-century refrain song *Presens festum laudat clerus*, sung at Matins in an Austrian abbey and copied uniquely into the St. Pölten Processional (fol. 9^{r-v}), provides internal evidence of its vocal performance. It begins in its first strophe with a call to the clergy to sing sweet melodies "with one voice" ("una voce"). This cue for a unified voice leads into the refrain, which repetitively and rhetorically plays with the stem "mir-," or "wonderful":[4]

1. Presens festum laudat clerus	1. The clergy praise the feast at hand and
Dulce melos dat sincerus	give a sweet melody with one voice, eia
Una voce eya et eya.	and eia.
Mirum mirum	*Wonderful, wonderful*
Mirum nimirum	*exceedingly wonderful,*
Mirum festum	*wonderful feast*
Mira gaudia.	*wonderful joys.*

---

[4] The twelfth-century *Mira dies oritur* (St-M C, fol. 38^v) similarly plays with the stem "mir-" in ways that lend it a refrain-like function (termed by Haug a "virtual" refrain); see Haug, "Ritual and Repetition," 96; Switten, "Versus and Troubadours," 117, text and music edited at 142–143, and Caldwell, "Texting Vocality."

2. Quisquis adest ut exultet
Canat plaudens ut resultet
Bis intonet eya et eya.
  Ref.

2. Whoever attends in order to exult, let him sing with applause in order to resound, let him twice intone eia and eia.
  Ref.

3. In hac die Christo nato
In salute nobis dato
Exultemus et letemur.
  Ref.

3. On this day on which Christ is born, given for our salvation, let us exult and rejoice.
  Ref.

4. Omnis etas omnis homo
Sollempnizet in hac domo
Bis intonet eya et eya.
  Ref.

4. Let all generations, all mankind keep the solemn feast in this house [church] and twice intone eia and eia.
  Ref.

5. Eya lector sic incipiat
Atque presul benedicat
Totus chorus sic respondeat
  Ref.

5. Eia, thus, let the lector begin and let the bishop bless, [and] thus let the whole choir answer:
  Ref.

Repetition saturates this song beyond the refrain; the five strophes share portions of repeated text (such as "bis intonent eia et eia" in strophes 2 and 4) as well as similar exhortations to sing and rejoice on the feast day, named in the third strophe as Christ's Nativity. While the rubrication of the song, "conductus infra noctem," suggests a functional role in the Matins liturgy adjacent to a reading (*lectio*), the final strophe of the song formulaically cues the lector to begin following a final iteration of the "wonderful" refrain.[5]

A responsorial performance for *Presens festum laudat clerus* is overtly cued in this final strophe as the whole choir is directed to respond ("totus chorus sic respondeat") with the refrain. In previous strophes, implicit performance cues frame the refrain as a vocalic choral response, a semantically simplistic manifestation of the joyous song repeatedly elicited in the strophes by commands to let "everyone," "all mankind," and the "church" express their joy. The framing of the first strophe, however, is key: the clergy is asked to sing their sweet, sincere melodies "with one voice" ("una voce"). While in literal terms this could refer to the monophonic (literally unison) performance of *Presens festum laudat clerus*, the expression originates in Daniel 3:51 with the three boys who were thrown into the furnace singing the canticle *Benedictus es* "as with one

---

[5] On lectionary formulas in Latin song, see Everist, *Discovering Medieval Song*, 52–56; Hiley, *Western Plainchant*, 248–250; and Ahn, "Exegetical Function," 128–131.

mouth" ("quasi ex uno ore").[6] The doctrine of singing *quasi una voce* became integral to how liturgical chant and, indeed, the aural performance of sacred texts more generally, was understood by the Church Fathers and liturgical commentators throughout the Middle Ages.[7] As Clement of Rome states, "we too assembled with one accord should earnestly cry out without ceasing to him as with one voice";[8] in this he is followed by Clement of Alexandria, who asserts that "the union of many, which the divine harmony has called forth out of a medley of sounds and divisions, becomes one symphony."[9]

The doctrine of *quasi una voce* pertains both to performance practices – specifically monophonic chant – and to the metaphor of performance. As Judith Peraino writes regarding Augustine's views on devotional song, the doctrine leads to "many bodies coming together as one voice, producing one sound, and becoming one body (the Church)."[10] The music that results – namely, chant – is seen as a "solution to the dangers of song, for the words are completely controlled … by preventing individuality."[11] Univocal song and praise are a way for the church to control and divert the individual voices of a community (i.e. the church) into a shared expressive goal. And while chant as a whole can be conceived as a form of singing *una voce*, liturgical responses and refrains (e.g. "amen") are especially rich moments of explicit participation by the totality of the community, bringing a greater number of voices into alignment literally and figuratively.

The example of liturgical responses, however, brings up an important point. Singing *quasi una voce*, as if with one voice, does not necessarily mean everyone (choir, school, clergy, congregation) participates equally or at the same time; as Richard Crocker observes, "more than one Christian cannot sing literally with one voice; the doctrine is some kind of spiritual direction for 'performance practice.'"[12] To sing with one voice is to imagine a collective voice being expressed by singers regardless of their number. Steven Connor employs the term "chorality" to think about these sorts of

---

[6] Dan. 3:51 "Tunc hi tres quasi ex uno ore laudabant, et glorificabant, et benedicebant Deum in fornace."

[7] Quasten, *Music and Worship*, 66–72; Peraino, *Listening to the Sirens*, 41–43 and note 131; and Crocker, *Introduction*, 24–25.

[8] Quasten, *Music and Worship*, 68.

[9] Ibid., 67. As Crocker summarizes, "singing *una voce* is regarded by the Fathers as the proper way in which Christians praise their God, the way in which they address God: they are to sing all together, at once, in unison, using the same words and the same intonation." "Two Recent Editions," 90.

[10] Peraino, *Listening to the Sirens*, 41. See also Peraino, "Listening to the Sirens," 441–447.

[11] Peraino, *Listening to the Sirens*, 41.   [12] Crocker, "Two Recent Editions," 90.

collective speech and musical acts, which include prayers, statements of fealty, protest songs, and learning songs, and how what he terms the "choric voice" most often builds solidarity – a sense of singing *as if with one voice* – within communities, however delineated.[13] Importantly, chorality does not simply mean a "collective voice," or many voices coming together, but rather a voice that is understood as representing the whole.[14]

The Latin refrain and refrain song resonate with Connor's "choric voice." Mirroring the ideal of liturgical chant to produce a single, unified voice for the church, the refrain song is constructed around the voice of the community and its rhetorically anticipated, if not actual, participation cued by the refrain. Whether or not an entire choir responds with the refrain of *Presens festum laudat clerus* as cued in the final strophe, the entire Augustinian community in St. Pölten – and, indeed, the entire church – is ventriloquized through performance in the collective voice of the song and its responsorial form. Although a collective yet unified voice resonates throughout Latin song, chant, and liturgical tropes, the refrain is a specific signal. Repeating over the course of a song and, in some cases, across songs, refrains belong to a register of voice capable of eliciting both real and imagined community participation.[15]

A Grammar of Performance and Plurality

The poetry of the refrain song – grammar, language, rhetoric – illustrates through the use of plural and collective nouns and verbs the ways in which communities of singers are linked through a unified voice in song. Like many medieval songs that range across language and register, the Latin refrain song is self-reflexive; references to song and singing, as exemplified

---

[13] Connor, "Choralities," 5. See also Applegate, "The Building of Community" and Ahlquist, ed., *Chorus and Community.* This differs from William McNeill's thesis that "moving our muscles rhythmically and giving voice consolidate group solidarity by altering human feelings"; as Connor suggests, and I describe here, participation (muscular or vocal) is not required to produce a sense of solidarity and community. *Keeping Together*, viii.

[14] As Connor writes, chorality "is the means whereby we allow ourselves the collective hallucination of collectivity." "Choralities," 17 and 20.

[15] I am building in this chapter on the implications for performance described by Haug of the refrain as it moves on the spectrum between "real" and "virtual": "Whilst [the switch from strophe to refrain] may not point to an actual change in performance resources from solo singer to group, it does, however, suggest the idea of communal participation in the song: of the extension of sung performance across a growing number of singers: of an excrescence in song." "Ritual and Repetition," 88.

in *Presens festum laudat clerus*, are commonplace.[16] Interest in song itself most often arises around the issue of a song's performance, whether imagined or actual. Initial strophes of Latin song often offer an assertion of the implied performing forces; as I discuss in Chapter 1, incipits can also position the performance of song within the calendar and seasonal year. Accounting for elements of performance in the language and grammar of refrain songs reveals a repertoire of songs focused on communal song, repeatedly evoking, if implicitly, the doctrine of singing *una voce*. This manifests in two ways in refrain songs, often, albeit not exclusively, within the confines of the refrain itself: first, through repeated returns to the idea of a community, and second, through a consistent emphasis on plurality by means of the widespread use of the plural first-person and collective nouns. The poetry of Latin refrain songs creates a link between performance and the expression of a unified voice of the church through consistent terminological and grammatical choices.

The contribution of language to the creation and maintenance of feelings of community is not a new concept but has been well explored by cultural and social historians, as well as musicologists. Peter Burke in particular has examined the role of language in the process of community formation for the early modern period.[17] His insights regarding the role of Latin as a shared, albeit second, language within communities across Europe and the significance of plural grammar as signifier of identity have relevance for the high Middle Ages and the lyrics under consideration here. The resolute Latinity of these songs situates them within literate, clerical, and monastic milieus, and gives them the potential, in Burke's words, of creating "a sense of distance from everyday life and a sense of universality" as well as "a sense of tradition."[18] Close associations with the Latin liturgy (including direct and indirect borrowings of prayers, chants, biblical passages, etc.) further enhance Latin song's ties with the linguistic communities created and supported by the church. The largest community circumscribed by the Latinity of Latin song is, consequently, that of the Catholic church writ large. This is not surprising; the spheres in which Latin song was principally cultivated were also ones in which Latin served as the key mode of communication and education within and without the liturgy.

---

[16] On self-reflexivity in song, see Zumthor, "On the Circularity of Song"; Leach, "Nature's Forge"; Peraino, *Giving Voice to Love*; Dillon, "Unwriting Medieval Song"; and Levitsky, "Song Personified." The psalmodic trope of the "new song" is one locus for Latin song's self-reflexivity, particularly acute for twelfth- and early thirteenth-century *nova cantica*, although the "new song" trope has a wide currency in Latin song; see Caldwell, "Singing, Dancing, and Rejoicing," 116–132.

[17] Burke, *Languages*. In the context of print culture, see also Anderson, *Imagined Communities*.

[18] Burke, *Languages*, 49.

While language delineates the church at the broadest level, the refrain song repeatedly evokes performance by groups of singers through the consistent use of collective nouns and first-person plural verb forms attached to self-referential descriptions of performance. The systematic use of the first-person plural sets refrain-form songs apart from the grammatical practices of Latin song more broadly in ways that have yet to be examined.[19] The final two fascicles in F serve as a case study for the way in which grammatical choices differ between songs with and without refrains. The collection of *conducti* in Fascicle X in F begins with a highlighting of singular voices in *Homo natus ad laborem* (fol. 415[r–v]), attributed to Philip the Chancellor.[20] In a dialogue that alternates between the voice of the body and soul by strophe, *Homo natus ad laborem* dramatically privileges the subjectivity of individual voices. By contrast, an Easter song, *De patre principio*, begins Fascicle XI (fol. 463[r]). Its five strophes and two-part refrain are markedly different in tone and grammar than *Homo natus ad laborem*, emphasizing the unified voice of the church, as the first strophe illustrates:

1. De patre principio	1. From the Father as origin,
Gaudeamus eȳa	*let us rejoice, eia!*
Filius principium	The Son is an origin,
Cum gloria	*with glory,*
Novum pascha predicat	*the Church proclaims a new*
ecclesia.	*Passover.*
Gaudeamus eȳa.	*Let us rejoice, eia!*

The Easter *rondellus* repeats "gaudeamus eya" twice in each strophe as part of the two-part refrain, whose subject is identified as the church ("ecclesia"); the song is not the expression of an individual, subjective voice, but instead reflects the voice of the collective church celebrating Christ's Resurrection. *De patre principio* sets the grammatical tone for the entire final fascicle of F. Only two songs out of sixty consistently employ a singular voice; the remaining fifty-eight are grammatically unified around either the first-person plural or collective nouns (e.g. "contio") that take the third-person singular.[21] By contrast, the *conducti* of

---

[19] Switten has observed this grammatical emphasis in the twelfth-century *versus* repertoire, noting the frequency with which verbs are in the first-person plural and describing this as a reflection of the "communal nature of the celebration for those participating." Switten, "Versus and Troubadours," 109.

[20] Rillon-Marne, *Homo considera*, text, transcription, and further bibliography at 267–270.

[21] *Vineam meam plantavi* (fol. 466[v]) and *Breves dies hominis* (fol. 469[r]), both unique to F.

Fascicle X, beginning with *Homo natus ad laborem*, showcase a wider variety when it comes to verbal person and number, with a notable emphasis on the first-, second-, and third-person singular rather than plural forms. Fascicles X and XI in F offer a striking opportunity to compare the poetic grammar of songs that take different forms and subject matter. In addition to ordering according to form and the liturgical calendar, the refrain songs of Fascicle XI also show an undeniable poetic and grammatical tendency toward voicing the collective rather than the individual.[22]

Throughout devotional Latin refrain songs, certain verbs occur more often than others in the first-person plural imperative, most significantly "gaudeamus," "exultemus," "iubilemus," "celebremus," and "psallamus" (let us rejoice, exult, sing out joyously, celebrate, and sing, respectively). Over half the time, these calls to the community can be found in the refrain itself, as in *De patre principio*. In three songs, "gaudeamus" comprises the entirety of the refrain, marking it as a refrain word, or response, comparable to the "alleluia" or "amen." Like these liturgical refrains, "gaudeamus" also implicitly supports group participation. The three songs with the "gaudeamus" refrain were closely linked to, or performed within, the liturgy.[23] *Voce resonantes* is a neumed *Benedicamus Domino* song-trope transmitted in the thirteenth-century troper and songbook from a Swiss cloister, Stuttg, also known as the Stuttgart Cantionale (fols. 52^v–53^r and 74^v–75^r); *Salve festa dies veneranda* is rubricated "conductum sancti Iacobi" in the twelfth-century troped liturgy for St. James in the Codex Calixtinus (fol. 132^{r-v}); and *Exultantes in partu virginis* survives unnotated in the twelfth-century *versarium* St-M A and also serves as a Matins *conductus* for the Feast of the Circumcision in sixteenth-century manuscripts from Le Puy Cathedral.[24] In each case, the invariable, single-word refrain is treated differently, showcasing a range of approaches to the

---

[22] At the risk of reinscribing a dichotomy between the Latin and the French *refrain*, the latter demonstrates little of the poetic communality foregrounded in the former. On the whole, French *refrains* are cued in narrative contexts as the product of a single singer/character, and grammatically tend to focus on the individual, subjective "I." See Doss-Quinby, *Les Refrains*, 37; Butterfield, *Poetry and Music*, 48; and Mullally, *Carole*, 84–87.

[23] Switten writes, in comparing refrains of varying lengths in the *versus* repertoire, that shorter refrains "arguably ... are linked to ritual." "Versus and Troubadours," 102.

[24] *Voce resonantes* was also added with neumes, but lacking reference to the *Benedicamus Domino*, to a manuscript containing Thomas Aquinas's *De sortibus* (Brugge 111/178, fol. 32^v), from Ter Doest Abbey; see Mannaerts, "Musiek en musiektheorie," 18. For additional sources of *Exultantes in partu virginis*, including Le Puy B, see the Appendix.

composition and performance of refrain forms and, importantly, the potential of the refrain to be performed by a soloist or larger ensemble.

In *Voce resonantes*, "gaudeamus" repeats between each line of the *Benedicamus Domino* song-trope, the brevity of the refrain at odds with the way it textually dominates the brief work:[25]

Voce resonantes	With a resonant voice,
Gaudeamus	*let us rejoice.*
Corde concordantes	with a harmonious heart,
Gaudeamus	*let us rejoice.*
Omnes ei	let all to him,
Gaudeamus	*rejoice.*
Quam ius rei	To the degree that is just in the matter
Gaudeamus	*let us rejoice*
Qui cuncta fecit	with regard to him who made everything
Ex nichilo	out of nothing,
Gaudeamus	*let us rejoice.*
BENEDICAMUS DOMINO.	LET US BLESS THE LORD.
Gaudeamus	*Let us rejoice*
Deo soli	to God alone
Gaudeamus	*let us rejoice*
Regi poli	to the king of heaven,
Gaudeamus	*let us rejoice*
Laudes canentes ?ymnizonas	singing praises and hymns
Gaudeamus	*let us rejoice*
DEO DICAMUS GRATIAS	LET US GIVE THANKS TO GOD,
Gaudeamus	*let us rejoice.*

The poem includes repeated references to song and singing, the incipit immediately signaling its performance by means of a "resonant voice." At times, the "gaudeamus" refrain appears to fit grammatically into the poem; at other times, it sits apart from the simplistic text of praise and thanksgiving that tropes the Office versicle. The structure of the poem is uncommon, but not unique among tropes; within Stuttg alone, Marian refrains are inserted across liturgical chants in a pattern similar to the "Gaudeamus" refrain in *Voce resonantes*.[26] Significantly, in *Voce resonantes* the

---

[25] *Voce resonantes* is copied twice in Stuttg, the first time (fol. 52ᵛ–53ʳ) only partially up to the fifth repetition of "gaudeamus"; fol. 74ᵛ–75ʳ transmit the poem as transcribed here.

[26] On Marian refrains in Stuttg, see Purcell-Joiner, "Veil and Tonsure," 125–166. Outside of Stuttg, a comparable format obtains in the troped Feast of Circumcision in Le Puy, first in a troped *Pater noster* and, more widely disseminated, the refrain-trope *fulget dies* and *fulget dies ista* is inserted between lines of Office hymns (in Le Puy A the hymn is *Iam lucis orto sidere*); the Codex Calixtinus, discussed below, also transmits several *conducti* and a *Benedicamus Domino*

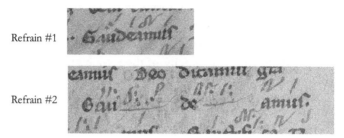

Refrain #1

Refrain #2

Figure 3.1 Neumed "gaudeamus" refrain in Stuttg, fol. 75ʳ. Reproduced by kind permission of the Württembergische Landesbibliothek, Stuttgart

"gaudeamus" refrain is textually identical throughout, but musically variable, alternating between two melodic profiles, one brief and neumatic and the other melismatic (see Figure 3.1). The refrain mirrors the musical style of the nonrefrain material, matching it in complexity and style; the neumes make it challenging, however, to discern whether melodic repetition occurs among the textual elements.

Considering the weight of the refrain in terms of repetition and its frequent melismatic setting, it is unclear what performance practices the "Gaudeamus" refrain entailed. The refrain text itself, "let us rejoice," might provide some slight grammatical support for the implied choral versus soloistic performance of the refrain. The liturgical context is also noteworthy here. The *Benedicamus* versicle is comprised of both a verse, typically performed by two or more soloists, and a choral response; the structure of the verse and response is outlined in the text of *Voce resonantes* above by the citation of *Benedicamus Domino* midway through and "Deo dicamus gratias" at the end. While the refrain runs throughout the song-trope, the implied responsorial format may reflect the versicle's associated liturgical practices – certainly, the choir would have been ready to participate.

A *conductus* for St. James in the Codex Calixtinus, *Salve festa dies veneranda*, shares with *Voce resonantes* the textually identical yet musically variable repetition of "gaudeamus" following each verse line, yet with details regarding performance added by the rubricator (see Figure 3.2):

---

song-trope (the latter with the *fulget dies* refrain) that take a similar form. The troped *Pater noster* in Le Puy A is edited in Chevalier, *Prosolarium*, 11. On hymns troped with "fulget dies," see Caldwell, "Troping Time."

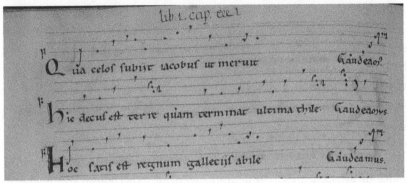

Figure 3.2 Codex Calixtinus, fol. 132^{r-v}, *Salve festa dies veneranda* with "gaudeamus" refrain. Copyright © Cabildo de la Catedral de Santiago de Compostela – all rights reserved. Partial or whole reproduction is prohibited

1. Salve festa dies veneranda
per omnia dies.
Gaudeamus.
2. Qua celos subiit Iacobus,
ut meruit.
Gaudeamus.
3. Hic decus est terre quam
terminat ultima Thile.
Gaudeamus.

4. Hoc satis est regnum
Galleciis abile.
Gaudeamus.

. . .

1. Hail, festive day, a day to be revered by
all things.
Let us rejoice.
2. On which James rose to heaven,
as he deserved.
Let us rejoice.
3. He is the glory of the land that ends
at distant Thule
[beyond the borders of the world].
Let us rejoice.
4. This kingdom is sufficiently suitable
for the Galicians.
Let us rejoice.

. . .

The musical settings alternate with the verses of variable lengths, lengthening or shortening as needed. Akin to *Voce resonantes*, the refrain shifts between two melodies, characterized by descending versus ascending figures on "gau-" of "gaudeamus" (the scribe gradually abbreviates the music of the refrain moving down the folio).

By contrast to *Voce resonantes*, however, the scribe in Codex Calixtinus includes a performance indication directly before the first iteration of the refrain: "the boy repeats this [refrain], going between two singers" ("puer hoc repetat pergens inter duos cantores"). The choral performance of the refrain suggested by its plural form and function as a response is rejected entirely – instead a single boy is seemingly directed to repeat it between the verses sung by the two singers. In *Salve festa dies veneranda*, "gaudeamus" is a boy soloist's response, not the expected communal interjection implied by the first-person plural form. In the Codex Calixtinus, *Salve festa dies veneranda* concludes a series of five *conducti* with liturgical functions as *Benedicamus Domino* tropes and lectionary introductions, functions suggested by rubrics and their poetry.[27] All five employ refrains, and three include similar rubrication to *Salve festa dies veneranda*, prescribing the refrain's solo performance by a boy. The performance practices of refrain songs in the Codex Calixtinus thus invert the expectations of the choral refrain, although not the responsorial framework – the boy soloist still responds to other singers. Moreover, by repeatedly proclaiming "let us rejoice," a single boy takes on the voice of those around him; in the case of the Codex Calixtinus, we might imagine this would involve not only clergy, but possibly also the imagined voices of pilgrims.

A *conductus* sung during the first Nocturne of Matins during the troped Circumcision liturgy transmitted in Le Puy A, *Exultantes in partu virginis*, presents an entirely different structure and performance situation than *Voce resonantes* and *Salve festa veneranda*:[28] The one-word refrain is sung between longer strophes and, in Le Puy A alone, the texture changes between strophe and refrain, with the refrain functioning as a monophonic interjection in a polyphonic setting:[29]

---

[27] Codex Calixtinus, fol. 130[r]–132[r–v]. *Exultet celi curia, Iacobe sancte, In hac die laudes, Resonet nostra*, and *Salve festa dies veneranda*. On these works (excluding the first one, *Exultet celi curia*), see Asensio Palacios, "Neuma, espacio y liturgia," 136–140; on *Exultet celi curia*, see Caldwell, "Troping Time."

[28] On Le Puy A, see Arlt, "Office." Text edited in Chevalier, *Prosolarium*. Also transmitted in Le Puy B, fol. 16[r]/103[v].

[29] The rubrication of *Exultantes in partu virginis* also indicates in a later hand the folios at the end of the manuscript in which a second voice is copied, transforming the monophonic strophes into polyphony (fol. 162[r]).

1. Exultantes in partu virginis	1. Exulting in the birthing of the Virgin
Quo deletur peccatum hominis	by which the sins of man are expunged,
Ad honorem superni numinis	to the honor of the supreme divinity,
Gaudeamus.	*let us rejoice.*
2. Facta parens, non viri coitu	2. Made a parent without congress with a man,
Quem concepit de Sancto Spiritu	the Virgin gives birth to the one she conceived
Virgo parit sed sine genitu.	through the Holy Spirit, but without generation;
Gaudeamus.	*let us rejoice.*
. . .	. . .

The single-word refrain, combined with a monophonic setting, under-scores the responsorial structure of the song, and may have suggested the deliberate juxtaposition of polyphony and monophony for a composer who added a polyphonic line in an appendix at the end of the manuscript; as it occurs initially in Matins, the entire work is monophonic.[30] The invariable musical setting of the refrain is short and simple, outlining a descent of a third, including a lower neighbor extending the gesture to a fourth, by means of small clusters of pitches (see Figure 3.3). The voices of the choir

Figure 3.3 Le Puy A, fol. 28ʳ, monophonic "gaudeamus" refrains. Reproduced by kind permission of the Bibliothèque municipale, Grenoble

---

[30] On the polyphonic additions in Le Puy A (and B), see Arlt, "Einstimmige Lieder" and "Office."

come together both literally in monophony and figuratively here on "let us rejoice," the musical setting affirming the communal message of the refrain. Alternating textures work at the poetic as well as musical level in *Exultantes in partu virginis* to convey meaning in the ritual act of celebrating Christ's birth. Whether the soloists come together in unison for the refrain or they are joined by the choir (and other *conducti* sung at Matins do specify the choir, *chorus*, in rubrics), the "gaudeamus" refrain in *Exultantes in partu virginis* functions as a moment of singing *quasi una voce*.

A variety of performance practices are implied by text, form, and rubrication among songs employing "gaudeamus" as a refrain, ranging from the unison response of *Exultantes in partu virginis* to the explicitly singular performance of the refrain in the Codex Calixtinus. Less clearly attuned to performance, Latin refrain songs invoke three particular communities as the "we" in their plural grammar. The communities who rejoice and sing together are nearly always identified as *cleri* and *pueri* (clergy and choirboys); more generally as a *contio/concio* (assembly, company, or congregation); and, most broadly, as *ecclesia* (the church). The first category pertains both to the clerical milieu of the repertoire's creation and dissemination and to the performative aspect of collectivity, while the latter two are far more general in scope, although always bounded by the limits of the church. While this terminology is not surprising given the religious milieus and institutions in which Latin song was created, the usage of such language in refrain songs specifically frames ideas of performance. *Cleri*, *contio*, and *ecclesia* are not passing references or invoked as subjects alone, but are positioned in the poetry (and in some cases in rubrics) as the agents responsible for producing song on behalf of their community.

When clergy are positioned as singers and listeners in Latin song, they are typically identified by the plural *cleri* or the diminutive *clericuli* (choirboys).[31] The clergy is seldom far removed from the larger assembly of which they are a part, leading to the linking of *cleri* and *concio*, as in phrases from refrain songs including "letatur cleri concio" or "clericalis concio."[32] Returning regularly throughout individual songs and across the repertoire, the refrain frequently serves as the locus for the clergy's self-identification. Communities of faithful, moreover, are rarely silent; instead, their verbal actions emphasize the sounding of devotion: the clergy *resonet*,

---

[31] When the singular appears, as in *clerus*, it still retains its collective sense (as in the English "clergy").

[32] In *Nicholai sollempnio* (St-Victor Miscellany, fol. 186ᵛ) and *Nicholae, presulum* (F, fol. 471ʳ), respectively.

gaudeat, psallat, congaudeat, and *exultet.*[33] Notably, verbs are nearly always in the hortatory subjunctive mood, expressing the poet's desire for communities to convey their devotional joy through sound and song.

Since examples of this formulaic combination of collective noun and subjunctive verb are abundant, a small selection of songs readily illustrates how this linguistic practice works poetically. The first is an Aquitanian *versus, Promat chorus hodie,* often described as a formal precursor to the French *rondeau* and Latin *rondellus* due to its internal refrain:[34]

1. Promat chorus hodie	1. Let the chorus bring forth today,
O contio	*o assembly,*
Canticum letitie	a song of joy.
O contio	*O assembly.*
Psallite contio	*sing, assembly,*
Psallat cum tripudio	*let [the assembly] sing with joy.*
2. Regum rex et dominus	2. King of Kings and Lord,
O contio	*o assembly,*
Quem non claudit terminus.	whom no bound encloses.
O contio	*O assembly.*
Psallite contio	*sing, assembly,*
Psallat cum tripudio	*let [the assembly] sing with joy.*
. . .	. . .

The expected subjunctive mood appears twice in the first strophe of four in the incipit and in the refrain. The imperative mood also appears in the refrain, varying the repetition of the verb *psallere* between "psallite" and "psallat." From the initial line, the *versus* frames itself as a communal outpouring of praise (for Christ, although this is not explicit until the second strophe). The "chorus" is immediately made central to its imagined performance as "bringing forth" joyous song, underscored by the repetition of "contio" in each strophe thanks to the internal refrain. The final three refrain lines bring the sound back to the *contio* once again, with the psalmic verb providing the action for the assembly.

The second example is not a single song, but rather a refrain that appears, similar to "gaudeamus," in different songs and sources: *gaudeat ecclesia.* As a generic expression of the church's joy, "gaudeat ecclesia"

---

[33] Haines has also observed the performative vocabulary saturating refrain songs, specifically those in Fascicle XI of F; see Haines, *Medieval Song*, 71. On performative language in liturgical chant, particularly verbs used in reference to singing, see Iversen, "Le Son de la lyre," "Verba canendi," and *Laus angelica.*

[34] St-M A, fol. 51ᵛ, edited and transcribed in Marshall, "A Late Eleventh-Century Manuscript," 85. See also Chapter 4 for a discussion of this and the closely related *Puer natus hodie.*

occurs dozens of times in Latin poems, not always functioning as a structural refrain, but instead a formulaic invocation of the church. Altogether, nearly one dozen Latin refrain songs utilize "gaudeat ecclesia" as all or part of their refrain (including the variation "*congaudeat* ecclesia").[35] The refrain of a Nativity song in the Moosburger Graduale, *Gaudeat ecclesia inventa*, fol. 232^v–233^r, intertwines the phrase with vocalic repetition and an expanded description of the church in question: "Eya et eya, | regia egregia, | gaudeat ecclesia!" ("eia and eia, let the splendid royal church rejoice"). A well-known song employing the vocabulary of music theory in honor of Christ's Resurrection, *Diastematica vocis armonia* (Later Cambridge Songbook, fol. 2v [1v], twelfth century), features a longer refrain that concludes with "gaudeat ecclesia":[36]

Sanctus sanctorum	*Holy of holies,*
Festa festorum	*feast of feasts,*
Resurrexit	*he has arisen,*
Eya eya eya	*eia, eia, eia,*
Plebs fidelis iubilet	*let the faithful people jubilate,*
Gaudeat ecclesia.	*let the church rejoice.*

In a similar fashion to *Gaudeat ecclesia inventa* in the Moosburger Graduale, the vocalic repetition of "eya" precedes the church's rejoicing; unlike the later *cantilena*, this earlier twelfth-century song includes a reference to the people who comprise the *ecclesia*: the "plebs fidelis" (faithful people).

Collective nouns and verbs of identity and collectivity form a grammatical and poetic trope throughout Latin refrain songs, one heightened and emphasized through the repetition of the refrain itself. The deliberate choice of the first-person plural (as well as collective nouns) is part of the delineation of communities, solidifying a sense of togetherness that might already exist, while also serving to redefine and fortify boundaries. In the context of song, this community formation and/or maintenance occurs within the space of the lyric and its performance, with the potential to interact with performance practice.

In other words, pluralizing language in song may reflect a song's performance by a plurality of voices within a community – who better to sing "let us rejoice" than the community as a whole? Yet the language of song does not always neatly connect to its performance forces or practices, as alluring as the language of refrains might be in this regard. The rubric of

---

[35] See Chapter 4 for this and other itinerant refrains.

[36] Edited and translated in Stevens, ed., *Later Cambridge Songs*, 72–74; see also the discussion on 31.

Salve festa dies veneranda makes this point by asking a single boy to represent the community in his plural "we" refrain. Grammar and language construct the actual as well as imagined performance of this repertoire in ways that always refer to the plural and collective. When one boy sings "gaudeamus," listeners understand that he performs a kind of ventriloquism of the group to which he belongs. Form, manuscript context, and poetics work together to convey information about song's performance in time and space, underscoring how song and refrain functioned as an expression of a community's unified voice, regardless of whose voices, and how many, were actually heard.

All as One and Many Together: Musical Settings of Refrain Songs

Musical texture plays a significant role in shaping the performance of refrains. Above all, the combinations of voices in either monophony or polyphony provides a commentary on the performance of refrain forms that speaks to the question of responsorial performance and the communal identity of the refrain. For Latin song, the greater part of the repertoire is monophonic; only a small percentage survives for two and three voice parts. Scholarly assumption has been that the performance of the repertoire generally involved a choir or group of soloists, by contrast to the soloists required for the frequently more complex polyphonic *conductus*.[37] However, not all Latin refrain songs lend themselves to a choral performance in which the ideal of singing *quasi una voce* can be achieved. The survival of polyphonic settings of Latin refrain songs, alongside several exceptional works that alternate monophonic and polyphonic textures between strophes and refrains, offers different perspectives on the performance of the Latin refrain as an expression of the choric voice and as a soloist's art.

Several songs alternate polyphonic and monophonic textures between strophe and refrain, creating a sonic contrast between the two formal elements.[38] Although examples are scarce and predominantly date from

---

[37] As I noted earlier in this chapter, scant work has been done on the performance practices around *conducti*; however, it seems likely the multi-voice *conducti* were performed by soloists just as soloists performed contemporaneous polyphonic genres, most especially *organum*. On the performance of *organum* at Notre Dame in Paris and its status as a "soloist's art," see Wright, *Music and Ceremony*, 335–344.

[38] Everist discusses five *conducti* that alternate between two and three voices; these are not refrain forms (with the possible exception of *Salvatoris hodie*): *Naturas Deus regulis, Ortu regis*

the fourteenth century and beyond, four extant songs set strophes polyphonically and interpolate monophonic refrains. Three are preserved in Swiss sources chiefly transmitting liturgical contents, tropes, and some polyphony, while one is found in a French source for the Feast of the Circumcision. Two are uniquely preserved in the Engelberg Codex, *Unicornis captivatur* (fol. 150ᵛ–152ʳ) and *Ovans chorus scholarium* (fol. 153ʳ–153ᵛ); a third is the more widely transmitted *Nove lucis hodie* in SG 392, pp. 88–89 (see Chapter 4); and the fourth is *Exultantes in partu virginis* (fols. 27ᵛ–28ᵛ and 162ʳ) in the Le Puy Feast of the Circumcision sources, discussed in the previous section.[39] Only *Nove lucis hodie* is set for three voices in SG 392 (notated successively); the others feature strophes for two voice parts. The two songs in the Engelberg Codex are notated in score format, and the lower of the two voices in *Exultantes in partu virginis* is transmitted in an appendix to Le Puy A. In all cases, refrains are set monophonically. The alternation of texture between strophes and refrain is unambiguous across all the sources, further enhanced by scribal cueing of the refrain in the Engelberg Codex and SG 392.

The transition from polyphonic strophes to monophonic refrain is exemplified by *Unicornis captivatur* in the Engelberg Codex, in which the refrain is visually marked by a textural change and textual cue in red ink. The layout is noteworthy, since the upper voice drops out before the end of a system and the lower line alone continues, leaving the upper stave blank (see Figure 3.4). A textual abbreviation of *et repetitur* cues the monophonic refrain, and capital letters emphasized with red figuration further distinguish refrain from strophe.

1. Unicornis captivatur	1. The Unicorn is captured [and]
Aule regum presentatur	presented to the royal court
Venatorum laqueo	in the trap of the hunter;
Palo serpens est levatus	a serpent is raised upon a stake;
Medicatur sauciatus	a wounded man is cured
Veneno vipereo.	by the viper's venom.
Alleluia canite	*Sing Alleluia*
Agno morienti	*to the dying lamb;*
Alleluia pangite	*cry out Alleluia,*
Alleluia promite	*acclaim Alleluia*
Leoni vincenti.	*to the victorious Lion.*

---

evanescit, Relegentur ab area, Salvatoris hodie, and *Transgressus legem Domini.* See Everist, "Le conduit" and "Variable-Voice Conductus."

[39] On *Nove lucis*, see Chapter 4.

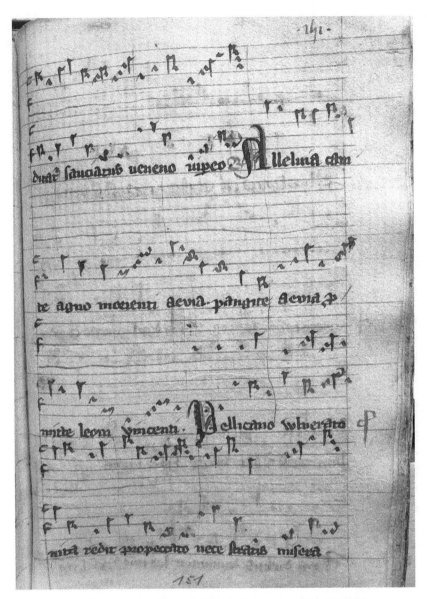

Figure 3.4 Engelberg Codex, fol. 151ʳ, *Unicornis captivator*, from "[me]dicatur sauciatus" in strophe 1 to "misera" in strophe 2. Reproduced by kind permission of Stiftsbibliothek Engelberg

2. Pelicano vulnerato	2. Life returns to the wounded
Vita redit pro peccato	Pelican after miserable slaughter
Nece stratis misera.	in its nest for sin.
Phos fenicis est exusta	The Phoenix's light is burnt out,
Concremanturque vetusta	and the ancient sins of the universe
Macrocosmi scelera.	are consumed by fire.
Ref.	*Ref.*
3. Idrus intrat crocodillum	3. The Hydrus penetrates the
Extis privat, necat illum	crocodile, robs its entrails, kills it,
Vivus inde rediens	and comes back alive.
Tris diebus dormitavit	The Lion slept three days
Leo, quem resuscitavit	until the Basilisk awakened it
Basileus rugiens.	with a roar.
Ref.	*Ref.*

The differing performing forces for strophes and refrain are not indicated; the monophonic refrain could have been performed by the same singers responsible for the polyphonic strophes. The coming together as one voice in the refrain is one that could occur not only by means of a choral interjection, but also by the coming together in unison of previously independent polyphonic voices.

The musical setting and poetry of the refrain in *Unicornis captivatur* work together to create a moment of song framed within a well-known collective response, "Alleluia." The poetry of *Unicornis captivatur* as a whole is striking, employing animal allegories familiar from medieval bestiaries to construct a poem about Christ's Resurrection. Unambiguous animal signifiers of Christ, real or mystical, are introduced in quick succession throughout the poem: The strophes name the unicorn, pelican, phoenix, hydrus, lion, and basilisk, while the refrain names the lamb and the lion.[40] The poem rehearses the traditional allegorical meanings of the animal symbols in turn, each strophe narrating the period between the Passion and Resurrection. The strophic narrative is bounded by the refrain, which provides a two-part summary of Easter – first Christ as the dying paschal lamb and then second as the risen, victorious lion. The summative effect of the refrain within the Easter narrative is enhanced by its imperative to sing alleluia. Refrains in narrative song, as I show in Chapter 2, often invoke song; *Unicornis captivatur* further invokes the singing of a familiar liturgical refrain, "Alleluia," which was removed from the liturgy during Lent and reintroduced on Easter Sunday. The textural shift from

---

[40] On the medieval symbolism of animals and creatures in bestiaries, including several cited in *Unicornis captivatur*, see Hassig, *Medieval Bestiaries*.

polyphony to monophony, in other words, mirrors the textual shift from narrative to invocations of song and refrain.

A New Year's song transmitted in St-M A and the Le Puy Feast of the Circumcision sources, *Annus novus in gaudio*, upsets the textural affiliation of the refrain with monophony exemplified by *Unicornis captivatur* by setting the refrain polyphonically alternating with monophonic strophes.[41] Much discussed due to the successive notation of its polyphonic refrain in St-M A, *Annus novus in gaudio* stands as the sole example in either manuscript context, and more broadly among medieval Latin songs, to invert the expected texture of refrain versus strophes (see Example 3.1).

Annus novus in gaudio is unquestionably a song about singing, framed as the simultaneous celebration of the New Year (understood as the Feast of the Circumcision on January 1) and its octave and the cantor, leader of the choir (see Chapter 1). The strophes follow the model of the first two underlaid in Example 3.1, beginning with a statement on the New Year and then prescribing sung praise in honor of the cantor. The message of the strophes is emphasized in the refrain, which asks the assembled worshippers to raise their voices in honor of the cantor. Performative language characterizes the entirety of the poem as does the collective voice, making the playful move from monophony to polyphony a musical complement to the poetry. The singers make their voices heard ("sonantia") in a special way when the refrain enters, joining together ("concurrent") in harmony, that is, polyphony. While the monophonic "gaudeamus" of *Exultantes in partu virginis* utilizes monophony to signify communal rejoicing and singing *quasi una voce*, in *Annus novus in gaudio* the conjoining of voices in polyphony is deployed to express the collective sentiments of the refrain.[42]

Apart from the unusual witness of *Annus novus in gaudio*, a preference emerges for monophonic over polyphonic settings of refrain forms, brought into relief through the alternation of musical textures. In some cases, focusing on musical texture reveals the seeming elimination of repeating structures in polyphonic versions of monophonic refrain songs. While monophonic textures do not universally correlate to communal performance, simpler, monophonic settings of refrains increase the potential for group, rather than solo,

---

[41] On this song and its polyphonic refrain, see Fuller, "Hidden Polyphony," edited and transcribed from St-M A in 3:2–3; "Aquitanian Polyphony"; Treitler, "The Polyphony of St. Martial"; Arlt, "Einstimmige Lieder" and "Nova cantica," 37–44. A recently discovered contrafact is discussed in Colette, "*Leta cohors fidelium.*" See also Caldwell, "Singing Cato."

[42] The polyphonic refrain in Le Puy A, moreover, has been suggested as an example of improvised polyphony, with the potential for two additional vocal lines around the two in Example 3.1. See Jans, "Ad haec sollempnia."

Example 3.1 Le Puy A, fols. 1ᵛ–2ʳ and 171ʳ, strophes 1–2 and refrain of *Annus novus in gaudio*

performance. Variable texture works likewise to highlight an affiliation between monophony and refrains, showcased through *alternatim* performance based on the division between strophe and refrain. The interjection of the refrain offered composers, in many cases, a poetic "break" that could be exploited texturally by shifting from, more commonly, polyphony to monophony, or more rarely, monophony to polyphony.[43]

---

[43] On the refrain as a break etymologically, see the Introduction, and Hollander, "Breaking into Song."

Only a small number of Latin refrain songs were set polyphonically for two or three voices across strophes and refrain.[44] Perhaps most surprisingly, only one Latin *rondellus* survives in a polyphonic setting, *Luto carens et latere* (W1, fol. 80[r]); all other polyphonic textures occur in settings of strophic songs with refrains. *Luto carens et latere*, moreover, is a unique case study.[45] Extant in five sources, its text appears alone in Tours 927 (fol. 18[v]), with one voice in F (fol. 463[v]), LoB (fol. 48[r]), and Bord 283 (fol. 134[v]), and for three voices in W1 (fol. 80[r]); all the polyphonic versions share their bottom-most voices with the monophonic settings. Notably, in the one-voice and unnotated sources, a minimum of three strophes are included, with eight surviving in Bord 283. As evidenced by the monophonic sources, *Luto carens et latere* is a *rondellus*, with one line of the refrain inserted between the first two lines of the strophe. Yet in its polyphonic form in W1, only the first strophe is copied.

Strophic Version (monophonic)

1. Luto carens et latere
    Transit Hebreus libere
Novo novus charactere
    In sicco mente munda
    Transit Hebreus libere
    Baptismi mundus unda.

2. Servus liber ab opere
    Transit Hebreus libere
Culpe recluso carcere
    In sicco mente munda
    Transit Hebreus libere
    Baptismi mundus unda.

Single Strophe in W1 (polyphonic)

Luto carens et latere
Transit Hebreus libere
Novo novus charactere
In sicco mente munda
Transit Hebreus libere
Baptismi mundus unda.

[44] Most often, the musical setting of a poem remains stable across sources, with poems only rarely surviving with both monophonic and polyphonic settings. See, for instance, the polyphonic setting of the otherwise monophonic *Congaudeat turba fidelium* in the Engelberg Codex, fol. 180[r–v], or the two-part version of *Gregis pastor Tityrus* in St-M D, fol. 13[v] versus the single-voice setting in the Moosburger Graduale, fol. 232[r], as well as the example of *Luto carens et latere*, below. The refrain song *Cum animadverterem*, conversely, is transmitted only polyphonically, but for two voices in W1 (fol. 108[r–v] [117[r–v]]) and three voices in F (fol. 225[v]–226[r]), and as text only in ORawl (fol. 15[r–v]).

[45] The three-part versicle trope *Custodi nos Domine* in StV, fol. 281[r–v], also takes a shape reminiscent of a one-strophe *rondellus*; however, a monophonic version with further strophes is not extant, making it difficult to argue a similar case.

1. Casting aside bricks and mortar,   Casting aside bricks and mortar, the
   the Hebrews freely crossed,   Hebrews freely crossed; renewed
renewed with a new character.   with a new character on dry land
   On dry land with a clean mind   with a clean mind, the Hebrews
   the Hebrews freely crossed   freely crossed cleansed by baptismal waters.
   cleansed by baptismal waters.

2. The slave is free from toil,
   the Hebrews freely crossed,
with the prison of sin unlocked.
   On dry land with a clean mind
   the Hebrews freely crossed
   cleansed by baptismal waters.

. . .

The continuation of the text from a previous *conductus* in the upper right-hand corner of the folio and the space below makes it clear, however, that the scribe had space to copy additional strophes if desired to the right of the systems (see Figure 3.5).[46] Throughout W1, multiple strophes of poly-phonic songs are typically included, making the single strophe of *Luto carens et latere* an outlier. Either the scribe of W1 did not have access to a version with multiple strophes or they deliberately chose to exclude further strophes.

The effect of W1's poetically foreshortened polyphonic transmission of *Luto carens et latere* is an effacement of the *rondellus* form. As transmitted in W1, the reoccurrence of lines 2 and 4–6 in subsequent strophes is elided, leaving only the repetition of line 1 as line 5. Moreover, while the lower voice repeats the melody of the A-line of the refrain, the upper voices present different music at the repetition of the refrain text (lines 1 and 5), further obscuring the repetition of the text.[47] In its polyphonic form, *Luto carens et latere* resembles any other short, rhymed, rhythmical poem set for multiple voices in W1 and elsewhere. In performance, it is possible that the shared tenor line with its repetitive patterning and the repetition of text may have clued the listener into the *rondellus* form of the song that becomes obvious when further strophes are present; it is also possible

---

[46] As far as layout is concerned, it is clear from Figure 3.5, however, that the planning did not work out smoothly, since staves needed to be extended into the margins to accommodate the final two words and their music.

[47] The music of the three-voice version is edited in Anderson, ed., *Notre-Dame and Related Conductus*, 2:1. The monophonic version is edited in 8:3. Note that the musical setting differs in Bord 283.

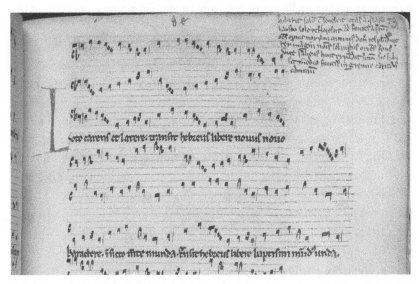

Figure 3.5 W1, fol. 80ʳ (73ʳ), *Luto carens et latere*. Reproduced by kind permission of the Herzog August Bibliothek Wolfenbüttel

that singers could have supplied additional strophes as they performed.[48] As it stands in W1, however, *Luto carens et latere* resembles less a strophic refrain song than a through-composed setting of a short poem.

Assuming the scribe of *Luto carens et latere* in W1 deliberately left out additional strophes, which seems likely considering the wider – and in the case of Tours 927, earlier – transmission of the song, did the textural shift to polyphony motivate the obscuring of the underlying refrain form? In other words, does the polyphonic rendering of *Luto carens et latere* in W1 align it better with other polyphonic *conducti* since refrains were more commonly the purview of chorally performed monophony rather than soloist-performed polyphony? Of the over 400 songs listed in the Appendix, fewer than 40 (depending on source and reading) survive in polyphonic settings for part or all of the poem. Sources for the *versus* transmit the greatest number of polyphonic refrain forms, and in these the refrain is typically cued consistently. Moreover, the transmission of polyphonic refrain forms is often complicated by absent or inconsistent cueing of

---

[48] As in, for example, a recording of the three-voice version by the ensemble Sequentia in which the remaining strophes are supplied from the monophonic setting; Sequentia, *Philippe le Chancelier: Notre-Dame-Schule*, directed by Benjamin Bagby (Deutsche Harmonia Mundi RD77035, 1990, CD).

refrains, as well as inclusion of only one strophe or a single iteration of the refrain, as in *Luto carens et latere*.

The refrain-form lament *Eclypsim patitur* exemplifies the ambiguities around polyphonic refrain forms in two particular sources, W1 and F.[49] By contrast to the transmission of *Luto carens et latere*, which survives mono-phonically in F with seven strophes and polyphonically in W1 with one, all four strophes of the two-voice *Eclypsim patitur* are included in W1 (fol. 110[r]) (the first notated, and the following ones copied below the final system). At no point, however, is the refrain (beginning "Mors sortis") indicated as such, nor is its return indicated textually after strophes 2–4. The only evidence of a refrain is the poetic and musical form itself in W1, which suggests by means of the contrasting scansion and musical setting of the refrain that it is indeed a refrain, and not the continuation of the strophe or an entirely new one.[50] The situation is more obscure in F, where only one strophe and one statement of the refrain are included (fol. 322[v]–323[r]), making the refrain structure impossible to derive from this manuscript alone.

A similarly ambiguous situation obtains for many of the polyphonic *conducti cum* refrains transmitted in W1 and F, calling into question the very identification of polyphonic refrains in these polyphonic settings. Only a few polyphonic *conducti* include refrains and multiple strophes (eight between W1 and F), and not all cue the return of the refrain with any regularity, similar to *Eclypsim patitur*.[51] Works like *Luto carens et latere* are indicative of this ambiguity, the addition of voices and subtraction of strophes essentially erasing the refrain form. In the absence of extant monophonic versions that clearly indicate a repeating refrain, single strophes and single iterations of refrains in polyphonic settings can only be tentatively labeled refrain forms. The differing treatment of a single refrain form in monophonic and polyphonic settings points toward a correlation of monophony with specifically repeating refrain forms, as

---

[49] *Eclypsim patitur* has drawn attention due its "datable" status; see Mazzeo, "Two-Part Conductus," 165–168; and Payne, "Datable 'Notre Dame' Conductus." It has also been attributed to Philip the Chancellor; Traill, "More Poems," 173–175.

[50] As Mazzeo argues, the tone of what is probably a refrain heightens the lamenting character of the *conductus* overall; "Two-Part Conductus," 167.

[51] Three-voice *conducti* with unambiguous refrains in F and W1 include: *Ortus summi peracto gaudio*; *Novus annus hodie* [A]; *Cum animadverterem* (in F); and *Veris ad imperia*. For two voices, although not always unambiguous, the *conducti* are: *O qui fontem*; *Eclypsim patitur*; *Sol sub nube latuit*; *Nove geniture*; and *Cum animadverterem* (in W1). I should note that these numbers disagree with Everist's tabulation of poetic form and voice, since I am limiting the list here to F and W1. See Everist, *Discovering Medieval Song*, table 1.1.

opposed to single strophes and refrains set polyphonically. The performance implications of such an association relate to choral versus solo performance – monophonic songs and refrains are more likely, albeit not exclusively, sung by groups whereas polyphonic settings, at times eliminating refrains, are more likely to be sung by soloists. Indeed, this resonates with Anonymous IV's association of *conducti* without *caudae*, or musically less complex *conducti*, with performance by "minores cantores."[52]

Shaping Performance: Strophic Refrain Songs and *Rondelli*

The noticeable lack of polyphonic settings of *rondelli* and the ambiguous example of *Luto carens et latere* in W1 points toward a larger divide in terms of performance and transcription between *rondelli* and strophic+refrain songs. Textual cues for refrains in manuscripts, including "chorus," "repetitio," and others, are exclusively associated with strophic+refrain songs, as opposed to *rondelli*. As I detail in the Introduction, all Latin refrain songs fall into one of these two camps, with strophic+refrain songs more common. Given the marked preference to indicate form and performance for strophic+refrain songs alone, what does this suggest concerning the performance of the Latin refrain song more generally?

Historiographically, the *rondellus* has been understood as inherently responsorial. Musical evidence for the responsorial performance of *rondelli* rests on the assumption that the soloist's introduction of all the melodic material before the refrain enters familiarizes the choir with the melody – if the form is that of the early *rondeau* or *rondet*, aAabAB – thereby enabling a choral response. As far as this argument goes, the initial statements by the soloists would serve as a reminder to the chorus, who then sing their refrain (the text of which is not introduced by a soloist) to the same melody.[53] Evidence for such a performance has been shaped by the reception of the repertoire over time and the gradual solidification of this perspective by means of contemporary performance and recording practices; no primary evidence of which I am aware, theoretical, manuscript, or otherwise, suggests that *rondelli* were necessarily performed *alternatim* between soloist and chorus.

---

[52] "Est et quintum volumen de quadruplicibus et triplicibus et duplicibus sine caudis, quod solebat esse multum in usu inter minores cantores, et similia." ("And there is a fifth volume of quadruple, triple and duple [*conducti*] without *caudae*, which used to be much used by minor singers, and similar things.") Latin edition and English translation in, respectively, Reckow, *Der Musiktraktat des Anonymus 4*, 1:82, and Yudkin, *Music Treatise of Anonymous IV*, 73.

[53] See, for example, this argument in Stevens, *Words and Music*, 191.

Conversely, manuscript evidence does exist for the *alternatim* performance of strophic+refrain songs. Although the forms of refrains interjected between strophes vary more widely than those in *rondelli* since they lack the same structural constraints of syllable count and rhyme, rubrication in several manuscript sources points both to their identity as refrains (by means of cues such as "repetitio") and their choral performance.[54] In the *cantionale* of the Moosburger Graduale, which also furnishes a preface attributed to the dean of the song school, Johannes de Perchausen, in which he discusses the songs, textual cues for refrains are widely employed (see Chapter 1).[55] In two *Benedicamus Domino* song-tropes, *Christus vicit resurgendo* (fol. 248[r–v]) and *Florizet vox dulcisonans* (fol. 249[v]–250[r]), refrains are marked off according to both their refrain forms and performance. In *Christus vicit resurgendo* the cue for the refrain changes from "R." to "chorus" midway through the song, before the third repetition of the refrain, as a page turn occurs. For the remainder of the song, the fourfold repetition of the liturgical refrain "alleluia" is cued with first "chorus" and then the abbreviation "chor" (see Figure 3.6).[56] Nowhere does the scribe specify performing forces for the strophes. Instead, the "chorus" cue implies the potential for the nonchoral performance for the strophic material. The use of "chorus" as a refrain cue also speaks to the community addressed by Johannes in his preface – the songs were an offering to the *clericuli* of the song school, the very choir we could imagine singing the refrain in *Christus vicit resurgendo*.

An identical refrain cue is attested to in the Seckauer Cantionarium, a mid-fourteenth-century liturgical book with a musical *cantionale* featuring neumed songs and tropes from the collegiate church in Seckau.[57] The scribe of the songs and tropes in the Seckauer Cantionarium, unlike in the Moosburger Graduale, only periodically included rubrication and cues for refrains. Only one song, *Stella nova radiat*, includes thoroughgoing cueing

---

[54] Rubrics identifying the choral performance of refrains appear in the Moosburger Graduale, Engelberg Codex, Seckauer Cantionarium, SG 392, Aosta Cod. 11 and 13, Autun S 175[10] and an early sixteenth-century liturgical book, the Antiphonarium Lausannense from Freiburg. On this last, whose multiple volumes were copied in duplicate for use by the choir, see Leisibach, *Die liturgischen Handschriften*, 34–52.

[55] The textual cue "repetitio" appears most often, alongside its abbreviation as "Rep." or "R." On refrain cues in medieval song more broadly, see Caldwell, "Cueing Refrains."

[56] A similar use of the choral rubric for a paschal "Alleluia" refrain occurs in *Florizet vox dulcisonans*, in which every return of the refrain is preceded by the performance cue "chorus."

[57] Irtenkauf, "Das Seckauer Cantionarium"; and Brewer, "In Search of Lost Melodies." For one further example of the "chorus" cue, albeit with a variable refrain, see *Quanto decet honore* in LoA, fol. 26[r]–26[v], which has a textually variable but musically stable refrain sung by the "chorus." Arlt, *Ein Festoffizium des Mittelalters*, 2:60–61 (transcription) and 227 (notes).

Figure 3.6 Moosburger Graduale, fol. 248ᵛ, *Christus vicit resurgendo*, excerpt.
Reproduced by kind permission of the Universitätsbibliothek, Munich

of the refrain.[58] Beginning "ergo novis laudibus," the refrain's choral performance is indicated by the red abbreviated "Chor." for "Chorus" appearing prominently before its first iteration (see Figure 3.7).

The case of *Stella nova radiat*, moreover, becomes more interesting after the page turn. Only the first occurrence of the refrain on fol. 186ʳ is preceded by a prompt for the choir; while it is not uncommon for cues to disappear in the course of a song's inscription (see Chapter 4), the continuation of *Stella nova radiat* onto fol. 186ᵛ also marks a change in the refrain's prescribed performance. From "chorus" the scribe switches to "pueri" for the remaining iterations of the refrain (see Figure 3.8). This is an unusual moment in which a scribe not only changes a cueing strategy, but also clarifies the performance forces in question. "Chorus" could mean boys, but not necessarily; by using "pueri" the precise subgroup of performers is made explicit. Given the possible connections of the Seckauer Cantionarium to the bishop's school in Seckau, it may be that the "pueri" in question were, like Johannes's *clericuli* in Moosburg, local students and choirboys.

---

[58] *Stella nova radiat* is also transmitted in the Moosburger Graduale (fol. 245ʳ) and the St. Pölten Processional (fol. 14ʳ); its refrain is cued in both manuscripts with "R." In Graz 409 (fol. 72ʳ), the refrain is not cued, but instead copied after the final strophe (see Chapter 4).

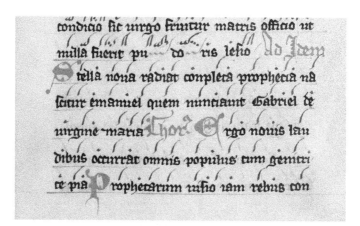

Figure 3.7 Seckauer Cantionarium, fol. 186ʳ, *Stella nova radiat*. Reproduced by kind permission of the Universitätsbibliothek, Graz

A final example is an early sixteenth-century antiphonary produced for the Monastery of St. Nicolas in Freiburg and whose contents reflect the use of the Lausanne diocese.[59] A liturgical source, the antiphonary includes accretions in the form of songs rubricated as *prosae* that function as *Benedicamus Domino* substitutes. On Vespers for the Feast of St. Stephen (December 26), the somewhat widely transmitted refrain song and *Benedicamus Domino* song-trope *Dulcis laudis tympano* is included along with performance instructions that place boys (*pueri*) in musical conversation with the choir (see Figure 3.9).[60] A rubric precedes the song, reading "in place of the *Benedicamus Domino*, the boys sing the following prosa" ("Loco de benedicamus domino pueri canunt prosam sequentem"). Another rubric appears before the refrain, beginning "Oy mira virtus stephani," directing the choir to sing it as a response ("Chorus respondet"). After the refrain, a third rubric appears, this time directing the singers (boys and choir) to continue as follows for the remaining verses, until after the final verse when the choir sings the conclusion of the *Benedicamus Domino* versicle, "Deo dicamus gratias alleluia" ("et sic de versibus consimilibus; post ultimum versum Chorus respondet").

---

[59] See Ladner, "Ein spätmittelalterlicher Liber Ordinarius Officii."

[60] See the Appendix for concordances, as well as a closely related song with the incipit *Martyr fuit Stephanus. Dulces laudes [Dulcis laudis] tympano* was fairly widely disseminated in German and Swiss liturgies and may have been performed polyphonically; see the reference to the singing of *Dulcis laudis tympano* "cum melodis organo" ibid., 21 and 22.

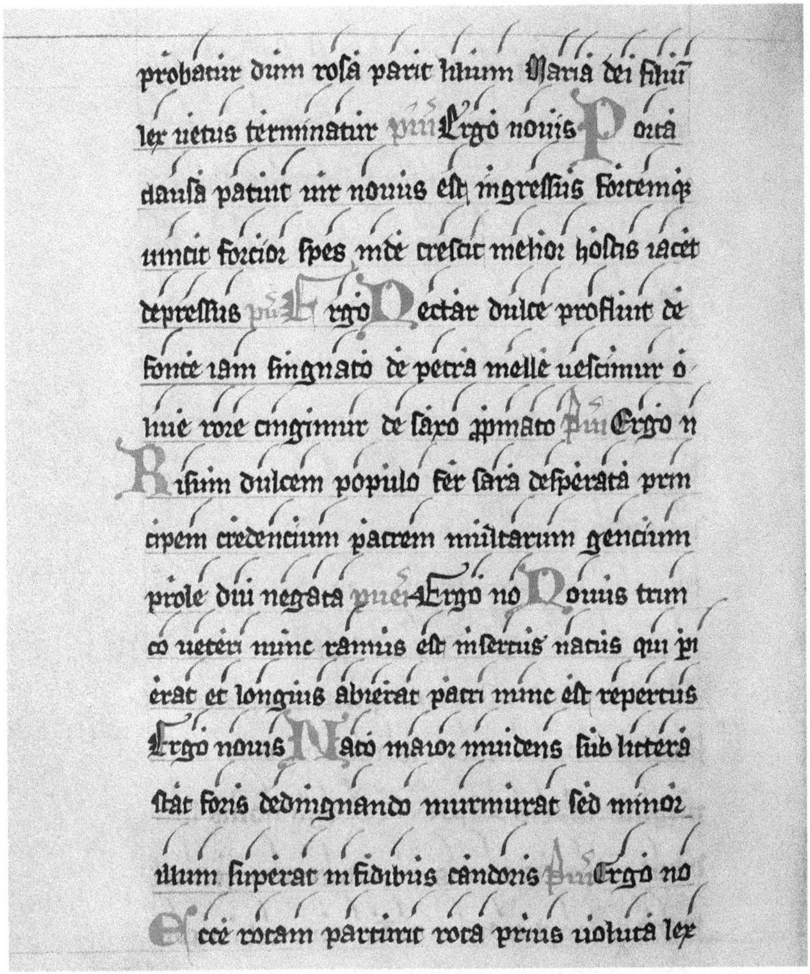

probatur dum rosa parit lilium Maria dei filius

lex vetus terminatur ... Ergo novis ... ota

clausa patuit vir novus est ingressus fortemque

vincit fortior spes mea crescat melior hostis iacet

depressus ... Ergo Nectar dulce profluit de

fonte iam signato de petra melle vescimur o

huius rore cingimur de saxo ... Ergo n

...stum dulcem populo per sara desperata prin

cipem credencium patrem multarum gencium

prole diu negata ... Ergo no Novus trun

co veteri nunc ramus est insertus natus qui pri

erat et longius abierat patri nunc est repertus

Ergo novis ... sco maior invidens sub littera

stat fons dedignando murmurat sed minor

illum superat in fidibus candens ... Ergo no

ecce totam partitur rota prius voluta lex

Figure 3.8 Seckauer Cantionarium, fol. 186ᵛ, *Stella nova radiat* continued. Reproduced by kind permission of the Universitätsbibliothek, Graz

The responsorial framework of the *Benedicamus* versicle is reflected in a detailed way in the performance structure outlined for *Stella nova radiat*. Compared to most items in the antiphoner for the Feast of St. Stephen, and indeed for most other feasts, greater attention is given to the performance of *Dulcis laudis tympano*. A striking aspect of this example, moreover, is that boys were tasked with singing the strophes, while the whole choir sang the refrain – a contrast to the boy soloist's performance of the refrain in *Salve festa dies veneranda* in the Codex Calixtinus and *Stella nova radiat* in the Seckauer Cantionarium.

Figure 3.9 Antiphonarium Lausannense III.3.1, p. 103, *Dulcis laudis*
[*Dulces laudes*] *tympano.* Reproduced by kind permission of the Archives de l'État de Fribourg

The question remains whether the performance practices indicated by scribes in these examples, all dating from the fourteenth century and later, can be applied to other sources and repertoire. Notably, the manuscripts just discussed transmit more than a single Latin refrain song or song-trope, but scribes did not systematically indicate the choral or group performance of refrains in these. Is the absence of similar performance indications for other Latin refrain songs merely an accident or oversight? What was special about certain songs that demanded clearer performance directions? Significantly, refrain songs that include scribal performance directions each carry liturgical designations. In these examples, *Christus vicit resurgendo* and *Dulcis laudis tympani* are *Benedicamus Domino* song-tropes, and *Stella nova radiat* is rubricated for performance "in die nativitatis Domini super magnificat," suggesting its performance at Vespers before the

Magnificat.[61] The liturgical orientation of these songs is noteworthy since similar performance indications, whether referring to the choir, or even boys, were not uncommon in liturgical manuscripts, especially for special feast days.

Scribes seemed to have adapted practices used in copying chant and applied them to devotional song, with the intention of clarifying the performance of songs added, in many cases, to the Office. Conversely, rubrics or annotations specifying performing forces are absent for songs and sources that lack liturgical ties. While this does not mean comparable performance practices could not have been shared with Latin refrain songs absent liturgical ties, it does mean that, as far as scribal intentions are concerned, details concerning the performance of refrain forms were only deemed important to include when songs were integrated into the liturgy. *Rondelli*, significantly, are all devotional but never explicitly incorporated into the liturgy and, consequently, never received scribal intervention in terms of their prescribed performance. In manuscripts such as F, scribes were not concerned with outlining the performance of *rondelli*, or other Latin songs, leaving little material evidence concerning possible performance practices.

Yet what these scribal cues offer is a glimpse into the variety of performance practices around strophic+refrain songs as well as into the specific communities tasked with singing Latin song in liturgical contexts. Boys, whether junior clergy, choirboys, or students, were clearly the intended performers for a portion of the refrain song repertoire, their vocal engagement overtly dictated by scribes. Moreover, for strophic+refrain songs, the balance of poetic and manuscript evidence points toward the choral performance of refrains. When exceptions occur, as with the single boy in the Codex Calixtinus or the polyphonic refrain of *Annus novus in gaudio*, it is nevertheless possible to point to the ways in which the poet, composer, and scribe through language, grammar, and form intended the refrain to be heard as a reflection of the choric voice, the collective voice singing *una voce*.

---

[61] Although *Stella nova radiat* is rubricated as "Ad item.," the longer rubric appears before the previous song, *Pater ingenitus*. For another example from the fifteenth century, see the antiphoner Autun S 175[10] (probably from the Cathedral of Autun) in which two *Benedicamus Domino* song-tropes are rubricated in a way that designates the choral performance of refrains. For *Patrem parit filia*, fol. 198[r], "chorus" is used to cue the refrain, while in *In laudem innocentium*, fol. 200[v], for the Feast of the Holy Innocents, "innocentes" are assigned the strophes (presumably choirboys representing the Holy Innocents) while the larger "chorus" sings the refrain.

Reimagining the Clerical Dance Song

The ability of the refrain to participate through performance, grammar, poetry, and music in implicit and explicit discourses of community does not account for a central strand of scholarship that sees the Latin refrain as generating chorographic meaning in performance. Scholarship on the Latin refrain song as early as the eighteenth century has steadfastly connected it to the devout circling, stepping, and twirling choreographies of religious men and women across Europe, repeatedly privileging its lyric-choreographic meaning. As the general absence of dance in this chapter and elsewhere in the book suggests, however, movement was not a central performance referent for the Latin refrain song on the part of poets, composers, scribes, and compilers. Yet the association of the Latin refrain song with dance has extensive roots and, in some cases, seemingly strong evidence that supports the "clerical dance song" label. The strongest evidence has been historically located in the refrain songs of the final fascicle of F, initially argued by Yvonne Rokseth in 1947 and reiterated in a half-century of subsequent scholarship.[62] I turn to this fascicle now in order to reevaluate the lyric-choreographic identity of the refrain songs of F and align their perceived choreographic potential with their vocal realization and invocation of community.

The collective identity of the songs in the eleventh fascicle of F is strikingly signaled on the initial folio by a historiated initial depicting a group of tonsured clerics. The five clerics appear to hold hands, or, more accurately, link fingers, with feet turned out and positioned as if in motion, in parallel to depictions of social dancing in sources of vernacular song and romance (see Figure 3.10).[63] The image is evocative, but not the sole evidence called upon to label the works that follow "clerical dance songs." In addition to iconography, the abundance of *rondelli* and a thematic focus on Easter and festive and liturgical occasions associated with dance have been interpreted as markers of a choreographic function. Given this confluence of details, few dance scholars or musicologists have critically evaluated the probability that the eleventh fascicle transmits such a large number of dance songs in relation to the relatively few surviving instrumental dance works and vocal dances in other sources.[64] If the refrain songs in F were intended to be danced to, the

---

[62] Rokseth, "Danses cléricales." The earliest citation I have located to the songs' choreographic function is Aubry, *La Musique et les musiciens d'église*, 45. Recent citations include Knäble, *Eine tanzende Kirche*, 310.

[63] Page, *Voices and Instruments*, 89.

[64] See, however, Edward Roesner's caution in *Antiphonarium*, 30–31. See also Aubrey, "The Eleventh Fascicle," 37, and Rillon-Marne, "*Exultemus sobrie.*"

Figure 3.10 F, fol. 463ʳ, illustrated "D-" of *De patre principio*. Reproduced by permission of Florence, Biblioteca Medicea Laurenziana, MiBACT. Further reproduction by any means is prohibited

manuscript represents an atypical source within the history of medieval dance music, and the only source for Latin refrain songs that explicitly signals a choreographic function.[65]

A reevaluation, however, of the evidence deriving from the iconography, form, and poetry of the refrain songs in F weights the relationship of song to dance more on the side of the symbolic than the functional. These songs may have invoked the idea of dance, but a primary function as the accompaniment of clerical dance in thirteenth-century Paris cannot be assumed; poets, composers, scribes, and compilers in F, and in sources for the refrain song more broadly, show a greater interest in the voice, and the poems and melodies it realized, than in the body and its movements.[66] Apart from infrequent, highly localized witnesses, manuscript sources for the Latin refrain song are silent when it comes to rubricating or otherwise gesturing textually or iconographically toward dance – with the exception of the image in F.[67]

---

[65] For an overview, with an emphasis on instrumental dance music, see McGee, *Medieval Instrumental Dances*.

[66] Of the two authority figures who provide textual and contextual framing for Latin refrain songs, the dean of the Moosburg song school Johannes de Perchausen and Bishop Richard Ledrede of the Ossorian Diocese, only the former references dance as part of the festal practices for the Feast of the Boy Bishop "in many churches." See Chapter 1.

[67] This is by contrast to vernacular song, for which manuscript sources more often include rubrication, poetic or literary references, and iconography that is highly suggestive of dance, although even in these cases the relationship is challenging to determine and analyze. Other

In addition to the opening historiated initial, the internal evidence of the refrain songs themselves in F has most often been called upon to support an association with movement.[68] Although the poetic register and vocabulary of the songs have been called upon as evidence of function, a vocabulary of sobriety infuses the refrain songs of F, illustrating the conservative and vocal performance-focused poetics of the fascicle, as I argue in Chapter 1.[69] When it appears in the fascicle, dance-related vocabulary metaphorically frames the voice and signals a festive register. Similarly, the presence of a refrain has been interpreted as a signal of register, and especially a so-called "Lower Style," characterized by links to dance and popular song.[70] Formal parallels of the Latin refrain with vernacular song forms, most especially French *rondeaux*, have consequently underpinned the choreographic identification of the Latin *rondellus* in particular, even though the identity of the French *rondeau* as a "dance song" is itself precarious.[71] In Latin or French, the *rondeau* form does not supply incontrovertible evidence of a choreographic function.

The existence of Latin and vernacular contrafact pairs has also supplied evidence in support of the Latin refrain song as clerical dance music – if a Latin song is modeled after a vernacular dance song, the assumption has been that the two share a function. Yet, even if Latin contrafacts hypothetically shared the function of vernacular dance models – which is debatable – the paucity of vernacular contrafacts in Fascicle XI of F is noteworthy. Of the nearly sixty refrain songs in F alone, only two have vernacular contrafacts: *Decet vox letitie* and *Fidelium sonet vox sobria*.[72] Of these, neither can

contexts for the rubrication of devotional dancing are chiefly liturgical and do not involve refrain songs. See, for instance, the troped liturgy for the Feast of the Circumcision in Le Puy A, which includes rubrics indicating the dancing of choirboys ("clericuli tripudiant"), but not associated with the singing of refrain songs per se; see Arlt, "Office" and Caldwell, "Texting Vocality," 55–60.

[68] For a recent complementary approach to mine, see Rillon-Marne, "*Exultemus sobrie.*"

[69] This reading differs from that of John Haines, who observes that "the most compelling connection of these sixty *conductus* [in F] to the ring-dance corpus lies in their texts," pointing to themes occurring in the songs that yoke them to a repertoire of festive vernacular love songs. Haines, *Medieval Song*, 68. For similar justifications for labeling the Latin refrain song a dance genre rooted in the poetry, see Page, *Voices and Instruments*, 88–91; Stevens, *Words and Music*, 178–186; and Wright, *Maze and the Warrior*, 151–154.

[70] See Aubrey, "Reconsidering 'High Style' and 'Low Style.'" The expression "Lower Style" is derived from the work of Christopher Page; see for example his typology in *Voices and Instruments*, 16.

[71] See, for instance, Stevens, *Words and Music*, 181.

[72] Only one other song in the final fascicle of F shares its music with a vernacular work, the strophic *In hoc statu gratie*. I do not include here the misidentified contrafacture of *Ecce mundi gaudium* (see Chapter 2), nor *Iam lucis orto sidere*, which is a troped hymn; see Caldwell, "Troping Time."

be unproblematically associated with dance via its vernacular counterpart. *Decet vox letitie*, for instance, has a Latin contrafact, *Ave mater salvatoris*, in St-M D, and together the songs share music with a French *refrain* in the *motetus* of the motet *Tout leis enmi les prez/DOMINUS*, a refrain found also in an unnotated *rondet* from Jean Renart's *Le Roman de la Rose*, *C'est la gieus, en mi les prez*.[73] The paths and chronologies of transmission and contrafacture among these four contexts are convoluted, to say the least, and there is little evidence to suggest that the *rondet* was danced to, or that either Latin song serves a choreographic function.[74]

Fidelium sonet vox sobria, by contrast, shares its music, but not *rondellus* form, with a contemporaneous strophic+refrain Galician-Portuguese *cantiga*, *Maldito seja quen non loará* from the Cantigas de Santa María (fol. 260^r): It is unlikely that either song is a contrafact of the other; instead, a third, unknown song probably served as an intermediary.[75] Although the *cantiga* may have been a dance song, or may have borrowed a dance song melody, it would be a stretch to see dance as a shared function between *Maldito seja quen non loará* and *Fidelium sonet vox sobria*, especially in the absence of an additional work connecting the two songs.[76] Latin-vernacular contrafacture, in other words, offers little support to the identification of the refrain songs of F as dance songs.

Where *Fidelium sonet vox sobria*, uniquely among the refrain songs of Fascicle XI, gains potential meaning as a clerical dance song is in its complicated reception history outside of F. Since the publication of an anonymous French article published in 1742 identifying *Fidelium sonet vox sobria* as an example of a song danced to at Easter at the collegiate church of St. Mary Magdalene in Besançon, France, in the fifteenth century, scholars have repeatedly linked this song with clerical dance.[77] This identification,

---

[73] This family of contrafacts was discovered by Saint-Cricq, "Formes types," 1:155–156. The motet is transmitted in W2, fol. 247^v, and Munich Cg. 42, fol. 6^r. The text is edited in Everist, *French Motets*, 115. On the *refrain* in relation to the *rondet*, see Page, "Performance of Ars Antiqua Motets"; Everist, *French Motets*, 115–116; and Ibos-Augé, *Chanter et lire*, 86.

[74] Butterfield, for instance, has argued for an understanding of the *rondets* in *Le Roman de la Rose* as "a literate, fictionalised piece of rhetorical description that stands at one remove from the actualities of live performance." *Poetry and Music*, 47–48. See also Saltzstein, *Refrain*, 8–16.

[75] *Maldito seja quen non loará* is Cantiga 290; see Mettman, ed., *Afonso X, o Sábio*, 97–98. Edited and translated in Cunningham, ed., *Alfonso X, el Sábio*, 209–212. The Latin and vernacular contrafact pair has been edited in parallel several times over; see, for instance, Wulstan, *Emperor's Old Clothes*, 36. Wulstan (p. 37) suggests a third intertext.

[76] Wulstan, "Contrafaction and Centonization," 89. On recreation and entertainment, including dance in the Cantigas manuscripts, see Keller and Cash, *Daily Life*, 43–44.

[77] "Lettre écrite de Besançon." The letter could be believably attributed to historian Jean Lebeuf, who wrote on related subjects during the same time period. *Fidelium sonet vox sobria* is copied in solfège syllables ibid., 1942. This song is cited in nearly every study of medieval clerical dance

however, is rooted in layers of historiographical reinterpretation and misreading and the witness of several lost manuscripts; moreover, the possible – if unlikely – role of *Fidelium sonet vox sobria* as a dance song in fifteenth-century Besançon has little bearing on its choreographic identity in thirteenth-century Paris.[78]

Although the internal evidence – poetry, form, and contrafacture – of the refrain songs as dance songs is ambiguous at best, the image of the clerical dancers at the head of Fascicle XI might provide clearer proof of function (see Figure 3.10). Not only is the image strikingly similar to contemporary depictions of *caroles*, the visual program in F also often showcases thematic links between miniatures and the music of the fascicles (or works) they introduce.[79] Importantly, however, none of the other historiated initials allude to the function or performance of the songs that follow. The question, then, is whether the refrain songs dominating the final fascicle motivated the illustrator to switch from thematically related illustrations for the previous openings to this sole instance of an image suggestive of performance practice. Considering that the artist probably drew on stock images, and in at least one case misjudged the thematic match between illustration and the work that followed,[80] one such factor may be the frontispiece of the manuscript depicting the Boethian division of music (*musica universalis, humana,* and *instrumentalis*) (see Figure 3.11).[81] Enthroned in panels on the left side, Lady Music gestures to the panels on the right representing each division in turn: The heavenly firmament represents *musica universalis*; a group of four dancers represents *musica humana*; and a vielle player in an *instrumentarium* represents *musica instrumentalis.*

A unique visual elaboration of Boethius's tripartite division, the frontispiece philosophically frames the music contained within F, only indirectly relating to the music folios that follow. For instance, the artist chose instruments to depict the only audible music in Boethius's division, *musica instrumentalis*, yet the manuscript transmits solely vocal music. The male figures reflect *musica humana* through synchronized motions symbolizing

---

music; the earliest I have located is Fleury-Husson (dit Champfleury), "Danses dans les églises." More recently, see Wright, *Maze and the Warrior*, 152–154.

[78] I am grateful to the librarians and staff at the municipal library in Besançon who assisted me in my search for the manuscripts cited in "Lettre écrite de Besançon."

[79] On the miniatures in F, see Baltzer, "Thirteenth-Century Illuminated Miniatures" and Masani Ricci, *Codice Pluteo 29.1*, 59–63. See also Branner, "Johannes Grusch Atelier."

[80] Baltzer, "Thirteenth-Century Illuminated Miniatures," 9 and 12.

[81] On this image, see ibid., 3; Seebass, "Prospettive," 79–81; and Masani Ricci, *Codice Pluteo 29.1*, 60.

Figure 3.11 F, frontispiece, Boethian division of music. Reproduced by permission of Florence, Biblioteca Medicea Laurenziana, MiBACT. Further reproduction by any means is prohibited

the harmonization of body and soul and, as Anne-Zoé Rillon-Marne has suggested, social harmony, by combining clerical and lay figures.[82] Moreover, by employing dancers in this context, the artist accessed a long-standing tradition in which dance mirrored celestial harmonies, exemplified by the heavenly ring dance described by Honorius of Autun and others.[83]

The images in the frontispiece and at the head of Fascicle XI, the final unit of music in the manuscript, while not identical, visually bookend the source. How might we interpret the illuminator's reuse of the type of image associated with *musica humana* in the frontispiece for introducing devotional Latin refrain songs later in the manuscript? Is the image of dancers transformed over the course of hundreds of folios from a metaphorical to a literal representation of movement?[84] Rather than assume the artist recognized the refrain songs of Fascicle XI as dance music and chose to represent them functionally – rejecting the working procedure of the visual program throughout the manuscript – a simpler answer might be that the scribe was thematically illustrating the poetry on fol. 463ʳ. Considering the collective spirit of the songs and refrains that follow, perhaps the artist was inspired to depict clerics absorbed in an activity deeply linked with the act of harmoniously rejoicing together, thereby thematically, rather than functionally, linking image with content. Clerics caught in a moment of bodily and communal rejoicing may have seemed an apt choice, considering that the songs copied on the folio celebrate Easter in highly communal and festive terms.

What is more, the artist had only to look to the frontispiece for a visual prototype of *musica humana*, the bodies of individuals moving together as symbolic of a higher order of harmony. In this interpretation, an image of group dance becomes another way of signaling the community-building enacted by the songs' vocal performance, using a familiar image of *musica humana* to cue the "social harmony" of the clerical community represented visually by the dancers and sonically by the refrain songs.

While evidence in support of the "clerical dance songs" of F is less convincing than scholars have hoped, the songs and iconography in Fascicle XI could still evoke the idea, if not the reality, of dance for medieval singers and audiences. Just as the polyphonic *rondeaux* of Adam de la Halle

[82] Knäble, "L'Harmonie des sphères," and Rillon-Marne, "*Exultemus sobrie.*"
[83] See the discussion of the image in Seebass, "Prospettive," 79–81. Seebass suggests that the middle image is a representation of vocal music, and that the entire frontispiece reflects an attempt to reconcile theory (Boethius) and practice (the contents of F).
[84] See also Aubrey, "The Eleventh Fascicle," 37, and Rillon-Marne, "*Exultemus sobrie.*"

and Guillaume de Machaut, or the later English carol evoke the idea of dance without its accompanying physical movements, so too could the Latin refrain songs of F resonate musically and formally with the gestures of dance.[85] Their vocal, rather than bodily, performance manifests in the choreography implied by the poetry's "joyful leaps" of the voice, with the voices of singers comprising a choreography of togetherness. Formulated in this way, the Latin refrain song might be understood as shaped by medieval perceptions of collective, social dance and its cultural associations with refrain forms, without necessarily serving as the accompaniment to dance.

If the refrain song, and those in F in particular, are demoted in import-ance within the narrative of the "clerical dance song," what remains? Rather than relying on broad stylistic and formal markers such as the refrain, detailed archival research of local contexts and communities will best afford a richly textured, and historically accurate, understanding of devotional dance and its music in medieval Europe. This necessitates returning to the manuscripts and archives that have been repeatedly featured in histories of devotional dance, yet are mediated by layers of prior scholarship, hypotheses, and assumptions. For the Latin refrain song in particular, the label of "dance song" should not be applied without first reevaluating the reasons for so doing. Letting go of predetermined associ-ations of refrains with dance allows the Latin refrain song to be resituated within a broader range of performance contexts in the Middle Ages.

Singing the Refrain: Form, Performance, and Community

Interrogating the poetry, form, inscription, and performance of the Latin refrain song reveals the invocation of communal, unified performance through different means and at different levels. The partiality of material evidence is an important caution: Rubrics or iconography in individual sources, or the relatively limited number of songs with variable musical textures between refrain and strophe, cannot speak to the performance of the repertoire writ large. Yet the identity of the refrain as either a real or imagined choral response – literally sung by a group or ventriloquized by a single singer or soloists – plays a role in fostering a sense of togetherness and community. Singing *quasi una voce* is powerful, as the chanted liturgy of the medieval church demonstrates. The refrain

---

[85] I am indebted to Chaganti, *Strange Footing*, for this formulation.

fosters a similar, even heightened, sensation of togetherness in devotional Latin song, underscoring through form and repetition the church's doctrine of singing as if with one voice.

An implicit theory of collective song and performance develops in the poetry of the refrain song, rooted in a linguistic emphasis on communities of singers and grammatical preference for the first-person plural. Poetic, terminological, and grammatical choices made throughout the repertoire alert us to the implications of the refrain imagined by their creators for meaning and performance. However, the theory of collective performance expressed in the poetry of the refrain song does not uniformly correspond with performance practices described by scribes and compilers. Reappraising the evidence for the performance practices around refrain forms demonstrates that, in practical terms, refrains were performed responsorially, but the performing forces responsible for the refrain varied. Responsorial practices, moreover, are only rarely detailed in manuscript sources, and scribal evidence for performance along with musical settings emphasizes further the distance between *rondelli* and strophic+refrain songs already witnessed in the organization and compilation of refrain songs.

Above all, the refrain was framed and experienced as an expression of the collective voice – a moment of singing as if with one voice. The refrain enacted a sense of togetherness by symbolically and literally emblematizing the choric voice in form and performance, emphasized through repetition and the ensuing familiarity. This is the power of the repeated refrain in Latin song, and what affords the regular repetition of text and music a hefty cultural weight and ability to be meaningful in so many ways. Perhaps most importantly in light of Chapters 1 and 2, the ability of the choric voice to unify a group of individuals is part of the regulative function of singing and moving together.[86] Implicitly and explicitly, the refrain coordinates, aligns, and even disciplines the voices of singers, while the words they sing persistently emphasize belonging in communities whose boundaries are defined by the church. The inclusiveness and plurality of the songs thus also speaks to those it excludes – for instance, those outside of the communities of clerics and choirboys in the collegiate churches and cathedrals of Moosburg, Seckau, Le Puy-en-Velay, and many other institutions and locales in medieval Europe where the Latin refrain song found willing singers and proponents. Finally, in this chapter I move away from the

---

[86] As Connor writes, "choric utterance is almost always concerned with the establishment of solidarity." "Choralities," 6.

previous association of the refrain song with devotional dance practices, although, as I suggest, dance emerges in F as a metaphor for the social harmony of the clerical performers of the refrain song, once again reinforcing the communal spirit of this repertoire.

4 | Remembering Refrains

Composition, Inscription, and Performance

> Thus we again observe that refrains are, and have, memories – of their
> prior strophes or stretches of text, of their own preoccurrences, and of
> their own genealogies in earlier texts as well.
>
> – Hollander, "Breaking into Song"

Recurring between strophes of a single song, "refrains are, and have,
memories" as John Hollander writes. This memory can extend beyond a
single song; refrains frequently are, and have, memories of "their own
genealogies in earlier texts as well."[1] As defined throughout this book, the
Latin refrain is chiefly structural, repeating within and between strophes,
its memories constituted within the space of an individual work. Yet,
although it is fixed in the sense of its structural identity, the Latin refrain
does not always lack a memory outside of its formal utterance and repetition between and within the strophes of a song. Latin refrains can and do
repeat beyond the boundaries of individual songs, resonating through time
and across place in memory, sound, and inscription.[2] The circulation, or
mouvance, of the Latin refrain shows how song and refrain were not always
conceived of as inseparable units of form and meaning; at the same time,
the mobile refrain also brings to the fore the ability of a repeated unit of text
and music to become anchored in the memory and further recalled,
deployed, reworked, and redeployed. Refrains, consequently, become
fixed not only within song, but also fixed within the individual and collective memories of singers and scribes as they repeat across songs, creating
rich genealogies of poetry and music.

In this chapter I explore Latin refrains with this key characteristic in
common: They each have genealogies and memories beyond the borders of
individual songs. Although it does not compare in complexity to the

---

[1] Hollander, "Breaking into Song," 77.

[2] This has already been glimpsed in Chapter 1 with the "annus novus" refrain employed as a
marker of time and its mediation in Latin song, and in Chapter 3 with the plural voicing of the
"gaudeamus" refrain across several songs. In Chapter 1, I related the "annus novus" refrain to
Andreas Haug's "virtual" refrain; I avoid the term here since it does not fully capture the mobility
of refrains among songs that I examine in this chapter.

intertextual, citational, and intergeneric French *refrain*, the Latin refrain participates in an extensive, and at times complicated, network of textual and musical borrowing, reworking, and repetition within medieval Latin song.[3] This intertextual and intermusical network includes refrains that are reworked from other genres, most often chant; refrains that do not always serve as structural refrains, but are recycled more freely among songs; and refrains that are employed structurally across different songs.[4] Importantly, even when not employed structurally, these intertextual and mobile refrains always remain tethered to, and are rooted within, repertoires of devotional, strophic, Latin songs – their movement is invariably circumscribed by the limits of form, function, and language. The interplay of performance and inscription also informs how these refrains came into being and how they circulate. Although I am reliant on the written side of the Latin refrain's transmission, the intertextuality I describe is underpinned by the lived experiences of the individuals and communities who performed, remembered, and wrote down Latin song and refrain.

Singers, scribes, and compilers are the typically unnamed agents driving the reworking, recycling, and reuse of Latin refrains. The intertextuality of Latin song and refrain reflects an origin within predominantly anonymous clerical and monastic communities, comprised of individuals who crafted, performed, and copied this repertoire as a form of devotional entertainment and, at times, incorporated it into their liturgies. By means of memory, inscription, or both, the wider circulation of the Latin refrain speaks to its role in expressing the unified voice of religious communities and its embeddedness within the rituals and language of the church. These refrains are not "owned," or even composed, by individual, named composers, nor tethered exclusively to particular songs, genres, or functions, but instead are part of a broader, communal culture of devotional song, one in which refrains travel and repeat in the textual and memorial archives of religious communities. As Elizabeth Hellmuth Margulis writes, "repeatability is how songs become the property of a group or a community instead of an individual, how they come to belong to a tradition, rather than to a moment."[5] For the Latin refrain, its repeatability within strophic song as well as in larger networks of Latin song and poetry situates it within the tradition of devotional music that is rooted in the real, imagined, and poetically constructed forms of participation explored in Chapter 3.

---

[3] On the intertextual French *refrain*, see Butterfield, *Poetry and Music* and Saltzstein, *Refrain*.

[4] All told, such refrains characterize nearly 20 percent of the songs listed in the Appendix, a significant proportion even if outweighed by songs with unique refrains.

[5] Margulis, *On Repeat*, 6.

Reworking Text and Music: Chant and the Latin Refrain

The intertextuality of music and poetry in the devotional Latin song frequently reveals intimate relationships with a range of texts and genres, even if rarely at the level found in contemporary genres such as the medieval motet or French *refrain*. For the refrain song, these relationships are strongest with chant, and especially with hymns and sequences, genres that share poetic, musical, and formal features with Latin song.[6] Office versicles, and the *Benedicamus Domino* versicle above all, represent additional points of contact between Latin song and the liturgy. Beyond formal and poetic parallels, textual, and more rarely melodic, references to and quotations of chant range from brief, passing allusions to sustained reworkings of entire lines and sections.[7] Unsurprisingly, these longer, more sustained, references tend to derive from familiar and widely sung chants – hymns such as *Ave maris stella* or sequences like *Veni sancte spiritus* are among the most often cited and reworked chants within the Latin refrain song repertoire.

The deliberate reuse and reworking of chant in the refrain song – as opposed to inadvertent parallels stemming from shared contexts and vocabulary – is always overt and underscored, in most cases, by how a poet-composer treats the borrowed text. The refrain serves as a particular locus for borrowed and reworked texts in refrain songs, effectively highlighting the reuse of a familiar text by embedding it in the repetitive structure of a new song. The communal associations of the borrowed chant, moreover, intersect with the responsorial performance practices and connotations of the refrain; the construction of "new" Latin refrains out of the "old" songs of the liturgy enables poets and composers to build on singers' associations with chant and its role within communal forms of worship. The reworking of familiar chant texts and melodies establishes a genealogy between Latin chant and Latin song that allows the ritual connotations of the former to resonate in the latter, recalling for singers the memory and knowledge of the original contexts of borrowed text and music. Repeating within the structural framework of new songs, refrains reworked from chant demonstrate not only the intergeneric mobility and fluidity of devotional Latin poetry and its music, but also an aesthetic

---

[6] Arlt, "Hymnus und 'Neues Lied'" and "Sequence," and Everist, *Discovering Medieval Song*, 181–213. See also Chapter 2.

[7] On the borrowing and reworking of preexistent material in Latin song, see, for example, Bukofzer, "Interrelations"; Everist, *Discovering Medieval Song*, 181–279; Caldwell, "Medieval Patchwork Song"; and Ciglbauer, "Quoting."

interest in repetition and recycling – the originality of songs that rework preexisting material rests in how they newly assemble familiar words, sounds, and phrases.[8]

Although borrowing and reworking is found across the refrain song repertoire, certain works, and collections of works in certain manuscripts, illustrate a higher degree of engagement with preexistent materials than others. To put it another way, composers and poets working in certain milieus were more interested and invested in connecting devotional song to the liturgy than those working in others, which is reflected in the contents of the manuscripts they produced.[9] One such manuscript is the mid-thirteenth-century Parisian source F, whose *conducti* and refrain songs showcase an acute awareness of how chant – and hymns and sequences in particular – could serve as a creative starting point for borrowed material. The hymns *Veni creator spiritus* and *Ave maris stella* are reworked in several polyphonic *conducti* in F, for instance, and individual lines of many other hymns are cited throughout the manuscript's fascicles of Latin song.[10] Sequences, too, are mined for their text and music in F, appearing either as single-line quotations or more fully fleshed-out reworkings of longer segments of text and music. Lines derived from chants and psalms appear with the greatest regularity in the final fascicle of largely refrain-form songs, with the majority of the sixty songs in Fascicle XI directly or indirectly referencing and reworking liturgical chant. The chanted liturgy resonates from the beginning of the fascicle, where the second song on the first folio (463ʳ), *Felix dies et grata*, draws its refrain from both the familiar psalmic text employed for Eastertide chants and a line of its first strophe from the Easter sequence *Zyma vetus expurgetur*.[11]

One *rondellus* from F's final fascicle, *Mors vite propitia* (fol. 464ʳ), demonstrates especially well the borrowing and reworking of the text and

---

[8] The borrowing and manipulation of chant in Latin song is also not dissimilar to the use of chant as motet tenors.

[9] See Chapter 5, where I discuss the relationship between Latin and vernacular refrains and refrain forms within localized contexts.

[10] *Veni creator spiritus spiritus*, fol. 207ᵛ (a3); *Ave maris stella virgo*, fol. 221ʳ (a3); *Veni creator spiritus et in me*, fol. 360ʳ (a2); and *Ave maris stella ave*, fol. 373ʳ (a2).

[11] These are "hec est dies quam fecit dominus" and "dies nostri doloris terminus." Edited in Anderson, ed., *Notre-Dame and Related Conductus*, 8:ii. Familiar lines from chant repeat as refrains throughout Fascicle XI, including "omnes gentes plaudite" in *Processit in capite* (fol. 466ʳ); "deus in adiutorium" in *Pater creator omnium* (fol. 467ʳ); and "veni sancte spiritus" in *Descende celitus* (fol. 467ᵛ), among others. On the versicle *Deus in adiutorium* and the construction of *Pater creator omnium*, see Caldwell, "Medieval Patchwork Song."

music of a sequence, in this case *Sexta passus feria* for Easter.[12] Transmitted in F and the closely related Tours 927, *Mors vite propitia* reflects the degree to which a sequence can both be reworked and yet still recognizably resonate within a new poetic and musical structure. The versions in F and Tours 927, importantly, are not identical; in Tours 927, *Mors vite propitia* is more elaborate musically and formally than in F, and the two versions have only four of eight total strophes in common. These differences have implications for how closely each version connects to the sequence *Sexta passus feria*. As transmitted in F, *Mors vite propitia* features seven strophes with a three-line refrain interpolated following the first and final lines of each strophe. The refrain introduces the sequence text, consisting of the initial three-line strophe of the rhymed, rhythmic sequence. Since the refrain quotes the sequence verbatim, it shares its syllable count, rhyme scheme, and accent pattern at the conclusion of lines, all of which is mirrored in the strophes (see Table 4.1).[13] The refrain text comprises the most significant borrowing from the sequence since it repeats throughout the strophic song, resulting in the initial strophe of the sequence being sung a total of seven times in the course of a single performance. Beyond the refrain, strophe 5 contains the only other verbatim quotation of the sequence, drawing its text from the second paired strophe of *Sexta passus feria*, beginning "surgens cum victoria." The remaining five strophes in F gloss the Easter narrative of *Sexta passus feria*, retelling the familiar story of Christ's Passion and Resurrection in a parallel fashion to the sequence.[14]

The straightforward manner in which the F version of *Mors vite propitia* adopts lines from *Sexta passus feria* speaks to the style and poetic form of the sequence itself. With rhymed aab strophes and a regular syllable count and accent pattern, the sequence already bears the typical features of the refrain songs in the final fascicle of F, making the process of borrowing smooth. Facilitated by the rhymed, rhythmical lines of the sequence, the poet not only incorporates full strophes of the sequence but also mirrors the scansion of the liturgical song throughout the song. All strophes of *Mors vite propitia* in F and Tours 927 repeat the 7pp+7pp+4pp strophic

---

[12] *Mors vite propitia* is edited in Anderson, *Notre-Dame and Related Conductus*, 8:viii, 4, comments at 53, where he identifies the borrowing of the sequence. The sequence is edited in *AH* 54:147, where it is attributed to Adam of St-Victor. Whether or not this attribution is accurate, the sequence does have Parisian origins; see Fassler, *Gothic Song*, 158 and 180.

[13] *Sexta passus feria* is edited and translated, adapted here, in Mousseau, ed., *Adam of Saint-Victor*, 76–79. For Tables 4.1 and 4.2, p = paroxytone (accent on penultimate syllable) and pp = proparoxytone (accent on antepenultimate syllable).

[14] For similar narrative structures, see Chapter 2.

Table 4.1 Comparison of *Sexta passus feria* (first two paired strophes) and *Mors vite propitia* (strophes 1 and 5)

Sequence		Song	
		1. Mors vite propitia	7pp
1. Sexta passus feria	7pp	*Sexta passus feria*	7pp
		Mortis a miseria	7pp
		Nos erexit.	4p
Die Christus tertia	7pp	*Die Christus tertia*	7pp
Resurrexit.	4p	*Resurrexit*	4p
		...	
2. Surgens cum victoria	7pp	5. Surgens cum victoria	7pp
		Sexta passus feria	7pp
Collocat in gloria	7pp	Collocat in gloria	7pp
Quos dilexit.	4p	Quos dilexit.	4p
		Die Christus tertia	7pp
		Resurrexit.	4p
		1. A death propitious to life,	
1. Having suffered on the		*having suffered on the sixth day,*	
sixth day [Friday],		has raised us from the misery	
		of death.	
Christ has risen		*Christ has risen*	
on the third day.		*on the third day*	
2. Arising with victory,		5. Arising with victory,	
		having suffered on the sixth day.	
He settles in glory		He settles in glory	
those he has loved.		those he has loved.	
		Christ has risen	
		on the third day.	

structure of the sequence, resulting in regular six-line strophes employing the same pattern.[15] Indeed, removing the refrain, which has its own internal 7pp+7pp+4p structure, reveals an identical form to *Sexta passus feria* in *Mors vite propitia* (see Table 4.2). The *rondellus*, in other words, nests two sequence-form strophes to arrive at six-line strophes with an interpolated refrain. The disyllabic rhyme scheme of the sequence is also imitated exactly in the *rondellus* throughout all six strophes, to the point of sharing the exact same disyllabic rhymes: -ia and -exit. Even in portions of

---

[15] On the forms of new sequences, many similar to *Mors vite propitia* and its sequence model, see Norberg, *Introduction*, 167–173; Björkvall and Haug, "Sequence and Versus"; and Kruckenberg, "Relationship" and "Two *Sequentiae Novae*."

Table 4.2 Text, scansion, rhyme scheme, and translation of *Mors vite propitia* in F

1. Mors vite propitia	7pp	a	1. A death propitious to life,
Sexta passus feria	7pp	A	*having suffered on the sixth day,*
Mortis a miseria	7pp	a	has raised us from the misery
Nos erexit.	4p	b	of death.
Die Christus tertia	7pp	A	*Christ has risen*
Resurrexit.	4p	B	*on the third day.*
2. Ad vite palatia	7pp	a	2. To the palaces of life,
Ref.			*Ref.*
Mortis a miseria	7pp	a	from the misery of death
Nos erexit.	4p	b	it has raised us.
Ref.			*Ref.*
3. Fracta sunt imperia	7pp	a	3. Empires are shattered;
Ref.			*Ref.*
Joseph a custodia	7pp	a	Joseph leaves prison
Liber exit.	4p	b	a free man.
Ref.			*Ref.*
4. Nove legis gratia	7pp	a	4. The grace of the new law
Ref.			*Ref.*
Veterum mysteria	7pp	a	has now revealed
Iam detexit.	4p	b	the mysteries of the ancients.
Ref.			*Ref.*
5. Surgens cum victoria	7pp	a	5. Arising with victory,
Ref.			*Ref.*
Collocat in gloria	7pp	a	he settles in glory
Quos dilexit.	4p	b	those he has loved.
Ref.			*Ref.*
6. Ad celi consortia	7pp	a	6. To the companies of heaven,
Ref.			*Ref.*
Nostra spes et gloria	7pp	a	our hope and glory,
Nos direxit.	4p	b	he has guided us.
Ref.			*Ref.*

the *conductus* not drawn from the sequence, the strophic material poetically mirrors its liturgical model.

As closely as the *rondellus* poetry models that of the sequence, the musical setting in F contributes an additional layer of borrowing and musical memory, by contrast to the version in Tours 927. In Tours 927, a slightly more elaborate melody circles around a different pitch center than F, resulting in a different melodic profile and text setting (see Example 4.1). The version in F is syllabic, featuring only three different melodic phrases versus the four in Tours 927. Differences such as these may signal regional preferences; different scribes recording whichever version of the tune they had access to in writing or by memory. In this instance, the contrasting

Example 4.1 Comparison of *Mors vite propitia* in Tours 927, fol. 10ᵛ (a) and F, fol. 464ʳ
(b)

(a)

(b)

versions gesture to a relationship deliberately constructed between song and sequence.

Notably, the melody in F draws on the musical material for the initial pair of strophes of *Sexta passus feria* as it survives in an early thirteenth-century notated missal from the Cathedral of Notre Dame in Paris (Paris lat. 1112; see Example 4.2), and more widely across Europe; in Tours 927, *Mors vite propitia* does not demonstrate any musical links with the sequence repertoire in Paris or elsewhere.[16] The music for the initial pair of sequence strophes is transplanted note-for-note to the song, enabling the incipital line of music and text of the sequence to sound as the refrain in *Mors vite propitia*. Although the second melodic phrase of the song diverges from the sequence, the tonal area is retained and the final four-syllable lines in song and

---

[16] Paris lat. 1112 is dated to the 1220s, with a *terminus post quem* of 1207; see Fassler, *Gothic Song*, 149–150, following Robert Branner, and Baltzer, "Performance Practice."

Example 4.2 Comparison of *Sexta passus feria* (Paris lat. 1112, fol. 267ʳ) (a) and *Mors vite propitia* (F, fol. 464ʳ) (b)

(a)

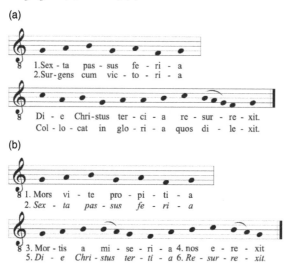

1. Sex - ta   pas - sus   fe - ri - a
2. Sur - gens cum vic - to - ri - a

Di - e Chri-stus ter - ci - a   re - sur - re - xit.
Col - lo - cat in glo - ri - a quos di - le - xit.

(b)

1. Mors vi - te   pro - pi - ti - a
2. Sex - ta   pas - sus   fe - ri - a

3. Mor - tis   a   mi - se - ri - a 4. nos   e - re - xit
5. Di - e Chri - stus ter - ti - a 6. Re - sur - re - xit.

sequence share a near identical descent from C to G, with only minor variants. Consequently, while both versions of *Mors vite propitia* poetically rework *Sexta passus feria*, only in F is the music also reworked to reflect a melody sung locally for the sequence.

The different melody of *Mors vite propitia* in F, which reflects the setting of the Easter sequence as it was sung in Paris and elsewhere, parallels other differences between F and Tours 927. Although both versions use the entire first strophe of *Sexta passus feria* as a refrain, only the Parisian version of *Mors vite propitia* borrows additional text from the second strophe of the sequence, in addition to the music shared by the first two paired strophes. It seems likely the composer-poet or scribe responsible for the version of *Mors vite propitia* in F linked the song more closely to the sequence by musically and textually emphasizing the poetic borrowing already taking place. Whether this has implications for the chronology and origins of each version is debatable, although Tours 927 was almost certainly copied *ca.* 1225, approximately a quarter of a century prior to the copying of F, *ca.* 1240s–1250s.[17] It is possible that *Mors vite propitia* was musically and textually adapted for inclusion in F and performance in Paris since the sequence melody borrowed for *Mors vite propitia* in F was that sung at Notre Dame in Paris.[18]

---

[17] See Chapter 1 on dating.

[18] A Victorine melody also circulated in Paris for *Sexta passus feria*; see Aubry and Misset, *Les Proses*, 186, 254–256.

The unambiguous relationship of this song to the sequence *Sexta passus feria* sheds light on the ways in which a composer-poet could retool parts of a sequence, itself a relatively new addition to the liturgy, into a new Latin song, and even rework this song further to adapt it to a specific locale and its chanted rites. *Mors vite propitia* highlights both the fluidity and intertextuality of the Latin refrain song; although termed concordances in F and Tours 927, the differences in music and poetry between the versions in these two sources illustrate the flexible, nonstatic identity of Latin song that allows it to be adapted to the needs and aesthetic preferences of different communities. The intimate relationship between song and sequence foregrounded in the version in F, moreover, shows how preexistent material persists on multiple levels of form, poetry, and music. The memory of the refrain in *Mors vite propitia* extends not only to another version of itself, but also to the sequence upon which it is modeled poetically and musically. The intergeneric and intertextual memory and mobility of refrains is emphasized in the refrain of *Mors vite propitia* as it repeats through the mechanisms of borrowing and reworking from chant to song, and from strophe to strophe.

Recycling Refrains and Signaling Performance

While the borrowing and reworking of preexistent material is a significant feature of how the Latin refrain song was constructed and reconstructed over time, single words, phrases, or occasionally entire strophes also circulate among songs, creating intertextual networks independent of other genres. These refrains are units of text, and more rarely music, that are fluidly reworked across many songs, refrains whose genealogies are diffuse but can be traced to within, as opposed to outside of, the diverse corpus of Latin song. What I termed a New Year's refrain in Chapter 1, "annus novus," is one such example, a brief but distinctive noun–adjective pair that operates throughout Latin song as a marker of temporal meaning and an intertextual refrain. "Annus novus" serves in some instances as a structural refrain, repeating within or between strophes, but is not tethered to that function as it circulates more widely. These characteristics are shared with a number of other refrains that I will identify as intertextual, and their mobility speaks to the role of the Latin refrain within a communal song repertoire. These refrains, in Margulis's formulation, "belong to a tradition" of Latin song by means of their repetition, and are not necessarily the unique, authorial products of individual poets and composers.[19] The tension between the fixity and fluidity of the Latin refrain song, moreover, is underscored in the repeated unmooring and reintegrating of the refrain in, and in between, song strophes.

Manuscript sources from the twelfth century onward transmit Latin refrains functioning intertextually among songs, with recycled refrains often clustered into certain sources, emanating from certain milieus, or associated with particular functions. Before I go on to discuss a group of shared refrains collected in two Austrian manuscripts, I begin with a simple, one-line refrain transmitted across several sources, a refrain whose identity is complex and complicated by its association with the liturgy and tropes. While the refrain is unchanging as it appears within individual songs, its movement across songs exhibits a lack of fixity to individual works that precisely enables the refrain to emerge as a locus for the production of intertextual meaning and an expression of *mouvance*, the mobility of medieval lyric.

The refrain is "psallat cum tripudio," a phrase that can be translated differently depending on context but means something like "sing with great joy." Although the term "tripudio" is often translated in a way that refers to dance, in poetic contexts and song it most often refers generically to exuberant rejoicing, and is also frequently associated with the voice and act of singing.[20] Like many Latin refrains, "psallat cum tripudio" overtly asserts its vocality, the hortative subjunctive form of *psallere* an example of what Gunilla Iversen terms "verba canendi" in tropes and sequences.[21] Notably, this precise connection emerges between Latin song and the liturgy – "psallat cum tripudio" recurs across not only Latin songs, but also sequences and song-form tropes of the *Benedicamus Domino* versicle. And although it appears in chant, its origins are ambiguous and it does not, by contrast to the refrain of *Mors vite propitia*, reflect the reworking of a preexistent biblical or liturgical material. The refrain line emerges instead from within a flourishing eleventh- and twelfth-century tradition of composing new devotional, rhymed, and rhythmic Latin songs.

As a refrain, "psallat cum tripudio" is memorable, easily recycled, and even formulaic; its seven-syllable structure with an antepenultimate accent and a closing vowel on "-o" make it easy to rhyme with the *Benedicamus Domino* versicle in particular. Its nonspecific, even generic, meaning and

---

[19] Margulis, *On Repeat*, 6.
[20] On the more general, celebrative sense of the term, see La Rue, "Tripudium." See also Mews, "Liturgists and Dance," 14–16, and Knäble, *Eine tanzende Kirche.*
[21] Iversen, "Verba canendi."

Table 4.3 Songs with "psallat cum tripudio"

Incipit	"Psallat cum tripudio" in refrain or strophe
Hodie splendor et lux	strophe
In hoc anni circulo	
Magno gaudens gaudio	
Martyr fuit Stephanus	
Mira dies oritur	
Natum regem laudat*	
Nos respectu gratie	
Patrem parit filia	
Promat chorus hodie	refrain
Puer natus hodie	
Solis iubar nituit	
Missus est Emmanuel	

* *Natum regem laudat* has no refrain.

allusion to singing also lends it the flexibility to appear across festive, devotional, and liturgical songs.[22] Putting aside liturgical sequences for the moment, the line survives as "psallat cum tripudio" in at least a dozen songs and *Benedicamus Domino* song-tropes, transmitted in sources that include Aquitanian *versaria*, troped liturgies, songbooks including the Carmina Burana and Later Cambridge Songbook, and liturgical books and tropers (see Table 4.3; sources listed in the Appendix).[23] Although textually stable, the refrain line does not transmit any musical information. Instead, it is a poetic marker, or even topos, of devotional Latin song, its iterability connecting songs and singers across diverse contexts in a shared expression of vocal joy.

With the exception of sequences, "psallat cum tripudio" has a special relationship to refrain forms, even when it does not serve as a refrain. Within the dozen or so songs in which "psallat cum tripudio" is included, it appears as a refrain, or part thereof, in only four, although all but one song employs a refrain. Two of the four songs in which the phrase is part of a refrain, moreover, are closely related, and may be contrafacts: *Promat chorus hodie* and *Puer natus hodie*.[24] The two songs, including three slightly

---

[22] See, for example, Caldwell, "Texting Vocality," 46–48 and 52–55.

[23] Sequences with the line include *AH* 9:202; 37:136; 55:254; 55:69; 55:53; 42:284; and 10:425.

[24] See Chapter 3; although the relationship due to the refrain between *Promat chorus hodie* and the later *Puer natus hodie* has been noted, the degree of textual and musical similarity has not. *Promat chorus hodie* has been instead hypothesized as a contrafact, or imitation, of the text-only *Companho, farai un vers*, attributed to Guilhem de Peiteu, edited in Jeanroy, ed., *Les Chansons*,

different versions of *Puer natus hodie*, share similarities beyond the refrain. The initial strophes of each illustrate the close relationship between the songs, including occasion (Nativity), scansion (7pp lines in each strophe), and the refrain (see Table 4.4).

The musical settings of these songs are challenging to compare, since the version in the thirteenth-century troper and songbook Stuttg is notated with unheightened neumes and the one in the fourteenth-century service book and troper Engelberg Codex is unnotated. Only *Promat chorus hodie* is transcribable, along with the fifteenth-century version of *Puer natus hodie* in the Wienhäuser Liederbuch, manuscripts separated by several centuries (see Example 4.3).[25] Despite this chronological (as well as geographical) gap, the melodies of these two songs are related, different starting and ending pitches notwithstanding. The initial gesture on "promat chorus" and "puer natus" is identical, if transposed, and the melodic contours of each closely track. The refrain is a locus for the most poetic, and apparently musical, play and variation too, as the Wienhäuser Liederbuch includes one further verse line ("nato dei filio") and a more ornate setting for the refrain as a whole.[26]

Most interesting is the treatment of "psallat cum tripudio" and its integration into longer refrains rife with repetition and vocalic play in two songs copied in chronologically and geographically disparate sources.[27] The inclusion of this refrain appears to cue a certain type of sonic and vocalic play that develops within each iteration of the longer refrain. This is taken to its fullest expression in the Engelberg Codex, where repeated vowels function both as anticipations and extensions of "contio" and "psallite"; as with all three versions, the refrains ultimately conclude with a full statement of "psallat cum tripudio." Although the syllable count of the strophic material is regular within and across the songs, the refrain is decidedly irregular. The length and contours of its lines bend and shift, adding, subtracting, and expanding words and vowels. In this case, although the refrain varies, it

---

1–3. See Spanke, "Zur Formenkunst," 75–76, and Marshall, "Pour l'étude des Contrafacta," 328–329. See, however, Haug, "Kennen wir die Melodie," 372, and a fuller analysis of *Promat chorus hodie* in Llewellyn, "Nova Cantica," 154–155.

[25] St-M A is one of several twelfth-century *versaria* from the Aquitanian milieu of the Abbey of St-Martial in Limoges, France (see Grier, "Some Codicological Observations"), while the Wienhäuser Liederbuch is a fifteenth-century songbook used by the sisters of the Cistercian Abbey of Wienhäusen, near Celle, Germany; see Sievers, ed., *Das Wienhäuser Liederbuch*, and Roolfs, "Das Wienhäuser Liederbuch."

[26] This is a phrase, however, that appears elsewhere alongside "psallat cum tripudio"; see later in this chapter.

[27] On similar forms of vocalic and vocabalic play, see Caldwell, "Texting Vocality."

Table 4.4 Comparison of *Promat chorus hodie* and *Puer natus hodie*

St-M A, 51ᵛ	Stuttg, 75ᵛ	Engelberg Codex, 130ᵛ	Wienhäuser Liederbuch, 2ᵛ
1. Promat chorus hodie	1. Puer natus hodie	1. Puer natus hodie	1. Puer natus hodie
O contio	*O o concio*	*O o concio*	*O o concio*
Canticum letitie.	Cantus est letitie.	Ex Maria virgine.	Ex Maria virgine.
O contio	*O concio psallite*	*O o concio*	*O o concio*
Psallite contio	*O concio o et o*	*Psallite e e*	*Psallite e e concio*
Psallat cum tripudio.	Psallat cum tripudio	*Concio o o*	Psallat cum tripudio
		Psallat cum tripudio.	Nato dei filio.
1. Let the chorus bring forth today,	1. A boy is born today,	1. A boy is born today,	1. A boy is born today,
o assembly	*o, o, assembly,*	*o, o, assembly,*	*o, o, assembly,*
a song of joy.	this is a song of joy.	from the Virgin Mary.	from the Virgin Mary.
O assembly,	*O, assembly, sing*	*O, o, assembly,*	*O, o, assembly,*
sing, assembly,	*o assembly, o and o,*	*sing, e, e,*	*sing, e, e, assembly,*
let the assembly sing	let the assembly sing	*assembly, o, o,*	let the assembly sing
with great joy.	with great joy.	let the assembly sing	with great joy, to the
		with great joy.	newborn son of God.

Example 4.3 Comparison of *Promat chorus hodie* (St-M A, fol. 51ᵛ) and *Puer natus hodie* (Wienhäuser Liederbuch, fol. 2ᵛ)

remains recognizable since it employs the same vocabulary and an identical final line ("psallat cum tripudio"), as well as an inner refrain that divides the two-line strophe in half.[28] The example of *Promat chorus hodie* and *Puer natus hodie*, in other words, speaks to the tension between sameness and variation, fixity and *mouvance*, which arises when refrains repeat beyond the boundaries of individual songs.

The three words "psallat cum tripudio" represent the most stable element in both the refrains of *Promat chorus hodie* and *Puer natus hodie*, as well as across the other ten songs in this refrain network. In several instances, the refrain line is fully integrated into strophes. This is how it appears in the first strophe of *Magno gaudens gaudio* in the twelfth-century Later Cambridge Songbook, for instance, and in select versions of the widely transmitted Christmas song *In hoc anni circulo*.[29] The refrain line appears most often, however, in the final strophes of songs, where it serves as part of a longer, formulaic marker of function and performance. The inclusion of "psallat cum tripudio" most often anticipates citations of the *Benedicamus Domino* versicle and its response, *Deo gratias*. In most cases comprising an entire strophe, this versicle formula typically begins with an invocation of a community of singers, identified as "contio," followed by "psallat cum tripudio" and then the versicle text; lines might also be repeated or added to complete the scansion of the song's strophes. The final strophe of *Patrem parit filia* illustrates the most basic shape of this versicle formula in several of its many sources: "ergo nostra contio | psallat cum tripudio | benedicat domino" ("therefore let our assembly sing with great joy and bless the Lord").[30] Variations on this formulaic strophe usually involve the inclusion of an additional line, as in *Martyr fuit Stephanus*: "ergo nostra concio | in chordis et organo | psallat cum tripudio | Benedicamus Domino" (Engelberg Codex, fol. 128[v]).

What results from these repeated, strophic formulations is a doxology of sorts for song-tropes of the *Benedicamus Domino*, comparable to the seasonal and ferial doxologies employed in hymnody.[31] Significantly, doxologies do not belong to single hymns, but instead are itinerant both in terms of specific hymns and liturgical seasons, just as this *Benedicamus*

---

[28] For a similar discussion of variation, formulas, and refrains, see Butterfield, "Repetition and Variation," 10–13.

[29] *Magno gaudens gaudio* is edited in Stevens, ed., *Later Cambridge Songs*, 96–97; sources and versions of *In hoc anni circulo* are listed in the Appendix and *CPI*.

[30] Sources that transmit *Patrem parit filia* (or the closely related *Pater matris hodie*) without "psallat cum tripudio" include Sens 46; LoA; Colmar 187; Basel B.XI.8; and the St. Pölten Processional.

[31] Hughes, *Medieval Manuscripts*, 56–57 at §409.

Domino "doxology" is reused throughout song-tropes with different texts and for different occasions. A key difference between the changing and itinerant doxologies, or closing prayers, of hymns and this versicle "doxology" is that the latter functions chiefly as a marker of genre and performance, indicating where and how a Latin song is supposed to be integrated into the liturgy as a trope. Pointing, moreover, to the fluidity of genre among Latin songs, this versicle doxology can be included or excluded depending on whether its attached song was intended to serve as a versicle trope, or simply as a devotional, festive work. In the case of *Patrem parit filia* in the St. Pölten Processional, for instance, the *Benedicamus Domino* formula is switched out for a different liturgical formula. In this fifteenth-century source, the final strophe invites the lector to begin the reading using formulaic language that occurs as a closing formula across Latin songs: "lector librum accipe | profer iube domine | lectionem incipe" ("let the reader take the book, saying 'iube domine,' and begin the reading").[32] Formulaic strophes like these were added to or removed from songs to alter their function and association with the liturgy, affirming the fluidity of Latin song in practice, performance, and transmission.

Formulaic or doxological strophes are, however, not refrains, and the integration of "psallat cum tripudio" into strophic formulas complicates and confuses its identity and identification. The repetition of this line as a stereotyped, even stock, invocation of vocalic rejoicing points to the broader tradition of Latin song and its performance. Repeated and recycled lines like "psallat cum tripudio" reflect a shared vocabulary and culture of devotional Latin song, a culture, moreover, that valued the reuse and the reworking of familiar material into new frameworks. Refrains that circulate in both expected and unexpected places were part of the poetic toolbox of poets and composers, indistinct from their poetic surroundings yet persistently recognizable and iterable; in this way, repeated lines like "psallat cum tripudio" come into closer alignment with the inherent tension between the indistinct and marked identity of the French *refrain* across diverse contexts.[33] Different from French *refrains* that can invoke different forms of *auctoritas*, however, the reuse of simultaneously common yet distinctive lines in Latin song instead derives its intertextual power from their genealogy, or perhaps even ontology, within the tradition of devotional Latin songs, chants, and tropes.[34] The

[32] On lectionary formulas in Latin song, see Chapter 3, n. 5.
[33] I am paraphrasing Butterfield, who remarks that "however indistinct and featureless many [French] refrains are, medieval poets and composers persistently recognize and re-cite them." "Repetition and Variation," 4.
[34] On *auctoritas* and the French *refrain*, see Saltzstein, *Refrain*.

auctoritas, if it can termed such, accessed by the reuse of "psallat cum tripudio" is rooted in collective knowledge and memory of song itself and its fluidity in performance and function. In what follows, the scribal cueing of refrains in two sibling sources offers a localized glimpse into the way refrains circulating among songs were further positioned at the intersection of not only memory and performance, but also inscription.

Cueing Refrains in an Austrian Abbey

Two fourteenth-century manuscripts from the Benedictine Abbey of St. Lambrecht in Austria, Graz 258 and 409, together transmit an assortment of practical and liturgical materials, as well as a sizable collection of Latin songs, many with refrains. As anthologies of Latin song – rubricated as *conducti* – the two Graz manuscripts map several networks of song and refrain transmission from the twelfth to the fourteenth century across Europe.[35] The intertextual and intermusical networks constructed by refrains in the Graz sources, however, are complex and derive from scribal practices around the cueing of refrains and the inscription of Latin song. The pair of manuscripts bring to the fore tensions around the fixity and fluidity, and memory and inscription, of the Latin refrain and refrain song.

The smaller and more streamlined of the two in size, number of folios, and contents is Graz 258.[36] The majority of the manuscript comprises a neumed antiphoner for the liturgical year dating to the late twelfth century; devotional Latin songs on the recto and verso of a single folio (fol. 2) are among various additions made over time to the main liturgical contents. Graz 409 is larger both in size and number of folios, and its contents (apart from Latin songs) are entirely textual and devotional, reflecting a provenance within a pedagogical and religious institution.[37] Its Latin songs are copied in three different locations in the manuscript, always in a different

---

[35] The total of fifty-four texts includes three sequences not considered in the following discussion. See Anderson, "Thirteenth-Century Conductus"; Brewer, "In Search of Lost Melodies"; and Lipphardt, "Zur Herkunft der Carmina Burana." On liturgical sources from St. Lambrecht, see Engels, "Handschriften aus St. Lambrecht." Seckau Abbey has also been proposed as an origin; see Lipphardt, "Zur Herkunft der Carmina Burana," 214.

[36] The manuscript measures 20 × 29 centimeters and includes 176 total folios, along with bindings from other manuscripts. The contents are listed in the Graz library catalogue: sosa2.uni-graz.at/sosa/katalog/katalogisate/258.html.

[37] Graz 409 measures 34 × 25 centimeters and includes 274 folios, with the contents listed in the Graz library catalogue: sosa2.uni-graz.at/sosa/katalog/katalogisate/409.html.

hand from the nonmusical texts – on the initial flyleaves (fol. 1ʳ–2ᵛ), at the end of a gathering (fol. 70ᵛ–72ᵛ), and on a final leaf (fol. 273ʳ).

In both manuscripts, the copying of songs appears to be at least partly driven by the opportunity of empty space. The songs were not part of the planned contents of the antiphoner of Graz 258 or the textual miscellanea of 409; rather, they were added at some point in each manuscript's history. The reasons for their inclusion in Graz 258 seem somewhat clearer and more understandable; the musical nature of the liturgical manuscript aligns with devotional Latin songs, some of which may have served a liturgical function.[38] For Graz 409, the reasons are less obvious. While the contents as a whole are devotional, the addition of music and poetry is somewhat out of place, although they align with the theological focus of the other contents. Given the close relationship between the hands responsible for copying the songs in both manuscripts, perhaps what we see in this pair of sources is a monastic scribe taking advantage of blank folios in manuscripts he had at hand, rather than attempting to match the contents therein.[39]

Above all, the Graz sources represent a repository of Latin refrains and refrain songs. Of the total number of fifty-four songs between the two sources, twelve out of fourteen songs in Graz 258 and thirty-two out of the forty in Graz 409 include refrains of varying forms and lengths. Within this combined total of forty refrain-form songs, six are concordant between the two sources. At least twenty-two have concordances outside of the Graz sources, although not all concordances have the same, or even any, refrain (see Table 4.5).[40]

The collection of strophic songs gathered in Graz 258 and 409 is unusual, first and foremost for its remarkably high ratio of songs with refrains. More unusual, although the songs were copied on the page in a relatively clear fashion, is that refrains are consistently cued irregularly and inconsistently, in a fashion not found in contemporary manuscript sources.

---

[38] Two songs, *Umbram destruxit penitus* and *Tribus signis deo dignis*, not in Table 4.5, include formulaic calls to the lector, suggesting the possible role of certain of the songs in the liturgy itself or as part of monastic reading practices. Graz 409 also preserves a single work citing the *Benedicamus Domino* versicle (*Serena virginum*, not in Table 4.5).

[39] Anderson, "Thirteenth-Century Conductus," 356.

[40] Alphabetical organization according to refrain allows for comparison among works sharing identical (or nearly identical) refrains. The refrain as it appears in the context of each individual work is included, with the longest version only indicated here if it is cued differently. The "concordant refrain" column indicates whether concordant sources transmit the refrain from the second column, not whether the song itself has a refrain prior to its copying into the two Graz manuscripts.

Table 4.5 Inventory and concordances for songs with refrains in Graz 258 and 409**

Incipit	Refrain in Graz sources	Graz 258	Graz 409	Concordances	Concordant refrain
Ave maris stella divinitatis	Apparuit apparuit quem virgo pia genuit Maria	2^r	71^v	Piae Cantiones (1582), no. 27, and (1625), no. 11	Yes
Dies ista dies pretiosa	Apparuit	2^r	273^r	Zurich C. 58, 148^v*	No
Mirabatur antiquitas	Apparuit		72^r		
Umbram destruxit penitus	Apparuit	2^r	72^r		
Nos respectu gratie	Audi audi audi nos, audi audi audi nos, audi audi nos, rex eterne salva nos		71^v	Colmar 187, 45^v; Laon 263, 141r^†; Prague XIII.H.3c, 262^v; St. Pölten Processional, 12^r; Vienna 4494, 68^r	Mixed [with variants]
Ruga dure vetustatis	Domine dominus noster quam admirabile		1^r		
Ecce venit de Syon	[258] Eia et eia iubilando resonet ecclesia. Gaudet. [409] Gaudeat	2^v	71^v	Engelberg 102, 139^r; Hortus Deliciarum, 27^r [destroyed]; Moosburger Graduale, 233^v; SG 1397, p. 21; St. Pölten Processional, 11^r; Stuttg. 25^r	Mixed [all exclude "Gaudet"/ "Gaudeat"]
Nuntio dum credidit	Eia et eia iubilando resonet ecclesia		71^r		
Primus homo cum pro pomo	Eia		2^r	Le Puy A, 65^r/166^r; Le Puy B., 36^v/116^v*	No
Salve maris stella	Eia et eia		72^v		
Tres signatas calculo	Eia, dicit canticum, baculum per typicum mundi transit per lubricum durus ferens dura	2^v			
Stella nova radiat	Ergo novis laudibus occurrat omnis populus cum genitrice pia		72^r	Moosburger Graduale, 245^r; Seckauer Cantionarium, 186^r; St. Pölten Processional, 14^r	Yes

Table 4.5 (cont.)

Incipit	Refrain in Graz sources	Graz 258	Graz 409	Concordances	Concordant refrain
Ecce novus annus est	*Exultandi tempus dies est venit lex venit rex venit fons gratie*		2ᵛ	Le Puy A, 53ʳ Le Puy B, 30ʳ* Moosburger Graduale, 244ʳ St. Pölten Processional, 7ᵛ	Mixed
Dies ista colitur	*Felix est egressio per quam fit salvatio*	2ᵛ	273ʳ	A-Wn frag. 660, 1b Bobbio, 334ᵛ Colmar 187, 45ᵛ Engelberg 1003, 117ʳ Leipzig 225, 178ᵛ LoA, 18ʳ Moosburger Graduale, 236ᵛ Sens 46, p. 33 St. Pölten Processional, 8ʳ Stuttg, 25ᵛ/81ʳ	Yes [minor variants]
Sol sub nube latuit	*Gaude nova nupta fides est et veritas, quod a carne deitas non fuit corrupta*		1ʳ	Bekynton Anthology, 80ʳ Berlin 1996, 292ᵛ F, 354ᵛ Leipzig 225, 178ᵛ Paris lat. 4880, 83ᵛ Royal 7.A.VI, 107ᵛ Saint Omer 351, 20ʳ SG 383, p. 169 W1, 119ᵛ (110ᵛ)	Mixed
Agnus pugnat cum dracone	*Gaudeat*		71ᵛ	Brussels 5649–5667, 7ᵛ	No
De sinu patris verbum emicuit	*Gaudeat*		1ᵛ		
Glomerat in aula	*Gaudeat*		72ᵛ		
In natali summni regis	*Gaudeat*		72ʳ	Later Cambridge Songbook, 7ʳ (4ʳ) [as *In natali novi regis*] Moosburger Graduale, 238ᵛ	No

Iubilemus cordis voce	*Gaudeat*		2^r	Laon 263, 123^{r‡}	No
Lac de silice	*Gaudeat*		1^v	[all as *Latex silice*] F, 230^v ORawl, 240^v (11^v) Stuttg, 30^v W1, 81^r (74^r)	No
Novi partus gaudium	*Gaudeat gaudeat gaudeat ecclesia*		1^r	Charleville 190, 158_v ORawl, 241^v (12^v) Paris lat. 4880, 83^r	No
Rimetur mens hominis	*Gaudeat*		2^v		
Sata tria fert Maria [Sancta pia fert Maria in 258]	*Gaudeat omnis homo*	2^r	273^r		
Stupeat natura	*Gaudeat*		2^r	Bekynton Anthology, 129^r Munich 16444, IIa^v Tort, 140^r W2, 177^v [motet]	No
Verbum patris humanatur	*Gaudeat gaudeat gaudeat ecclesia*		71^r	Later Cambridge Songbook, 7_r (4^r) Moosburger Graduale, 237^v Paris lat. 4880, 84^v St-M C, 91^r St. Pölten Processional, 13^v	No/mixed
Deinceps ex nulla	*Hei in ista die meta prophetie partus est Marie*		71^r	Moosburger Graduale, 238^r	Yes
Paris [Parit] preter morem$	*Hei in ista die*		72^r	F, 232^r Hu, 103^v Ma, 123^r ORawl, 245^r (16^r)	No
Pater filie	*Hinc concinere est et nova psallere letitia*	2^r		Le Puy A, 144_v5 Le Puy B, 89^r	?No
Lux optata claruit	*Hoc in hoc, hoc in hoc, hoc in hoc solempnio, concinat hec contio*		2^r	Klagenfurt Perg. 7, 6_r LoA, 29^v Sens 46, p. 36	Yes

Table 4.5 *(cont.)*

Incipit	Refrain in Graz sources	Graz 258	Graz 409	Concordances	Concordant refrain
Novi partus gratia	*Laudet ecclesia quem parit conscia castitatis*		71ʳ		
Gaude Syon iubila	*Sonet vox leticie in gloria nova sint ecclesie tripudia. virginis hon- orem frequentemur et laudemur gratie et venie datorem*		2ᵛ	St. Pölten Processional, 12ᵛ	Yes [minor variants]
Hostis perfidus et invidus•	*Sonet vox leticie*		2ᵛ		
Nove geniture	*Sonet vox leticie*		1ᵛ	Brugge 111/178, 32ᵛ Cambridge R.9.11, 152ᵛ F, 355ʳ Moosburger Graduale, 233ʳ Tort, 81ᵛ W1, 117ᵛ (108ᵛ)	No

** A single asterisk indicates that I was unable to consult the source personally and am relying on information provided in *CPI* and/or Anderson, "Notre Dame and Related Conductus."

† *Nos respectu gratie* also appears in a late thirteenth-century ordinal from the Cathedral of Metz, where it was sung as a trope at the beginning of Mass for Epiphany, introducing and interpolating the introit antiphon *Ecce advenit Dominator Dominus*; see McGrade, "Enriching," 45.

‡ Robert Lagueux refers to this as a "rare sequence"; according to the *Analecta Hymnica* (AH54:165) and reiterated by Anderson and in *CPI*, it appears to be transmitted as a sequence in two later sources, the 1497 *Breviarium Tornacense* and the 1519 *Missale Nidrosiense*. See Lagueux, "Glossing Christmas," 363. Lagueux cites Fassler's identification of the melody of *Iubilemus cordis voce* as that of a *conductus* in the Daniel play in LoA, fol. 96ᵛ, *Iubilemus regis nostro*; see Fassler, "Feast of Fools," 88–89.

§ The bottom-most voice, or tenor, in the polyphonic settings of Hu, Ma, and F is shared with the song.

¶ Le Puy A, fol. 144 is missing, although no refrain appears at the conclusion of strophe 3 on fol. 145ʳ.

• Related to *Pater filie* (Graz 258, fol. 2ᵛ).

Significantly, attention was paid by the scribes to the song as a defined unit of poetry and, when neumed, of music. Most, though not all, songs begin with a large initial flush left on the folio, and are followed by neat lines of text, heavy with abbreviation, which are highly legible. Red rubrics also proclaim the songs to be "conductus" and within songs, strophes are frequently rubricated with "V."

Yet, in Graz 409 in particular, refrains are typically cued only once for each song, generally following the final strophe of the song, with only three exceptions where the end refrain is complemented by internal cues for refrains between strophes.[41] In Graz 258, refrain cues in half of its twelve refrain songs appear following each strophe, while in the other half the refrain is appended solely at the end of all strophes, as in Graz 409. The scribe in Graz 258 does utilize the cue word "repetitio" before the refrain of *Dies ista colitur* (fol. 2^v), the only unambiguous reference in either manuscript to repetition, although the refrain and its accompanying textual cue occur solely at the end of the poem, and not between strophes. In most cases, without knowledge of the songs or access to concordant sources, the songs in both manuscripts would appear to lack refrains based on how they were copied, unless scribal cueing practices across both sources are closely examined.

What I identify as "refrains" in Table 4.5, in other words, look more like poetic "tags" on the manuscript page, ranging from one to several words copied at the end of songs, at times bleeding into the margin.[42] The first letter of the refrain "tag" is typically capitalized and highlighted with red (see Figure 4.1). As an example, in Graz 409, all four strophes of *Umbram destruxit penitus*, a song unique to these two sources, are copied, and only after the final strophe is the single word "apparuit" copied, seemingly an acclamative conclusion much like the "amen" that concludes many Latin hymns and devotional songs. Its only concordance is in Graz 258, where the cueing is still somewhat ambiguous, but a scribe has more regularly included the word "apparuit," or its abbreviation "app.," after each strophe (each signaled by the capital "V") (see Figure 4.2). Due to the witness of Graz 258, the "tag" in Graz 409 can be more accurately identified as a refrain, intended to be sung between each of the four strophes of *Umbram destruxit penitus*. In both manuscripts, however, only the word

---

[41] These exceptions all have concordances outside the Graz sources: *Lux optat claruit, Verbum patris humanatur,* and *Nove geniture.*

[42] One of the few musicologists to address the refrain tags in these two sources refers to the appended refrains as "acclamations [that] frequently occur at the end of these pieces." Anderson, "Thirteenth-Century Conductus," 361, n. 18. See also Lipphardt, "Zur Herkunft der Carmina Burana," 217–218.

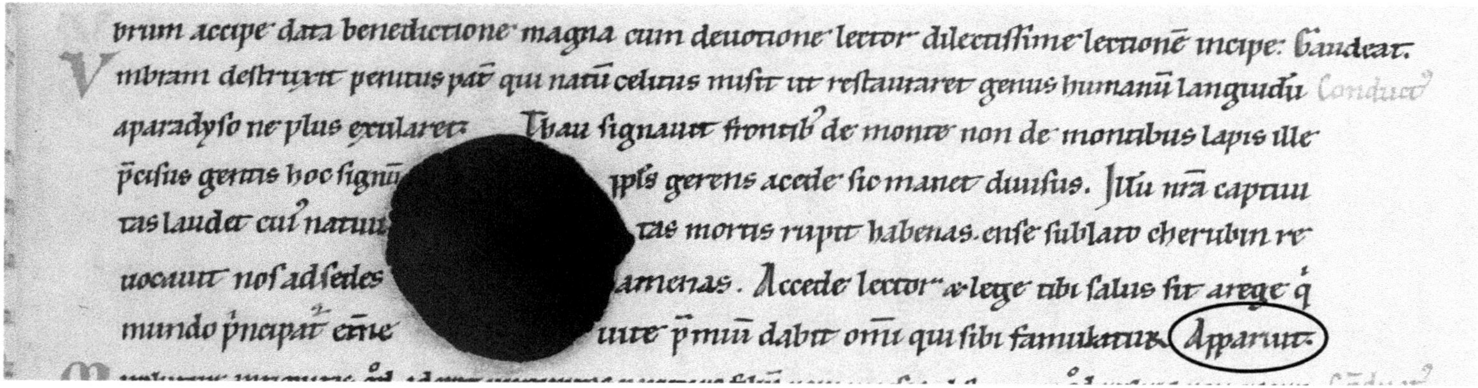

Figure 4.1 Graz 409, fol. 72ʳ, *Umbram destruxit penitus*, refrain cue circled. Reproduced by kind permission of the Universitätsbibliothek, Graz

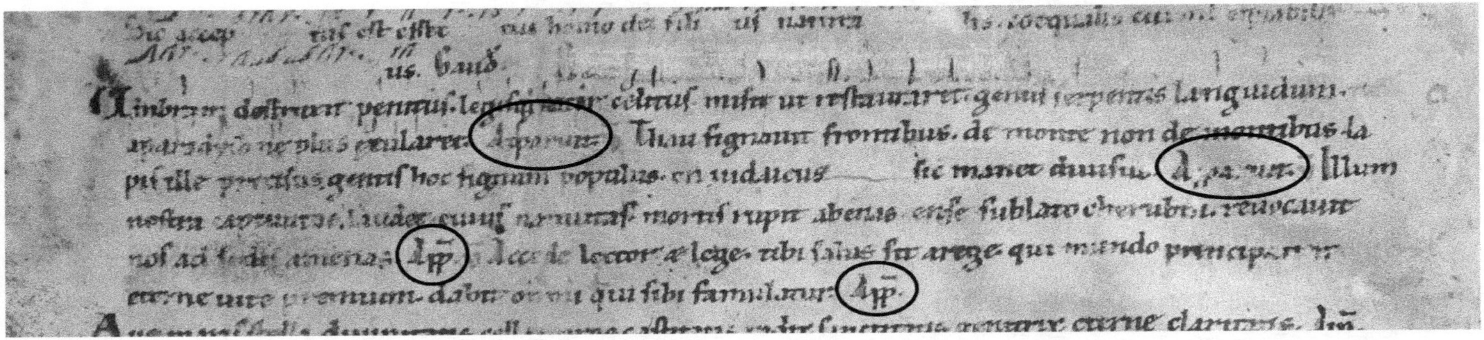

Figure 4.2 Graz 258, fol. 2ʳ, *Umbram destruxit penitus*, refrain cues circled. Reproduced by kind permission of the Universitätsbibliothek, Graz

"apparuit" ("he appeared") is included, suggesting a one-word refrain sung between the four strophes of *Umbram destruxit penitus*. Yet Table 4.5 includes seven instances between the two sources of refrains beginning with "apparuit" and, among these, five include only this one-word incipit or its abbreviation "app." One time in each source, however, the refrain expands to become the lengthier "apparuit, apparuit quem virgo pia genuit Maria" ("he appears, he appears, who was brought forth from the Holy Virgin Mary"), in both manuscripts in the song *Ave maris stella divinitatis*. The single word "apparuit" thus seems to function as a cue not only for the refrain within an individual lyric, but also for the longer version of the refrain found elsewhere in each source. Of the thirty-four total refrain songs in the Graz sources, the lion's share of twenty-six songs – when eliminating concordances – includes refrains beginning with only five distinctive words, with the majority of these reusing only four of these refrain incipits, "apparuit" among them (see Table 4.6). In Latin contexts, the sharing of refrains among works to this degree is exceedingly rare. Approximately 20 percent of the songs in the Appendix share refrains between two or more works, with the Graz sources transmitting the greatest number of shared refrains of any extant source. Unlike "psallat cum tripudio," however, these refrains are more variable in length or word order, as I discuss below, although they invariably retain an identical incipit or cue word.

The manner in which the refrains are inscribed in Graz 258 and 409 is key; since they were cued only once, and typically incompletely, singers and users of the manuscript were required to not only extrapolate the insertion of refrains between strophes, but also either connect the refrain incipits to longer versions within the manuscript or concordant sources, or simply recall them from memory. Conversely, if recording local song practices, the cueing suggests that scribes did not feel the need to fully outline familiar

Table 4.6 Shared refrains in Graz 258 and 409 (concordances not counted in totals)

Refrain incipit	Occurrences		TOTALS
	258	409	
Gaudeat	1	13	12
Apparuit	3	4	4
Eia	2	4	5
Sonet	0	3	3
Hei in ista die	0	2	2
TOTAL			26

practices and forms. The cueing practices around refrains in Graz 258 and 409, in other words, suggest a collective body of remembered refrains, a common currency of responses that could be deployed in performance or added at will by a scribe.

Sharing, Adding, and Subtracting Refrains

Of the five shared refrain incipits in the two Austrian sources listed in Table 4.6, none presents a straightforward case. Variation characterizes each refrain both in terms of how it appears in the Graz sources and among external concordances; the degree of similarity that must obtain to label refrains as identical is a central, indeed crucial, question for these shared refrains. The Graz sources do not make this easy, since the partial cueing of refrains leaves only incipits or brief multi-word phrases in many cases. Moreover, while in certain cases songs and refrains have concordances elsewhere, some of the songs transmitted outside of the Graz sources do not include refrains at all or include entirely different refrains. The songs in the two manuscripts exhibit ties through concordances to sources such as twelfth-century *versaria*, thirteenth-century festive liturgies, songbooks and poetic anthologies, thirteenth- and fourteenth-century service books and tropers, and many other sources in between. Some of the songs copied in the Graz sources survive in polyphonic settings, others in text-only sources. Yet, due to their particular approach to sharing, adding, and subtracting refrains, this pair of fourteenth-century manuscripts do not appear to copy or draw from any one source or intertext, instead transmitting a relatively unique arrangement, and versions, of many widely transmitted songs.

The most stable of the five refrains in terms of its shape and repeats across songs, the refrain beginning "apparuit" nevertheless has a complex history, appearing in over a half-dozen songs, with the songs in the Graz sources included. Most notably, the "apparuit" refrain belongs to a famous complex of Christmas song-tropes known by the Latin incipit *Resonet in laudibus* that originated in tropes of the *Nunc dimittis* for Christmas and which became a widely known Christmas song in Latin and with a German text.[43] In the Graz sources, however, the "apparuit" refrain is unmoored from any liturgical context and is instead linked to four strophic songs

---

[43] On the dissemination of this trope/song complex, see Ameln, "Resonet in Laudibus," 52–112; Lipphardt, "Magnum nomen Domini Emanuel," 194–204; and Brewer, "In Search of Lost Melodies," 98.

celebrating Christ's nativity, paralleling the survival of the refrain in several strophic songs transmitted elsewhere, including *Fulget dies hec pre ceteris*, *Nove lucis hodie*, *Resonemus laudibus*, and some strophic reworkings of *Resonet in laudibus*.[44] The textual stability of the refrain is rooted in the incipit "apparuit," a core sentiment, and a recognizable if variable sequence of words; when variation within the refrain occurs, it usually involves word order or the elimination of words. In the Graz sources, a fully realized form of the "apparuit" refrain appears twice, once each in Graz 258 and 409 as "apparuit, apparuit, quem virgo pia genuit Maria." In the other three songs with which it is associated in the Graz manuscripts, *Dies ista dies pretiosa*, *Mirabatur antiquitas*, and *Umbram destruxit penitus*, only the incipit "apparuit," or the even briefer "app.," appear. Of these four songs, *Dies ista dies pretiosa* has one concordance that lacks any refrain, and *Ave maris stella divinitatis* appears in the later printed Finnish/Swedish *Piae Cantiones* of the late sixteenth and early seventeenth centuries. In these later sources, the word order of the refrain is slightly changed ("apparuit quem pia virgo genuit Maria").

Since all four songs with the "apparuit" refrain in the Graz sources are unnotated, a comparison of musical settings is impossible. However, because the refrain survives outside of the Graz sources, including in later settings of *Ave maris stella divinitatis*, it is possible to compare the music of the refrain as it circulates more widely. One complication is the integration of the "apparuit" refrain in the *Resonet in laudibus* song-trope complex where it repeats within strophes, but not always as a structural refrain (similar to the behavior of "psallat cum tripudio"). In the comparison in Example 4.4, I have included only instances in which the "apparuit" refrain serves as a structural refrain outside of, although in some cases related to, the *Resonet in laudibus* complex in *Fulget dies hec pre ceteris*, *Resonemus laudibus*, *Ave maris stella divinitatis*, and *Nove lucis hodie*.[45] Sources for notated versions of these songs are transmitted in predominantly fourteenth-century sources; across these songs, the melodic setting of the refrain exhibits similar contours, especially among certain manuscripts and between select songs. In particular, the *Piae Cantiones*, Moosburger Graduale and SG 392 all transmit a similar melody for the refrain, while in the two fourteenth-century service books and tropers from Aosta (possibly copied for the Cathedral) the refrain is markedly

---

[44] See the Appendix for sources.

[45] *Nove lucis hodie* is frequently part of the *Resonet in laudibus* song-trope complex; see n. 43.

different. In terms of specific songs, among the first three songs in Example 4.4, the refrain shares the same tonal space, beginning and ending on E and outlining a range of a fifth from D to A (with an added lower neighbor to C in the *Piae Cantiones*). The refrain melody in *Ave maris stella divinitatis*, *Fulget dies hec pre ceteris*, and *Nove lucis hodie*, in other words, is similar enough across four sources to be recognizably the same; the refrain as it appears in *Resonemus laudibus* in the Aosta manuscripts sits at the farthest remove melodically and textually. Only the Moosburger Graduale transmits the refrain in two different songs in one source, and in this case the text and music of the refrain are nearly identical, although the music and poetry of each song's strophic material are not shared.

Example 4.4 Comparison of "apparuit" refrain in *Ave maris stella divinitatis*, *Fulget dies hec pre ceteris*, *Nove lucis hodie*, and *Resonemus laudibus*

Ave maris stella divinitatis

Piae cantiones (1582), no. 27 and (1625), no. 11 (*mensurally notated)

Ap - pa - ru - it, ap - pa - ru - it quem pi - a vir - go ge - nu - it Ma - ri - a.

Fulget dies hec pre ceteris

Moosburger Graduale, fol. 235r

Ap - pa - ru - it, ap - pa - ru - it quem vir - go pi - a ge - nu - it Ma - ri - a.

Nove lucis hodie

Moosburger Graduale, fol. 239v

Ap - pa - ru - it, ap - pa - ru - it quem vir - go pi - a ge - nu - it Ma - ri - a.

CH-SGs 392, p. 89

Ap - pa - ru - it, ap - pa - ru - it quem vir - go pi - a ge - nu - it Ma - ri - a.

Resonemus laudibus

Aosta Cod. 11, fol. 80v

Ap - pa - ru - it___ quem ge - nu - it___ Ma - ri - a.

Aosta Cod. 13, fol. 66v

Ap - pa - ru - it___ quem ge - nu - it___ Ma - ri - a.___

Indeed, the four songs whose refrains are compared in Example 4.4 are not contrafacts; their strophic material shares neither the same poetic scansion nor the same musical settings. Along with the other three unnotated songs in the Graz sources employing the "apparuit" refrain, these seven Latin songs are linked solely by means of the text and, in some cases, the music of the "apparuit" refrain alone. This external network of concordances has implications for the series of four unnotated songs in the Graz sources and their one-word "apparuit" cues, in addition to further confirming the identity of the cues seen in Figures 4.1 and 4.2 as markers of repeated refrains. The wider, and relatively stable, transmission of the refrain across songs featuring different strophic forms illustrates that the "apparuit" refrain was not tethered to particular poems, melodies, or even to the *Resonet in laudibus* song-trope complex. That is not to say that several of the Latin songs employing the "apparuit" refrain could not have served a liturgical function; the final strophe of *Umbram destruxit penitus*, for instance, begins with a formulaic invitation to the reader to begin the reading "accede, lector, et lege," and *Resonemus laudibus* in the Aosta manuscripts is a *Benedicamus Domino* song-trope. However, the "apparuit" refrain circulates within the broader sphere of devotional Latin song that includes tropes, not only of the *Nunc dimittis* in the *Resonet in laudibus* complex, but for other parts of Mass and especially the Office. Finally, the origins of the refrain are ambiguous. Akin to "psallat cum tripudio," the language and vocabulary of the "apparuit" refrain are familiar, even generic, but not related to a specific liturgical, biblical, or theological text; instead, it emerges from within the tradition and poetic conventions of devotional Latin song and trope.

Within this song tradition, certain refrains formed a special currency of familiar and communal responses, refrains that communities of singers and scribes knew from other songs or tropes and could insert or add on to other works. Testifying to the choral, if not also communal, nature of several of the refrains included in Graz is the rubrication and scribal cueing in two sources with concordances, the fourteenth-century Seckauer Cantionarium and the fifteenth-century service book with devotional songs and tropes, SG 392.[46] In both these contexts, refrains in common with the Graz sources are preceded by the rubric "chorus," a marker of performance practice. In SG 392, the song is the mensurally notated *Nove*

---

[46] On the songs in the Seckauer Cantionarium, see Irtenkauf, "Das Seckauer Cantionarium" and Brewer, "In Search of Lost Melodies." On SG 392, see Fischer, "Neue Quellen," 296–301; *Nove lucis hodie* is edited on 298–299.

lucis hodie, in which the "apparuit" refrain is sung as a choral, monophonic response following polyphonic strophes. The first polyphonic strophe is notated successively, culminating not with the refrain, but instead with the text-only recording of the following two strophes. The refrain is written after this *residuum*, doubly cued in the left and right margins by scribes as a choral response (see Figure 4.3). The incipit alone of the refrain appears after the third entry of the first strophe ("apparuit," at the end of the fourth system on p. 89); the complete music and text of the refrain, as seen in Figure 4.3, arrive only at the conclusion of the strophes in a manner similar to the Graz sources.

In another manuscript with concordances in the Graz sources, the Seckauer Cantionarium, the song *Stella nova radiat* (which appears as Figures 3.7 and 3.8 in Chapter 3) cues its refrain beginning "ergo novis" first by means of "chor." (chorus) and then "pueri." Considering the concordances for these performative refrains in the Graz collections, it is tempting to imagine a similarly choral performance practice in the Abbey of St. Lambrecht, one in which a curated collection of familiar, perhaps even memorized, refrains could serve a range of songs, readily recalled and interjected by the choir. The circulation of the "apparuit" refrain in particular, along with its monophonic choral performance inscribed in SG 392, certainly points in the direction of a refrain practice that was rooted equally in performance and inscription.

The other four shared refrains in the Graz sources present a more challenging perspective on the mobility of music and text than the "apparuit" refrain. The "gaudeat" refrain cued most often across the two Graz sources, and especially in Graz 409, is the slipperiest of all the shared refrains in the two manuscripts in terms of its identity and repetition. In eight songs, only the single word "gaudeat" appears as a cue; for the remaining three songs, two possible "gaudeat" refrains are provided: "gaudeat, gaudeat, gaudeat ecclesia" in *Novi partus gaudium* and *Verbum patris humanatur*, and "gaudeat omnis homo" in *Sata tria fert Maria*. Moreover, of the twelve total songs with the "gaudeat" refrain cue, seven have concordances, and none of these transmit anything resembling a refrain beginning "gaudeat." Only two songs, *Verbum patris humanatur* and *Ecce venit de Syon*, have concordances in sources outside of Graz 409 that employ structural refrains, in neither case beginning with "gaudeat."

What kind of refrain, then, is "gaudeat"? It is unquestionably different from the "apparuit" refrain, however similarly the two refrains are treated and cued in the Graz sources. Thanks to its distribution throughout twelve songs, concentrated especially in Graz 409, the "gaudeat" refrain connects a

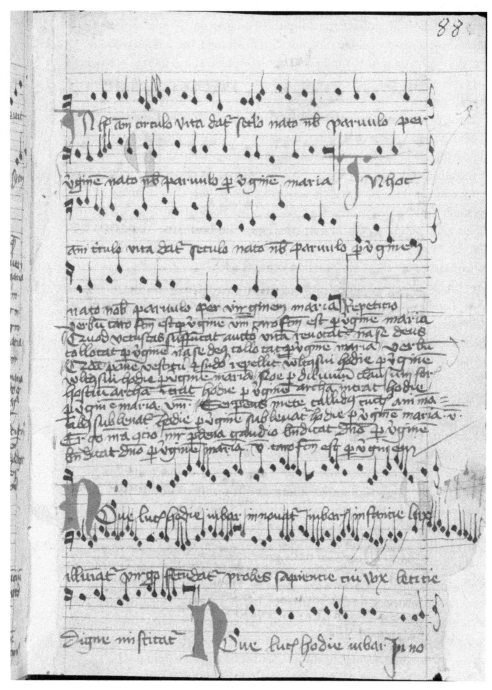

Figure 4.3 SG 392, pp. 88–89, *Nove lucis hodie*. Reproduced by kind permission of the Stiftsbibliothek St. Gallen

Figure 4.3 (cont.)

significant network of songs and concordances outside of the Graz manuscripts. Moreover, the refrain itself – or at least its incipit – occurs across a
trio of songs in the twelfth-century Aquitanian *versarium* St-M A. In these
three songs, the refrain is both musically and textually variable, linked by
means of the incipit "gaudeat." In *Nunc clericorum concio* and *Congaudeat
ecclesia* (fols. 33^v and 51^r), the refrain is "gaudeat homo" and in *Regi nato
Domino* (fol. 41^v), the refrain is "gaudeat omnis homo," the same textual
refrain found in the Graz sources for *Sata tria fert Maria*.[47] The "gaudeat"
refrain serves a structural role in each song in St-M A, as well as in *Sata tria
fert Maria*, although it manifests differently in each. The similarity, as
Margaret Switten observes, relates "songs in a wider universe"; the fact
that they are not identical does not matter as much as their recognizable
similarity, or family resemblance. These "gaudeat" refrains are generic in
sentiment; their repetition – or better, perhaps, their resonance – across
songs is less the act of direct quotation or citation, and more about a shared,
responsorial vocabulary of rejoicing.

Within the Graz sources alone, the "gaudeat" refrain links a disparate
group of songs. Unlike "psallat cum tripudio" and "apparuit," "gaudeat" is
not connected primarily to refrain forms; in fact, a striking characteristic of
this refrain tag in the Graz manuscripts is that it is appended to songs
whose concordances do not feature refrains. Only two songs, cited above,
include structural refrains outside of Graz, and in neither instance does the
refrain resemble any version of the "gaudeat" refrain. *Ecce venit de Syon* in
particular is illustrative both of how refrains functioned independently of
song and how a song's strophes could be ordered, copied, and probably
sung in a similarly fluid manner. Eight manuscript sources transmit the
Christmas song *Ecce venit de Syon* (or *Sion*, depending on source); of these,
five transmit the refrain "eia et eia iubilando | resonet ecclesia," and the
remaining three transmit either no refrain or, in the case of Graz 409, the
single-word cue "gaudeat." Moreover, in only two sources are an identical
number of strophes arranged identically (Engelberg 102 and Stuttg); across
all other sources, the strophes are variable in number and order, although
they share several core strophes.[48] The modular construction of *Ecce venit
de Syon* is readily apparent, the stability of the song's identity resting on the
transmission of certain core elements rather than on an identical number

---

[47] Switten, "Versus and Troubadours," 102.

[48] For a similarly modular approach, see *Congaudeat turba fidelium*, analyzed in Chapter 2. There
are nine distinct strophes in *Ecce venit de Syon* distributed differently across eight sources, each
with between five and seven total strophes and with four strophes in common across all sources;
the final strophe in SG 1397 uniquely includes a lectionary formula.

and ordering of strophes – or, for that matter, on the presence or absence of a refrain.[49]

The inclusion and exclusion of refrains in the transmission of *Ecce venit de Syon* from the twelfth-century Hortus Deliciarum to the fifteenth-century St. Pölten Processional suggest that the refrain was a modular, fluid component of the song. Since the song is strophic and not a *rondellus*, the addition or subtraction does not disturb the scansion of the poem; indeed, all Latin refrains circulating with a degree of independence are attached to strophic songs and not *rondelli*. What is unusual about *Ecce venit de Syon* is not necessarily that some versions are transmitted without a refrain, but that there are two possible refrains with which it is sung. In the case of songs with the "apparuit" refrain, by comparison, the refrain is reused, but the songs themselves do not employ different refrains in different sources. Yet between Graz 258 and 409, a scribe has chosen to include the "eya et eya" refrain of *Ecce venit de Syon* in the former, rubricated with a capital "V" following the formatting of the previous strophes, and "gaudeat" in the latter. In Graz 258, a different hand has then added a single word after the "eya et eya" refrain, "gaudet" (see Figure 4.4). Is it possible the scribe who added "gaudet" did not notice that the song already had a refrain and he was adding a cue based, for instance, on the refrain cue included in Graz 409? In Graz 409, the "eya et eya" refrain is not included, and therefore the scribe does not "double up" on refrains.[50] Another question might be whether the "gaudet" of Graz 258 can be understood as a cue for the "gaudeat" refrain; the missing vowel and different scribal hand could suggest a later addition made in error, or even a mistaken attempt to copy the strophe beginning "Gaudet asinus et bos." In either case, it remains true that the refrain of *Ecce venit de Syon* varies between the two Graz sources, and that these two refrains themselves circulate more broadly.

The written-out "eya et eya" refrain of *Ecce venit de Syon* in Graz 258 is, in fact, also appended to a song unique to Graz 409, *Nuntio dum credidit*,

---

[49] Only the Moosburger Graduale and St. Pölten Processional transmit transcribable musical notation, both bearing a recognizably similar melody for strophes and refrain. Two other Christmas songs, *Puer natus in Betlehem* and *Puer nobis nascitur*, are similarly transmitted with variable strophes and both with and without a refrain, which is itself also variable.

[50] Similarly, the song *Verbum patris humanatur* travels with an identical refrain across all concordances ("eia et eia, | nova gaudia," sometimes with minor variants), yet in Graz 409 the scribe has added "gaudeat" after the final strophe. The layout of *Verbum patris humanatur*, however, does not indicate the function of the "eia et eia" repetition as a refrain with rubrication, capital letters, or ink color, methods employed for refrains that uniquely travel with individual songs.

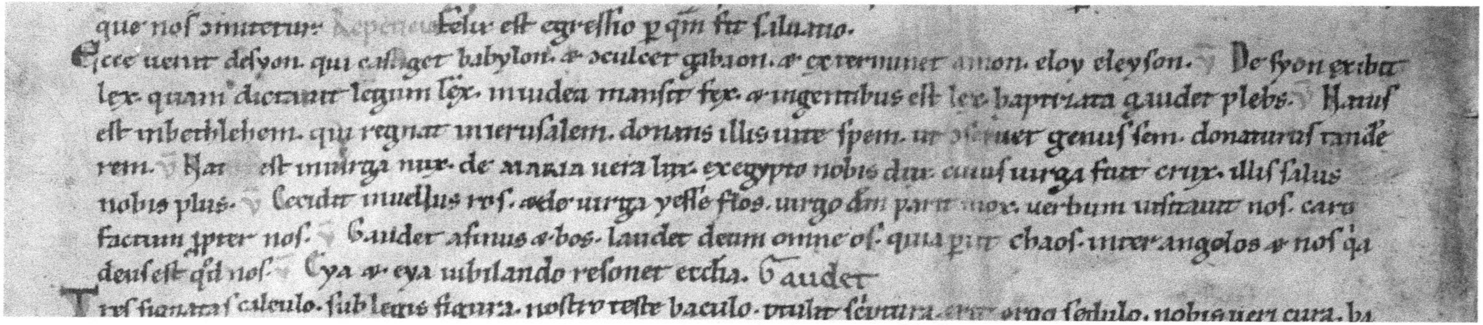

Figure 4.4 Graz 258, fol. 2ᵛ, *Ecce venit de Syon*. Reproduced by kind permission of the Universitätsbibliothek, Graz

where it is copied in full following its final strophe. Three other songs in the Graz sources also have refrains similarly beginning with "eia." Two songs – *Salve maris stella* and *Primus homo cum pro pomo* – include either the abbreviation "eia et eia" in the former, or "eia" in the latter; the third, *Tres signatas calculo*, transmits a longer, unique refrain beginning "eia dicit canticum." Considering the presence of two longer refrains beginning with "eia," the abbreviated cues are ambiguous.[51] The "eia et eia" refrain cue of *Salve maris stella* probably points to the refrain of *Ecce venit de Syon* and *Nuntio dum credidit* thanks to the duplicated "eias" linked by "et"; the single "eia" in *Primus homo cum pro pomo*, on the other hand, could indicate either refrain. Since the "eia et eia iubilando | resonet ecclesia" refrain appears to be more widely known, at least by the scribal community at St. Lambrecht, then I would suggest that this was the intended realization of the cue in *Primus homo cum pro pomo*. Significantly, this is yet another song whose concordances in two later manuscripts of the troped Feast of the Circumcision (Le Puy A and B) lack a refrain. The only song that circulates beyond the Graz sources with the "eia et eia" refrain is *Ecce venit de Syon*. One possible scenario is that this refrain was initially familiar from *Ecce venit de Syon* and then recycled by singers and scribes at the Abbey of St. Lambrecht. Although this does not explain the absence of the refrain in *Ecce venit de Syon* transmitted in Graz 409, it might explain why it became associated with two songs unique to the Graz sources (*Salve maris stella* and *Nuntio dum credidit*), as well as with a song that was circulating more widely without a refrain, *Primus homo cum pro pomo*.

The final two shared refrains, beginning "sonet vox leticie" and "hei in ista die," exhibit some of the same characteristics and ambiguities as the "gaudeat" and "eia et eia" refrains. The refrain beginning "hei in ista die" is attached to only two songs in Graz 409, one of which, *Deinceps ex nulla*, is found in the Moosburger Graduale with the same refrain. The other song, *Paris preter morem*, is transmitted more widely in both text-only and polyphonic settings, but never with a refrain. Moreover, what appears in concordant sources as a single strophe of *Paris preter morem* is copied by the scribe of Graz 409 in such a way as to suggest that the lengthy strophe was chopped up in performance into shorter units, using capital letters and red highlighting to apply internal, if irregular, divisions. What results is a pseudo-strophic form for *Paris preter morem* that would have enabled the

---

[51] Notably beyond the songs in the Graz sources, refrains in over a dozen different Latin songs begin with some permutation or repetition of "eia," although never identical to the two discussed here. "Eia" was simply one of the most popular ejaculatory refrains in Latin songs and tropes; Iversen, "Verba canendi," 1:455, and Caldwell, "Texting Vocality."

scribe's added refrain, "hei in ista die," to be performed between these newly created strophic divisions.[52] The scribe of Graz 409, in other words, adapts and reworks the song's form on multiple levels.

A similar situation obtains for the refrain beginning "sonet vox leticie." Three songs, all in Graz 409, carry a refrain cue, and in the case of *Gaude Syon iubila*, a written-out refrain beginning "sonet vox letitice." *Gaude Syon iubila*, moreover, has a concordance in the St. Pölten Processional, where the same refrain is regularly cued between strophes. Of the other two songs, *Hostis perfidus et invidus* is unique to Graz, and *Nove geniture* survives in several sources as text-only and for one or two voices. In all its sources, *Nove geniture* includes a short repeating line at the end of each strophe, "nato Christo"; in the majority of sources, including Graz 409, this line is not marked off as a refrain, however, and instead is grammatically and scribally integrated into each strophe.[53] Only in the Moosburger Graduale does rubrication identify "nato Christo" as a refrain in a variant version of the song. It seems likely that the scribe of Graz 409, like most scribes who copied this song in other sources, did not consider "nato Christo" to function as a refrain, and so – in keeping with the broader project of adding structural refrains to strophic songs in both Graz sources – they appended the cue "sonet vox letitice" to suggest the performance of this refrain between the five strophes of *Nove geniture*. As with the "eia et eia" refrain, we might envision a similar process by which the refrain from a better-known song, in this case *Gaude Syon iubila*, is repurposed for other songs, even those that may already carry their own refrain in some sources.[54]

Throughout the Latin song collections of Graz 258 and 409, we witness the malleability, fluidity, and transformability of Latin song and refrain. Whether reflecting performing practices at the Abbey of St. Lambrecht or a more personalized agenda, the almost excessive interest in Latin refrains on the part of the scribes is a local phenomenon with reverberations

[52] As Thomas Payne notes regarding its textual form in F, *Parit preter morem* is "perhaps the most ostentatiously fashioned *rithmus* in the Parisian corpus," which might be attributable to its musical and poetic relationship to the trouvère song *Pieça que savoie* in Trouv U. Payne, "Latin Song II," 1054. *Parit preter morem* survives with music in three polyphonic settings; the lowermost voice is related to the French *chanson Pieça que savoie*, in Trouv U, fol. 48ᵛ. See Spanke, "Studien," 222–224 and Gennrich, "Lateinische Kontrafakta," 196–201. The irregularity of *Parit preter morem* may also have more easily permitted the scribe of Graz 409 to manipulate its strophic form.
[53] On the polyphonic settings of *Nove geniture*, see Anderson, "Nove Geniture." Edited and translated in Anderson, ed., *Notre-Dame and Related Conductus*, 4:xiv.
[54] The refrain-line "sonet vox leticie" (or "letitie") also travels among Latin song in a formulaic manner similar to "psallat vox tripudia"; see Caldwell, "Texting Vocality."

throughout sources of Latin song. One of the key features of the refrains shared and recycled among songs in the Graz sources and elsewhere is their origins; unlike those reworked and borrowed from the liturgy and biblical texts, these refrains emanate from and are constructed around the performative vocabulary and grammar of Latin song. The origins of these refrains are, consequently, diffuse and unspecific. The mobility of individual refrains, moreover, speaks to the wider orbit of Latin song and refrain and the role of memory and inscription in performance, transmission, and adaptation. Most strikingly, Latin refrains emerge from the Graz sources as both the remembered and transferable parts of song, initiated in the abbreviated repetition of the refrain across folios. The regularly irregular refrain cues mark the ability of refrains to be cued from memory while also potentially reflecting performing practices that involved the addition, subtraction, and reworking of refrains in strophic Latin song.

Cueing practices inevitably reveal something about the workings of the refrain at the level of performance, as well as expectations concerning form and genre, and this is taken to an extreme in the Graz sources.[55] As Ingrid Nelson writes with respect to the English lyric, "written lyrics often bear witness in their very incompleteness to their survival in other contexts: in the popular memory, for instance, and in performance."[56] The material life of the Latin refrain in the Graz sources suggests most acutely its existence in the memory of its performers and through the very act of performance itself. As refrains circulate within and beyond the Graz sources, they bear witness to wider intertextual networks within repertoires of Latin song, linking songs and sources separated by centuries and regional borders, and highlighting how different communities adopted, adapted, performed, and copied a corpus of Latin song that belonged both to everyone and to no one.

Conclusion: Refrains in Song, Memory, and Text

Although often overlooked, the complexities of the Latin refrain and its genealogies highlight tensions in medieval Latin song between fixity and fluidity, repetition and variation, and memory and inscription. This chapter has explored the Latin refrain from several related perspectives that

---

[55] See especially Caldwell, "Cueing Refrains." In the context of vernacular song, see Butterfield, *Poetry and Music*.

[56] Nelson, *Lyric Tactics*, 8. See also Butterfield, "Poems without Form?," 194.

reveal intertextual networks of song and refrain rooted in, and expressed through, composition, performance, and inscription. Importantly, examining the ways in which the Latin refrain serves as a locus for practices of reworking and intertextuality both shifts it closer and pushes it farther away from the cultural workings of the intertextual French *refrain*. While the Latin refrain mirrors some of the mobility of the French *refrain*, the reworking and recycling of refrains in Latin song are not signals of a citational poetic and musical practice, nor are they invocations of *auctoritas*, as has been argued for the intertextual French *refrain*. The Latin refrains I discuss in this chapter are self-referential; they chiefly emerge from and belong to the repertoire of Latin song itself; its language, conventions, poetic and musical contours, and meaning as an expression of the collective yet unified voice of devotional communities.

As the examples throughout the chapter demonstrate, and perhaps most especially the gatherings of songs in the Graz manuscripts, intertextuality and mobility go hand in hand with memory and inscription. A tension emerges within networks of Latin song and refrain between memory, performance, and inscription, revealed in scribal habits around refrains. When copied on the manuscript page, refrains inevitably sit at the edge of the written record, inscribed and cued incompletely and inconsistently in ways that gesture toward the realization of refrains beyond the witness of the written page. Even absent the scribal ambiguities in the Graz sources, the Latin refrain is the part of song that simultaneously remains firmly in the ear and in performance, even while disappearing off the page, as it is progressively abbreviated by scribes upon each return, cued with briefer and briefer textual gestures.[57]

I have continually returned to the idea that refrains are inherently memorable. Refrains are memorable not only through their relative simplicity and brevity, a feature of many Latin refrains, but also through their repetition, much in the same way that earworms embed themselves in one's aural memory.[58] When refrains repeat across a repertoire of songs, or are themselves reworked from snippets of familiar songs, they become memorable on a different plane, housed in the multigenerational and collective memory of the scribes and singers responsible for crafting, performing, and

---

[57] This is typical for most manuscript sources of Latin refrain songs; see Caldwell, "Cueing Refrains."

[58] Margulis, *On Repeat, passim* but especially ch. 4.

copying devotional Latin song. In the next chapter, I continue following the refrain as it traverses the boundaries of individual songs. Yet, rather than focusing on Latin contexts alone, I consider the ways in which refrains move across language through contrafacture, extending the memories and genealogies of the refrain into repertoires of French, German, and English song.

5 | Retexting Refrains

Latin and Vernacular Refrains in Contact

Language is key to the identity and meaning of the Latin refrain song, delineating the communities for whom Latin is a shared language of education, devotion, and communication. In the previous chapter I explored the mobility and memorability of refrains, showing how text and music travel from liturgy to song, and among songs, and circulate by both written and unwritten means. Importantly, these itinerant refrains are all Latin. The Latinity of the refrain song fosters its mobility and wide-reaching transmission, the shared language of the church and its texts making it possible for disparate communities and institutions to adopt the refrain song for their own purposes or create entirely new devotional songs.[1] Yet these communities of clerics, monks, and students learned Latin as a second language; their first language was that of their family, town, and region.[2] In other words, a vernacular language.

The Latin refrain song reflects the varied vernacular contexts of its composers, poets, and performers chiefly through contrafacture, the sharing of a melody by two or more texts in the same or different languages.[3] Although contrafacture is not a core feature of medieval Latin song in the same way that it is for the motet or liturgical sequence, for instance, clusters of Latin contrafacts (both pairs of Latin songs, and Latin and vernacular songs) emerge in certain manuscripts, associated with particular poets or narrative works, or emanating from specific milieus.[4] The refrain in Latin song represents a special formal nexus for contrafacture across language; through contrafacture, refrains repeat across the boundaries not only of individual songs, but also language, time, and place. Although a close relationship between Latin and vernacular refrain forms is often assumed due to the formal parallels between the French *rondeau* and Latin *rondellus*,

---

[1] See, for instance, the example of the final strophe of *Qui passus est pridie*, which is altered in its three concordant sources to better designate the local context; Caldwell, "*Pax Gallie*," 121–122.

[2] Murphy, "Teaching of Latin."

[3] For a clear definition and overview of contrafacture, see O'Sullivan, "Contrafacture."

[4] O'Sullivan, "On connaît la chanson"; Deeming, "Music, Memory and Mobility" and "Multilingual Networks"; Everist, *Discovering Medieval Song*, 248–262; Murray, *Poetry in Motion*, 27–83; and Quinlan, "Repetition as Rebirth."

the similarity of form does not necessarily suggest the more intimate relationship implied by contrafacture, which involves the sharing of music as well as formal characteristics. Contrafacture – instances in which music is shared explicitly or implicitly across texts – provides a more nuanced perspective on these oft-cited formal parallels and the ways in which the Latin refrain song was, or was not, influenced by vernacular song and refrain, and vice versa.

In this chapter I explore the refrain as an axis between Latin and vernacular song, focusing on what the concentration of contrafacts in a small number of unique manuscripts reveals concerning the interpenetration of song cultures and their languages across Europe. Reflecting highly localized processes of production and transmission, three manuscripts are at the center of Latin refrain song contrafacture: the late thirteenth-century St-Victor Miscellany, copied in the environs of Paris and its schools; the fourteenth-century Engelberg Codex, copied in an abbey scriptorium in Engelberg, Switzerland; and the late fourteenth-century Red Book of Ossory, originating from the diocese of Ossory in Ireland.[5] These manuscripts demonstrate limited connections to the broader transmission of Latin song, with few concordances, although the poetry and, when extant, music share numerous formal, stylistic, and thematic features with the wider repertoire of Latin refrain songs.

While the three manuscripts are chronologically and geographically disparate, they are linked by the way their collections of Latin refrain songs are transmitted on the page. In each manuscript, Latin refrain songs are accompanied by scribal rubrics and marginalia that cue the text, form, and music of vernacular song. Before or beside Latin poems, in other words, scribes copied short, lyrical fragments in French, German, and English, transforming intertexts into paratexts and alluding to the sharing of poetic form and music; importantly, these fragments are, in the majority of cases, vernacular refrains that correspond directly to Latin refrains. However, two of the three sources – the St-Victor Miscellany and the Red Book of Ossory – transmit only unnotated songs, while the Engelberg Codex lacks notation for six of its nine marginally annotated songs. Since the practice of contrafacture is rooted in the sharing of melodies, the absence of notation is unsurprising. The vernacular fragments, or refrains, behave in many ways like musical notation; knowledge of the melody attached to a given vernacular text enables the musical realization of the Latin poem. Independently of one another, the St-Victor Miscellany, Engelberg Codex, and Red Book of Ossory

---

[5] Bibliographic details for each manuscript are provided in the individual sections below.

treat the Latin and vernacular refrain in similar ways by using a formal component of song to initiate formal links and generate musical meaning in the absence of notation.

Although scribal and textual practices in these manuscripts make musical notation unnecessary, they assume an audience familiar with the melodies of vernacular song and refrain. Contrafacture always signals a layer of meaning accessible only to individuals belonging to communities within which sets of texts, melodies, and contrafacts already circulated; even when scribal paratexts elucidate a particular relationship, the audience still requires prior knowledge of vernacular music, form, and poetry. A singer's relationship to an individual song in any of the three manuscripts discussed in this chapter would change depending on their familiarity with each work in the contrafact pair, or in some cases, cluster, shaping meaning, interpretation, and ultimately performance.[6] Moreover, the textual persistence of the vernacular in these collections of Latin song and poetry is a reminder that, however deeply embedded through liturgy and education, Latin was a learned language and always circulated alongside vernacular tongues for the creators, scribes, and singers of the Latin refrain song. The St-Victor Miscellany, Engelberg Codex, and Red Book of Ossory bear witness to the multilinguality of medieval song communities, blurring through the lens of the refrain the linguistic boundaries that often define and divide medieval song repertoires.

Contrafacture and the Latin Refrain Song

What counts as a contrafact? Most often, identification of contrafacts derives from recognition of a shared melodic material by sight or sound. How much must be shared to "count" is part of the question, as is the degree to which the text and its poetic and formal characteristics must also be shared.[7] The degree of sameness is important in terms of distinguishing between contrafacture and other forms of borrowing and citation, in which music might be shared but other elements such as form are not. Judging sameness is especially challenging for the Latin refrain songs in the three

---

[6] See, for example, O'Sullivan's proposal of the term "kaleidoscopic" to describe the at-times "dizzying" ways in which links could have been made between and among songs through contrafacture; "On connaît la chanson," 120.

[7] On the historiography of contrafacture, including efforts to create typologies and criteria beginning with Friedrich Gennrich, see O'Sullivan, "Contrafacture."

manuscripts at the center of this chapter. Although Latin and vernacular song is textually linked by scribes, music rarely survives, and never for both a Latin song and its vernacular counterpart – the degree of musical correspondence, in other words, is impossible to determine. Situating the process of contrafacture in the refrain, however, offers insight into the formal and, to a degree, poetic parallels between Latin and vernacular works. The refrain creates an expectation of form and poetic structure that fosters a degree of similarity across language.

The potential of the refrain to produce certain formal expectations in the process of contrafacture is a likely factor in its popularity among poets and composers: Latin–vernacular contrafacts cluster decidedly around refrain forms. Of the total number of songs in the Appendix, around 12 percent are part of contrafact pairs or families; this compares to roughly 8 percent of all medieval Latin song being identified as contrafacts, of which over 4 percent represent refrain forms.[8] Refrain-form songs unquestionably participate in contrafacture more often than non-refrain forms. This can partially be attributed to the weightiness of refrains. Although typically representing only a small portion of text, the refrain carries a great deal of information. Refrains convey something about form, namely the presence of repetitive structures, and in many cases the poetry and musical settings of refrains mirror or anticipate those of surrounding strophes; this is certainly the case for the *rondellus*. The refrain is also a memorable part of a song, perhaps more so than its incipit. As illustrated in the previous chapter, Latin

---

[8] Outside of the St-Victor Miscellany, Engelberg Codex, and Red Book of Ossory, I am aware of only nine refrain-form Latin–vernacular contrafact pairs: *Beata viscera* and two French songs by Gautier de Coinci (*De la Saint Leocade* and *Entendez tuit ensemble*); *Decet vox letitie*, *Ave mater salvatoris*, and the French *refrain Tout leis enmi les prez*; *Fidelium sonet vox sobria* and the Galician-Portuguese *Maldito seja quen non loará*; Adam de la Bassée's *Nobilitas ornata moribus* on the melody of the unidentified *Qui grieve ma cointise*; *Salve virgo virginum parens* and *Veine pleine de ducur*; *Sol sub nube latuit*, *Chanter et renvoisier seuil* (Thibaut de Blason), and *Por mon chief* (Gautier de Coinci); *Veni sancte spiritus* [C] and the French *refrain En ma dame ai mis mon cuer*; and *Veris ad imperia* and *A l'entrada del tens cler*. *Veni sancte spiritus* [A] is followed in Basel B.XI.8 by a German text, although it does not appear to retain the refrain. Most of these works are listed in Everist, *Discovering Medieval Song*, 257–258, and the Appendix lists these and other Latin contrafacts with their sources, but not the related vernacular works. The refrain song *In hoc statu gratie* has been identified as a contrafact of the French *pastourelle Huimain par un ajournant* by Friedrich Gennrich, a view which was echoed by later scholars, although there does not appear to be any melodic relationship. Additionally, Anderson and others have posited *Ecce mundi gaudium* as a contrafact of *Lonc tens ai use ma vie* (Trouv P, fol. 195ʳ–195ᵛ and the Chansonnier de Clairambault, fol. 262ʳ–262ᵛ); Anderson, ed., *Notre-Dame and Related Conductus*, 8:59. Little melodic evidence supports this claim either.

On contrafacture and Latin song, see specifically Gennrich, "Lateinische Kontrafakta" and *Lateinische Liedkontrafaktur*, 75; Tischler, *Conductus and Contrafacta*, 75; and Everist, *Discovering Medieval Song*, 248–262.

refrains were both constructed from familiar texts and circulated among songs and communities; through different means, the French *refrain* also circulated among genres and contexts, marked off as distinctive, recognizable, and memorable. Refrains offered something special to scribes and singers – a unit of text (and in some cases music) rich with potential meaning as it repeats within and across song and language.

In the retexting of refrains, meaning is not only transmitted, but shared between two or more songs, knowledge of each work in a contrafact complex informing the understanding of the other(s). With contrafacture, cross-song resonances are always possible, although resonances vary depending on the access a scribe, singer, or listeners has to all the works in a contrafact network and the order in which they are exposed to each work.[9] For contrafacts lacking textual cues or markers, it is possible to be unaware of relationships to other works via the melody and form. When contrafacture is inscribed on the page, however, an immediate visual, textual, and aural connection is engendered that persists for each new user of the manuscript. Even if – as for modern scholars – the songs cued in rubrics and the margins are unfamiliar, the sensation of hearing more than one song is nevertheless produced.[10] Moreover, when cued songs are unknown, the new texts and, when available, musical settings, allow us to extend our hearing into this lacuna, however imperfectly – the exchange of information goes in both directions. In our trio of manuscripts, this bidirectional flow enables glimpses into, for instance, repertoires of German and English *rondeaux*, as well as the early history of certain French *refrains*.

One well-examined resonance between contrafacts relates to poetic register, and specifically between sacred and secular texts. Contrafacture can enable the implicit or explicit conversion of secular texts toward devotional purposes, as was the case for Gautier de Coinci's widely transmitted *Miracles de Nostre Dame*.[11] By extension, secular vernacular texts can be replaced by pious Latin texts, further magnifying the process of conversion not only by thematic redirection, but also by linguistic change. This has remained a frequent interpretation for the Latin songs of the St-Victor Miscellany,

---

[9] Deeming, "Multilingual Networks." See also O'Sullivan, "Contrafacture," on contrafacture as "kaleidoscopic."

[10] Helen Deeming has termed the resonance produced by contrafacture "virtual polyphony" for those who knew both works; the substitution of one text for another to a single melody does not erase the existence of the original text or vice versa. "Music, Memory and Mobility," 67.

[11] Butterfield, *Poetry and Music*, 104–115; Switten, "Borrowing, Citation, and Authorship"; Duys, "Performing Vernacular Song"; and Quinlan, "Repetition as Rebirth."

Engelberg Codex, and Red Book of Ossory. However, although the Latin song poems they transmit are entirely devotional, the vernacular songs with which they are associated are not so clearly secular, as I discuss later in this chapter. While the textualization of vernacular song may be interpreted as confirmation of, and emphasis on, the textual conversion from secular to sacred, vernacular to Latin, in these three manuscripts this is only one possibility, and not a fully convincing one. Instead, the regularity and persistence of the vernacular alongside Latin refrain song contrafacts ensures that works are repeatedly read and heard against one another in a way that suggests a continuing discourse rather than a moment of conversion.

Finally, the textual cues and markers found in these three manuscripts are rare among medieval song sources more generally.[12] In the case of Latin–vernacular contrafacts, cueing happens almost exclusively in the absence of music for one or both works in the contrafact pair, and is overwhelmingly concentrated in the witnesses of the St-Victor Miscellany, Engelberg Codex, and Red Book of Ossory.[13] Scribal paratexts indicating contrafacture represent an exceptional rather than quotidian practice. Yet the highly localized songs and scribal habits in these three sources simultaneously speak beyond their disparate points of origin to a trans-European interest in the refrain as a point of formal contact between Latin and vernacular song repertoires. Their parallel treatment of the relationship between Latin and vernacular song attests to the agency of refrains and refrain forms in larger cultural discourses around song, language, and meaning. In what follows, I examine each manuscript in turn, beginning with the St-Victor Miscellany in the late thirteenth century and ending with the Red Book of Ossory in the fourteenth century, exploring how song and refrain interact on the page and the implications

---

[12] For references to the textual cueing of contrafacture, with an emphasis on the developing nomenclature of the procedure, see Falck, "Parody and Contrafactum."

[13] Two additional Latin refrain song contrafacts survive with manuscript cues outside of the trio of manuscripts discussed here (see also n. 8, above): *Salve virgo virginum parens* and *Veine pleine de ducur*, copied one after the other in Arundel 248, fol. 155^r, and *Nobilitas ornata moribus* in Adam de la Bassée's thirteenth-century *Ludus super Anticlaudianum*, headed by a descriptive rubric reading "Cantilena de chorea super illam que incipit *Qui grieve ma cointise se iou l'ai? Ce me font amouretes c'au cuer ai*" ("Song of the dance upon that which begins *Qui* ... "). *Ludus super Anticlaudianum*, fol. 36^r. On the former, see Deeming, "Multilingual Networks," 130–131. On contrafacture in the *Ludus*, see Hughes, "Adam de la Bassée"; Barnard, "Journey of the Soul"; and O'Sullivan, "On connaît la chanson." One further manuscript includes a vernacular annotation in the margins of a bilingual (Latin and French) song; however, this refrain appears within the song itself (*De papa scholastico* in Paris lat. 11331, fol. 12^r). See Butterfield, *Poetry and Music*, 187 and 305, and Latzke, "Zu dem Gedicht 'De papa scolastico.'" Finally, ORawl transmits a fragment of a sacred English lyric in the midst of its Latin *conducti* on fol. 232^r; Hunt, "Collections," 34.

of this for our understanding of Latin as well as vernacular song and refrain throughout medieval Europe.

French *Refrains* as Rubrics in a Parisian Miscellany

The earliest of the three sources for Latin contrafacts of vernacular refrain songs, the St-Victor Miscellany, dates from after 1289, a date provided by the poetry copied in its final folios alongside epistolatory materials – letters – pertaining in many cases to the abbey school of St-Denis, its teachers, and its students.[14] Rather than organized according to type, Latin and bilingual (Latin, French, and Greek) poems and Latin letters alternate freely, with individual items numbered sequentially in the margins by a later hand. While the letters deal with more practical matters than the poems, thematic links do appear, as with references across texts to particular feast days (notably St. Nicholas, a patron saint of students). The collection of verse and epistolary materials in the Miscellany suggests a compiler working in a milieu that was multilingual and intellectual. Several of the poems include words, lines, or partial strophes in French and Greek and details in the letters point to the figure of a grammar school master, capable, among other things, of citing Horace.[15]

While notation is neither included nor was space left for its addition, the musical identity of the Latin poems in the St-Victor Miscellany has long been acknowledged. In part, this is due to the nature of the poems themselves as *rithmi*, which conveys a degree of inherent musicality and performance. A more revealing feature is the presence of French *refrains* in the form of rubrics, frequently accompanied by a brief Latin phrase that describes the relationship between the *refrain* and subsequent text: "contra in latino" ("conversely in Latin"). Identified by Robert Falck as "a kind of 'prehistory' for the term contrafactum," the combination of French *refrain*

---

[14] "Anno Christi millesimo | Et quater quinquagesimo," fol. 182ᵛ; 1288 is in the Old Style, making the date 1289 in the context of the modern calendar; the same lyric discusses the flooding of the Seine River in Paris. On the dating of the miscellany, see Hauréau, *Notice*, 268–269, and Thomas, "Refrains français," 499–500. Further confirmation of a post-1288 date may be offered by one of the more unusual refrains that mentions the burning of Jews; on this, see later in this chapter and ibid., 507, n. 1. For the broader context of the letters, including reference to Orleans, see Haskins, "Life of Medieval Students."

[15] Hauréau, *Notice*, 272. On the bilingual poems in the miscellany, see Meyer, "Chanson" and "Chansons religieuses"; and Zumthor, "Un problème d'esthétique médiévale," 329–331.

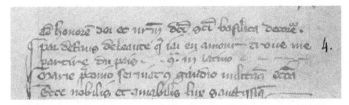

Figure 5.1 St-Victor Miscellany, fol. 177ʳ, *Marie preconio* with French *refrain* and "contra in latino." Reproduced by kind permission of the Bibliothèque nationale de France

and the term "contra" in the rubrics of the Miscellany has established its Latin poems as integral to the tradition of medieval contrafacture, if not as prime examples of the practice.[16]

Each rubricated Latin poem in the St-Victor Miscellany, moreover, employs a refrain; poems lacking rubrication invariably lack refrains. It is not only remarkable that these seventeen refrain-form poems are associated with French song; in this case explicit scribal cues for vernacular song uniformly predict the presence of a refrain (see Table 5.1).[17] As the *mise en page* makes clear, the French *refrains* were copied at the same time as the poems they introduce by the same hand (see Figure 5.1). Rather than additions or emendations, the *refrains* are integral to poems as they uniquely survive in the St-Victor Miscellany. In the layout of the poems, the French *refrains* are neither marginal nor visually subordinated to the Latin texts. Rather, the layout underscores the importance of the *refrains* as an interpretive, formal, and musical framework for the Latin poems that follow.

From the perspective of form, the French *refrains* and the works they signal outside of the Miscellany appear to correspond with the poetic and formal structures of the Latin poetry. To take *Marie preconio* from Figure 5.1 as a further example, the French *refrain* serving as its rubric survives in Douce 308 (fol. 214ʳ⁻ᵛ [226ʳ⁻ᵛ]) in the context of a *ballette à refrain*, a courtly love song.[18] Comparing the French

---

16 Falck, "Parody and Contrafactum," 15. See also Gennrich, "Lateinische Kontrafakta" and Stevens, *Words and Music*, 181.

17 Since the songs begin with an iteration of the refrain, I use the refrain's incipit as the title here and throughout. French *refrains* are listed according to their number in van den Boogaard, *Rondeaux et refrains*, 316. See also Thomas, "Refrains français" and Meyer, "Table" and "Chansons religieuses."

18 Edited and translated in Doss-Quinby, Rosenberg, and Aubrey, eds., *Old French Ballette*, 102–107.

Table 5.1 Poems with *refrain* rubrics in the St-Victor Miscellany

	Refrain	Incipit of first strophe	Occasion	Rubric	Folio	vdB #
1	Marie preconio / Serviat cum gaudio / Militans ecclesia	Ecce nobilis	Virgin	Par defaus de leaute que j'ai en amour trove me partire du pais. contra in latino	177^r	vdB 1476
2	Syon concio / Ana iubilet / Cum tripudio	Ecce sanctorum	All Saints' Day	De tele heure vi la biaute ma dame que ne puis sanz li. contra in latino	178^r	vdB 484
3	Ad sancte Katerine / Decus Syon concine	Virgo gemma gracie	Katherine	La tres grant biaute de li ma le cuer du cors ravi. contra in latino	178^{r-v}	vdB 1205
4	Sancti Nicholai / Vacemus titulis / Cum summa leticia / Pangentes Alleluia	Ille puerulus jacens cunabulis	Nicholas	Joi te rossignol chantez de sus .i. rain u jardinet m'amie de sus l'ante florie. contra in latino	178^v	vdB 1159
5	Gallia cum leticia / Eximia / Ana pangat Alleluia	Ecce festum egregii	Denis the Martyr	E jolis cuers se tu t'en vas s'onques m'amas pour dieu ne m'antroblie pas. contra in latino	181^r	vdB 847
6	Letare mater ecclesia	Ecce festum beate Katerine	Katherine	Ci aval querez amour-eites. contra in latino	181^v	vdB 355
7	Nicholai laudibus / Cum gaudio / Eximio / Nos decet convacare	Hic fulgens virtutibus	Nicholas	Je fere mentel taillier cousu de flours, ourle d'amours fourre de vio-leite. contra in latino	182^r	vdB 1044
8	Iherusalem / Iherusalem / Letare mater ecclesia	Ecce venit insigne	Virgin/Pentecost	Amours amours amours ai qui m'ocient et la nuit et le iour	183^r	vdB 150

#					
9	Alleluia Regi regum omnium Concinat ecclesia	Ecce festum nobile	Pentecost	Au bois irai pour cullir la violeite mon ami i trouverai. contra in latino	183ᵛ	vdB 191
10	Ave regina celorum Regis regum triclinium	Ave, plena gracia	Virgin	Dex quar haiez merci de m'ame si con j'e envers vous mespris. contra	184ᵛ	vdB 488
11	Superne matris gaudia Represente ecclesia	Universorum orgio	All Saints' Day	Amez moi douce dame amez, et je fere voz voulentez	186ʳ	vdB 117
12	Militans ecclesia Beate Katerine Gaudeat sollempnio	Virgo costi filia	Katherine	Unques mes ne fu seurpris du mal d'amoueites mes or le sui orandroit	186ʳ⁻ᵛ	vdB 1423
13	Nicholai sollempnio Letetur cleri concio	Hic Dei plenus gracia	Nicholas	Unques en amer leaument ne conquis fors que mal talent	186ᵛ	vdB 1420
14	Pange cum leticia Iherusalem incola	Pulsa noxe scoria	Pentecost	Honniz soit qui mes ouan beguineite devendra	187ᵛ	vdB 881
15	Mater ecclesia Cantet Alleluia	Ecce orgium	Pentecost	Bonne amoureite m'a en sa prison pieca	188ʳ⁻ᵛ	vdB 288
16	Syon presenti sollempnio Deo iubilet corde pio	Ecce virginis Marie	Virgin	Dex donnez me joie de ce que jain l'amour a la belle ne puis avoir	188ᵛ	vdB 515
17	Laudibus Nicholai dulcibus Vacemus cum cantibus	Ille civis Pathere	Nicholas	Rois gentis faites ardoir ces juiis pendre ou escorcher vis	189ʳ	vdB 1635

refrain with the Latin refrain, the mirroring of syllable count and rhyme across languages is readily apparent (pp = proparoxytonic accent):

Par fate de lëaultei	7	a	*Marie preconio*	7pp	a
Ke j'ai an amors trovei	7	a	*Serviat cum gaudio*	7pp	a
Me partirai dou païx.	7	b	*Militans Ecclesia.*	7pp	b

Due to the lack of loyalty I have found in love, I will leave the region.	*May the militant church preserve with joy praise of Mary.*

The same holds true for the strophic material of the *ballette à refrain* in Douce 308 and Latin poem in the Miscellany: The latter corresponds in syllable count and rhyme scheme with the vernacular song. This refrain concordance is especially helpful due to the inconsistent cueing of the Latin refrain in *Marie preconio*. Despite a relatively high degree of scribal attention to layout in the poetic assemblage of the St-Victor Miscellany in general, cues for regularly recurring refrains do not always appear. In this case, the alternation of strophes and refrains can be extrapolated from knowledge of the French *ballette à refrain*.[19] What the survival of the French *refrain* in Douce 308 does not provide, however, is a possible musical realization for *Marie preconio*, since this sole refrain concordance is unnotated.

Of the seventeen *refrains* preserved in the St-Victor Miscellany, five (including the one just discussed) have concordances as *refrains* in *ballettes à refrain*, *dits entés*, and narratives.[20] Of these, three survive with notation in at least one source. Two of these notated *refrains* appear in the early thirteenth-century interpolated Fauvel manuscript attributed to Jehannot de Lescurel, while the third occurs in the late thirteenth-century *romance Renart le Nouvel* (see Table 5.2).[21] Given the existence of notated concordances, it is possible to underlay some of the Latin poems to the melodies of French *refrains*, as scholars have previously attempted.[22] A parallel

---

[19] Problematically, however, the refrain's repetition similarly lacks a cue in Douce 308; this is not uncommon in the source. See the varieties of refrain cueing detailed ibid., cxxxii–cxxxvii.

[20] The *refrain* "Ci aual querez amoureites" in the St-Victor Miscellany is most unlike, although still similar to, its potential concordances in two copies of *Le Livre d'amoretes*, where the refrain reads "droit au cuer querez amoretes en mon sain ie les i uing metre" (Paris lat. 13091) and "droit au cuer querez amoretes en mon sain ie les uing metre" (Paris fr. 23111); see Table 5.2.

[21] On Lescurel's corpus in Fauvel, see Wilkins, ed., *Works Jehan de Lescurel*; Plumley, *Art of Grafted Song*, 57–88; Regalado, "The Songs of Jehannot de Lescurel"; and Arlt, "Jehannot de Lescurel." On the *refrains* in *Renart*, see Peraino, "*Et pui conmencha a canter*"; Ibos-Augé, *Chanter et lire*; and Haines, *Satire*.

[22] Gennrich, "Lateinische Kontrafakta," 205–206, and Anderson, *Notre-Dame and Related Conductus*, 8:41–50. Anderson supplies melodies for all the refrain-form poems in the St-Victor Miscellany using melodies from *refrains* he perceives as metrical matches.

Table 5.2 *Refrain* concordances in the St-Victor Miscellany

French *refrain* incipit in the St-Victor Miscellany	Concordances	Date	Context	Notated
Par defaus de leaute	Douce 308, 214^{r-v} (226^{r-v}) and 225^{r} (236^{r})	after 1309	*Ballette à refrain*	No
Joi te rossignol chantez	Fauvel, 61^{r}	1314–1317	*Dit enté*, "Gracïeus temps" (Lescurel)	Yes
Ci aual querez amoureites	Paris fr. 23111, 212^{v} Paris lat. 13091, 151^{r}	late 13th 1380–1400	*Le Livre d'amoretes*	No
Amez moi douce dame	Fauvel, 61^{v}	1314–1317	*Dit enté*, "Gracïeus temps" (Lescurel)	Yes
Unques en amer leaument	Douce 308, 227^{v} (238^{v})	after 1309	*Ballette à refrain*	No
	Paris fr. 372, 34^{v}	*ca.* 1292	*Renart le Nouvel*	Yes
	Paris fr. 1593, 33^{v} (34^{v})	*ca.* 1290		
	Trouv W, 147^{v}	after 1288		
	Paris fr. 1581, 33^{v}	late 13th		No

transcription of the *refrain Ames moi douce dame amez* from Fauvel cited in the rubric for *Superne matris gaudia* appears in Example 5.1; the close relationship between syllable count and rhyme scheme is readily apparent. For this *refrain*, a musico-poetic insertion in a *dit enté* attributed to Jehannot de Lescurel and not part of a larger song structure, the only music preserved is that of the refrain itself. Indeed, all three concordant refrains presented with notation survive as refrain melodies alone, serving as insertions into poetic and literary texts (a *dit* and *romance*) rather than as part of fixed song forms, such as a *ballette à refrain*. In the two contexts for which the concordant refrain belongs to a song (in both cases *ballettes à refrain* in Douce 308), notation is unfortunately lacking.

Consequently, the music for the *refrains* alone survives as a clue to the melodic realization of certain Latin poems in the St-Victor Miscellany. In each case, the *refrain*'s music can nevertheless be underlaid to the entirety of the Latin poem due to the shared scansion between strophes and refrain. Following Grocheio's description of a *rotundellus*, "the parts of which do not have a melody different from the melody of the response or refrain," for these Latin poems with notated *refrain* concordances, the music of the whole could be derived solely from the refrain.[23] In the case of the three songs with

---

[23] Grocheio, *Ars musice*, 68–69. See also the Introduction and Butterfield, *Poetry and Music*, 48–49.

Example 5.1 Underlay of *Superne matris gaudia* to *Amez moi douce dame* (St-Victor Miscellany, fol. 186ʳ and Fauvel, fol. 61ᵛ)

	A	-	mez	moi	dou	-	ce	dame	a	- mez
1. Su	-	per	-	ne	ma	-	tris	gau	di	- a
3. U	-	ni	-	ver	- so	-	rum	or	gi	- o
4. San	- cto	-	rum	et	so	-	sol	- lemp	ni	- o
5. Sit	laus	de	cus	et	glo	ri	- a
7. Su	-	per	-	ne	ma	-	tris	gau	di	- a

et	je	fe	-	rai	vouz	vou	-	len	- tez.
2. Re	-	pre	-	sen	-	tat	ec	cle	-	si	- a.
6. Il	-	li	qui	re	-	git	o	-	mni	- a
8. Re	-	pre	-	sen	-	tat	ec	cle	-	si	- a.

extant melodic material for the French *refrains, Superne matris gaudia, Nicholai sollempnio,* and *Sancti Nicholai,* the regular scansion and form of each poem allows for the reuse of the *refrain*'s melody throughout; in the other poems with refrain rubrics but without surviving musical material, the scansion is varied enough to make such a realization unlikely. In other words, only in certain cases does the music of the French *refrain* accompany both strophic and refrain material. The survival of notated *refrain* concordances nevertheless supports interpretation of the French *refrain* rubrics in the St-Victor Miscellany as musical, as well as formal, cues. Even without notated concordances one could understand the cues as musical – the absence of notation does not necessarily correlate to the absence of music.[24] Moreover, the refrains themselves rhetorically convey musical performance, repeatedly calling on the church and its community to sing using the imperative and subjunctive forms of verbs including "concinere," "cantare," and "pangere" (see Chapter 2 on similar verbiage suggesting musical performance in refrain songs).

Why provide solely refrain-form poems with such explicit cues? It seems unlikely that the other, strophic poems would have lacked a similar life in performance, and there are certainly examples of strophic contrafacts outside of the Miscellany. One answer might be found in the itinerant nature of *refrains* during the thirteenth and fourteenth centuries. As Ardis Butterfield notes, the vernacular *refrain*'s identity as a "small, independent and culturally distinctive [element]" affords it weighty currency in the circulation of

---

[24] See, for instance, Leach's argument with respect to the unnotated songs of Douce 308 in "A Courtly Compilation," 233–245.

medieval music and text. The privileging of the refrain as an epicenter of musical and poetic meaning speaks, too, to the broader context of the intertextual refrain and its citation in clerical and monastic contexts. As Jennifer Saltzstein argues, "vernacular refrains were treated as valued sources of knowledge," and "the treatment of intertextual refrains in these contexts reveals a preoccupation among clerical writers with the status and authority of the vernacular song tradition, even when measured directly against the authority of the Latin."[25] In the St-Victor Miscellany, Latin and vernacular interact explicitly through the refrain, serving as yet another form of intertextual citation and as an acknowledgment of the wider song culture of which Latin song is a part.

The *refrain* rubrics in the St-Victor Miscellany certainly suggest a poet and/or scribe conversant enough in the culture of vernacular song such that *refrains* could serve as a musico-poetic shorthand. Given the Parisian milieu of Lescurel, the sole name attached to the *refrains* copied in the Miscellany – albeit copied more than a quarter of a century later in Fauvel – and the circulation of the other *refrains* in northern French sources, responsibility for the collection of *refrains* and Latin contrafacts in the Miscellany probably resides with an individual or community not only affiliated with a pedagogical institution, but with ears tuned to French lyric. This is all the more evident considering the network of refrain concordances in *Renart*, *Le Livre d'amoretes*, Douce 308, and the *dits* of Lescurel in Fauvel that form the core of the refrains cited in the St-Victor Miscellany.[26]

The timeline of these sources for the concordant *refrains* in the St-Victor Miscellany, however, is notable – none of the *refrains* is transmitted in any manuscripts earlier than the late thirteenth century. In other words, the rubrics in the St-Victor Miscellany reflect the earliest copying dates for five *refrains*, and the unique witness for the remaining twelve. What might this reveal about the citational network of *refrains* in the later thirteenth century? If the *refrains* were known prior to their inclusion in the rubrics of the St-Victor Miscellany, how and where were they circulating? Conversely, if these *refrains* were newly created for the Miscellany, through which intermediary texts did they make their way, for instance, into Lescurel's *dits entés* or Douce 308?

While these questions may remain unanswerable, the subject matter of the French *refrains* offers some insight into the milieu of the creator and/or

---

[25] Saltzstein, *Refrain*, 7. See also Saltzstein's discussion of French *refrains* in the context of a clerical miscellany, a textual milieu reminiscent of the intellectual character of the St-Victor Miscellany, 69–79.

[26] Gennrich, "Lateinische Kontrafakta," 207, and Plumley, *Art of Grafted Song*, 83–84.

compiler of the poems, as well as the earlier history of *refrains* otherwise only attested in later sources. Courtly love comprises the principal theme of the refrains on the whole, with the conventional vocabulary of French song and romance fully present. With themes of courtly love amply represented, most of the *refrains* with and without concordances transmitted in the St-Victor Miscellany would be at home in any of the expected contexts, from song and motet to narrative *romance*, as evidenced by the list of concordances in Table 5.2. Amid the predominantly love-themed *refrains*, two stand out for their lack of engagement in this courtly vocabulary. The first, "Honniz soit qui mes ouan beguineite devendra" ("Evil be to her who will now become a beguine"), rubricating *Pange cum leticia*, references the beguines, and the second, "Rois gentis faites ardoir ces juiis pendre ou escorcher vis" ("Noble king, make the Jews burn, hang, or be skinned alive"), rubricating *Laudibus Nicholai*, is an alarming invective against Jews. While both appear to be unique, the *refrains* nevertheless display striking resonances with the broader cultural context of thirteenth-century France and its literary and musical sources.

The first of the two unique *refrains* curses a woman entering the lay sisterhood of the beguines, a community whose numbers increased dramatically over the course of the thirteenth century before reforms in the early fourteenth century.[27] With communities across Europe, especially the Low Countries and in major cities such as Paris, beguines received both positive and negative attention from religious and civic institutions and individuals. Beguines (as with other religious figures, especially women) make repeated appearances in medieval French song and poetry, which refer to them in pejorative ways.[28] The *refrain* of the *motetus* in a *rondeau-motet* in the Chansonnier de Noailles, *Ja n'avrés deduit de moi/SECULUM* exemplifies one of the more common attitudes toward beguines, situating

---

[27] On beguines, especially in France, see Miller, *Beguines*.

[28] See, for instance, the figure of the beguine in two *chansons de rencontre, Amors m'anvoie a mesaige* and *J'antrai en lai ruwelette* in Douce 308, edited and translated in Doss-Quinby, Rosenberg, and Aubrey, eds., *Old French Ballette*, xxvii, 216–219 and 478–481. See also O'Sullivan, *Marian Devotion*, 66–67. Other references to beguines can be seen in the motet repertoire; see, for example *A Cambrai/SOIER* in Mo, fol. 84ᵛ. At least one trouvère was also possibly a male beguin, Martin le Beguin, and lyrical texts in the lost manuscript Metz 535 appear to have been part of the musical activities of a beguine community; on the latter, see Meyer, "Notice du ms. 535"; Långfors, *Notices des manuscrits*; and most recently, Hasenohr, "Aperçus sur la forme et la reception des textes" and Grossel, "Trouveresses messines." My thanks to Jennifer Saltzstein for alerting me to several of these references.

an anonymous beguine as a hypocrite, only offering her affections after entering the (celibate) lay order:

Motetus	*Ja n'avrés deduit de moi*	*You will never take your pleasure with me*
	se je ne sui beguine,	*unless I become a Beguine;*
	par la foi ke je vous doi.	Take my word for it.
	Ja n'avrés deduit [de moi]	*You will never take your pleasure with me*
	se je ne sui beguine.	*unless I become a Beguine.*[29]

In a similar vein, the *refrain* in the St-Victor Miscellany focuses not on the hypocrisy of beguines, but on the perceived wrongness of the lay order. Reflecting an attitude of censure often held by clerics and monastics, the inclusion of an anti-beguine *refrain* in a collection of devotional Latin texts serves as another possible indicator of the institutionally religious, and potentially conservative, milieu of the compiler.

The second of the two non-courtly love *refrains*, beginning "rois gentis," expresses a markedly darker sentiment than most contemporary *refrains*, although not necessarily darker than texts in contemporary genres. Hostility toward Jews akin to what appears in the *refrain* from the St-Victor Miscellany is scattered throughout medieval French narrative sources, sermons, and numerous other texts. Throughout the thirteenth century in France, under the rule of Louis IX followed by Philip III and Philip IV, Jewish communities experienced increasing antisemitism and violence, culminating in the expulsion of Jews from France in 1306.[30] However, as far as I am aware, no parallel poem or song exists featuring such strikingly violent language. References to Jews do occur, often in the context of conversion, and the song culture of medieval France included a number of Jewish composers and poets.[31]

I have located a possible model for the language of this violent *refrain* in an Old French *Evangile de l'enfance*, an example of a subtype of vernacular religious writing that takes Christ's infancy as its focus.[32] Although sources for the Old French *Evangile* all date from after the turn of the fourteenth century, the origins of the text have been placed in the late thirteenth century, if not earlier.[33] With a *terminus post quem* of 1289 for the St-Victor Miscellany, the composition of the *Evangile* and the Latin poems may be roughly contemporaneous. Significantly, the *Evangile de l'enfance*

---

[29] Text and translation in Saint-Cricq, Doss-Quinby, and Rosenberg, eds., *Motets*, lviii.

[30] On the relationship more broadly between Jews and Christians in the thirteenth century, see Baumgarten and Galinsky, eds., *Jews and Christians*.

[31] Jordan, "Exclusion," and Paden, "Troubadours and Jews."

[32] For an overview, see Boulton, ed., *The Old French Évangile de l'Enfance*, 1–6.

[33] Ibid., 16–17.

includes a passage whose language mirrors (or is mirrored by?) the *refrain* in the St-Victor Miscellany:

Evangile de l'enfance	St-Victor Miscellany, fol. 189ʳ
Vivre ne devroit o nous chi,	Rois gentis **faites ardoir** ces juiis
Ansi **le doit on** crucfier	**pendre ou escorcher vis**
Pendre ou ardoir ou eschorchier,	
Car il confront toutes nos loys;	
Je veul gue il soit mis en crois.	
He [Jesus] should not live with us here,	Noble king, **make** the Jews **burn,**
But **we should** crucify him	**hang or be skinned alive.**
Hang him or burn him or skin him	
Because he is destroying all our laws;	
I want him to be put on a cross.[34]	

Both texts list the same horrors – burning, hanging, and flaying. The key difference is the intended recipient of the torture in each context.[35] In the *Evangile de l'enfance*, the speaker is a Jew addressing Jesus, while the invectives of the *refrain* are explicitly directed *at* Jews. In the *Evangile de l'enfance*, the anti-Jewish sentiment surrounds the excerpted passage, including in the authorial explanation that directly follows: "this was the first root [cause] | why God had hatred for the Jews."[36] In both contexts, then, Jews are ultimately situated in negative terms, whether as the aggressor in the *Evangile* or object of aggression in the poem. Whatever the relationship between the sources (including the possibility of an unknown intermediary), the shared vocabulary of the two texts undeniably participates in the deeply anti-Semitic culture of thirteenth-century France.[37]

The *refrain* rubrics of the St-Victor Miscellany represent a varied, if at times problematic, interpretive frame for the relationship between Latin

---

[34] Edited and translated in Vitz, "Apocryphal," 128. An edition of entire *Evangile de l'enfance* is in Boulton, *The Old French Évangile de l'Enfance*; passage here on p. 60.

[35] Another difference rests in voice and mood of each text. In the *Evangile de l'enfance*, the passage conveys direct speech, while in the St-Victor Miscellany the *refrain* uses the imperative form of "faire."

[36] Vitz, "Apocryphal," 128.

[37] As Thomas observed in one of the initial overviews of the French *refrains* of the St-Victor Miscellany, a further link to a contemporary event might also speak to the relevancy of the *Rois gentis refrain*, namely the burning of thirteen Jews in Troyes on April 24, 1288. Thomas, "Refrains français," 507, n. 1, where Thomas attributes this connection to David Blondheim. While the relationship of the *refrain* to this event is a matter of speculation alone, violent antisemitism was a reality across France by the 1280s. On the Troyes martyrdom, see Einbinder, *Beautiful Death*, 126–154. For the broader context of this event prior to the expulsion of the Jews in the fourteenth century, see Jordan, *French Monarchy and the Jews*, 179–199.

and vernacular song. Situating the collection of unnotated Latin poems within a deeply bilingual setting, the use of French *refrains* points not only to the compiler's or scribe's familiarity with vernacular song, but their assumption of an audience equally familiar with the vernacular repertoire. With *refrains* serving as formal and melodic mnemonics for the Latin poems, a collection that is otherwise lacking music is provided with a musical subtext, even if the sound of many of the songs remains inaccessible due to the lack of notated concordances. Yet *refrains* with and without concordances paint a picture of a working environment for the compiler and/or writer of the poems that is of his time – a complaint about beguines and a brutal cry to arms against Jews place the poetry firmly within the cultural setting of late thirteenth-century France. Finally, refrain-form poems comprise only part of the poetic contents of the Miscellany, yet these are the sole works whose ties to vernacular song are made visually and textually explicit. The *refrains* of the St-Victor Miscellany bear witness to the multivalence of the refrain, bridging language and register, and cueing music and form.

German Song in the Margins in the Engelberg Codex

The late fourteenth-century/early fifteenth-century service book and troper for the Benedictine Abbey of Engelberg, the Engelberg Codex, sits at a sharp chronological, geographical, and repertorial remove from the St-Victor Miscellany.[38] Alongside polyphonic works, tropes of Office and Mass chants, and an Easter play, numerous Latin songs are preserved in this unique source produced by and for the use of a single community in Switzerland.[39] Also particular to the Engelberg Codex is its transmission of German-texted works, both liturgical and extraliturgical, including several German contrafacts of hymns, sequences, and songs.[40] In addition to offering insight into late medieval troping practices, the Engelberg Codex

---

[38] Along with various codicological details, the dating of the Engelberg Codex is discussed in the most recent study of the manuscript by Arlt, Stauffacher, and Hascher, eds., *Engelberg.* While the manuscript and its contents represent a collaborative effort undertaken over decades, the date 1372 appears twice in the manuscript. Ibid., 11.

[39] For information on the historical context of the manuscript and those involved in its production, see ibid., 62–80.

[40] The Engelberg Codex also transmits a significant number of polyphonic works; see Handschin, "Angelomontana polyphonica," 65–84. On the vernacular contents, see Bartsch, "Alt- und Mittelhochdeutsches aus Engelberg"; Arlt, Stauffacher, and Hascher, *Engelberg,* 64–65 (inventory), and *passim*; and März, "Pange lingua."

also serves as a witness to the use of the vernacular within and alongside the liturgy. Although the liturgical orientation of this Swiss Codex contrasts with the intellectual milieu of the St-Victor Miscellany, the contents of both manuscripts reveal an interest in multilinguality and song.

Refrain songs are among the varied works copied into the twelfth and final gathering of the Codex (fol. 168^r–182^v), a grab bag in terms of genre and function.[41] Since the gathering existed independently before being compiled with the other eleven, trimming of the edges resulted in the loss of some textual information. Specifically, for nine unique Latin songs with refrains – eight of which are *rondelli* – marginal notes added by two different scribes have been partially lost. What remains are jotted fragments of German lyric, included in Table 5.3 along with corresponding Latin poems, refrains, rubrics, and occasions.[42]

In addition to belonging to a single gathering, the nine songs appear within the space of relatively few folios (168^r–176^r), with the *rondelli* (songs 1–8) copied almost back-to-back. Only three songs survive with notation, a not uncommon situation for this codex. For each song, visible stave lines indicate a single melodic line, with the *residuum* copied below. With respect to musical style, the eight *rondelli* are unusual among Latin refrain songs since they feature melismatic passages, typically at the beginning and end of verse lines.[43] Even for the unnotated songs, text underlay suggests similar melismatic treatments. For the only strophic+refrain song, *Nato celorum Domino*, the textual underlay of this unnotated song suggests a syllabic rather than melismatic setting. Form, rubrication, and, in nearly all cases, musical style mark these songs as different from others within the Engelberg Codex and among the wider repertoire of Latin refrain songs.

Yet, these songs are still devotional; Latin rubrics indicating feast or saint introduce all nine songs. The poems cover conventional topics for refrain songs (Christmas, Pentecost, the Virgin), with the addition of two unusual saints for the repertoire, Margaret and Michael; neither saint appears with any regularity in medieval Latin song, and both must have been of special interest to the community in Engelberg. While the Latin poems are unique, several rework liturgical chant texts, including sequences and hymns preserved elsewhere in the Engelberg Codex. Most notable is *Flore vernat virginali* for John the Evangelist, which shares its incipit and textual

---

[41] Arlt, Stauffacher, and Hascher, *Engelberg*, 59–61.

[42] The works are inventoried ibid., 98–99. See also Everist, *Discovering Medieval Song*, 255. The German text here follows Arlt and Stauffacher's readings.

[43] See also the example of *Congaudeat turba fidelium* in Chapter 2, for which a more ornate musical setting is transmitted in the Engelberg Codex compared to other sources.

Table 5.3 Engelberg Codex, refrain songs with marginal German annotations

	Incipit	Refrain	Occasion	Rubric	Marginal German lyric	Folio	Notation
1	Veni sancte spiritus	Veni sancte spiritus Illustra cecam mentem Ut plebs devota maneat.	Pentecost	De spiritu sancto	Sol mi [ ] dienst sin	168^r	YES
2	O virgo pelle	O virgo pelle vitia Nobisque sis propicia Alleluia Tuum placando filium	Marian	De sancta Maria	Dissen ich [ ] vs	168$^{r–v}$	NO
3	Pusillus nobis nascitur	Pusillus nobis nascitur Gaude gaude Gaude gaude plebs Israhel.	Nativity	De nativitate domini	[ ]kúnd	168^v	NO
4	Flore vernat	Flore vernat virginali Et doctrina spiritali Iohannes pre ceteris.	John the Evangelist	De Iohanne ewangelista	[ ]ten sehen [ ]cherli	168^v	YES
5	O stirpe regis filia	O stirpe regis filia Tu scala penitencium Solamenque miserorum.	Marian	De sancta Maria	[ ] dich alle [ ] so bin ich	168^v	NO
6	Salve virgo Margaretha	Salve virgo Margaretha Nigra tu es sed formosa Castitatis lilium Bonum certamen certasti.	St. Margaret	De sancta Margaretha	Ein wild [ ]vf [ ] gen	169^r	NO
7	Congaudent omnes angeli	Congaudent omnes angeli In festo Michahelis Qui fecit victoriam Ob laudem salvatoris.	St. Michael	De angelis	[ ] wilduang [ ] f genaden	169^v	YES

Table 5.3 (*cont.*)

	Incipit	Refrain	Occasion	Rubric	Marginal German lyric	Folio	Notation
8	Ave stella maris Maria	Ave, stella maris Maria Trinitatis cellaria Que das dona varia Nobis in hac miseria En ad te confugimus.	Marian	De sancta Maria	[ ] mimpt mir [ ]l der fræd	169ᵛ	NO
9	Nato celorum Domino	Natus est in Betlehem salvator Regum rex facinorum laxator Gaudent milia milium.	Nativity	De nativitate domini conductus	[ ] bluendes [ ]s aller selikeit	175ᵛ – 176ʳ	NO

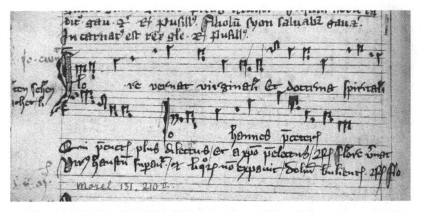

Figure 5.2 Engelberg Codex, fol. 168ᵛ, *Flore vernat virginali* with marginal lyric. Reproduced by kind permission of Stiftsbibliothek Engelberg

material with a sequence of the same name appearing earlier in the manuscript.[44] Other refrain songs in the Engelberg Codex similarly appear to be reworkings, although less closely tied to their models than *Flore vernat virginali*. These include *Veni sancte spiritus* [B] and *Ave stella maris Maria*, both of which borrow from well-known chants, namely a Pentecost sequence and a Marian hymn, respectively.

Notably, the melodies for both sequence and song versions of *Flore vernat virginali* survive in the Engelberg Codex, and they are markedly different. The song reworks only the text, not the musical setting. Instead, the melody for the refrain song appears to derive from outside of the manuscript, cued by means of a marginal note made unintelligible by trimming undertaken when the gathering was joined with the previous eleven to form the current Engelberg Codex (see Figure 5.2).[45] The German text as it appears here is "[]ten sehen[]cherli," which offers little in terms of poetic meaning and has no witnesses outside of the Engelberg Codex. Nevertheless, the marginal notes in this gathering of refrain-form songs suggest that they were modeled on the melodies and perhaps also poetic forms of vernacular songs – in this case, chiefly German songs that take the poetic and musical form of a *rondeau* (ABaAabAB). Certain of the refrain song contrafacts in the Engelberg Codex, in other words, are doubly constructed from borrowed material – text from liturgical chant and

---

[44] Fol. 55ʳ–56ʳ, edited in *AH* 55:192.

[45] As Arlt and Stauffacher note, the twelfth gathering containing the Latin contrafacts was compiled separately before being trimmed and put together with the rest of the manuscript gatherings; *Engelberg*, 59–61.

music from vernacular song. This may explain, too, the more unusual musical, melismatic style for the *rondelli* in the Codex compared to other notated *rondelli*, such as those in the thirteenth-century F and Tours 927; earlier *rondelli* are generally not contrafacts, while these later fourteenth-century *rondelli* appear to be musically related to German song.

Although the nine pairs of German lyric and Latin contrafacts are unique to the Engelberg Codex, the existence of these *rondelli* has not escaped the notice of scholars seeking German counterparts to the French *formes fixes*. Indeed, the contrafacts in the Engelberg Codex have long been positioned as early witnesses to a tradition of German song modeled after northern French forms.[46] Notably, the relationship between Latin and German *rondeau*-form songs occurs in at least one other source that makes the relationship between the two languages explicit, albeit with no surviving music: the Erfurt Codex.[47] A fourteenth-century manuscript originating in England before being owned and annotated by rector Johannes Barba of the St. Katherine Chapel at Aachen's collegiate church of St. Mary, the Erfurt Codex transmits a series of unnotated German songs with similarly unnotated Latin contrafacts in *rondeau* form all added by Barba. Rubrication cues the relationship, with Latin poems preceded by rubrics such as "Kantilena Latinalis super isto" (referring to the German poem just prior) or "Sequitur kantilena primo in Teutonico, post in Latino." All told, the Erfurt Codex transmits six German *rondeaux* with five Latin contrafacts, in addition to an assortment of poetic texts in both languages.[48] While the Erfurt Codex contains no musical notation, its pairing of German and Latin *rondeaux* provides a fuller picture of the diglossic tradition gestured to in the marginal inclusion of German lyrical fragments in the Engelberg Codex. Moreover, the existence of the full text in both languages in Barba's pairings sheds light on the nature of the poetry itself; akin to the Engelberg Codex, the Latin poems are chiefly devotional in register, while the German songs reflect a worldlier outlook. The

---

[46] Gennrich, "Deutsche Rondeaux"; Handschin, "Die Schweiz, welche sang," 113–118; and Kornrumpf, "Rondeaux." More generally, see Petzsch, "Ostschwäbische Rondeaux vor 1400."

[47] On this source and Barba's added lyrics, see Gennrich, "Deutsche Rondeaux," 136; Nörrenberg, "Ein Aachener Dichter"; Frantzen, "Ein spätes Zeugniß"; and Kornrumpf, "Rondeaux," 65. See also the catalogue entry in Schum, *Beschreibendes Verzeichnis*, 566–568. Notation is included for two polyphonic works, both for Christmas: the Latin *Gloria in excelsis Deo* and the German *Syß willekomen heire Kerst*.

[48] Many of the texts added by Barba reflect his milieu and position in Aachen, including more pedagogically oriented poems such as *Modus est indicativus*, which employs Latin verb forms in a rhetorical and exegetical way, and *Cosmi proch inicium*, which does the same with noun cases. Frantzen, "Ein spätes Zeugniß," 134–136.

phrasing and position of the songs in the manuscript is also notable; the German poems provide the models for the Latin poems, the latter in each case designated "super," "to the tune of," the former.[49]

The existence of Barba's bilingual poetic addendum, however, does not offer insight into the specific German songs cued in the margins of the Engelberg Codex. For the most part, scholars have lamented the fragmentary nature of the German lyrics in the margins. Even the interpretation of these fragments is subject to debate; readings of the marginal lyrics vary considerably, although general consensus is that the German texts from which they are derived are unique.[50]

One promising avenue has emerged in a study attempting to locate German lyrics cited in the early fifteenth-century Limburg Chronicle attributed to Tilemann Elhen von Wolfhagen, in which Gisela Kornrumpf outlines a network of largely unnotated German *rondeaux* surviving from the fourteenth and early fifteenth centuries. With the marginal lyrics preserved in the Engelberg Codex and the more complete texts in the Erfurt Codex among her examples, Kornrumpf has uncovered a concordance for three of the German marginalia in the Engelberg Codex, those lyrical fragments attached to *Salve virgo Margaretha*, *Congaudent omnes angeli*, and *O virgo pelle* (see Table 5.3). With respect to the first two songs, Kornrumpf makes the case that they share the same German lyric, linking "Ein wild []vf [] gen" beside *Salve virgo Margaretha* to "[] wilduang [] f genaden" beside *Congaudent omnes angeli*. Kornrumpf identifies a possible match with this German lyric in a *rondeau* transmitted as text only in Munich cgm. 1113, *Ein wildfanch auf genad*.[51] As she demonstrates, the extant poetry of the German *rondeau* aligns neatly with that of the Latin *rondelli* in the Engelberg Codex, making her identification of the marginal lyric highly possible. Consequently, it seems that the German song lyrics familiar to the scribes of the Engelberg Codex circulated beyond the immediate milieu of the manuscript. One could also move in the other direction and interpret the musical setting of *Congaudent omnes angeli* as preserving the melody of an otherwise unnotated German song.

More directly connecting to Tilemann's Chronicle is the refrain song *O virgo pelle*, its accompanying lyrical fragment reading, according to

---

[49] On "*super*" to cue contrafacture, see Falck, "Parody and Contrafactum," 15.

[50] See, for instance, the readings in Arlt, Stauffacher, and Hascher, *Engelberg*, 98–99, versus those in Bartsch, "Alt- und Mittelhochdeutsches aus Engelberg," 64–65 or Everist, *Discovering Medieval Song*, 255. See also Kornrumpf, "Rondeaux," 67, n. 41.

[51] Kornrumpf, "Rondeaux," 65–66.

Kornrumpf, as "<Des?> | dispa< . . . > | ich vs(g)< . . . >."[52] What this new interpretation of the German text affords is a link to a lyric cited in the Limburg Chronicle, beginning "Des dipans bin ich ußgezalt."[53] As Kornrumpf argues, the texts in the Limburg Chronicle (sung by the "Barfüßers vom Main") may be refrains of longer German *rondeaux*.[54] In this case, the marginal lyric beside *O virgo pelle* could provide confirmation that the lyric in the Chronicle is, in fact, a refrain. Conversely, a concordance for a second of the German songs cited in the Engelberg Codex points to the borrowing of musical and poetic materials in circulation more widely, either in writing or orally. As these examples illustrate, information flows not only from the vernacular to Latin, but from Latin to German, painting a fuller picture not only of Latin song culture in medieval monasteries, but of a multilingual song culture.

To sum up, of the nine unique Latin contrafacts in the Engelberg Codex, at least three may be modeled after German *rondeaux* surviving in other sources compiled in German-speaking areas, paralleling similar practices found in contemporary, albeit unnotated, sources. The lack of notation in these other sources, however, sets the Engelberg Codex apart. While the existence of the lyrics elsewhere affirms the wide dissemination of the German songs, their inscription in the Engelberg Codex means that their music may also have survived, retexted with devotional Latin poetry. The engagement of the scribes of the Engelberg Codex with German songs in wider circulation also speaks to the integral bilingualism of the manuscript. As in the St-Victor Miscellany, in which Latin and French freely rub shoulders and complement one another, German and Latin continually inform one another throughout the Engelberg Codex. With movement from Latin to German, and vice versa, represented, the manuscript offers a window into the linguistic fluidity of high medieval musical life and, indeed, its song culture.

The gathering of refrain-form Latin songs with their marginal German lyrical citations further situates the refrain as a node through which linguistic transformations could take place. With the identification of at least three of the lyrical fragments as likely German *rondeaux*, it is clear that

---

[52] This conflicts with earlier readings, such as that of Arlt, Stauffacher, and Hascher, *Engelberg*, 67–68 and Table 5.3, above.

[53] The chronicle is edited in Wyss, ed., *Die Limburger Chronik*. See also Kornrumpf, "Rondeaux," 57–58.

[54] Unlike Kornrumpf's identification of the German lyric for *Congaudent omnes angeli* and *Salve virgo Margaretha*, the poetic match between the Chronicle's lyric and *O virgo pelle* is inexact, if still convincing; see "Rondeaux," 67–68.

the refrain was not only the most memorable part of the song (and therefore provided the richest textual and visual clue), but also that it encoded melodic information. Kornrumpf in fact has suggested that the marginal lyrics were cues for the music scribe, indicating solely through the incipit of German refrains the melodic structure to which the new Latin poems were to be fitted.[55] This would certainly go a far way toward explaining why these songs required notation in the first place, since it is often the case that the citation of a musical model eliminates the need for musical notation. However, a degree of inconsistency obtains throughout the Engelberg Codex with respect to how contrafacts were inscribed. In the case of German reworkings (or more accurately, translations) of hymns and sequences, at times text alone is preserved with rubrics pointing to the textual and musical model (i.e. "*Ut queant laxis* verbo et melodia," fol. 10[r]); at other times, both rubric and music appear (as in "Sicut *Letabundus* verbo et melodia," fol. 89[r]).[56] In other words, the scribes of the Engelberg Codex did not preclude notation for works they probably knew (such as the sequence beginning *Letabundus*). Instead, as in the refrain-form songs in the final gathering, the scribes doubled up on information for works that crossed linguistic boundaries, including rubrics, marginal notes, and musical notation. Regardless of the reasons for the seeming overlap between textual and musical information, the marginal annotations of Latin refrain songs in the Engelberg Codex provide further testimony to the encoding of melodic and poetic meaning in refrains, however fragmentary and brief their inscription and accidental their survival.

Multilinguality in the Red Book of Ossory

Approximately 1,000 miles away during the same decades that the scriptorium at Engelberg actively copied and compiled the Engelberg Codex, a different group of scribes began work on what would become known as the "Red Book of Ossory." Copied from the last quarter of the fourteenth century and into the fifteenth century, the Red Book of Ossory preserves a variety of materials, including documents pertaining to the Ossorian diocese, chapters of the Magna Carta, various statutes and ordinances, proverbs, and a collection of sixty largely unique, unnotated, devotional

---

[55] Ibid., 65.
[56] See the inventory of works, with rubrication indicated, in Arlt, Stauffacher, and Hascher, *Engelberg*, 85–99.

Latin poems.[57] Although predominantly Latin, the manuscript as a whole is multilingual, with contents in French and, to a lesser degree, English. Due to its wide-ranging contents, the Red Book of Ossory has drawn the attention of scholars for over a century; the Latin poems in particular (often dubbed "hymns") have received frequent mention and were edited in their entirety three times in the early 1970s, in a somewhat bizarre coincidence.[58]

The modern fame of the poems in the Red Book of Ossory derives from two features of the manuscript source: the authorial framing of a textual preface on the first folio of the collection; and the inclusion of "snatches" of lyric in English, French, and in one case Latin, preceding and alongside thirteen of the poems and widely interpreted to be melodic cues (see Table 5.4).[59] The layered paratexts of the preface and lyrical fragments afford a range of possible interpretations and allude to a dense network of possible allusions (musical and poetic) operating within this fairly large group of poems. Beyond the presence of such textual and poetic materials, the poetry of the Red Book of Ossory finds a place in this book due to the prevalence of refrains: over eighty percent of the poems (forty-nine out of sixty) feature refrains or highly repetitive structures with internal repeats. Of these, just over half (twenty-five) are *rondelli*, making the Ossorian manuscript one of the largest repositories of *rondelli* alongside thirteenth-century sources such as F and Tours 927.[60] Yet, akin to the German milieu of the Engelberg Codex, the context for these Latin poems lies at a linguistic and geographical remove from the French *forme fixe* tradition, signaled by the inclusion of English lyrical cues and the Ossorian origins of the manuscript and its compilation. With

---

[57] For an overview of the manuscript's contents and dating, see Colledge, *Latin Poems*, xiii–xiv; Stemmler, *Latin Hymns*, xiv–xvii; and Lawlor, "Calendar." The poems are copied on fol. 70^r–77^r.

[58] Greene, *Lyrics*; Stemmler, *Latin Hymns*; and Colledge, *Latin Poems*. For a critical review of these editions, see Rigg, "Red Book." Musicologists have engaged infrequently with this collection, although it receives mention in several key works, such as Stevens, *Words and Music*, 183–184.

[59] Stemmler, "Vernacular Snatches." The songs are most often termed contrafacts due to the presence of these lyrical incipits. See, for instance, Greene's comparison to Continental examples of contrafacture (including in the St-Victor Miscellany) in the introduction of *Lyrics*, xxiii–xxx.

[60] Due to the late date of the Red Book of Ossory and (presumably) lack of notation, Anderson does not include these in his edition of Latin *rondeaux* (*Notre-Dame and Related Conductus*, vol. 8).

Table 5.4 Poems with rubrics or marginal annotations (repeated rubrics in bold) in the Red Book of Ossory

	Incipit	Refrain	Occasion	Rubric or marginal note	Language of rubric	Folio
1	*Laus Christo regi nato*	–	Epiphany	**Haue mercy of me frere**	English	70^v
2	*Peperit virgo*	–	Nativity	*Mayde y[n] the moore [l]ay*	English	71^r
3	*Succurre mater Christi*	–	Marian	*Alas hou shold y syng, Yloren is my playnge Hou shold y wiþ þat olde man To leven and let my leman Swettist of al þinge*	English	71^v
4	*Jhesu lux vera seculi*	Yes	Christ	*Harrow ieo su trahy par fol amor de mal amy*	French	71^v
5	*Jam Christo moriente*	–	Easter	**Haue mercie on me frere Barfote þat y go**	English	71^v
6	*Dies ista gaudii*	Yes	Easter	**Do do nightyngale synge ful myrie Shal y neure for þyn loue lengre karie**	English	72^r
7	*Plangentis Cristi uulnera*	Yes	Easter	*En Christi fit memoria*	Latin	72^r
8	*Resurgenti cum gloria*	Yes	Easter	*Haue god day my lemon &c*	English	72^v
9	*Maria noli flere*	–	Easter	**Haue merci of me frere**	English	73^r
10	*Verum est quod legi satis plene*	–	Moral / Judgment Day	*Gayneth me no garlond of greene Bot hit ben of wythoues ywroght*	English	73^v
11	*Regem adoremus*	Yes	Nativity	**Do do nightyngale synge ful myrie Shal y neure for þyn loue lengre karie**	English	74^r
12	*Vale mater virgo pura*	–	Marian / Presentation at the Temple	*Heu alas pur amour Qy moy myst en taunt dolour*	French	74^v
13	*En parit virgo regia*	Yes	Nativity	*Hey how þo cheualdoures wokes al nyght.*	English	74^v

its formal and material linking of devotional Latin poetry, refrains, and vernacular lyric, the Red Book of Ossory reflects an intertextual culture of song production and performance, one in which the refrain once again serves as an axis for linguistic, musical, and poetic exchange.

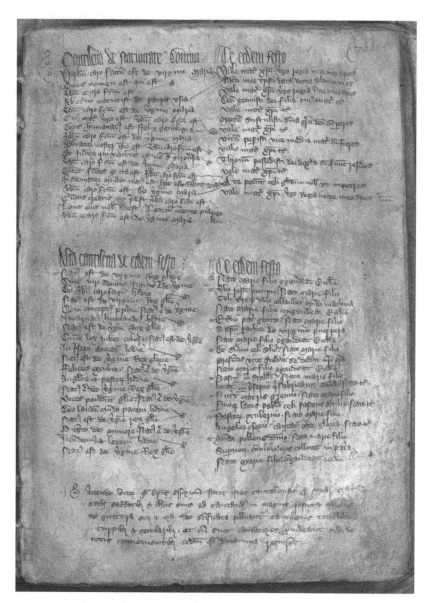

Figure 5.3 Red Book of Ossory, fol. 70ʳ, preface. Reproduced by kind permission of the Representative Body Library of the Church of Ireland

Unusually for songbooks or gatherings, the collection includes a preface at the foot of the first four poems on fol. 70ʳ (see Figure 5.3 and Chapter 1). In this brief "nota" (as it is rubricated in the manuscript), the songs are identified as the work of an unnamed Bishop of Ossory, who is assumed to be Richard Ledrede based on the approximate dates of copying (1360s) and of his tenure as bishop (1317–1360):[61]

Be advised, reader, that the Bishop of Ossory has made these songs for the vicars of the cathedral church, for the priests, and for his clerks, to be sung on the important holidays and at celebrations in order that their throats and mouths, consecrated to God, may not be polluted by songs that are lewd, secular, and associated with the theatre, and, since they are singers, let them provide themselves with suitable tunes according to what the poems require.[62]

The preface attributes the making ("fecit") of the songs to the bishop for the benefit of his clergy; it continues by decrying the singing of lewd, secular songs, thereby positioning the collected songs as a kind of pious entertainment for "great feasts."[63] The final phrase has proved the most interesting for scholars due to its resonance with the largely vernacular cues that appear throughout the song collection: "since they are singers, let them provide themselves with suitable tunes [notes] according to what the poems require" ("et cum sint cantatores prouideant sibi de notis conuenientibus secundum quod dictamina requirunt").[64] With this reference to the music of the poems in mind, the lyrical fragments interspersed throughout have thus been understood as references to the melodies suited to the poems.

What often seems to be missed, however, is the preface's abnegation of responsibility to supply the melodies "required" by the poems. Most frequently, attempts to grapple with the poems focus on linking the Latin texts attributed to Ledrede to the fragmentary citation of vernacular lyrics. Consequently, one argument sees the inclusion of vernacular snippets as examples of the kinds of lewd and secular song Ledrede aimed to erase from the mouths of his clergy; another argument sees the situation instead as one of compromise, with Ledrede acknowledging the popularity of

---

[61] On Ledrede, see Colledge, *Latin Poems*, xv–xxxiv; Stemmler, *Latin Hymns*, xviii–xx; Butterfield, "Poems Without Form?," 182–183; and Echard, "Ledred." He probably did not write all the poetry, witnessed by the fact that a group of poems are in fact reworkings of Walter of Wimborne's *Carmina Marie*. The contents of the miscellaneous manuscript certainly point to the compilation of the Red Book of Ossory as a diocesan record of materials related to Ledrede's lengthy term as bishop, with his own statutes included among the contents. For a detailed look at the contents, including Ledrede's statutes, see Lawlor, "Calendar."

[62] "Attende, lector, q[uo]d Episcopus Ossoriensis fecit istas cantilenas pro vicariis Ecclesie Cathedralis sacerdotibus et clericis suis ad cantandum in magnis festis et solaciis, ne guttura eorum et ora Deo santificata polluantur cantilenis teatralibus, turpibus et secularibus, et cum sint cantatores prouideant sibi de notis conuenientibus secundum quod dictamina requirunt." Edited and translated, with minor changes here, in Greene, *Lyrics*, iii–iv.

[63] See Chapter 1.   [64] See later in this chapter.

vernacular song and offering pious textual substitutes for the melodies his clergy enjoyed.[65] However, the preface seems to suggest that the bishop himself is not overly concerned with the melodies, and instead expects singers to provide "suitable" ones themselves. The implications of this shift in the interpretation of the preface concern the nature of the relationship between the song citations and devotional Latin poems, and the question of the users of, and audience for, the songs in their material form.

Although Ledrede is rhetorically framed in scholarship as the author of the songs in the Red Book of Ossory, and this is conflated with the work of scribes and/or copyists, the extent of his responsibility for the writing and compilation of the songs is unknown (and, indeed, the poems may have been compiled posthumously).[66] Several of the Latin texts, moreover, are not original but instead are extracted from a longer work by Walter of Wimborne.[67] At least three scribal hands – none of which are likely to be that of Ledrede himself – contributed to the copying of the folios, with poems written tidily, albeit with errors, in two neat columns with plenty of empty space; the preface was added by yet another hand. The *mise en page* immediately signals the poetic contents by means of blocks of text demarcating each work, and within each block the use of a variety of textual and symbolic annotations to clarify (and, in some cases, inadvertently confuse) formal features. In addition to the preface on fol. 70[r], rubrics precede the first four songs indicating their identity as songs ("cantilenae") for the Feast of the Nativity (see Figure 5.3). While rubrication of this type disappears after the first folio, the lyrical tags are added in such a way that they function as rubrics comparable to the French *refrains* in the St-Victor Miscellany. In Figure 5.4, for instance, two poems copied one after the other begin with a boxed lyric copied at the same time as the main text. The manner in which the scribe boxed off the fragmentary vernacular lyrics (in this case French and English) as a kind of title suggests an intention for the Latin poem to be read in relation to this header. Akin to the fully integrated French *refrains* of the St-Victor Miscellany, effort was made to incorporate the lyrical cues into the inscription of the songs in the Red Book of Ossory.

Of the thirteen instances of song cueing, seven (including the two in Figure 5.4) are inscribed in this planned fashion.[68] The remaining six are

---

[65] For these views, see Stevens, *Words and Music*, 183.

[66] On the copying order and dates of the manuscript, see Stemmler, *Latin Hymns*, xv–xvii and Lawlor, "Calendar," 159–160.

[67] See Greene, *Lyrics*, vii–viii and Rigg, "Red Book."

[68] See, for instance, the light pen decorations around the English lyric "Hey, how, þo cheualdoures wokes al nyght" on fol. 74[v]. The seven planned poems can be seen on fols. 70[v], 71[r], 72[r–v], 73[r], and 74[r].

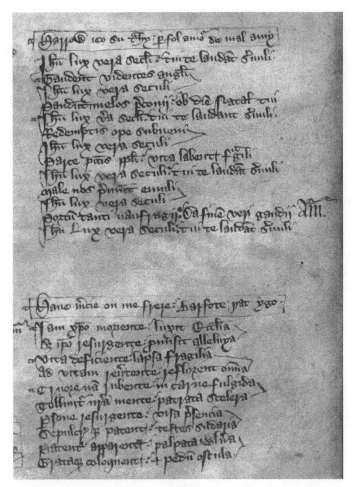

Figure 5.4 Red Book of Ossory, fol. 71ᵛ, *Jhesu lux vera seculi* and *Jam Christo moriente*. Reproduced by kind permission of the Representative Body Library of the Church of Ireland

not only less clearly a part of the original planning of the folios, but in many cases were later additions and/or the work of a different scribe. That several hands were involved in the copying of these folios is clear, with at least two text hands identified for the Latin poems alone (with a division in the first column on fol. 75ʳ marking a distinctive turn in the types of texts being copied).[69] At least one other hand annotated the collection, adding "amen" at the conclusion of many of the poems and also adding additional citations of vernacular – and one Latin – texts in the margins.

---

[69] Lawlor, "Calendar," 159–160, and Greene, *Lyrics*, iii. Only one other lyric within the Red Book is copied more than once, "Do do nightingale," and so on, discussed later in this chapter.

(a)

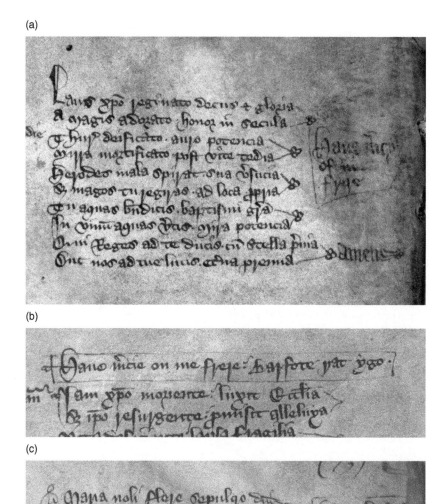

(b)

(c)

Figure 5.5 Red Book of Ossory, fols. 70ᵛ (a), 71ᵛ (b), and 73ʳ (c) (details). Reproduced by kind permission of the Representative Body Library of the Church of Ireland

The different hands can be seen in a comparison of the threefold appearance of the English line (or part thereof) "Haue mercie on me frere | Barfote þat y go" in Figure 5.5. Copied with a poem for Epiphany and two for Easter, this is one of only two English textual snippets with a concordance outside of the Red Book of Ossory (the other is the well-known *Mayde yn the moore lay*).[70]

Only the lengthier version of "Haue mercie on me frere" on fol. 71[v] is fully incorporated into the *mise en page* in a way that suggests it was copied at the same time as the Latin poem that follows. By contrast, a different scribal hand boxed off the shorter forms of the lyric in the margins on fols. 70[v] and 73 r. On fol. 70[v] in particular, the hand responsible for the boxed lyric also seems to have added the concluding "amen." In both of these shorter, marginal annotations, there are spelling changes too – "of" instead of "on," and "mercy" (on fol. 70[v]) instead of "mercie" or "merci."[71] Rather than added uniformly and at the same time as the Latin texts themselves, nearly half of the song cues appear to be a product of a process of adding to and editing the songs, undertaken by different hands at different times.

The recycling of this English lyrical fragment may witness the use and performance of the Latin poems by singers themselves, who, responding to the direction in the preface to provide suitable tunes ("notis"), added references to familiar songs as reminders of melodies that fit the formal contours and scansion of a given poem. This reinforces the impression of the song gathering as its own independent *libellus*, whose well-worn leaves indicate a degree of use that does not characterize the other gatherings of the Red Book of Ossory.[72] Perhaps similarities between songs (whether based on rhyme scene, meter, or form, etc.) caught the eye of a singer or scribe using the *libellus*, who then made note of this by adding new, marginal citations of musical models. Certainly, the Latin poems attached to "Haue mercie on me frere" all share the same general form – quatrains with a 7676 syllabic structure and ABAB rhyme scheme – making it plausible they could share the same melodic profile.[73]

If some of the song cues resulted from an ongoing process initiated by use, this may explain mismatches between the poetic and formal features of the Latin texts and their vernacular models.[74] This certainly seems to be the case for the other vernacular lyric employed twice in the songbook, first planned and boxed off like a rubric on fol. 72[r] as "Do do nihtyngale synge ful myrie | Shal y neure for þyn loue Lengre karie," and then in the upper

---

[70] On this concordance, see Wenzel, "New Occurrence."

[71] In the phrasing "mercy of me," the lyric is a closer match to the sermon concordance identified, ibid.

[72] Greene, *Lyrics*, iii, notes that "the condition of this last part of the manuscript shows that the pages with the songs have been fingered many times oftener than the rest of the volume."

[73] The three poems are edited ibid., 11–12, 27–28, and 41; Stemmler, *Latin Hymns*, 15, 32–33, and 51–52; and Colledge, *Latin Poems*, 18–21, 42–45, and 70–71.

[74] As Butterfield notes in "Poems Without Form?," *passim*, but particularly 183–184.

margin on fol. 74^r as "Do do ny3tyngale Syng wel mury | Shal y neure for þyn loue Lengre kary." The orthographic differences between the two citations are striking, and the Latin texts with which they are associated also do not match in syllable count or rhyme scheme: *Dies ista gaudii* on fol. 72^r and *Regem adoremus* on fol. 74^r.[75] Only *Regem adoremus* has a refrain indicated in the manuscript, while *Dies ista gaudii*, by contrast, has no refrain cued, although editor Edmund Colledge argues that the first quatrain (beginning "Dies ista gaudii") probably served as a recurring refrain.[76] Colledge is guided in this by the English lyrical cue for the song of the nightingale, which he interprets as a refrain whose melody and implied formal structure shaped the performance of both *Dies ista gaudii* and *Regem adoremus*.

Despite the formal mismatch between the two Latin songs on the page, the addition of a shared English lyric may gesture toward a parallel form realized in performance – namely, a strophic form with a regularly recurring refrain. The English nightingale lyric and its remembered melody, in this case, are adapted to fit the two newly composed Latin songs while also, in turn, inflecting and informing their poetic structures. The process of annotation throughout the poetic collection emerges through examples such as this as one motivated by the needs and interpretations of singers and scribes, as well as a process that was inherently fluid in its application. Curiously, the fact that many of the song cues in the Red Book of Ossory were added over time seems to have been largely overlooked in favor of attributing authorship of the Latin texts and their lyrical cues to Ledrede. While Ledrede himself may have contributed to the creation and compilation of some of the Latin poems, he was almost definitely not responsible for all, if any, of the vernacular song cues. In other words, the collection probably represents a collaborative, rather than individual, effort.

As in the St-Victor Miscellany and the Engelberg Codex, citations to vernacular song in the Red Book of Ossory sketch a picture of the broader song culture within which the scribes, copyists, and singers were enmeshed. The presence of song cues in not only one vernacular but two, English and French, reflects the multilingual milieu of Ledrede's clerical community in the Ossorian diocese of the fourteenth century.[77] Although

---

[75] Edited in Greene, *Lyrics*, 32 and 49–51; Stemmler, *Latin Hymns*, 38–39 and 61–62; and Colledge, *Latin Poems*, 50–53 and 82–83.

[76] Colledge, *Latin Poems*, 52 notes to lines 7–8.

[77] On the relationship between Ireland and England in relation to Ledrede, see ibid., xv–xix.

the only English in the manuscript is attached to lyrics, the question of language, and English in particular, is not absent from the other contents of the Red Book of Ossory. In a 1360 Latin letter on fol. 55ʳ from Edward III (r. 1327–1377) to the Sheriff of the Cross of Kilkenny and Seneschal of the Liberty of Kilkenny, English people living in Ireland who were speaking and raising their children in the Irish language were reprimanded and directed to learn English "on pain of loss of English liberty."[78] French is not mentioned, although it was spoken and used in written communication and for transactions and official records in Ireland and England throughout the fourteenth century.[79] Ledrede was himself English, and as Colledge writes, his "stormy career has been represented as one chapter in the centuries-long chronicle of the struggle between the Irish and the English."[80] The presence of Latin, French, and English in the poems of the Red Book of Ossory thus further marks the collection not as Irish, but rather as an effort closely linked to the influence of the English Bishop Ledrede and a longer history of language politics in Ireland.

The fragments of English song identify the Red Book of Ossory as a unique witness to a vernacular song practice with scant material remains – little survives of English-language song from this period. Notably, the transmission of *rondelli* with English song cues potentially supplements the otherwise lacking evidence for the English reception of the French *rondeau*.[81] In the Red Book of Ossory, three poems with song tags are *rondelli*: *Jhesu lux vera seculi* (fol. 71ᵛ); *Plangentis Christi ulnera* (fol. 72ʳ⁻ᵛ); and *Resurgenti cum gloria* (fol. 72ᵛ). Of these, the first is accompanied by a French lyric, the second by a Latin incipit, and the third an English lyrical snippet, respectively. The French lyric has no concordances where one might expect to find them in the *refrain* tradition, although – as with the second of the two French cues in the Red Book of Ossory – it has all the poetic characteristics of a *refrain*. In this, the French cues in the Red Book of Ossory are close in spirit to the *refrains* in the St-Victor Miscellany, several of which likewise remain

<hr/>

[78] Cited in Lawlor, "Calendar," 184.
[79] On the prominence of French as a spoken and written language in Ireland, see Neville, "French Language." Although now dated, see also Curtis, "Spoken Languages."
[80] Colledge, *Latin Poems*, xvi.
[81] A later fifteenth-century look at English *rondeaux* can be seen in Fallows, "English Song Repertories." More generally on the relations between England and France with a focus on literature and the works of Chaucer, which included an English *rondeau*, see Butterfield, *Familiar Enemy*. On lyrical imports into England and the transmission of French song forms, see Nelson, *Lyric Tactics*, 92–107, and Leach, "Learning French."

(a)

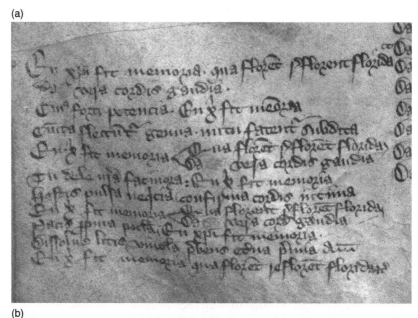

(b)

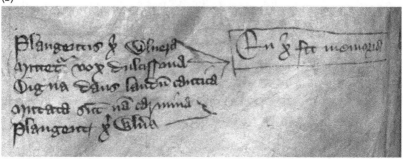

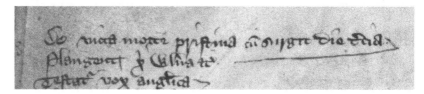

Figure 5.6 Red Book of Ossory, *En Christi fit memoria*, fol. 70^v (a), and *Plangentis Christi ulnera*, fol. 72^{r-v} (b) (details). Reproduced by kind permission of the Representative Body Library of the Church of Ireland

unidentified.[82] No concordances survive for the English lyric either, which is unsurprising considering its brevity and generic identity.

---

[82] The parallels between the French *refrains* in the St-Victor Miscellany and Red Book of Ossory have been noted several times; see, for instance, Greene, *Lyrics*, xxv–xxvi.

The marginal incipit of the Latin lyric, however, has a concordance within the Red Book of Ossory as the initial line of the refrain for another *rondellus*, *En Christi fit memoria* on fol. 70ᵛ (see Figure 5.6):[83]

rubric: **En Christi fit memoria**

En Christi fit memoria	*Plangentis Christi ulnera*
Qua florent reflorent florida	*Nittetur vox dulcisona*
Da vera cordis gaudia.	*Digna dans laudum cantica.*
Cuius forti potencia	Mutata sunt nam carmina
En Christi fit memoria	*Plangentis Christi ulnera*
Cuncta flectentur genua	De victa morte pristina
Nutu fatentur subdita.	Cum surgit die tercia.
En Christi fit memoria	*Plangentis Christi etc.*
Qua florent reflorent florida	
Da vera cordis gaudia.	

rubric: **Let there be remembrance of Christ**

Let there be remembrance of Christ,	*The sweetly sounding voice shines forth*
whereby all blossoms bloom and bloom again.	*of one who is mourning Christ's wounds.*
Give us our hearts' true joys.	For the songs are changed,
Before his great might,	*of one who is mourning Christ's wounds,*
let there be remembrance of Christ,	when on the third day he rises from a
all knees will be bent, all things confess	previous death that he has conquered.
themselves subject to his will.	*Of one who is mourning Christ's, etc.*
Let there be remembrance of Christ,	
whereby all blossoms bloom and bloom again.	
Give us our hearts' true joys.	

The Latin lyrical cue seems to be a later addition to *Plangentis Christi ulnera* based on its positioning and scribal hand, suggesting that a singer or scribe noted the formal and poetic parallels between the two *rondelli*. The melody for *En Christi fit memoria*, then, is reused for *Plangentis Christi ulnera*. Unfortunately, we have no indication of the original melody for *En Christi fit memoria*. What we do have is another *rondellus*, *Resurgenti cum gloria*, which survives with the English incipit "Haue god day my lemon &c" directly following *Plangentis Christi ulnera* on fol. 72ᵛ. *Resurgenti cum gloria* takes

---

[83] Texts edited and translated (adapted here) in Colledge, *Latin Poems*, 16–19 and 54–58.

a near-identical form to both *En Christi fit memoria* and *Plangentis Christi ulnera* with respect to syllable count and rhyme scheme:

rubric: Haue god day my lemon &c

Resurgenti cum gloria	In him who rises with glory,
Gaudeat ecclesia	let the church rejoice
Digne cantans alleluia.	appropriately singing Alleluia.
Rumpenti mortis vincula	In him who breaks the chains of death,
Resurgenti cum Gloria	in him who rises with glory,
Pede calcanti tartara	in him who treads down hell with his foot,
Vite reddenti premia	in him who restores the rewards of life,
Resurgenti cum Gloria etc.	in him who rises with glory etc.

As Greene notes concerning the relationships between these three *rondelli*, the use of the first line of "En Christi fit memoria" as the cue for *Plangentis Christi ulnera* points to the similar refrain identity for the English marginal cue for *Resurgenti cum gloria*.[84] To put it another way, it is possible that "Haue god day my lemon &c" records the initial words of a longer *rondeau* refrain, mirroring the use of the refrain incipit of *En Christi fit memoria* at the head of another *rondellus*. For *rondelli* in the Red Book of Ossory, marginal cues are probably comprised of refrains, just as they are in the St-Victor Miscellany and the Engelberg Codex. Finally, if this is the case, then "Haue god day my lemon &c" may bear witness to a yet-unidentified English *rondeau*, just as the marginal annotations in the Engelberg Codex did to German *rondeaux* unknown until the discoveries of Kornrumpf. At any rate, it is clear that a scribe or singer recognized the underlying *rondeau* form of several poems and made an effort to visually and musically link poems capable of being realized using a single shared melody.[85]

The fragmentary cues annotating Latin poems in the Red Book of Ossory bring to the fore once again the centrality of the refrain in the practice of contrafacture. This is the case even though, of the three manuscripts discussed in this chapter, the English, French, and Latin paratexts of this Irish compilation engage the least with refrain forms. Only six of the thirteen annotated Latin poems employ structural refrains; one other, *Peperit virgo*, features a highly repetitive (and frequently debated) form similar to several others in the Red Book of Ossory.[86] That nearly half of the Latin poems accompanied by lyrical paratexts feature refrains, however, is significant, as is the fact that refrains

---

[84] Greene, *Lyrics*, xvii–xviii.

[85] O'Sullivan's term "kaleidoscopic" for the "complex associative webs created in the minds of listeners" by means of contrafacture might apply here, as singers and scribes generated associations among songs in the collection. *Marian Devotion*, 79.

[86] For the most recent edition of the text and exploration of the issues surrounding its structure as it relates to its vernacular song cue, *Mayde yn the moore lay*, see Butterfield, "Poems Without Form?"

dominate the formal structures of the collection as a whole. Refrains are central to the lyrical and musical endeavors represented in the Red Book of Ossory, in addition to serving as the cornerstone in the textual inscription of contrafacture.

Despite the preface's reference to melodies, no music survives for any of the Latin poetry in the Red Book of Ossory, nor for the vernacular cues and their concordances.[87] On the whole, it is a frustratingly *un*musical collection, which goes a long way toward explaining its relative absence in musicological literature. Even in comparison with the similarly unnotated St-Victor Miscellany, the Red Book of Ossory offers far less in terms of sounding music, since certain of the French *refrains* transmitted in the Parisian collection survive with musical settings. Nevertheless, the Latin poetry of the Red Book of Ossory points to the ability of material manifestations of contrafacture to serve as a shorthand for music. Textual cues like those in all three manuscripts discussed here take the place of musical notation or, in the case of the Engelberg Codex, function as a placeholder before notation is added. While such a technique is employed in different ways across these three sources, the textual signaling of contrafacture virtually always denotes the existence of music in some form, even if its sonic contours are lost, audible only to those who once held the repertoire in their aural memories. For the poems of the Red Book of Ossory, this partly material, partly memorial practice affirms their identity as songs, even if the melodic component remains out of our reach and hearing. Moreover, the link between the preface and the following song cues frames contrafacture as inherently performative. Although inscription initiates the link, remembered melodies and new and old texts come together not on the page but through performance.[88]

Refrains Across Language

This chapter has explored the interplay between Latin and vernacular song and refrain evidenced by cueing in and around the songs themselves in the form of rubrics and lyrical fragments. As the three manuscripts explored here uniquely showcase, refrains sit at the center of this practice of inscribing contrafacture. As the locus for linguistic and registral exchange and

---

[87] A still-cited article by Joan Rimmer, "Carole, Rondeau and Branle," asserts that some of the poems can be "fitted exactly to contemporary music" using melodies from Italian, French, and English sources, although no evidence supports this.

[88] See also Strohm, "Late-Medieval Sacred Songs," 145, where he notes that the textual signaling of contrafacts "was not necessarily a primarily *textual* manipulation but a *performative* one, where a poet or musician would sing the song with newly invented words, or the words with a newly invented tune, fitting them together in his head."

melodic sharing, refrains inscribed on the manuscript page encapsulate the underlying processes of contrafacture. This speaks to the weight of musical and poetic material embodied by the refrain – refrains can signal the overriding poetic structure (syllable count, rhyme scheme, etc.) for an entire song, just as the refrain's melody can be employed across strophic material and refrain. Refrains, in other words, can serve as a stand-in for the entirety of a song as the "sticky," memorable parts of song that readily embed themselves in the ear and memory.

While contrafacture often describes movement from secular to sacred, the examples discussed in this chapter neither affirm nor overtly contradict this registral directionality. Although the preface in the Red Book of Ossory advocates for replacing "secular" songs with "pious" substitutes, the intimate sharing of formal and musical structures manifested in the inscription of vernacular song across all three manuscripts argues against a strict dichotomy between the sacred and the secular. Song and refrain paratexts instead ensured the continued resonance of vernacular song regardless of register in the performance of Latin poetry. This is the case, indeed, for all contrafacts – the sharing of music by more than one text enables texts to be heard and interpreted against one another. Through the inscription of the vernacular texts on the page, moreover, the interaction of old and new, Latin and vernacular, silent and sounded, becomes more potent and direct.

The St-Victor Miscellany, Engelberg Codex, and Red Book of Ossory, in diverging yet parallel ways, testify to a link between Latin and vernacular song that orbits around the refrain. Across all three sources, moreover, rubrics and marginal lyrical fragments denote in some cases the sole surviving or earliest records of vernacular song and its refrains, whether the earliest French *refrains* in the St-Victor Miscellany or the refrains of German and English *rondeaux*. Above all, the trio of sources reflects the needs, song cultures, and conventions of circumscribed, local communities – an abbey school in Paris, a monastery in Engelberg, and a clerical community headed by an English bishop in the diocese of Ossory. Although most Latin refrain songs are not explicitly linked to vernacular song practices, these sources show how the refrain could be exploited as a site for the meaningful intersection of Latin and vernacular song. Scribes, copyists, and compilers provided material evidence for this relationship as it emerged from within localized and multilingual communities of song and singers, whether schools, monasteries, or regional dioceses. Despite the emphasis on inscription in all three manuscripts, the refrain emerges as a site of memory once again, namely the memory of melodies circulating across language within religious communities throughout Europe.

6 | Conclusion

I began this book with a question: What does the refrain do in Latin song? What meanings and discourses does the repeated refrain generate within the broader repertoire of devotional Latin song in the Middle Ages? I have made the case for the significance of the Latin refrain within discourses of devotional song, time and temporality, inscription, performance, community, memory, intertextuality, and language, among other interwoven threads. Without claiming a monolithic interpretation for the Latin refrain, I have identified many points of connections and shared meanings among songs and sources for a repertoire widely distributed over time and place.

A thread running throughout the book is the amorphous concept of community. The devotional Latin refrain song was a tool of devotional sociability for medieval communities of clerics, female and male monastics, and students, closely aligning with the ritual sociability engendered by the liturgy. The communities within which the Latin song was cultivated were varied, and the names of only a few individuals emerge from a sea of anonymity. Johannes de Perchausen and Bishop Richard Ledrede are two authority figures who feature prominently in the compiling and copying of localized repertoires of refrain songs, bearing witness to the power hierarchies underlying the creation and transmission of the refrain song. Latin refrains at times may have bubbled up within religious communities as part of a shared culture of devotional singing, but they were also part of disciplinary agendas in which communities of singers were defined by rank and age, their voices carefully controlled by means of devotional song. The refrain in particular functions as a meaningful instrument of community formation and maintenance, whether by mediating the experience of time, creating a sense of unity and togetherness through song, or sketching the linguistic parameters of one's community.

By virtue of its repeatability and memorability, the refrain also resides in the collective memories of religious communities, becoming a site of intertextual and linguistic play through composition, inscription, and performance. The circulation of refrains across song and language testifies to the mobility, or *mouvance*, as well as the generic flexibility of medieval Latin song. While the refrain structurally fixes the form of a text, bounding its strophic movement and controlling its temporal pacing, it is also a formal locus for movement and mobility. The refrain and its surrounding strophic material could be recreated, reworked, reinterpreted, and retexted to fit different contexts and serve different functions, always with an awareness of the devotional underpinning of the repertoire. Latin song and refrain were part of an active practice of devotional song, a form of medieval musicking shaped by the participation of scribes, singers, compilers, poets, and composers.

In this active process of music making, place matters. Medieval song constantly navigates the tension between local practices and transregional transmission, unique styles and conventional forms. Concordances allow for the tracing of long histories for certain songs and refrains across time and place, while the significant number of *unica* suggests equally an ongoing interest in creating new works in the same form alongside the transmission of established ones. Certain manuscripts have figured more prominently, most often sources reflecting richly textured, local approaches to the creation, compilation, and performance of the refrain song. In many cases, manuscript sources suggest shared performance contexts and practices that connect with the festive calendar of the European Middle Ages, even when demonstrating no other connections beyond preserving refrain-form Latin songs. The three disparate manuscripts examined in Chapter 5, for instance, underscore how different communities – pedagogical, monastic, clerical – distributed across thirteenth- to fourteenth-century Europe might nevertheless approach the Latin retexting of vernacular refrains in similar ways. Conversely, the locality of the refrain song is signaled by the variable, even modular, reorganization of its strophic texts, the addition and subtraction of liturgical formulas indicating its use within the liturgy, reworkings of texts, and the sheer number of *unica* recorded in the Appendix.

The locality of the Latin refrain song can be seen in scribal approaches to its inscription. I have repeatedly returned to the manuscript page in order to locate indirect traces of how scribes, and by association the communities within which they were working, understood the performance, function, and meaning of the refrain song. Although the inscription of the refrain song was inflected by performative orality and processes of oral transmission, scribal practices nevertheless reveal certain attitudes toward refrains. Scribes tell us that the refrain is an important formal feature of some Latin songs by setting songs with refrains apart from those without; providing a logic for the gathering and compilation of song; offering a link between vernacular and Latin song; and serving as a performance cue. Each chapter explores insights offered by scribal practices through the material witnesses of compilation, rubrication, and paratexts. Yet the interplay of orality and inscription also plays out in Latin song in ways that resonate with the patterns of transmission similarly witnessed in vernacular song repertoires. The refrain and refrain song were not fixed, nor can an "original" version be readily identified; traces of change, adaptation, and variation – whether introduced by singers or scribes – repeatedly signal the generic and performative fluidity, or *mouvance*, of the Latin refrain song within medieval communities.

Further Contexts

With over 400 songs listed in the Appendix transmitted in dozens of sources, much more can be explored in the context of individual songs and sources. Further contexts for performance within the liturgy, for instance, and the full extent of musical and textual relationships to tropes, hymns, and sequences are only beginning to be fully worked out for Latin song, including those with refrains. Additional performance possibilities already posited for medieval Latin song might also have accommodated refrain forms, including devotional plays and representational rites, processions, monastic reading practices, or *lectio publica*, preaching, pedagogy, and personal or communal forms of prayer, such as litanies. The degree of participation by men and women, boys and girls, also remains a question, answers to which rest in the witness of individual manuscripts and their histories of use within particular communities. Moreover, at the risk of reinscribing an anachronistic dichotomy between the sacred and the secular, refrains in a less devotional register demand consideration apart from those examined in this book. Refrains featuring in laments, moralizing and historical poems, and love songs, to list a few topical areas, operate differently than devotional refrains in repertoires of Latin song in terms of how they were composed, where they are transmitted, and their contexts for performance.

The chronological endpoint of this book with the printing of refrain songs in the Finnish/Swedish *Piae Cantiones* in the sixteenth and early seventeenth centuries represents only a glimpse into the early modern and contemporary reception and performance of the medieval Latin refrain song. Manuscript and print collections of devotional Latin and vernacular songs from the fifteenth century onward, especially across German-speaking lands, include Latin songs, or vernacular contrafacts, whose histories can be traced to the twelfth and thirteenth centuries.[1] The *cantionale* of the Moosburger Graduale offers an early witness to this later devotional song tradition, yet its contents are embedded within song repertoires reaching back to the twelfth century. Most often, *cantiones* revolve around the Christmas season, the New Year, and the Virgin Mary, reflecting a growing interest in compiling festive collections of songs for the liturgical and seasonal year.

The Latin, vernacular, and bilingual carol repertoire of fourteenth- to sixteenth-century England also exhibits several formal and poetic links with the Latin refrain song, as well as rare concordances. Most saliently, the English carol shares with the Latin refrain song the formal attribute of the refrain, either in the form of a refrain attached to each strophe, or a burden that typically repeats between strophes.[2] Occasionally, carols either rework the same liturgical texts as earlier Latin songs (including popular hymns and sequences like *Ave maris stella* or *Veni sancte spiritus*), employ similar refrains (or, in the case of the carol, burdens), or include textual formulas suggestive of the same liturgical functions fulfilled at times by the Latin refrain song (namely, as *Benedicamus Domino* song-tropes). The most notable connection of the Latin refrain song to the carol derives from the poems of the Red Book of Ossory, which are often cited as proto-examples in histories of the English carol. The medieval Latin refrain song, in other words, is intimately connected to later multilingual repertoires of religious song throughout Europe, its texts, form, and festive scope resonating throughout centuries of devotional music making.

Afterlives

The enduring afterlife of the Latin refrain song can be best identified in the widespread tradition of singing and recording Christmas songs, or more colloquially, Christmas carols. As I note in Chapter 2, the refrain song transmitted uniquely in F, *Ecce mundi gaudium*, is one example of a Christmas song whose transmission in the Middle Ages was apparently limited, yet it has entered into the modern recording repertoire of Christmas carols. Songs whose earliest occurrences are in the thirteenth and fourteenth centuries, like *Puer nobis nascitur* and *Puer natus in*

---

[1] For overviews, see Schlager, "Cantiones" and Strohm, "Sacred Song."

[2] On the carol, see most recently Fallows, *Henry V*, and the still-seminal Greene, ed., *The Early English Carol.*

Betlehem, both translated into an array of vernaculars, continue to be recorded on Christmas albums. Although it would be anachronistic to label medieval Latin refrain songs "Christmas carols," this repertoire provides many of the earliest witnesses to a form of widespread, perhaps even popular, devotional singing designed to foster the communal commemoration of the major feasts of the church year, with a special focus on the feasts of Christmastide.

Finally, medieval Latin refrain songs are delightful, appealing pieces of music, featuring singable melodies and accessible poetry that draw singer and listener into the space and time of the song. The refrain plays no small part in this, becoming anchored in the ears and memory of listeners, measuring their temporal progress through the song, and offering a moment ripe for participation, whether actual or imagined. The appeal of the refrain song has not been lost on contemporary performers of early music. By contrast to a history of benign neglect in scholarship – not including its foregrounding in histories of religious dance – the Latin refrain song has become a staple in the concert and recording repertoire of several ensembles. While interpretations and realizations vary, performance practices in concert and recordings overwhelmingly highlight the festive orientation, approachable music and poetry, and participatory potential of the refrain song. Through its prominence in contemporary performances and recordings, the medieval Latin refrain song continues to belong to an active culture of devotional song, shaped in the twenty-first century by performers, editors, and scholars who are repeatedly drawn to its rich history and engaging words, melodies, and refrains.

Appendix Latin Refrain Songs

Songs are listed alphabetically by incipit, with folio and page numbers indicating starting position alone. Numbers in parentheses indicate alternative foliation or pagination. A forward slash between numbers indicates that the song occurs on additional folios or pages. Only songs with refrains in at least one source are included here; contrafacts, when discussed, can be located in the Index of Works. Sources not included in the list of Manuscript Sigla are indicated here using the conventions employed by the Répertoire International des Sources Musicales (RISM): https://rism .info/community/sigla.html.

Incipit	Source
A dextris Dei	*Piae Cantiones* (1582), no. 56
A patre genitus	Saint Omer 351, 14^v
A sinu patris mittitur	F, 465^v
A solis ortus cardine	F, 464^r
Ad cultum tue laudis	Moosburger Graduale, 241^r
Ad infantum triumfantum	St-M C, 43^v
Ad sancte Katerine	St-Victor Miscellany, 178^r
Adam quia vetitum	ORawl, 259^r (30^r)
Adest dies optata socii	Luxembourg 27, 75^v
Agnus pugnat cum dracone	Brussels 5649–5667, 7^v
	Graz 409, 71^v
Agnus sine macula	Tours 927, 13^r
Alleluia regi regum omnium	St-Victor Miscellany, 183^v
Amor habet superos	Carmina Burana, 37^{r*}
Amoris vinculo	Red Book of Ossory, 71^v
Angelus emittitur	*Piae Cantiones* (1582), no. 1
	Piae Cantiones (1625), no. 1
Anni novi novitas	Moosburger Graduale, 232^r
Anni novi prima diie	Hortus Deliciarum, 30^v
Anno revirente	Saint Omer 351, 19^r
Annus gaudia	Codex Calixtinus, 215^v
Annus novus in gaudio	Le Puy A, 1^v/171^r
	Le Puy B, 1^r
	St-M A, 36^v
Annus renascitur	F, 468^r
Argumenta faluntur fiscie	Later Cambridge Songbook, 2^r (1^r)

(*cont.*)

Incipit	Source
Ascendit Christus hodie	Moosburger Graduale, 249^r
	Piae Cantiones (1625), no. 48
Assunt festa Paschalia	Red Book of Ossory, 72^v
Ave inquit angelus	Bobbio, 335^r
Ave Maria virgo virginum	F, 469^v
Ave maris stella ave	F, 373^r
Ave maris stella celi	Bobbio, 336^v
Ave maris stella divinitatis	Graz 258, 2^r
	Graz 409, 71^v
	Piae Cantiones (1582), no. 27
	Piae Cantiones (1625), no. 11
Ave mater piissima	Engelberg Codex, 168^v
Ave mater salvatoris	St-M D, 16^v
Ave mater stella maris	Saint Omer 351, 16^v
Ave plena gracia	Bobbio, 336^r
Ave regina celorum	St-Victor Miscellany, 184^v
Ave salus hominum	F, 247^r
Ave stella maris, Maria	Engelberg Codex, 169^v
Ave virgo mater intemerata	Moosburger Graduale, 240^r
Ave virgo mater Jesu Christi	Moosburger Graduale, 239^v
Ave virgo stella maris	Bobbio, 335^v
Bacche bene venies	Carmina Burana, 89^r
Beata nobis gaudia	Tours 927, 10^r
Beata viscera	Bekynton Anthology, 19^r
	Charleville 190, 159^r
	D-DS 2777, 4^r
	Engelberg Codex, 82^v (binding strip)
	F, 422^r
	F-T 990, 112^v
	GB-Ob Auct. 6 Q 3.17, ii^r
	I-Bc Q.11, 5^r
	I-TOD Fondo Antico No. 2, 178^v
	SG 383, p. 174
	US-Wc 1281, 32^r
	W2, 156^v
Beatus qui non abiit	Bekynton Anthology, 139^v
	F, 424^r
Benedicte tres personas	*Piae Cantiones* (1582), no. 65
	Piae Cantiones (1625), no. 50
Breves dies hominis	F, 469^r
	Tours 927, 19^r
Canite canite uultu iocundo	Red Book of Ossory, 75^v
Cantat omnis creatura	Tours 927, 11^v
Caritate nimia	Red Book of Ossory, 77^r
Castis psallamus mentibus	Moosburger Graduale, 231^r

238   *Appendix*

(cont.)

Incipit	Source
Castitatis lilium effloruit / Incorrupta Virgo	LoA, 10^r
	Mad 288, 165^v
	Mad 19421, 106^r
	Sens 46, p. 28
	St-M A, 42^r
Christe redemptor omnium	Red Book of Ossory, 74^r
Christi parentele	Red Book of Ossory, 71^r
Christi sit nativitas	Moosburger Graduale, 242^r
Christi sponsa Katharina	Carmina Burana (4660a), III^r
Christo psallat eccelsia	F, 464^v
Christo sit laus in celestibus	F, 468^r
Christus iam misit inclitum	Moosburger Graduale, 249^r
Christus patris gratie	F, 465^v
Christus vicit resurgendo	Moosburger Graduale, 248^r
Circa canit Michael	Tours 927, 13^v
Cohors leta ducat chorus	F-LG 2, 256^v
Congaudeant catholici	Codex Calixtinus, 185^r
Congaudeat ecclesia	Le Puy A, 28^v/162^v
	Le Puy B, 16^v/104^v
	St-M A, 51^r
Congaudeat turba fidelium	Aosta Cod. 11, 85^v
	Aosta Cod. 13, 62^v
	Apt 6, 115^r
	Cologne 196, 63^r
	Engelberg Codex, 130^r/180^r/182^r
	Le Puy A, 107^r
	Le Puy B, 60^r
	Mad 19421, 107^v
	Mad 288, 188^r
	Mad 289, 128^r
	Piae Cantiones (1582), no. 10
	Piae Cantiones (1625), no. 6
	St-M A, 61^v
	Stuttg, 71^v
Congaudent omnes angeli	Engelberg Codex, 169^v
Congaudentes ludite	Carmina Burana, 49^v
Congratulare et letare	Engelberg Codex, 169^r
Cosmi proch inicium	Erfurt Codex, 106^r
Culpe purgator veteris	F, 466^r
	Tours 927, 19^v
Cum animadverterem	F, 225^v
	ORawl, 244^r (15^r)
	W1, 117^r (108^r)
Cum sit omnis caro fenum	LoB, 27^v
	Piae Cantiones (1582), no. 38
	Piae Cantiones (1625), no. 71
	extensive circulation; see CPI Database

(*cont.*)

Incipit	Source
Cuncti simus concanentes	Llibre Vermell, 24^r
Cur suspectum me tenet domina	Carmina Burana, 49^v
Custodi nos	StV, 281^r
Da da nobis nunc	Red Book of Ossory, 70^v
Da laudis homo nova cantica	Le Puy A, 12^r
	Le Puy B, 6^r
	Mad 289 141^r
De papa scholastico	Paris lat. 11331, 12^r
De patre principio	F, 463^r
	Tours 927, 18^v
De radice processerat	*Piae Cantiones* (1582), no. 53
	Piae Cantiones (1625), no. 5
De radice virginis	Red Book of Ossory, 71^r
De sinu patris verbum emicuit	Graz 409, 1^v
De supernis affero	Engelberg Codex, 168^r
	St-M A, 32^r
De supernis sedibus	Moosburger Graduale, 237^r
Debacchatur mundus pomo	Carmina Burana, 16^v
Decet vox letitie	F, 463^r
Dei matris cantibus	Luxembourg 27, 21^r
Dei patris unice	Mad 289, 146^v
Deinceps ex nulla	Graz 409, 71^r
	Moosburger Graduale, 238^r
Descende celitus	F, 467^v
Deus pater filium	Tours 927, 14^r
Diastematica vocis armonia	Later Cambridge Songbook, 2^v (1^v)
Dies felix et gloria (see also *Felix dies et grata*)	Tours 927, 11^r
Dies ista colitur	A-Wn frag. 660, 1^b
	Bobbio, 334^v
	Colmar 187, 45^v
	Engelberg 1003, 117^r
	Graz 258, 2^v
	Graz 409, 273^r
	Leipzig 225, 178^v
	LoA, 18^r
	Moosburger Graduale, 236^v
	Sens 46, p. 33
	St. Pölten Processional, 8^r
	Stuttg, 25^v/81^r
Dies ista dies pretiosa	Graz 258, 2^r
	Graz 409, 273^r
	Zürich C. 58, 148^v
Dies ista gaudii	Red Book of Ossory, 72^r
Dies ista gaudium	Mad 289, 148^r
Dies salutis oritur	F, 466^r
Dies venit dies tua	Red Book of Ossory, 73^r
Dire mortis datus pene	Red Book of Ossory, 72^r
Disciplinae filius	*Piae Cantiones* (1582), no. 42

(*cont.*)

Incipit	Source
	Piae Cantiones (1625), no. 76
Diva summi gracia	Erfurt Codex, 101^r
Divinum stillant	St-M D, 8^r
Dogmatum falsas species	F, 438^r
	F-CECad 3. J. 250, 7^r
Domum obedentie	F-LG 2, 255^v
	F-Pn lat. 3237, 113^v
Dulce dignum melodia	St-M D, 11^r
Dulces laudes [*Dulcis laudis*] *tympano* [see also *Martyr fuit Stephanus*]	Antiphonarium Lausannense III.3.1, p. 103
	Antiphonarium Lausannense III.3.2, 55^f
	Antiphonarium Lausannense vol. 1, 47^v
	CH-Fcu Z 4, 83^v
	Moosburger Graduale, 241^v
Dum medium silentium componit	F, 422^v
	ORawl, 249^r (20^r)
Dum medium silentium tenerent	B-Br II.1019, 126^v
	Bekynton Anthology, 65^r
	CH-SGs 551, p. 49
	D-DS 2777, 4^v
	F, 422^v
	GB-Ob Bodl. 603, 57^r
	GB-Ob Digby 166, 56^v
	ORawl, 248^v (19^v)
	Royal 7.A.VI, 107^v
Dum pater familias	Codex Calixtinus, 222^r (193^r)
Dum Philippus moritur	Carmina Burana, 52^r
Dum prius inculta	Carmina Burana, 36^r
Ecce chorus virginum	Carmina Burana, 19^v
Ecce iam celebria	Moosburger Graduale, 242^v
Ecce mundi gaudium	F, 470^r
Ecce nomen Domini	Moosburger Graduale, 234^v
Ecce novum gaudium	Piae Cantiones (1582), no. 7
	Piae Cantiones (1625), no. 13
Ecce novus annus est	Graz 409, 2^v
	Le Puy A, 53^r
	Le Puy B, 30^r
	Moosburger Graduale, 244^r
	St. Pölten Processional, 7^v
Ecce tempus gaudii	F, 468^v
Ecce torpet probitas	Bekynton Anthology, 65^v
	Carmina Burana, 43^r
	Later Cambridge Songbook, 2^v (1^v, 298^r)
	Saint Omer 351, 19^v

(*cont.*)

Incipit	Source
Ecce venit de Syon	Engelberg 102, 139^r
	Graz 258, 2^v
	Graz 409, 71^v
	Hortus Deliciarum, 27^r
	Moosburger Graduale, 233^v
	SG 1397, p. 21
	St. Pölten Processional, 11^r
	Stuttg, 25^r
Eclypsim patitur	F, 322^v
	W1, 110^r (101^r)
Eia musa propera	Le Puy A, 63^r/164^v
	Le Puy B, 35^v/112^v
	St-M A, 79^v
En Christi fit memoria	Red Book of Ossory, 70^v
En parit virgo regia	Red Book of Ossory, 74^v
Estas non apparuit	Carmina Burana, 61^v
Estivali gaudio tellus renovator	Carmina Burana, 34^v/105^r
Eva cunctos perdidit	F-Pn lat. 1343, 63^r
Evangelizo gaudium	Moosburger Graduale, 243^r
Ex legis observantia	*Piae Cantiones* (1625), no. 32
Exceptivam actionem	Bekynton Anthology, 138^v
	F, 444^r
	SG 1397, p. 21
	SG 382, p. 87
	Stuttg, 70^r
	extensive circulation; see CPI Database
Exemplum [Templum] veri salomonis	Saint Omer 351, 16^r
Exultantes in partu virginis	F-RS 1275, 190^r
	Le Puy A, 27^v/162^r
	Le Puy B, 16^r/103^v
	St-M A, 52^v
Exultemus et letemur	Later Cambridge Songbook, 7^r (4^r)
Exultemus et letemur hodie	F-LG 2, 276^v
Exultemus sobrie	F, 468^r
Exultet celi curia	Codex Calixtinus, 130^r
Exultet hec concio	F, 471^v
Exultet nostra concio	Mad 19421, 108^r
	Mad 289, 127^v
Exultet plebs fidelium	F, 464^v
Fas legis prisce	Stuttg, 34^v
Felix dies et grata	F, 463^r
Festa dies agitur mundo	LoB, 47^r
Festa dies agitur qua	Saint Omer 351, 15^r
Fidelium sonet vox sobria	F, 465^r

(cont.)

Incipit	Source
Filii calvarie	F, 463$^\text{v}$
Flore vernat virginali	Engelberg Codex, 168$^\text{v}$
Floret silva nobilis	Carmina Burana, 60$^\text{v}$
Florizet vox dulcisonans	Moosburger Graduale, 249$^\text{v}$
Flos campi profert lilium	Moosburger Graduale, 240$^\text{v}$
Fons salutis nostre plene	Red Book of Ossory, 70$^\text{v}$
Frigescente caritatis	Saint Omer 351, 16$^\text{v}$
Frigus hinc est	Carmina Burana, 35$^\text{r}$
Fulget dies hec pre ceteris	Moosburger Graduale, 235$^\text{r}$
Fulget hodie	Aosta Cod. 11, 83$^\text{r}$
	Aosta Cod. 13, 59$^\text{r}$
Gallia cum leticia	St-Victor Miscellany, 181$^\text{r}$
Gaude Syon iubila	Graz 409, 2$^\text{v}$
	St. Pölten Processional, 12$^\text{v}$
Gaude Syon devoto gaudio	F, 469$^\text{v}$
Gaude virgo mater Christi	Red Book of Ossory, 74$^\text{r}$
Gaudeat ecclesia inventa	Moosburger Graduale, 232$^\text{v}$
Gaudeat ecclesia presulis	F, 471$^\text{r}$
Gaudeat hec concio	F, 466$^\text{v}$
Glomerat in aula	Graz 409, 72$^\text{v}$
Gratulemur dies est leticie	Later Cambridge Songbook, 1$^\text{r}$ (2$^\text{r}$)
Gregis pastor Tytirus [Tityrus]	Moosburger Graduale, 232$^\text{r}$
	St-M D, 13$^\text{v}$
Hac in anni ianua	ORawl, 246$^\text{r}$ (17$^\text{r}$)
Hac in die salutari	F, 363$^\text{v}$
Hec est turris	Engelberg Codex, 152$^\text{r}$
Hec nova gaudia	Carmina Burana, 105$^\text{v}$
Hic verus Dei famulus	LoA, 99$^\text{r}$
Hoc in sollempnio	Later Cambridge Songbook, 7$^\text{r}$ (4$^\text{r}$)
Hodie splendor et lux	Bobbio, 334$^\text{v}$
	I-Ma C 243 inf. [as *Puer nobis natus est*], p. 613
Hospes laudatur	Carmina Burana, 90$^\text{v}$
Hostis perfidus et invidus	Graz 409, 2$^\text{v}$
Hunc diem leti ducamus	LoA, 55$^\text{v}$
Iam missum est per angelum	Seckauer Cantionarium, 203$^\text{r}$
Iam ver aperit terre gremium	F, 469$^\text{r}$
Iam ver exoritur	Tours 927, 12$^\text{v}$
Ianus annum circinat	Carmina Burana, 18$^\text{v}$
Ich was ein kint so wol [bilingual]	Carmina Burana, 72$^\text{r}$
Ignis in rubo cernitur	Tours 927, 12$^\text{v}$
Iherusalem Iherusalem letare	St-Victor Miscellany, 183$^\text{r}$
Illuxit lux celestis gratie	F, 468$^\text{r}$
Imperator rex Grecorum	Carmina Burana, 16$^\text{v}$
Impleta sunt omnia	St-M C, 83$^\text{v}$
In domino confidite	F, 464$^\text{r}$

(*cont.*)

Incipit	Source
In hac die Dei	F, 463^r
	OBod 937, 446^v
	Tours 927, 11^v
In hac die gloriosa	Bobbio, 336^r
In hoc anni circulo [see also *Verbum caro factum est*]	Bobbio, 334^r
	F-Pn lat. 1343, 40^r
	I-Ma C 243 inf., p. 613
	I-Vsmc 71, 67^v
	Le Puy A, 31^r
	Le Puy B, 18^r
	Mad 289, 147^r
	Piae Cantiones (1582), no. 2
	Piae Cantiones (1625), no. 4
	SG 392, p. 88
	St-M A, 48^r
	extensive circulation; see CPI Database
In hoc festo breviter	St-M A, 33^v
In hoc statu gratie	F, 470^r
In laudes debitas	Tours 927, 9^v
In laudes [*laudem*] *innocentium*	Autun S 175^{10}, 200^v
	St-M A, 40^r
In natali Domini	Piae Cantiones (1625), no. 26
In natali summi regis	Graz 409, 72^r
	Later Cambridge Songbook [as *In natali novi regis*], 7^r (4^r)
	Moosburger Graduale, 238^v
In rerum principio	F, 469^r
Incomparabiliter cum iucunditate	St-M A, 46^v
Inportana veneri	Saint Omer 351, 17^v
Integra inviolata	GB-Occc 489, 2^r
Intonent hodie [see also *Personent hodie*]	Moosburger Graduale, 232^v
Iocundemur socii	Carmina Burana, 95^r
Iubila rutila mater Ecclesia	Red Book of Ossory, 71^r
Iubilemus cordis voce	Graz 409, 2^r
	Laon 263, 123^r
Iuvenes amoriferi	Carmina Burana, 49^v
Jacobe sancte tuum	Codex Calixtinus, 131^r/186^v
Jhesu lux vera seculi	Red Book of Ossory, 71^v
Jhesu lux vera mencium	Red Book of Ossory, 74^v
Johelius prophetiae	*Piae Cantiones*, no. 33
Jugi voce cum iubilo	Bobbio, 336^v
Lac de silice	F [as *Latex silice*], 230^v
	Graz 409, 1^v
	ORawl [as *Latex silice*], 240^v (11^v)
	Stuttg [as *Latex silice*], 30^v

(cont.)

Incipit	Source
	W1 [as *Latex silice*], 81^r (74^r)
Laetetur Ierusalem	*Piae Cantiones* (1582), no. 54
	Piae Cantiones (1625), no. 8
Latebata in scriptura	Saint Omer 351, 16^v
Laudes canamus virginis	Luxembourg 27, 23^v
Laudibus Nicholai	St-Victor Miscellany, 189^r
Letare mater ecclesia	St-Victor Miscellany, 181^v
Letatur turba puerorum	Moosburger Graduale, 243^v
Letetur orbis hodie	St-M D, 23^r
Leto leta concio	F, 470^v
	Hortus Deliciarum, 90^v
Lilium floruit	St-M C, 43^r
Lingua manu opere	Red Book of Ossory, 70^v
Los set gotxs (bilingual)	Llibre Vermell, 23^v
Luce qua letatur	Red Book of Ossory, 73^v
Lumen patris resplenduit	St-M A, 40^r
Luto carens et latere	Bord 283, 134^v
	F, 463^v
	LoB, 48^r
	Tours 927, 18^v
	W1, 80^r (73^r)
Lux optata claruit	Graz 409, 2^r
	Klagenfurt Perg. 7, 6^r
	LoA, 29^v
	Sens 46, p. 36
Magno gaudens gaudio	Later Cambridge Songbook, 4^v (297^v)
Magnus qui factus erat	Tours 927, 12^r
Mariam matrem virginem	Llibre Vermell, 25^r
Marie preconio	St-Victor Miscellany, 177^r
Martyr fuit Stephanus [see also *Dulces laudes*	Engelberg Codex, 128^v
tympano]	SG 392, p. 90
Mater ecclesia	St-Victor Miscellany, 188^r
Mater summi domini	Seckauer Cantionarium, 193^v
	St. Pölten Processional, 9^v
	Moosburger Graduale, 238^v
Militans ecclesia	St-Victor Miscellany, 186^r
Mira dies oritur	St-M C, 38^v
Mira lege miro modo	St-M A, 78^r
Mira sunt prodigia	F-R 666, 92^v
	Le Puy A, 153^r
Mirabatur antiquitas	Graz 409, 72^r
Miro modo concepisti	Bobbio, 335^v
Miserans miserans	Red Book of Ossory, 74^r
Missus est Emmanuel	St. Pölten Processional, 15^r
Missus est per sidera	Wienhäuser Liederbuch, 5^r
Mittendus predicitur	Tours 927, 13^v
Modus est indicativus	Erfurt Codex, 101^r

(*cont.*)

Incipit	Source
Morbis heu gravissimis	Erfurt Codex, inside cover
Mors vite propicia	F, 464^r
	Tours 927, 10^v
Mos florentis venustatis	Moosburger Graduale, 231^v
Multiformi succendente	Carmina Burana, 80^r
Mundi princeps eicitur	F, 464^v
Nato celorum Domino	Engelberg Codex, 175^v
Nato Marie filio	Red Book of Ossory, 70^r
Natus est de virgine	Red Book of Ossory, 70^r
Natus est rex	St-M C, 43^v
Nicholae presulum	F, 471^r
Nicholai laudibus	St-Victor Miscellany, 182^r
Nicholai sollempnio	St-Victor Miscellany, 186^v
Nicholaus inclitus	Tours 927, 11^v
Nicholaus pontifex	F, 471^r
Nobilis mei miserere, precor	Carmina Burana, 81^v
Nobilitas ornata	Ludus super Anticlaudianum, 36^r
Noe noe iterumque noe	Aosta Cod. 11, 84^r
	Aosta Cod. 13, 60^r
Nomen a solemnibus	Carmina Burana, 17^r
	St-M B, 164^r
	St-M C, 41^r
Non contrecto quam affecto	Carmina Burana, 36^v
Nos respectu gratie	Graz 409, 71^v
	Colmar 187, 45^v
	Laon 263, 141^r
	Prague XIII.H.3 c, 262^v
	St. Pölten Processional, 12^r
	Vienna 4494, 68^r
Nostri festi gaudium	Le Puy A, 12^v
	Le Puy B, 6^v
	LoA, 24^v
	Moosburger Graduale, 244^r
Nove geniture	Brugge 111/178, 32^v
	Cambridge R.9.11, 152^v
	F, 355^r
	Graz 409, 1^v
	Moosburger Graduale, 233^r
	Tort, 81^v
	W1, 177^v (108^v)
Nove lucis hodie	Moosburger Graduale, 239^v
	Seckauer Cantionarium, 187^r
	SG 1397, p. 22
	SG 392, p. 88
Novi partus gaudium	Charleville 190, 158^v
	Graz 409, 1^r
	ORawl, 241 v (12^v)

(cont.)

Incipit	Source
	Paris lat. 4880, 83^r
Novi partus gratia	Graz 409, 71^r
Novum lumen apparuit	Red Book of Ossory, 74^v
Novum ver oritur	F, 468^v
	Tours 927, 12^v
Novus annus dies magnus	Le Puy A, 34^v
	Le Puy B, 20^v
	Mad 289, 147^v
	St-M A, 40^v
Novus annus hodie [A]	F, 218^v
	Sens 46, p. 54
Novus annus hodie [B]	Munich 21053, 5^v
Nunc angelorum gloria	Seckauer Cantionarium, 205^r
	Moosburger Graduale, 236^r
Nunc clericorum concio	St-M A, 33^v
Nunc floret	Piae Cantiones (1582), no. 71
	Piae Cantiones (1625), no. 63
Nuntio dum credidit	Graz 409, 71^r
Nuptialis hodie [*Nubcialis hodie*]	St-M D, 153^v
O Christi longanimitas	F-Pm 996, 181^r
	F-Pn lat. 14810, 327^v
	F-Pn lat. 14923, 229^v
	F-Pn lat. 15163, 218^v
	also transmitted in incunabula
O crux frutex salvificus	D-DS 2777, 44^r
	US-NHub 612, 100^v
	US-NHub 1001, 60^r
	extensive circulation; see CPI Database
O Deus sancte spiritus	Red Book of Ossory, 75^r
O dulces filii	St-M A, 32^v
O flos florens	MüC, 143^r
O labilis sortis	D-DS 2777, 3^v
	F, 427^v
	Fauvel, 11^r
O Maria stella maris	F, 445^v
O mi dilectissima	Carmina Burana, 71^r
O mira Christi pietas	GB-Cu Ee.VI.29, 33^r (29^r)
	GB-Lbl Royal 12.C.XII, 76^v
O mira clementia	Tours 927, 10^r
O nobilis virginitas	Basel B.XI.8, 155^v
	CH-Eins 171, p. 119
	CH-SGs 551, p. 59
	V-CVbav Vat. lat. 9991, I^v
O quam turpis	Erfurt Codex, 106^r
O quanto consilio	F, 470^v

(*cont.*)

Incipit	Source
O qui fontem gratie	F, 289^v
	GB-Lbl Cotton Nero C.IX, 226^r
	Mad 20486, 60^v
	ORawl, 240^r (11^r)
	W1, 158^r (149^r)
O salutaris hostia	Engelberg Codex, 157^r
O scholares voce pares	*Piae Cantiones* (1582), no. 46
	Piae Cantiones (1625) no. 81
O sedes apostolica	Tours 927, 14^r
O sepulchrum nobile	D-Sl Cod. Brev. 22, 26^v
	GB-Ob Lat liturg. f. 4, 2^v
O stirpe regis filia	Engelberg Codex, 168^v
O virgo pelle	Engelberg Codex, 168^r
Obtinente monarchiam	Saint Omer 351, 15^r
Offerat ecclesia	F, 467^v
Olim lacus colueram	Carmina Burana, 53^v
Olim sudor Herculis	Carmina Burana, 23^v
	Bekynton Anthology, 70^r
	F, 417^r
	GB-Ob Auct. 6 Q 3.17, 16 ext. b; 19 ext. a; 21 ext. a
	Later Cambridge Songbook, 5^r (300^r)
	V-CVbav Reg. lat. 344, 36^r
Omittamus studia	Carmina Burana, 29^v
Omnes gentes plaudite	F, 465^r
Omnipotens pater altissime	Tours 927, 1^v
Omnis curet homo	St-M A, 59^v
	St-M C, 79^v
	St-M D, 2^v
Omnis mundus iocundetur	Le Puy A, 90^v
	Le Puy B, 50^r
	Mad 289, 144^v
	Wienhäuser Liederbuch, 28^b
Orba suo pontifice	Saint Omer 351, 17^v
Orientis partibus	LoA, 1^r/43^r
	Mad 289, 146^v
	Sens 46, p. 3
Ortus dignis Christi signis	Engelberg Codex, 150^r
Ortus summi peracto gaudio	F, 218^r
Ovans chorus scholarium	Engelberg Codex, 153^r
Pange cum leticia	St-Victor Miscellany, 187^v
Parens partum peperisti	Red Book of Ossory, 73^v
Paris [parit] preter morem	F, 232^r
	Graz 409, 72^r
	Hu, 103^v

(cont.)

Incipit	Source
	Ma, 123^r
	ORawl, 245^r (16^r)
Partus per quem oritur	Bobbio, 334^v
Partus semiferos	F, 429^r
Parvulus nobis nascitur	Piae Cantiones, no. 28
Passionis emuli	F, 466^v
	Tours 927, 19^r
Pater creator omnium	F, 467^r
Pater filie	Graz 258, 2^r
Pater matris hodie [see also Patrem parit filia]	Le Puy A, 144^v
	Le Puy B, 89^r
	Colmar 187, 45^v
Patrem parit filia [see also Pater matris hodie]	Autun S 175^{10}, 198^r
	Basel B.XI.8, 156^r
	LoA, 65^v
	Sens 46, p. 13
	St. Pölten Processional, 10^v
	V-CVbav Vat. lat. 9991, I^v
	extensive circulation; see CPI Database
Pax in terris	F-Pn lat. 904, 12^r
	Later Cambridge Songbook, 5^v (300^v)
	Paris lat. 4880, 84^r
Per partum virginis	ORawl, 237^v (8^v)
	St-M B, 150^v
	St-M C, 64^r
	St-M D, 4^r
Personent hodie [see also Intonent hodie]	Piae Cantiones (1582), no. 5
Plangentis Cristi uulnera	Red Book of Ossory, 72^r
Plebs domini hac die	St-M B, 167^v
	St-M C, 39^v
Plurimorum vicia	Erfurt Codex, 106^r
Polorum regina	Llibre Vermell, 24^v
Presens festum laudat clerus	St. Pölten Processional, 9^r
Prima nostri generis	Saint Omer 351, 15^r
Primus homo cum pro pomo	Graz 409, 2^r
	Le Puy A, 65^r/166^r
	Le Puy B, 36^v/116^v
Procedenti puero [see also Verbum caro factum est eya annus]	Codex Sangallensis, IX^v
	F, 467^v
	SG 383, p. 172
	Sloane 2593, 15^v
	Tours 927, 19^r
Processit in capite	F, 466^r
	OBod 937, 446^v
	Tours 927, 13^r

(cont.)

Incipit	Source
Promat chorus hodie [see also *Puer natus hodie*]	St-M A, 15^v
Prophetatus a prophetis	St-M A, 42^v
Prothomartyr Stephanus	Luxembourg 27, 89^v
Psallat vox ecclesie	Le Puy A, 9^v
Psallite regi glorie	F, 469^r
Puer natus hodie [see also *Promat chorus hodie*]	Engelberg Codex, 130^v
	Stuttg, 75^v
	Wienhäuser Liederbuch, 2^v
Puer natus in Betlehem [*Bethlehem*]	Bobbio, 334^r
	Moosburger Graduale, 247^v
	Piae Cantiones (1582), no. 12
	Piae Cantiones (1625), no. 23
	SG 392, p. 87
	Stuttg, 46^r
	Wienhäuser Liederbuch, 4^r
	extensive circulation across Europe as Christmas song
Puer nobis nascitur	Moosburger Graduale, 247^r
	SG 392, p. 89
	Wienhäuser Liederbuch, 2^r
	extensive circulation across Europe as Christmas song
Pusillus nobis nascitur	Engelberg Codex, 168^v
Quam Natura ceteris	Carmina Burana, 71^r
Qui eminant in lacrimis	F, 425^r
Qui passus est pridie	D-Sl Cod. Brev. 22, 229^r
	OBod 937, 446^v
	Tours 927, 10^v
Qui pro nobis mori non respuit	F, 467^r
Qui seminant in loculis	F, 425^r
Quod spiritu David precinuit	Carmina Burana, 13^v
Ramus virens olivarum	*Piae Cantiones* (1582), no. 77
	Piae Cantiones (1625), no. 87
Redit estas preoptata	Saint Omer 351, 20^r
Reformatur forma iuris	Saint Omer 351, 17^r
Regem adoremus	Red Book of Ossory, 74^r
Regi nato Domino	St-M A, 41^v
Res nova principium	Le Puy A, 36^r
	Le Puy B, 21^r
	St-M A, 51^v
	St-M C, 15^r
Resonemus laudibus	Aosta Cod. 11, 80^v
	Aosta Cod. 13, 66^v
	Engelberg Codex, 129^v
Resonet in laudibus	Aosta Cod. 11, 80^v
	Moosburger Graduale, 246^r

(*cont.*)

Incipit	Source
	Piae Cantiones (1582), no. 3
	Piae Cantiones (1625), no. 14
	Seckauer Cantionarium, 187^r
	SG 392, p. 87
	Wienhäuser Liederbuch, 3^r
	see Ameln "Resonet in Laudibus" and Lipphardt "Magnum nomen Domini Emanuel" for wider circulation
Resonet intonet	Colmar 187, 45^v
	Harley 1010, x^r
	I-Nn VI G 34, 39^v
	Later Cambridge Songbook, 1^r (2^r)
	Mad 289, 101^r
	V-CVbav Barb. lat. 603, 3^r
Resultet plebs fidelis	Moosburger Graduale, 235^v
Resurexit a mortuis	Red Book of Ossory, 72^v
Resurexit Dominus	Red Book of Ossory, 72^r
Resurgenti cum gloria	Red Book of Ossory, 72^v
Resurrexit libere	Tours 927, 18^r
Rex omnipotentie	Tours 927, 11^r
	F, 464^r
Rimetur mens hominis	Graz 409, 2^v
Ruga dure vetustatis	Graz 409, 1^r
Rutilat ecclesia	Red Book of Ossory, 73^v
Saevit aurae spiritus	Carmina Burana, 35^v
Salutem iam de celis	I-Ma C 243 inf., p. 613
Salva nos stella maris	F, 470^r
Salve festa dies [A]	Codex Calixtinus, 116^v
Salve festa dies [B]	Later Cambridge Songbook, 5^v (300^v)
Salve maris stella	Graz 409, 72^v
Salve virgo Margaretha	Engelberg Codex, 169^r
Salve virgo virginum salve	Tours 927, 9^v
	F, 469^v
Salve virgo virginum parens	Arundel 248, 155^r
Sancti Nicholai	St-Victor Miscellany, 178^v
Sata tria fert Maria [*Sancta pia fert Maria*]	Graz 258, 2^r
	Graz 409, 273^r
Scandenti supra sidera	Red Book of Ossory, 75^r
Schola morum floruit	*Piae Cantiones* (1582), no. 44
	Piae Cantiones (1625), no. 79
Scribere proposui	*Piae Cantiones* (1582), no. 35
	Piae Cantiones (1625), no. 67
	Llibre Vermell, 26^v
	extensive circulation; see CPI Database

(*cont.*)

Incipit	Source
Si puer cum puellula	Carmina Burana, 71^v
Sol est in meridie	LoB, 47^v
Sol oritur occasus nescius	Hortus Deliciarum, 30^r
Sol polo in stellifero	Carmina Burana, 71^v
Sol sub nube latuit	Bekynton Anthology, 80^r
	Berlin 1996, 292^v
	F, 354^v
	Graz 409, 1^r
	Leipzig 225, 178^v
	Paris lat. 4880, 83^v
	Royal 7.A.VI, 107^v
	Saint Omer 351, 20^r
	SG 383, p. 169
	W1, 119^v (110^v)
Solis iubar nituit	Carmina Burana, 34^v
Spiritus sancti gracia	Red Book of Ossory, 75^v
Stella nova radiat	Graz 409, 72^r
	Moosburger Graduale, 245^r
	Seckauer Cantionarium, 186^r
	St. Pölten Processional, 14^r
Stella splendens	Llibre Vermell, 22^r
Stupeat natura	Bekynton Anthology, 129^r
	Graz 409, 2^r
	Munich 16444, Iia^v
	Tort, 140^r
	W2, 177^v [motet]
Summe Deus clemencie	Red Book of Ossory, 75^r
Superne matris gaudia	St-Victor Miscellany, 186^r
Surge vide gens misera	Tours 927, 12^v
Surrexit Christus Domine	*Piae Cantiones* (1625), no. 42
Surrexit Christus hodie	Moosburger Graduale, 248^r
	Piae Cantiones (1625), no. 43
Syon concio	St-Victor Miscellany, 178^r
Syon presenti sollempnio	St-Victor Miscellany, 188^v
Tempus adest gratie	F, 470^r
	LoB, 48^v
	Piae Cantiones (1582), no. 14
	Piae Cantiones (1625), no. 25
	Wienhäuser Liederbuch, 8^v
Tempus est iocundium	Carmina Burana, 70^v
Tempus instat floridum	Carmina Burana, 52^v
Thesaurus noue gracie	Mad 289, 134^v
Totius triclinium	F-Pn lat. 5132, 108^r
Transit nix et glacies	Carmina Burana, 81^r
Transite Syon filie	F, 467^r

(*cont.*)

Incipit	Source
Tres signata calculo	Graz 258, 2^v
Tribus signis deo dignis	D-Lk 11, 1^v
	Graz 258, 2^v
	Moosburger Graduale, 244^v
	SG 382, p. 14
	St. Pölten Processional, 11^v
Triformis relucentia	*Piae Cantiones* (1582), no. 14
	Piae Cantiones (1625), no. 52
Tronus regis instauratur	Berlin 1996, 87^v
	Later Cambridge Songbook, 1^v (2^v)
Tronus Salomonis vellus Gedeonis	ORawl, 243^v (14^v)
Tuum accidens plectentes	Erfurt Codex, 2^r
Umbram destruxit penitus	Graz 258, 2^r
	Graz 409, 72^r
Una trium deitas	St-M C, 26^v
Unicornis captivatur	Engelberg Codex, 150^v
Urbs salve regia	Carmina Burana, 90^v
Ut iam cesset calamitas	F, 467^v
Uterus hodie virginis floruit	St-M C, 38^v
Vacillantis trutine libramine	Carmina Burana, 80^r
	Later Cambridge Songbook, 2^r (1^r)
Vale mater Christi	Red Book of Ossory, 70^r
Vale virgo Christifera	Red Book of Ossory, 71^r
Veni creator spiritus et in me	A-ROU A 408, 171^v
	F, 360^r
	Graz 409, 1^r
Veni sancte spiritus [A]	Basel B.XI.8, 154^r
	CH-Bu AN.II.46, 102^v
	D-Mbs clm 14528, 192^v
Veni sancte spiritus [B]	Engelberg Codex, 168^r
Veni sancte spiritus [C]	LoB, 49^r
Verbum caro factum est eya annus [see also *Procedenti puero*]	Aosta Cod. 11, 80^r
	Aosta Cod. 13, 66^r
Verbum caro factum est … Dies	Aosta Cod. 11, 85^r
	Aosta Cod. 13, 61^v
Verbum caro factum est … Cuius	Red Book of Ossory, 70^r
Verbum patris humanatur	Graz 409, 71^r
	Later Cambridge Songbook, 7^r (4^r)
	Moosburger Graduale, 237^v
	Paris lat. 4880, 84^v
	St-M C, 91^r
	St. Pölten Processional, 13^v
Vergente mundi vespere	Saint Omer 351, 17^r
Veris ad imperia	F, 228^v
Veris dulcis in tempore	Carmina Burana, 36^v/64^r

(*cont.*)

Incipit	Source
Veris principium	F, 468^r
Versa et in luctum	Carmina Burana, 51^v
Veterem memorem pellite	F, 468^v
Vetus purgans facinus	F, 465^r
Videbitis qualis et quantus	Red Book of Ossory, 77^r
Vineam meam plantavi	F, 466^v
	Tours 927, 19^v
Virga Iesse floruit	F-LG 2, 255^r
Virgine nato rege beato	St-M A, 39^v
Virgo dei genitrix	Mad 289, 146^r
Virgo Galilea	A-M cod. 1087, 109^v
	Bobbio, 335^r
	I-Nn VI G 34, folio unconfirmed
Virgo parit filium	Seckauer Cantionarium, 194^v
Virgo quedam nobilis	Carmina Burana, 72^r
Vivere que tribuit	Tours 927, 18^r
	F, 463^v
Voce resonantes	Brugge 111/178, 32^v
	Stuttg, 52^v/74^v
Vocis tripudio	F, 465^v
	Tours 927, 13^r

Bibliography

Ahlquist, Karen, ed. *Chorus and Community*. University of Illinois Press, 2006.

Ahn, Dongmyung. "Beastly yet Lofty Burdens: The Donkey and the Subdeacon in the Middle Ages." In *L'Humain et l'animal dans la France médiévale (XIIe–XVe s.): Human and Animal in Medieval France (12th–15th c.)*, edited by Irène Fabry-Tehranchi and Anna D. Russakoff, 145–160. Rodopi, 2014.

"The Exegetical Function of the Conductus in MS Egerton 2615." PhD diss., The Graduate Center, City University of New York, 2018.

Ameln, Konrad. "'Resonet in Laudibus' – 'Joseph, lieber Joseph mein.'" *Jahrbuch für Liturgik und Hymnologie* 15 (1970): 52–112.

Anderson, Benedict. *Imagined Communities: Reflections on the Origin and Spread of Nationalism*. Revised ed. Verso, 2006 [1983].

Anderson, Gordon A. "Notre Dame and Related Conductus: A Catalogue Raisonné." *Miscellanea musicologica* 6–7 (1972–1974): 153–229 and 1–81.

"Nove Geniture: Three Variant Polyphonic Settings of a Notre Dame Conductus." *Studies in Music*, 9 (1975): 8–18.

"Thirteenth-Century Conductus: Obiter Dicta." *The Musical Quarterly* 58 (1972): 349–364.

Anderson, Gordon A., ed. *Notre-Dame and Related Conductus: Opera Omnia*. The Institute of Mediaeval Music, Ltd., 1979–.

Anderson, Michael Alan. "Enhancing the *Ave Maria* in the Ars Antiqua." *Plainsong and Medieval Music* 19 (2010): 35–65.

"Fire, Foliage and Fury: Vestiges of Midsummer Ritual in Motets for John the Baptist." *Early Music History* 30 (2011): 1–53.

Anglés, Higinio. "El 'Llibre Vermell' de Montserrat y los cantos y la danza sacra de los peregrinos durante el siglo XIV." *Anuario musical* 10 (1955): 45–78.

Applegate, Celia. "The Building of Community through Choral Singing." In *Nineteenth-Century Choral Music*, edited by Donna M. Di Grazia, 3–20. Routledge, 2013.

Arlt, Wulf. *Ein Festoffizium des Mittelalters aus Beauvais in seiner liturgischen und musikalischen Bedeutung*. 2 vols. Arno Volk Verlag, 1970.

"Das Eine und die vielen Lieder: Zur historischen Stellung der neuen Liedkunst des fruhen 12. Jahrhunderts." *In Festschrift Rudolf Bockholdt zum 60. Geburtstag*, edited by Norbert Dubowy and Sören Meyer-Eller, 113–127. Ludwig, 1990.

"Einstimmige Lieder des 12. Jahrhunderts und Mehrstimmiges in französischen Handschriften des 16. Jahrhunderts aus Le Puy." *Schweizer Beiträge zur Musikwissenschaft* 3 (1978): 7–47.

"Hymnus und 'Neues Lied': Aspekte des Strophischen." In *Der lateinische Hymnus im Mittelalter: Überlieferung – Ästhetik – Ausstrahlung,* edited by Andreas Haug, Christoph März, and Lorenz Welker, 133–136. Bärenreiter, 2004.

"Jehannot de Lescurel and the Function of Musical Language in the 'Roman de Fauvel' as presented in BN fr. 146." In *Fauvel Studies: Allegory, Chronicle, Music and Image in Paris, Bibliothèque Nationale de France, MS français 146,* edited by Margaret Bent, and Andrew Wathey, 25–34. Clarendon Press, 1998.

"Nova cantica: Grundsätzliches und Spezielles zur Interpretation musikalischer Texte des Mittelalters." *Basler Jahrbuch für historische Musikpraxis* 10 (1986): 13–62.

"The Office for the Feast of the Circumcision from Le Puy." In *The Divine Office in the Latin Middle Ages: Methodology and Source Studies, Regional Developments, Hagiography: Written in Honor of Professor Ruth Steiner,* edited by Margot E. Fassler and Rebecca A. Baltzer, translated by Lori Kruckenberg, Kelly Landerkin, and Margot E. Fassler, 324–343. Oxford University Press, 2000.

"Sequence and 'Neues Lied.'" In *La Sequenza Medievale: Atti del convegno internazionale, Milano, 7–8 aprile 1984,* edited by Agostino Ziino, 3–18. Libreria musicale italiana, 1992.

Arlt, Wulf, Mathias Stauffacher, and Ulrike Hascher, eds. *Engelberg Stiftsbibliothek Codex 314.* Schweizerische Musikdenkmäler 11. Amadeus Verlag, 1986.

Asensio Palacios, Juan Carlos. "Neuma, espacio y liturgia: La ordenación sonora en Compostela según el *Codex Calixtinus.*" *Medievalia* 17 (2014): 131–152.

Asensio Palacios, Juan Carlos, ed. *Symposium El Codex Calixtinus en la Europa del Siglo XII: Música, arte, codicología y liturgia.* Instituto Nacional de las Artes Escénicas y de la Música, 2011.

Aubrey, Elizabeth. "The Eleventh Fascicle of the Manuscript Florence, Biblioteca Mediceo-Laurenziana, Pluteus 29.1: A Critical Edition and Commentary." MM, University of Maryland, 1975.

"French Monophony." In *A Performer's Guide to Medieval Music,* edited by Ross W. Duffin, 134–143. Indiana University Press, 2000.

"Reconsidering 'High Style' and 'Low Style' in Medieval Song." *Journal of Music Theory* 52 (2008): 75–122.

Aubry, Pierre. *La Musique et les musiciens d'église en Normandie au XIIIe siècle, d'après le "Journal des visites pastorales" d'Odon Rigaud.* Minkoff Reprint, 1972 [1906].

Aubry, Pierre, and Eugène Misset. *Les Proses d'Adam de Saint-Victor: texte et musique. précédées d'une étude critique.* H. Welter, 1900.

Augustine, Bishop of Hippo. *Sermons on the Liturgical Seasons.* Translated by Sister Mary Sarah Muldowney. The Fathers of the Church: A New Translation 38. The Catholic University of America Press, 1959.

Bailey, Terence. *The Processions of Sarum and the Western Church.* Pontifical Institute of Mediaeval Studies, 1971.

Bakhtin, Mikhail. *The Dialogic Imagination: Four Essays.* Edited by Michael Holquist and translated by Caryl Emerson. University of Texas Press, 1981.

Baldwin, John W. "The Image of the Jongleur in Northern France around 1200." *Speculum* 72 (1997): 635–663.

Baltzer, Rebecca A. "Performance Practice, the Notre-Dame Calendar, and the Earliest Latin Liturgical Motets." Paper presented at conference, "Das musikgeschichtliche Ereignis 'Notre-Dame,'" Herzog August Bibliothek, Wolfenbüttel, April 1985; online in *Archivum de Musica Medii Aevi* (Musicologie Médiévale – Centre de médiévistique Jean Schneider, CNRS / Université de Lorraine) (2013): www.musmed.fr/AdMMAe/ Baltzer,%20Performance%20Practice.pdf.

"Thirteenth-Century Illuminated Miniatures and the Date of the Florence Manuscript." *Journal of the American Musicological Society* 25 (1972): 1–18.

Barnard, Jennifer A. "The Journey of the Soul: The Role of Music in the *Ludus super Anticlaudianum* of Adam de la Bassée." PhD diss., University of Bristol, 2008.

Bartlett, Robert. *Why Can the Dead Do Such Great Things? Saints and Worshippers from the Martyrs to the Reformation.* Princeton University Press, 2013.

Bartsch, Karl. "Alt- und Mittelhochdeutsches aus Engelberg." *Germania* 18 (1873): 45–72.

Basochis, Guidonis de. *Liber epistularum Guidonis de Basochis.* Edited by Herbert Adolfsson. Acta Universitatis Stockholmiensis: Studia Latina Stockholmiensia 18. Almqvist & Wiksell, 1969.

Baumgarten, Elisheva, and Judah D. Galinsky, eds. *Jews and Christians in Thirteenth-Century France.* Palgrave Macmillan, 2015.

Béthune, Evrard of. *Graecismus.* Edited by Johannes Wrobel. Olms, 1887.

Björkvall, Gunilla, and Andreas Haug. "Sequence and Versus: On the History of Rhythmical Poetry in the Eleventh Century." In *Latin Culture in the Eleventh Century: Proceedings of the Third International Conference on Medieval Latin Studies, Cambridge, September 9–12, 1998*, edited by Michael W. Herren, C. J. McDonough, and Ross G. Arthur, 57–82. Publications of the Journal of Medieval Latin 5/1–2. Brepols, 2002.

Blackburn, Bonnie, and Leofranc Holford-Strevens. *The Oxford Companion to the Year.* Oxford University Press, 1999.

Bonnin, Théodose, ed. *Regestrum visitationum archiepiscopi Rothomagensis: Journal des visites pastorales d'Eude Rigaud, archevêque de Rouen, MCCXLVIII–MCCLXIX*. A. Le Brument, 1852.

Boogaard, Nico H. J. van den. *Rondeaux et refrains du XIIe siècle au début du XIVe*. Éditions Klincksieck, 1969.

Boudeau, Océane. "La question des variantes dans les *nova cantica* de l'office de la Circoncision de Sens." In *Les Noces de philologie et musicologie: Textes et musiques du Moyen Âge*, edited by Christelle Cazaux-Kowalski, Christelle Chaillou-Amadieu, Anne-Zoé Rillon-Marne, and Fabio Zinelli, 97–124. Classiques Garnier, 2018.

Boulton, Maureen Barry McCann, ed. *The Old French Évangile de l'Enfance: An Edition*. Pontifical Institute of Mediaeval Studies, Studies and Texts 70. Pontifical Institute of Mediaeval Studies, 1984.

The Song in the Story: Lyric Insertions in French Narrative Fiction, 1200–1400. University of Pennsylvania Press, 1993.

Boynton, Susan. "Boy Singers in Monasteries and Cathedrals." In *Young Choristers, 650–1700*, edited by Susan Boynton and Eric Rice, 37–48. Boydell Press, 2008.

"Work and Play in Sacred Music and Its Social Context, *c.* 1050–1250." In *The Use and Abuse of Time in Christian History: Papers Read at the 1999 Summer Meeting and the 2000 Winter Meeting of the Ecclesiastical History Society*, edited by R. N. Swanson, 57–79. Boydell Press, 2002.

Bradley, Catherine A. "Contrafacta and Transcribed Motets: Vernacular Influences on Latin Motets and Clausulae in the Florence Manuscript." *Early Music History* 32 (2013): 1–70.

"Ordering in the Motet Fascicles of the Florence Manuscript." *Plainsong and Medieval Music* 22 (2013): 37–64.

Polyphony in Medieval Paris: The Art of Composing with Plainchant. Cambridge University Press, 2018.

Branner, Robert. "The Johannes Grusch Atelier and the Continental Origins of the William of Devon Painter." *The Art Bulletin* 54 (1972): 24–30.

Brewer, Charles E. "In Search of Lost Melodies: The Latin Songs of Graz 756." In *Dies est leticie: Essays on Chant in Honour of Janka Szendrei*, edited by David Hiley and Gábor Kiss, 93–109. Institute of Mediaeval Music, 2008.

"The Songs of Johannes Decanus." *Plainsong and Medieval Music* 20 (2011): 31–49.

Buettner, Brigitte. "Past Presents: New Year's Gifts at the Valois Courts, ca. 1400." *The Art Bulletin* 83 (2001): 598–625.

Bugyis, Katie Ann-Marie, A. B. Kraebel, and Margot E. Fassler, eds. *Medieval Cantors and Their Craft: Music, Liturgy and the Shaping of History, 800–1500*. York Medieval Press and Boydell and Brewer, 2017.

Bukofzer, Manfred F. "Interrelations Between Conductus and Clausula." *Annales musicologiques* 1 (1953): 65–103.

Burke, Peter. *Languages and Communities in Early Modern Europe*. Cambridge University Press, 2004.

Butterfield, Ardis. *The Familiar Enemy: Chaucer, Language, and Nation in the Hundred Years War*. Oxford University Press, 2009.

"Poems Without Form? *Maiden in the mor lay* Revisited." In *Readings in Medieval Textuality: Essays in Honour of A. C. Spearing*, edited by Cristina Maria Cervone and D. Vance Smith, 169–194. D. S. Brewer, 2016.

Poetry and Music in Medieval France: From Jean Renart to Guillaume de Machaut. Cambridge University Press, 2002.

"Repetition and Variation in the Thirteenth-Century Refrain." *Journal of the Royal Musical Association* 116 (1991): 1–23.

Caldwell, Mary Channen. "Cueing Refrains in the Medieval Conductus." *Journal of the Royal Musical Association* 143 (2018): 273–324.

"Litanic Songs for the Virgin: Rhetoric, Repetition, and Marian Refrains in Medieval Latin Song." In *The Litany in Arts and Cultures*, edited by Witold Sadowski and Francesco Marsciani. Studia Traditionis Theologiae 36, 143–174. Brepols, 2020.

"A Medieval Patchwork Song: Poetry, Prayer and Music in a Thirteenth-Century Conductus." *Plainsong and Medieval Music* 25 (2016): 139–165.

"'Pax Gallie': The Songs of Tours 927." In *The Jeu d'Adam: MS Tours 927 and the Provenance of the Play*, edited by Christophe Chaguinian. Early Drama, Art, and Music Monograph Series, 87–176. Medieval Institute Publications, 2017.

"Singing Cato: Poetic Grammar and Moral Citation in Medieval Latin Song." *Music & Letters* 102 (2021): 191–233.

"Singing, Dancing, and Rejoicing in the Round: Latin Sacred Songs with Refrains, circa 1000–1582." PhD diss., University of Chicago, 2013.

"Texting Vocality: Musical and Material Poetics of the Voice in Medieval Latin Song." In *Ars Antiqua: Music and Culture in Europe, c. 1150–1330*, edited by Gregorio Bevilacqua and Thomas Payne. Speculum Musicae 40, 33–70. Brepols, 2020.

"Troping Time: Refrain Interpolation in Sacred Latin Song, ca. 1140–1853." *Journal of the American Musicological Society* 74 (2021): 91–156.

Carlson, Rachel Golden. "Devotion to the Virgin Mary in Twelfth-Century Aquitanian *Versus*." 2 vols. PhD diss., University of North Carolina at Chapel Hill, 2000.

"Striking Ornaments: Complexities of Sense and Song in Aquitanian 'Versus'." *Music & Letters* 84 (2003): 527–556.

"Two Paths to Daniel's Mountain: Poetic-Musical Unity in Aquitanian *Versus*." *The Journal of Musicology* 23 (2006): 620–646.

Cazal, Yvonne. *Les Voix du peuple-Verbum Dei: Le bilinguisme latin–langue vulgaire au moyen âge*. Publications romanes et françaises 223. Droz, 1998.

Chaganti, Seeta. *Strange Footing: Poetic Form and Dance in the Late Middle Ages*. The University of Chicago Press, 2018.

Chaguinian, Christophe, ed. *The Jeu d'Adam: MS Tours 927 and the Provenance of the Play*. Early Drama, Art, and Music Monograph Series. Medieval Institute Publications, 2017.

Chambers, E. K. *The Mediaeval Stage*. 2 vols. Clarendon Press, 1903.

Fleury-Husson, Jules François (dit Champfleury). "Danses dans les églises et les couvents." *Le Bibliophile francais: Gazette illustrée des amateurs de livres, d'estampes et de haute curiosité* 3 (1869): 265–273.

Cheney, Christopher R. "Rules for the Observance of Feast-Days in Medieval England." *Bulletin of the Institute of Historical Research* 34 (1961): 117–147.

Chevalier, Ulysse. *Ordinaires de l'église cathédrale de Laon (XIIe et XIIIe siècles): Suivis de deux mystères liturgiques*. A. Picard, 1897.

   Prosolarium Ecclesiae Aniciensis: Office en vers de la Circoncision en usage dans l'église du Puy. A. Picard, 1894.

Ciglbauer, Jan. "Quoting, Rethinking and Copying: A Few Remarks on the Tradition of the Monophonic Cantio in Central Europe." *Hudebni Veda* 51 (2014): 21–32.

Colette, Marie-Noël. "*Leta cohors fidelium. Annus novus in gaudio*. Un air vagant en quête d'origine (XIe–XIIe siècle)." In *La rigueur et la passion: Mélanges en l'honneur de Pascale Bourgain*, edited by Cédric Giraud and Dominique Poirel, 199–216. Brepols Publishers, 2016.

Colledge, Edmund. *The Latin Poems of Richard Ledrede, O.F.M., Bishop of Ossory, 1317-1360*. Pontifical Institute of Mediaeval Studies, 1974.

Colton, Lisa. *Angel Song: Medieval English Music in History*. Routledge, 2017.

Connolly, Daniel K. *The Maps of Matthew Paris: Medieval Journeys through Space, Time and Liturgy*. The Boydell Press, 2009.

Connor, Steven. "Choralities." *Twentieth-Century Music* 13 (2016): 3–23.

Copeland, Rita, and Ineke Sluiter, eds. *Medieval Grammar and Rhetoric: Language Arts and Literary Theory, AD 300–1475*. Oxford University Press, 2009.

Corrigan, Vincent. "The Codex Calixtinus and the French Connection: The Office for St. James in Northern France." In *Music, Dance, and Society: Medieval and Renaissance Studies in Memory of Ingrid G. Brainard*, edited by Ann Buckley and Cynthia J. Cyrus, 3–18. Medieval Institute Publications, 2011.

Cressy, David. *Bonfires and Bells: National Memory and the Protestant Calendar in Elizabethan and Stuart England*. Weidenfeld and Nicolson, 1989.

Crocker, Richard L. *An Introduction to Gregorian Chant*. Yale University Press, 2000.

   "Two Recent Editions of Aquitanian Polyphony." *Plainsong and Medieval Music* 3 (1994): 57–101.

Cunningham, Martin G., ed. *Alfonso X, el Sábio: Cantigas de Loor*. University College Dublin Press, 2000.

Curtis, Edmund. "The Spoken Languages of Medieval Ireland." *Studies: An Irish Quarterly Review* 8 (1919): 234–254.

Curtius, Ernst Robert. *European Literature and the Latin Middle Ages*. Translated by Willard R. Trask. Princeton University Press, 2013 [1953].

Dahhaoui, Yann. "Enfant-évêque et fête des fous: Un loisir ritualisé pour jeunes clercs?" In *Freizeit und Vergnügen vom 14. bis zum 20. Jahrhundert*, edited by Beatrice Schumacher, Hans-Jörg Gilomen, and Laurent Tissot, 33–46. Chronos, 2005.

"Le pape de Saint-Étienne: Fête des Saints-Innocents et imitation du cérémonial pontifical à Besançon." In *Mémoires de cours: Études offertes à Agostino Paravacini Bagliani*, edited by Bernard Andenmatten, Catherine Chène, Martine Ostorero, and Eva Pibiri, 141–158. Université de Lausanne, 2008.

"Voyages d'un prélat festif: Un 'évêque des Innocents' dans son évêché." *Revue historique* 639 (2006): 677–693.

Damilano, Don Piero. "Fonti musicali della lauda polifonica intorno alla metà del sec. XV." In *Collectanea historiae musicae* 3, 59–90. Leo S. Olschki, 1963.

"Laudi latine in un Antifonario bobbiese del Trecento." In *Collectanea historiae musicae* 3, 15–90. Leo S. Olschki, 1963.

Davidson, Clifford. *Festivals and Plays in Late Medieval Britain*. Ashgate, 2007.

"Violence and the Saint Play." *Studies in Philology* 98 (2001): 292–314.

Davis, Adam J. *The Holy Bureaucrat: Eudes Rigaud and Religious Reform in Thirteenth-Century Normandy*. Cornell University Press, 2006.

Davis, Natalie Zemon. *The Gift in Sixteenth-Century France*. University of Wisconsin Press, 2000.

Society and Culture in Early Modern France: Eight Essays. Stanford University Press, 1975.

Deeming, Helen. "An English Monastic Miscellany: The Reading Manuscript of *Sumer is icumen in*." In *Manuscripts and Medieval Song: Inscription, Performance, Context*, edited by Helen Deeming and Elizabeth Eva Leach, 116–140. Cambridge University Press, 2015.

"Isolated Jottings? The Compilation, Preparation, and Use of Song Sources from Thirteenth-Century Britain." *Journal of the Alamire Foundation* 6 (2014): 139–152.

"Latin Song I: Songs and Songbooks from the Ninth to the Thirteenth Century." In *The Cambridge History of Medieval Music*, edited by Mark Everist and Thomas Forrest Kelly, 1020–1047. Cambridge University Press, 2018.

"Multilingual Networks in Twelfth- and Thirteenth-Century Song." In *Language in Medieval Britain: Networks and Exchanges: Proceedings of the 2013 Harlaxton Symposium*, edited by Mary Carruthers. Harlaxton Medieval Studies 25, 127–143. Shaun Tyas, 2015.

"Music and Contemplation in the Twelfth-Century *Dulcis Jesu memoria.*" *Journal of the Royal Musical Association* 139 (2014): 1–39.

"Music, Memory and Mobility: Citation and Contrafactum in Thirteenth-Century Sequence Repertories." In *Citation, Intertextuality and Memory in the Middle Ages and Renaissance*, edited by Giuliano Di Bacco and Yolanda Plumley, 67–81. Liverpool University Press, 2013.

Deeming, Helen, ed. *Songs in British Sources, c. 1150–1300*, Musica Britannica 95. Stainer & Bell, 2013.

Deeming, Helen, and Elizabeth Eva Leach, eds. *Manuscripts and Medieval Song: Inscription, Performance, Context.* Cambridge University Press, 2015.

Delale, Sarah, and Jean-Dominique Delle Luche. "Le Temps de la fête: Introduction." *Questes: Revue pluridisciplinaire d'études médiévales* 31 (2015): 11–32.

Denifle, Heinrich, and Aemilio Chatelain, eds. *Chartularium Universitatis Parisiensis.* 4 vols. Paris, 1889–1897.

Diehl, Patrick S. *The Medieval European Religious Lyric: An Ars Poetica.* University of California Press, 1985.

Dillon, Emma. "The Art of Interpolation in the 'Roman de Fauvel.'" *The Journal of Musicology* 19 (2002): 223–263.

"Unwriting Medieval Song." *New Literary History* 46 (2015): 595–622.

Doss-Quinby, Eglal. *Les Refrains chez les trouvères du XIIe siècle au début du XIVe.* American University Studies ser. II: Romance Languages and Literature. Peter Lang, 1984.

Doss-Quinby, Eglal, Samuel N. Rosenberg, and Elizabeth Aubrey, eds. *The Old French Ballette: Oxford, Bodleian Library, Ms Douce 308.* Droz, 2006.

Dronke, Peter. "The Lyrical Compositions of Philip the Chancellor." *Studi medievali* 28 (1987): 563–592.

The Medieval Lyric. 3rd ed. D. S. Brewer, 1996 [1968].

Drummond, Henry T. "Accommodating Poetic, Linear Narratives with Cyclical, Repetition-Based Musical-Poetic Structures in the *Cantigas de Santa Maria.*" DPhil thesis, University of Oxford, 2017.

"Linear Narratives in Cyclical Form: The Hunt for Reason in the Cantigas de Santa Maria." *Music Analysis* 38 (2019): 80–108.

Duffy, Eamon. *The Stripping of the Altars: Traditional Religion in England, c. 1400–c. 1580.* 2nd ed. Yale University Press, 2005 [1992].

Dunn, E. Catherine. "The Farced Epistle as Dramatic Form in the Twelfth-Century Renaissance." *Comparative Drama* 29 (1995): 363–381.

The Gallican Saint's Life and the Late Roman Dramatic Tradition. Catholic University of America Press, 1989.

Duys, Kathryn A. "Performing Vernacular Song in Monastic Culture: The *Lectio Divina* in Gautier de Coinci's *Miracles de Nostre Dame.*" In *Cultural Performances in Medieval France: Essays in Honor of Nancy Freeman*

Regalado, edited by Eglal Doss-Quinby, Roberta L. Krueger, and E. Jane Burns, 123–133. D. S. Brewer, 2007.

Echard, Siân. "Ledred, Richard." In *The Encyclopedia of Medieval Literature in Britain*, edited by Siân Echard and Robert Rouse, 1158–1159. John Wiley & Sons, Inc, 2017.

Einbinder, Susan L. *Beautiful Death: Jewish Poetry and Martyrdom in Medieval France*. Princeton University Press, 2002.

Engelhardt, Christian Moritz. *Herrad von Landsperg, Aebtissin zu Hohenburg, oder St. Odilien, im Elsass, in zwölften Jahrhundert und ihr Werk: Hortus deliciarum*. J. G. Cotta, 1818.

Engels, Stefan. "Die liturgischen Handschriften aus St. Lambrecht (Steiermark)." In *Cantus Planus: Study Group of the International Musicological Society: Papers Read at the 16th Meeting, Vienna, Austria, 2011*, edited by Robert Klugseder, 135–142. Österreichische Akademie der Wissenschaften, Kommission für Musikforschung, 2012.

Everist, Mark. *Discovering Medieval Song: Latin Poetry and Music in the Conductus*. Cambridge University Press, 2018.

French Motets in the Thirteenth Century: Music, Poetry and Genre. Cambridge University Press, 1994.

"Le conduit à nombre de voix variable (1150–1250)." In *Les Noces de philologie et musicologie: Textes et musiques du Moyen Âge*, edited by Christelle Cazaux-Kowalski, Christelle Chaillou-Amadieu, Anne-Zoé Rillon-Marne, and Fabio Zinelli, 329–344. Classiques Garnier, 2018.

"The Variable-Voice Conductus." In *Music and Instruments of the Middle Ages: Essays in Honour of Christopher Page*, edited by Tess Knighton and David Skinner, 195–219. Boydell & Brewer, 2020.

Falck, Robert. *The Notre Dame Conductus: A Study of the Repertory*. Musicological studies/Wissenschaftliche Abhandlungen 33. Institute of Mediæval Music, 1981.

"Parody and Contrafactum: A Terminological Clarification." *The Musical Quarterly* 65 (1979): 1–21.

"'Rondellus', Canon, and Related Types before 1300." *Journal of the American Musicological Society* 25 (1972): 38–57.

Fallows, David. "English Song Repertories of the Mid-Fifteenth Century." *Proceedings of the Royal Musical Association* 103 (1976–1977): 61–79.

Henry V and the Earliest English Carols: 1413–1440. Routledge, 2018.

Farmer, Sharon. *Communities of Saint Martin: Legend and Ritual in Medieval Tours*. Cornell University Press, 1991.

Fassler, Margot E. "Accent, Meter, and Rhythm in Medieval Treatises 'De Rithmis.'" *The Journal of Musicology* 5 (1987): 164–190.

"The Feast of Fools and *Danielis Ludus*: Popular Tradition in a Medieval Cathedral Play." In *Plainsong in the Age of Polyphony*, edited by Thomas Forrest Kelly, 65–99. Cambridge University Press, 1992.

Gothic Song: Victorine Sequences and Augustinian Reform in Twelfth-Century Paris. 2nd ed. Cambridge University Press, 2011 [1993].

"The Liturgical Framework of Time and the Representation of History." In *Representing History, 900–1300: Art, Music, History*, edited by Robert A. Maxwell, 149–171. Pennsylvania State University Press, 2010.

Filotas, Bernadette. *Pagan Survivals, Superstitions and Popular Cultures in Early Medieval Pastoral Literature.* Pontifical Institute of Mediaeval Studies, 2005.

Fischer, Kurt von. "Neue Quellen mehrstimmiger Musik des 15. Jahrhunderts aus Schweizerischen Klostern." In *Renaissance-Muziek 1400–1600: Donum Natalicium René Bernard Lenaerts*, edited by Jozef Robijns, 293–301. Katholieke Universiteit, Seminarie voor Muziekwetenschap, 1969.

Fowler, Maria Vedder. "Musical Interpolations in Thirteenth- and Fourteenth-Century French Narratives." 2 vols. PhD diss., Yale University, 1979.

Frantzen, Johann J. A. A. "Ein spätes Zeugniß deutscher lateinischer Klerikerdichtung." *Neophilologus* 6 (1921): 130–136.

Frith, Simon. *Performing Rites: On the Value of Popular Music.* Harvard University Press, 1996.

Fuller, Sarah. "Aquitanian Polyphony of the Eleventh and Twelfth Centuries." 3 vols. PhD diss., University of California, Berkeley, 1969.

"Hidden Polyphony, a Reappraisal." *Journal of the American Musicological Society* 24 (1971): 169–192.

Garlandia, Johannes de. *Concerning Measured Music (De mensurabili musica).* Translated by Stanley H. Birnbaum. Colorado College of Music Press Translations 9. Colorado College of Music Press, 1978.

Gazeau, Véronique, and Jacques Le Maho. "Les Origines du culte de saint Nicolas en Normandie." In *Alle origini dell'Europa: Il culto di San Nicola tra Oriente e Occidente, Italia–Francia. Atti del convegno Bari 2–4 dicembre 2010*, edited by Gerardo Cioffari and Angela Laghezza. Nicolaus Studi Storici, 143–160. Bari, 2011.

Genette, Gérard. *Narrative Discourse: An Essay in Method.* Translated by Jane E. Lewin. Cornell University Press, 1980.

Gennrich, Friedrich. "Deutsche Rondeaux." *Beiträge zur Geschichte der deutschen Sprache und Literatur* 72 (1950): 130–141.

"Lateinische Kontrafakta altfranzösischer Lieder." *Zeitschrift für romanische Philologie* 50 (1930): 187–207.

Lateinische Liedkontrafaktur; eine Auswahl lateinischer Conductus mit ihren volkssprachigen Vorbildern. Musikwissenschaftliche Studienbibliothek. 2 vols. Darmstadt, 1956.

Gilhus, Ingvild Salid. "Carnival in Religion: The Feast of Fools in France." *Numen* 37 (1990): 24–52.

Gillingham, Bryan. *A Critical Study of Secular Medieval Latin Song.* Institute of Mediaeval Music, 1995.

Giraldus, Cambrensis. *Giraldi Cambrensis Opera*. Edited by J. S. Brewer, James F. Dimock, and George F. Warner. 8 vols. Longman & Co, 1861–1891.

Golden, Rachel May. *Mapping Medieval Identities in Occitanian Crusade Song*. Oxford University Press, 2020.

Göllner, Marie Louise, ed. *The Manuscript Cod. lat. 5539 of the Bavarian State Library*, Musicological Studies and Documents 43. Hänssler-Verlag, American Institute of Musicology, 1993.

Gougaud, Louis. "La Danse dans les églises." *Revue d'histoire ecclésiastique* 15 (1914): 5–22, 229–245.

Green, Rosalie, ed. *Herrad of Hohenbourg: Hortus deliciarum*. 2 vols. Warburg Institute and Brill, 1979.

Greene, Richard L., ed. *The Early English Carols*. 2nd ed. Clarendon Press, 1977.
    The Lyrics of the Red Book of Ossory. Blackwell for the Society for the Study of Mediaeval Languages and Literature, 1974.

Grier, James. "Some Codicological Observations on the Aquitanian Versaria." *Musica Disciplina* 44 (1990): 5–56.

Griffiths, Fiona J. *The Garden of Delights: Reform and Renaissance for Women in the Twelfth Century*. University of Pennsylvania Press, 2007.

Grocheio, Johannes de. *Ars musice*. Edited by Constant J. Mews, John N. Crossley, Catherine Jeffreys, Leigh McKinnon, and Carol J. Williams. Medieval Institute Publications, 2011.

Gröninger, Eduard. *Repertoire-Untersuchungen zum mehrstimmigen Notre Dame-Conductus*. Kölner Beiträge zur Musikforschung 2. G. Bosse, 1939.

Gross, Guillaume. *Chanter en polyphonie à Notre-Dame de Paris aux 12e et 13e siècles*. Brepols, 2007.
    "Organum at Notre Dame in the 12th and 13th Centuries: Rhetoric in Words and Music." *Plainsong and Medieval Music* 15 (2006): 87–108.
    "L'Organum aux xiie et xiiie siècles: Le discours musical comme stratégie de communication ou la légitimation implicite de l'autorité épiscopale." *Revue historique* 659 (2011): 487–510.

Grossel, Marie-Geneviève. "Trouveresses messines: La lyrique courtoise dans les textes des beguines (autour du ms. perdu Bibl. Metz 535)." In *Uns clers ait dit que chanson en ferait: Mélanges de langue, d'histoire et de littérature offerts à Jean-Charles Herbin*, edited by Marie-Geneviève Grossel, Jean-Pierre Martin, Ludovic Nys, Muriel Ott, and François Suard, 331–342. Presses universitaires de Valenciennes, 2019.

Guérard, Benjamin Edme Charles, ed. *Cartulaire de l'église Notre-Dame de Paris*. 4 vols. Crapelet, 1850.

Gurevich, Aaron J. "Medieval Chronotope." *Theoretische geschiedenis* 22 (1995): 225–240.

Haggh, Barbara, and Michel Huglo. "Magnus liber: Maius munus. Origine et destinée du manuscrit F." *Revue de musicologie* 90 (2004): 193–230.

Hahn, Cynthia J. *Portrayed on the Heart: Narrative Effect in Pictorial Lives of Saints from the Tenth through the Thirteenth Century.* University of California Press, 2001.

Haines, John. "Le Chant vulgaire dans l'Église à la fête de saint Étienne." In *The Church and Vernacular Literature in Medieval France*, edited by Dorothea Kullmann, 161–175. Pontifical Institute of Mediaeval Studies, 2009.

Medieval Song in Romance Languages. Cambridge University Press, 2010.

Satire in the Songs of Renart le nouvel. Droz, 2010.

Halsberghe, Gaston H. *The Cult of Sol Invictus.* Brill, 1972.

Handschin, Jacques. "Angelomontana polyphonica." *Schweizerisches Jahrbuch für Musikwissenschaft* 3 (1928): 64–95.

"Die Schweiz, welche sang (Ueber mittelalterliche Cantionen aus schweizerischen Handschriften)." In *Festschrift für Karl Nef zum 60 geburtstag (22. August 1933) dargebracht von Schülern und Freunden*, edited by Hans Ehinger Edgar Refardt, Wilhelm Merian, and Ernst Mohr, 102–133. Kommissions-Verlag Gebrüder Hug, 1933.

Hankeln, Roman. "Reflections of War and Violence in Early and High Medieval Saints' Offices." *Plainsong and Medieval Music* 23 (2014): 5–30.

Harris, Max. "Claiming Pagan Origins for Carnival: Bacchanalia, Saturnalia, and Kalends." *European Medieval Drama* 10 (2006): 57–107.

"A Rough and Holy Liturgy: A Reassessment of the Feast of Fools." In *"Risus Sacer–Sacrum Risible": Interaktionsfelder von Sakralität und Gelächter im kulturellen und historischen Wandel*, edited by Katja Gvozdeva and Werner Röcke, 77–100. Peter Lang, 2009.

Sacred Folly: A New History of the Feast of Fools. Cornell University Press, 2011.

Harrison, Frank Ll. "Benedicamus, Conductus, Carol: A Newly-Discovered Source." *Acta Musicologica* 37 (1965): 35–48.

Harvey, Barbara. "Work and *Festa Ferianda* in Medieval England." The *Journal of Ecclesiastical History* 23 (1972): 289–308.

Hasenohr, Geneviève. "D'une 'poésie de béguine' à une 'poétique des béguines': Aperçus sur la forme et la reception des textes (France, XIIIe–XIVe s.)." *Comptes rendus des séances de l'Académie des Inscriptions et Belles Lettres* 150 (2006): 913–943.

Haskins, Charles H. "The Life of Medieval Students as Illustrated by Their Letters." *The American Historical Review* 3 (1898): 203–229.

Hassig, Deborah. *Medieval Bestiaries: Text, Image, Ideology.* Cambridge University Press, 1995.

Haug, Andreas. "Kennen wir die Melodie zu einem Lied des ersten Trobador? Ein Versuch in wissenschaftlichem Wunschdenken." In *Projektion – Reflexion – Ferne: Räumliche Vorstellungen und Denkfiguren im Mittelalter*, edited by Sonja Glauch, Susanne Köbele, and Uta Störmer-Caysa, 369–390. De Gruyter, 2011.

"Musikalische Lyrik im Mittelalter." In *Musikalische Lyrik*, edited by Hermann Danuser. Handbuch der musikalischen Gattungen, 59–129. Laaber-Verlag, 2004.

"Ritual and Repetition: The Ambiguities of Refrains." Translated by Jeremy Llewellyn. In *The Appearances of Medieval Rituals: The Play of Construction and Modification*, edited by Nils Holger Petersen, Mette Birkedal Bruun, Jeremy Llewellyn, and Eyolf Østrem, 83–96. Brepols, 2004.

"Tropes." In *The Cambridge History of Medieval Music*, edited by Mark Everist and Thomas Forrest Kelly, 263–299. Cambridge University Press, 2018.

Hauréau, Barthélémy. *Notice sur le numéro 15131 des manuscrits latins de la bibliothèque nationale*. Imprimerie nationale, 1889. Taken from the *Notices et extraits des manuscrits de la Bibliothèque Nationale et autres bibliothèques*, vol. XXXIII, 1st part.

Hiley, David. *Western Plainchant: A Handbook*. Clarendon Press, 1993.

Hiley, David, ed. *Moosburger Graduale: München, Universitätsbibliothek, 20 Cod. ms. 156*. H. Schneider, 1996.

Hollander, John. "Breaking into Song: Some Notes on Refrain." In *Lyric Poetry: Beyond New Criticism*, edited by Chaviva Hošek and Patricia Parker, 73–89. Cornell University Press, 1985.

Hughes, Andrew. "The 'Ludus super Anticlaudianum' of Adam de la Bassée." *Journal of the American Musicological Society* 23 (1970): 1–25.

Medieval Manuscripts for Mass and Office: A Guide to Their Organization and Terminology. University of Toronto Press, 1982.

Huglo, Michel. *Les Manuscrits du Processional*. Vol. 2. G. Henle Verlag, 2004.

Humphrey, Chris. *The Politics of Carnival: Festive Misrule in Medieval England*. Manchester University Press, 2001.

Hunt, Richard. "The Collections of a Monk of Bardney: A Dismembered Rawlinson Manuscript." *Mediaeval and Renaissance Studies* 5 (1961): 28–42.

Huot, Sylvia. *From Song to Book: The Poetics of Writing in Old French Lyric and Lyrical Narrative Poetry*. Cornell University Press, 1987.

Hutton, Ronald. *Stations of the Sun: A History of the Ritual Year in Britain*. Oxford, 1996.

The Rise and Fall of Merry England: The Ritual Year 1400–1700. Oxford University Press, 1996 [1994].

Ibos-Augé, Anne. *Chanter et lire dans le récit médiéval: La fonction des insertions lyriques dans les oeuvres narratives et didactiques d'oïl aux XIIIe et XIVe siècles*. 2 vols. Peter Lang, 2010.

Irtenkauf, Wolfgang. "Das Seckauer Cantionarium vom Jahre 1345 (Hs. Graz 756)." *Archiv für Musikwissenschaft* 13 (1956): 116–141.

Iversen, Gunilla. *Laus angelica: Poetry in the Medieval Mass*. Translated by William Flynn. Medieval Church Studies 5. Brepols, 2010.

"Le Son de la lyre des vertus: Sur la musique dans la poésie liturgique médiévale." In *La Place de la musique dans la culture médiévale: Colloque organisé à la*

Fondation Singer-Polignac le mercredi 25 octobre 2006, edited by Martine Clouzot, Michel Zink, and Olivier Cullin, 47–69. Brepols, 2007.

"'Verba canendi' in Tropes and Sequences." In *Latin Culture in the Eleventh Century: Proceedings of the Third International Conference on Medieval Studies, Cambridge, September 9–12, 1998*, edited by Michael W. Herren, C. J. McDonough, and Ross G. Arthur, 1:444–473. Brepols, 2002.

Jacobsson, Ritva, and Leo Treitler. "Tropes and the Concept of Genre." In *Pax et sapientia: Studies in Text and Music of Liturgical Tropes and Sequences in Memory of Gordon Anderson*, edited by Ritva Jacobsson, 59–89. Almqvist & Wiksell International, 1986.

Jans, Markus. "'Ad haec sollempnia': Zur Aufführungspraxis eines zweistimmig überlieferten Refrains in einer Handschrift von Le Puy." In *Beredte Musik: Konversationen zum 80. Geburtstag von Wulf Arlt*, edited by Martin Kirnbauer, 195–203. Schwabe Verlag, 2019.

Jeanroy, Alfred, ed. *Les Chansons de Guillaume IX, duc d'Aquitaine (1071–1127)*. 2nd ed. H. Champion, 1927.

Johnson, Susan M. "The Role of the Refrain in the Pastourelles *à refrain*." In *Literary and Historical Perspectives of the Middle Ages: Proceedings of the 1981 SEMA Meeting*, edited by Patricia Willett Cummins, Charles W. Connell, and Patrick W. Conner, 78–92. West Virginia University Press, 1982.

Jones, Charles W. "The Norman Cult of Sts Catherine and Nicholas, saec XI." In *Hommages à André Boutemy*, edited by Guy Cambier, 216–230. Latomus, 1976.

Saint Nicholas of Myra, Bari, and Manhattan: Biography of a Legend. The University of Chicago Press, 1978.

Jonsson, Ritva. "The Liturgical Function of the Tropes." In *Research on Tropes: Proceedings of a Symposium Organized by the Royal Academy of Literature, History and Antiquities and the Corpus Troporum, Stockholm, June 1–3, 1981*, edited by Gunilla Iversen, 99–123. Almqvist & Wiksell International, 1983.

Jordan, William C. "Exclusion and the Yearning to Belong: Evidence from the History of Thirteenth-Century France." In *Difference and Identity in Francia and Medieval France*, edited by Meredith Cohen and Justine Firnhaber-Baker, 13–24. Ashgate, 2010.

The French Monarchy and the Jews: From Philip Augustus to the Last Capetians. University of Pennsylvania Press, 1989.

Keller, John Esten, and Annette Grant Cash. *Daily Life Depicted in the Cantigas de Santa Maria*. University of Kentucky Press, 1998.

Kiening, Christian. "Mediating the Passion in Time and Space." In *Temporality and Mediality in Late Medieval and Early Modern Culture*, edited by Christian Kiening and Martina Stercken, 115–146. Brepols, 2018.

Kinney, Clare Regan. *Strategies of Poetic Narrative: Chaucer, Spenser, Milton, Eliot.* Cambridge University Press, 1992.

Klein, Dorothea, Brigitte Burrichter, and Andreas Haug, eds. *Das mittelalterliche Tanzlied (1100–1300): Lieder zum Tanz – Tanz im Lied.* Würzburger Beiträge zur deutschen Philologie 37. Königshausen & Neumann, 2012.

Knäble, Philip. *Eine tanzende Kirche: Initiation, Ritual und Liturgie im spätmittelalterlichen Frankreich.* Böhlau Verlag, 2016.

"L'Harmonie des sphères et la danse dans le contexte clérical au Moyen Âge." *Médiévales* 66 (2014): 65–80.

Knox, Philip. "Circularity and Linearity: The Idea of the Lyric and the Idea of the Book in the *Cent Ballades* of Jean le Seneschal." *New Medieval Literatures* 16 (2016): 213–249.

Kornrumpf, Gisela. "Rondeaux des Barfüßers vom Main? Spuren einer deutschen Liedmode des 14. Jahrhunderts in Kremsmünster, Engelberg und Mainz." In *"Ieglicher sang sein eigen ticht": Germanistische und musikwissenschaftliche Beiträge zum deutschen Lied im Spätmittelalter,* edited by Christoph März, Lorenz Welker, and Nicola Zotz, 57–73. Reichert Verlag, 2011.

Kruckenberg, Lori. "Neumatizing the Sequence: Special Performances of Sequences in the Central Middle Ages." *Journal of the American Musicological Society* 59 (2006): 243–317.

"The Relationship between the Festal Office and the New Sequence: Evidence from Medieval Picardy." *Journal of the Alamire Foundation* 5 (2013): 201–233.

"Two *Sequentiae Novae* at Nidaros: *Celeste organum* and *Stola iocunditatis.*" In *The Sequences of Nidaros: A Nordic Repertory and Its European Context,* edited by Lori Kruckenberg and Andreas Haug, 367–411. Tapir Academic Press, 2006.

La Rue, Donna. "Tripudium: Its Use in Sources from 200 BCE to 1600 CE." *ARTS* 7 (1995): 25–29.

Lacaze, Charlotte. *The "Vie de St. Denis" Manuscript: (Paris, Bibliothèque nationale, Ms. fr. 2090–2092).* Garland Publishing, 1979.

Ladner, Pascal. "Ein spätmittelalterlicher Liber Ordinarius Officii aus der Diözese Lausanne." *Zeitschrift für schweizerische Kirchengeschichte = Revue d'histoire ecclésiastique suisse* 64 (1970): 1–103.

Lagueux, Robert Charles. "Glossing Christmas: Liturgy, Music, Exegesis, and Drama in High Medieval Laon." PhD diss., Yale University, 2004.

Långfors, Arthur. *Notices des manuscrits 535 de la bibliothèque de Metz et 10047 des Nouvelles acquisitions du fond français de la Bibliothèque nationale.* Notices et extraits des manuscrits de la Bibliothèque nationale et autres bibliothèques 42. Académie des inscriptions et belles-lettres, 1933.

Lanham, Richard A. *A Handlist of Rhetorical Terms.* 2nd ed. University of California Press, 1991.

Larkowski, Charles Stephen. "The 'De musica mensurabili positio' of Johannes de Garlandia: Translation and Commentary." PhD diss., Michigan State University, 1977.

Latzke, Therese. "Zu dem Gedicht 'De papa scolastico' des Abaelardschülers Hilarius." *Mittellateinisches Jahrbuch* 13 (1978): 86–99.

Lawler, Traugott, ed. *The Parisiana Poetria of John of Garland*. Yale University Press, 1974.

Lawlor, Hugh Jackson. "Calendar of the Liber Ruber of the Diocese of Ossory." *Proceedings of the Royal Irish Academy. Section C: Archaeology, Celtic Studies, History, Linguistics, Literature* 27 (1908): 159–208.

Leach, Elizabeth Eva. "A Courtly Compilation: The Douce Chansonnier." In *Manuscripts and Medieval Song: Inscription, Performance, Context*, edited by Helen Deeming and Elizabeth Eva Leach, 221–246. Cambridge University Press, 2015.

"Learning French by Singing in 14th-Century England." *Early Music* 33 (2005): 253–270.

"Nature's Forge and Mechanical Production: Writing, Reading and Performing Song." In *Rhetoric beyond Words: Delight and Persuasion in the Arts of the Middle Ages*, edited by Mary Carruthers, 72–95. Cambridge University Press, 2010.

Sung Birds: Music, Nature, and Poetry in the Later Middle Ages. Cornell University Press, 2007.

Le Goff, Jacques. *In Search of Sacred Time: Jacobus de Voragine and the Golden Legend*. Translated by Lydia G. Cochrane. Princeton University Press, 2014 [2011].

Leisibach, Joseph. *Die liturgischen Handschriften des Kantons Freiburg (ohne Kantonsbibliothek)*. Universitätsverlag Freiburg Schweiz, 1977.

"Lettre écrite de Besançon sur un terme de la basse Latinité, et sur une Danse Ecclésiastique qui s'y faisoit le jour de Pâques." *Mercure de France* (September 1742): 1930–1955.

Leverage, Paula. *Reception and Memory: A Cognitive Approach to the Chansons de Geste*. Editions Rodopi, 2010.

Levitsky, Anne Adele. "Song Personified: The *Tornadas* of Raimon de Miraval." *Mediaevalia* 39 (2018): 17–57.

Le Vot, Gérard. "La Tradition musicale des épîtres farcies de la Saint-Étienne en langues romanes." *Revue de musicologie* 73 (1987): 61–82.

Linskill, Joseph. *Saint-Léger: Étude de la langue du manuscrit de Clermont-Ferrand. Suivie d'une édition critique du texte avec commentaire et Glossaire*. Droz, 1937.

Lipphardt, Walther. "'Magnum nomen Domini Emanuel': Zur Frühgeschichte der Cantio 'Resonet in laudibus.'" *Jahrbuch für Liturgik und Hymnologie* 17 (1972): 194–204.

"Zur Herkunft der Carmina Burana." In *Literatur und Bildende Kunst im Tiroler Mittelalter*, edited by Egon Kühebacher, 209–223. Kowatsch, 1982.

Llewellyn, Jeremy. "Nova Cantica." In *The Cambridge History of Medieval Music*, edited by Mark Everist and Thomas Forrest Kelly, 147–175. Cambridge University Press, 2018.

Longère, Jean. *La Prédication médiévale*. Etudes augustiniennes, 1983.

Ludwig, Friedrich. *Repertorium Organorum Recentioris et Motetorum Vetustissimi Stili*. 2 vols. M. Niemeyer, 1910.

Mannaerts, Pieter. "Musiek en musiektheorie in handschriften uit Ten Duinen en Ter Doest." *Novi Monasterii* 6 (2007): 3–20.

Margulis, Elizabeth Hellmuth. *On Repeat: How Music Plays the Mind*. Oxford University Press, 2014.

Marshall, John H. "Pour l'étude des *Contrafacta* dans la poésie des troubadours." *Romania* 101 (1980): 289–335.

Marshall, Judith M. "A Late Eleventh-Century Manuscript from St. Martial de Limoges: Paris, Bibliothèque nationale, fonds Latin no. 1139." PhD diss., Yale University, 1961.

Martène, Edmond. *Tractatus de antiqua ecclesiae disciplina in divinis celebrandis officiis . . . aliisque probatis auctoribus permultis*. Anisson & Joannis Posuel, 1706.

März, Christoph. "*Pange lingua per omnia verbo et melodia*: Zu den Anfängen poetischer Hymnennachbildung in deutscher Sprache." In *Der lateinische Hymnus im Mittelalter: Überlieferung – Ästhetik – Ausstrahlung*, edited by Andreas Haug, Christoph März, and Lorenz Welker, 279–299. Bärenreiter, 2004.

Masani Ricci, Massimo. *Codice Pluteo 29.1 della Biblioteca Laurenziana di Firenze: Storia e catalogo comparato*. Edizioni ETS, 2002.

Maurey, Yossi. *Medieval Music, Legend, and the Cult of St. Martin: The Local Foundations of a Universal Saint*. Cambridge University Press, 2014.

Mazzeo, Jacopo. "The Two-Part Conductus: Morphology, Dating and Authorship." PhD diss., University of Southampton, 2015.

McGee, Timothy J. *Medieval Instrumental Dances*. Indiana University Press, 1989.

McGrade, Michael. "Enriching the Gregorian Heritage." In *The Cambridge Companion to Medieval Music*, edited by Mark Everist, 26–45. Cambridge University Press, 2011.

McHale, Brian. "Beginning to Think about Narrative in Poetry." *Narrative* 17 (2009): 11–30.

McNeill, William H. *Keeping Together in Time: Dance and Drill in Human History*. Harvard University Press, 1995.

Messenger, Ruth Ellis. "Medieval Processional Hymns before 1100." *Transactions and Proceedings of the American Philological Association* 80 (1949): 375–392.

"Processional Hymnody in the Later Middle Ages." *Transactions and Proceedings of the American Philological Association* 81 (1950): 185–199.

Mettman, Walter, ed. *Afonso X, o Sábio: Cantigas de Santa Maria*, Vol. 3. Universidade, 1964.

Mews, Constant J. "Liturgists and Dance in the Twelfth Century: The Witness of John Beleth and Sicard of Cremona." *Church History* 78 (2009): 512–548.

Meyer, Paul. "Chanson à Jésus-Christ en sixains latins et français." *Bulletin de la Société des anciens textes français* 37 (1911): 53–56.

"Chansons religieuses en latin et en français." *Bulletin de la Société des anciens textes français* 37 (1911): 92–99.

"Notice du ms. 535 de la Bibliotheque Municipale de Metz." *Bulletin de la Société des anciens textes français* 11 (1886): 41–76.

"Table d'un ancien recueil de chansons latines et françaises." *Bulletin de la Société des anciens textes français* 24 (1898): 95–102.

Miller, Tanya Stabler. *The Beguines of Medieval Paris: Gender, Patronage, and Spiritual Authority*. University of Pennsylvania Press, 2014.

Milway, Michael. "Boy Bishops in Early Modern Europe: Ritual, Myth, and Reality." In *The Dramatic Tradition of the Middle Ages*, edited by Clifford Davidson, 87–97. AMS Press, Inc., 2005.

Mondschein, Ken, and Denis Casey. "Time and Timekeeping." In *Handbook of Medieval Culture: Fundamental Aspects and Conditions of the European Middle Ages*, edited by Albrecht Classen, 1657–1679. De Gruyter, 2015.

Morabito, Raffaele. "The Italian *Cantari* between Orality and Writing." In *Medieval Oral Literature*, edited by Karl Reichl, 371–386. De Gruyter, 2012.

Mousseau, Juliet, ed. *Adam of Saint-Victor: Sequences*. Peeters, 2013.

Muir, Edward. *Ritual in Early Modern Europe*. 2nd ed. Cambridge University Press, 2005.

Mullally, Robert. *The Carole: A Study of a Medieval Dance*. Ashgate, 2011.

Murphy, Diane. *Medieval Mystery Plays as Popular Culture: Performing the Lives of Saints*. The Edwin Mellen Press, 2006.

Murphy, James J. "The Teaching of Latin as a Second Language in the 12th Century." *Historiographia Linguistica* 7 (1980): 159–175.

Murray, David. *Poetry in Motion: Languages and Lyrics in the European Middle Ages*. Brepols, 2019.

Nelson, Ingrid. *Lyric Tactics: Poetry, Genre, and Practice in Later Medieval England*. University of Pennsylvania Press, 2016.

Neville, Grace. "French Language and Literature in Medieval Ireland." *Etudes irlandaises* 15 (1990): 23–35.

Norberg, Dag. *An Introduction to the Study of Medieval Latin Versification*. Translated by Grant C. Roti and Jacqueline de La Chapelle Skubly. Catholic University of America Press, 2004.

Nörrenberg, Constantin. "Ein Aachener Dichter des 14. Jahrhunderts." *Zeitschrift des Aachener Geschichtsvereins* 11 (1889): 50–66.

Norton, Michael L. *Liturgical Drama and the Reimagining of Medieval Theater*. Medieval Institute Publications, 2017.

O'Sullivan, Daniel E. "Contrafacture." In *Handbook of Medieval Studies: Terms – Methods – Trends*, edited by Albrecht Classen, 1478–1481. De Gruyter, 2010.

Marian Devotion in Thirteenth-Century French Lyric. University of Toronto Press, 2005.

"On connaît la chanson: La contrafacture des mélodies des trouvères dans le *Ludus super Anticlaudianum* d'Adam de la Bassée." *Cahiers de recherches médiévales et humanistes* 26 (2013): 109–127.

O'Sullivan, Jeremiah F., ed. *The Register of Eudes of Rouen*. Columbia University Press, 1964.

Pächt, Otto. *The Rise of Pictorial Narrative in Twelfth-Century England*. Clarendon Press, 1962.

Paden, William D. "Troubadours and Jews." In *Études de langue et de littérature médiévales offertes à Peter T. Ricketts à l'occasion de son 70ème anniversaire*, edited by Ann Buckley and Dominique Billy, 471–484. Brepols, 2005.

Page, Christopher. *Latin Poetry and Conductus Rhythm in Medieval France*. Royal Musical Association, 1997.

The Owl and the Nightingale: Musical Life and Ideas in France, 1100–1300. University of California Press, 1989.

"The Performance of Ars Antiqua Motets." *Early Music* 16 (1988): 147–164.

Voices and Instruments of the Middle Ages: Instrumental Practice and Songs in France, 1100–1300. J. M. Dent and Sons, Ltd., 1987.

Parkes, Malcolm B. "The Influence of the Concepts of *Ordinatio* and *Compilatio* on the Development of the Book." In *Medieval Learning and Literature: Essays Presented to Richard William Hunt*, edited by J. J. G. Alexander and M. T. Gibson, 115–141. Clarendon Press, 1976.

Payne, Thomas. "*Aurelianus civitas*: Student Unrest in Medieval France and a Conductus by Philip the Chancellor." *Speculum* 75 (2000): 589–614.

"Chancellor *versus* Bishop: The Conflict between Philip the Chancellor and Guillaume d'Auvergne in Poetry and Music." In *Philippe le Chancelier: Prédicateur, théologien et poète parisien du début du XIIIe siècle*, edited by Gilbert Dahan and Anne-Zoé Rillon-Marne. Bibliothèque d'histoire culturelle du Moyen Âge 19, 265–306. Brepols, 2017.

"Datable 'Notre Dame' Conductus: New Historical Observations on Style and Technique (*for Ernest Sanders*)." *Current Musicology* 64 (2001): 104–151.

"Latin Song II: The Music and Texts of the Conductus." In *The Cambridge History of Medieval Music*, edited by Mark Everist and Thomas Forrest Kelly, 1048–1078. Cambridge University Press, 2018.

"Poetry, Politics, and Polyphony: Philip the Chancellor's Contribution to the Music of the Notre Dame School." PhD diss., University of Chicago, 1991.

Payne, Thomas, ed. *Motets and Prosulas: Philip the Chancellor*. Recent Researches in the Music of the Middle Ages and Early Renaissance 41. A-R Editions, 2011.

Peraino, Judith A. "*Et pui conmencha a canter*: Refrains, Motets and Melody in the Thirteenth-Century Narrative *Renart le nouvel.*" *Plainsong and Medieval Music* 6 (1997): 1–16.

    Giving Voice to Love: Song and Self-Expression from the Troubadours to Guillaume de Machaut. Oxford University Press, 2011.

    "Listening to the Sirens: Music as Queer Ethical Practice." *GLQ: A Journal of Lesbian and Gay Studies* 9 (2003): 433–470.

    Listening to the Sirens: Musical Technologies of Queer Identity from Homer to Hedwig. University of California Press, 2006.

    "New Music, Notions of Genre, and the 'Manuscrit du Roi' circa 1300." PhD diss., University of California, 1995.

Petzsch, Christoph. "Ostschwäbische Rondeaux vor 1400." *Beiträge zur Geschichte der deutschen Sprache und Literatur* 98 (1976): 384–394.

Phythian-Adams, Charles. "Ceremony and the Citizen: The Communal Year at Coventry 1450-1550." In *Crisis and Order in English Towns, 1500–1700*, edited by Peter Clark and Paul Slack, 57–85. Routledge and K. Paul, 1972.

Plumley, Yolanda. *The Art of Grafted Song: Citation and Allusion in the Age of Machaut.* Oxford University Press, 2013.

    "French Lyrics and Songs for the New Year, ca. 1380–1420." In *The Cambridge History of Fifteenth-Century Music*, edited by Anna Maria Busse Berger and Jesse Rodin, 374–400. Cambridge University Press, 2015.

Poteat, Hubert McNeill. "The Functions of Repetition in Latin Poetry." *The Classical Weekly* 12 (1919): 139–142.

    "The Functions of Repetition in Latin Poetry (Concluded)." *The Classical Weekly* 12 (1919): 145–150.

Prévot, Brigitte. "*Festum baculi* : Fête du bâton ou fête des fous à Châlons, au Moyen Age." In *Poésie et rhétorique du non-sens: Littérature médiévale, littérature orale*, edited by Marie-Geneviève Grossel and Sylvie Mougin, 207–237. Éditions et Presses universitaires de Reims, 2004.

Purcell-Joiner, Lauren Elizabeth. "Veil and Tonsure: Stuttgart 95, Devotional Music, and the Discursive Construction of Gender in Thirteenth-Century Double Houses." PhD diss., University of Oregon, 2017.

Quasten, Johannes. *Music and Worship in Pagan and Christian Antiquity.* Translated by Boniface Ramsey. National Association of Pastoral Musicians, 1983 [1973].

Quinlan, Meghan. "Repetition as Rebirth: A Sung Epitaph for Gautier de Coinci." *Music & Letters* 101 (2020): 623–656.

Ragnard, Isabelle. "Les Chansons d'étrennes aux XIVe et XVe siècles." In *Poètes et musiciens dans l'espace bourguignon: Les artistes et leurs mécènes. Rencontres de Dordrecht (23 au 26 septembre 2004)*, edited by Jean-Marie Cauchies, 105–127. Publication du Centre européen d'Études bourguignonnes (XIVe–XVIe s.), 2005.

Reckow, Fritz. "Conductus." In *Handwörterbuch der musikalischen Terminologie*, edited by Hans Heinrich Eggebrecht and Fritz Reckow, 1–11. Franz Steiner Verlag, 1973.

    Der Musiktraktat des Anonymus 4. Beihefte zum Archiv für Musikwissenschaft 4–5. 2 vols. Franz Steiner Verlag, 1967.

    "Rondellus/rondeau, rota." In *Handwörterbuch der musikalischen Terminologie*, edited by Hans Heinrich Eggebrecht and Fritz Reckow, 1–7. Franz Steiner Verlag, 1972.

Regalado, Nancy Freeman. "The Songs of Jehannot de Lescurel in Paris, BnF, MS fr. 146: Love Lyrics, Moral Wisdom and the Material Book." In *Poetry, Knowledge and Community in Late Medieval France*, edited by Rebecca Dixon and Finn E. Sinclair, 151–172. D. S. Brewer, 2008.

Reimer, Erich, ed. *Johannes de Garlandia: De mensurabili musica. Kritische Edition mit Kommentar und Interpretation der Notationslehre.* 2 vols. Beihefte zum Archiv für Musikwissenschaft 10–11. Franz Steiner Verlag, 1972.

Rigg, A. G. "The Red Book of Ossory." *Medium Aevum* 46 (1977): 269–278.

Rillon-Marne, Anne-Zoé. "*Exultemus sobrie*: Gestualité et rythmique des rondeaux latins du manuscrit de Florence (Pluteus 29.1)." *Le Jardin de musique* 9 (2018): 25–48.

    Homo considera: La pastorale lyrique de Philippe le Chancelier. Une étude des conduits monodiques. Brepols, 2012.

Rimmer, Joan. "Carole, Rondeau and Branle in Ireland 1300–1800: Part 1. The Walling of New Ross and Dance Texts in the Red Book of Ossory." *Dance Research: The Journal of the Society for Dance Research* 7 (1989): 20–46.

Robertson, Anne Walters. "The Savior, the Woman, and the Head of the Dragon in the Caput Masses and Motet." *Journal of the American Musicological Society* 59 (2006): 537–630.

Robson, Charles Alan. *Maurice of Sully and the Medieval Vernacular Homily. With the Text of Maurice's French Homilies from a Sens Cathedral Chapter MS.* Basil Blackwell, 1952.

Rodgers, Edith Cooperrider. *Discussion of Holidays in the Later Middle Ages.* Columbia University Press, 1940.

Roesner, Edward H., ed. *Antiphonarium, seu, Magnus liber de gradali et antiphonario: Color Microfiche Edition of the Manuscript Firenze, Biblioteca Medicea Laurenziana Pluteus 29.1: Introduction to the "Notre-Dame Manuscript" F.* Codices illuminati medii aevi 45. H. Lengenfelder, 1996.

Rokseth, Yvonne. "Danses cléricales du XIIIe siecle." In *Mélanges 1945 des Publications de la Faculté des Lettres de Strasbourg*, edited by Université de Strasbourg Faculté des Lettres, 93–126. Les Belles Lettres, 1947.

Roolfs, Friedel Helga. "Das Wienhäuser Liederbuch: Eine kodikologische Annäherung." In *Passion und Ostern in den Lüneburger Klöstern: Bericht des VIII. Ebstorfer Kolloquiums, Kloster Ebstorf, 25. bis 29. März 2009*, edited by Linda Maria Koldau, 245–263. Kloster Ebstorf, 2010.

Ross, Leslie. *Text, Image, Message: Saints in Medieval Manuscript Illustrations.* Greenwood Press, 1994.

Rothenberg, David J. *The Flower of Paradise: Marian Devotion and Secular Song in Medieval and Renaissance Music.* Oxford University Press, 2011.

"The Marian Symbolism of Spring, ca. 1200–ca. 1500: Two Case Studies." *Journal of the American Musicological Society* 59 (2006): 319–398.

Saint-Cricq, Gaël. "Formes types dans le motet du XIIIe siècle: Étude d'un processus répétitif." 2 vols. PhD diss., University of Southampton, 2009.

Saint-Cricq, Gaël, Eglal Doss-Quinby, and Samuel N. Rosenberg, eds. *Motets from the Chansonnier de Noailles.* Recent Researches in the Music of the Middle Ages and Early Renaissance 42. A-R Editions, 2017.

Saltzstein, Jennifer. *The Refrain and the Rise of the Vernacular in Medieval French Music and Poetry.* D. S. Brewer, 2013.

"Songs of Nature in Medieval Northern France: Landscape, Identity, and Environment." *Journal of the American Musicological Society* 72 (2019): 115–180.

Sanders, Ernest H. "Rithmus." In *Essays on Medieval Music: In Honor of David G. Hughes,* edited by Graeme M. Boone, 415–440. Harvard University Press, 1995.

Schlager, Karlheinz. "Cantiones." In *Geschichte der katholischen Kirchenmusik. Unter Mitarbeit zahlreicher Forscher des In- und Auslandes,* edited by Karl Gustav Fellerer, 286–293. Bärenreiter-Verlag, 1972.

Schmidt, Victor M. "Painting and Individual Devotion in Late Medieval Italy: The Case of Saint Catherine of Alexandria." In *Visions of Holiness: Art and Devotion in Renaissance Italy,* edited by Andrew Ladis and Shelley E. Zuraw, 21–36. Georgia Museum of Art, University of Georgia, 2001.

Schmidt-Beste, Thomas. "Psallite noe! Christmas Carols, the Devotio Moderna, and the Renaissance Motet." In *Das Erzbistum Köln in der Musikgeschichte des 15. und 16. Jahrhunderts,* edited by Klaus Pietschmann, 213–231. Merseburger, 2008.

Schum, Wilhelm. *Beschreibendes Verzeichnis der Amplonianischen Handschriften-Sammlung zu Erfurt.* Weidmannsche Buchhandlung, 1887.

Seebass, Tilman. "Prospettive dell'iconografia musicale: Considerazioni di un medievalista." *Rivista italiana di musicologia* 18 (1983): 67–86.

Seville, Isidore of. *Isidore of Seville: De ecclesiasticis officiis.* Translated by Thomas L. Knoebel. Ancient Christian Writers 61. Newman Press, 2008.

Shahar, Shulamith. "The Boy Bishop's Feast: A Case-Study in Church Attitudes towards Children in the High and Late Middle Ages." In *The Church and Childhood: Papers Read at the 1993 Summer Meeting and the 1994 Winter Meeting of the Ecclesiastical History Society,* edited by Diana Wood, 243–260. Blackwell Publishers, 1994.

Sievers, Heinrich, ed. *Das Wienhäuser Liederbuch.* 2 vols. Möseler Verlag, 1954.

Silen, Karen. "Dance in Late Thirteenth-Century Paris." In *Dance, Spectacle, and the Body Politick, 1250–1750*, edited by Jennifer Nevile, 67–79. Indiana University Press, 2008.

Smith, Nathaniel B. *Figures of Repetition in the Old Provençal Lyric: A Study in the Style of the Troubadours*. University of North Carolina Studies in the Romance Languages and Literatures 176. Department of Romance Languages, University of North Carolina, 1976.

Smyth, Karen Elaine. *Imaginings of Time in Lydgate and Hoccleve's Verse*. Ashgate, 2011.

Spanke, Hans. "Das lateinische Rondeau." *Zeitschrift für französische Sprache und Literatur* 53 (1930): 113–148.

"Das Mosburger Graduale." *Zeitschrift für romanische Philologie* 50 (1930): 582–595.

"Studien zur Geschichte des altfranzösischen Liedes. II. Gautier de Coinci." *Archiv für das Studium der Neueren Sprachen und Literaturen* 156 (1929): 215–232.

"Tanzmusik in der Kirche des Mittelalters." In *Studien zur lateinischen und romanischen Lyrik des Mittelalters*, edited by Ulrich Mölk, 105–131. G. Olms, 1983.

"Zur Formenkunst des ältesten Troubadours." *Studi Medievali New Series* 7 (1934): 72–84.

Stein, Franz A. "Das Moosburger Graduale (1354–60) als Quelle geistlicher Volkslieder." *Jahrbuch für Liturgik und Hymnologie* 2 (1956): 93–99.

Stemmler, Theo. *The Latin Hymns of Richard Ledrede*. English Department (Medieval Section) of the University of Mannheim, 1975.

"The Vernacular Snatches in the Red Book of Ossory: A Textual Case-History." *Anglia* 95 (1977): 122–129.

Stevens, John E. *Words and Music in the Middle Ages: Song, Narrative, Dance, and Drama, 1050–1350*. Cambridge University Press, 1986.

Stevens, John E., ed. *The Later Cambridge Songs: An English Song Collection of the Twelfth Century*. Oxford University Press, 2004.

Strohm, Reinhard. "Late-Medieval Sacred Songs: Tradition, Memory and History." In *Identity and Locality in Early Modern Music, 1028–1740*, edited by Jason Stoessel, 129–148. Ashgate, 2009.

"Sacred Song in the Fifteenth Century: Cantio, Carol, Lauda, Kirchenlied." In *The Cambridge History of Fifteenth-Century Music*, edited by Anna Maria Busse Berger and Jesse Rodin, 755–770. Cambridge University Press, 2015.

Switten, Margaret. "Borrowing, Citation, and Authorship in Gautier de Coinci's *Miracles de Nostre Dame*." In *The Medieval Author in Medieval French Literature*, edited by Virginie Greene, 29–59. Palgrave Macmillan, 2006.

"*Versus* and Troubadours around 1100: A Comparative Study of Refrain Technique in the 'New Song.'" *Plainsong and Medieval Music* 16 (2007): 91–143.

Symes, Carol. *A Common Stage: Theater and Public Life in Medieval Arras.* Cornell University Press, 2007.

Szövérffy, Joseph. "The Legends of St. Peter in Medieval Latin Hymns." *Traditio* 10 (1954): 275–322.

Tanner, Norman P., ed. *Decrees of the Ecumenical Councils.* 2 vols. Georgetown University Press, 1990.

Thomas, Antoine. "Refrains français de la fin du XIIIe siècle tirés des poésies latines d'un maitre d'école de St-Denis." In *Mélanges de linguistique et de littérature offerts à m. Alfred Jeanroy par ses élèves et ses amis*, 497–508. Droz, 1928.

Tischler, Hans. *Conductus and Contrafacta.* Musicological Studies 75. The Institute of Mediaeval Music, 2001.

Traill, David A. "More Poems by Philip the Chancellor." *The Journal of Medieval Latin* 16 (2006): 164–181.

Traill, David A., ed. *Carmina Burana.* 2 vols. Dumbarton Oaks Medieval Library 48–49. Harvard University Press, 2018.

Treitler, Leo. "Homer and Gregory: The Transmission of Epic Poetry and Plainchant." *The Musical Quarterly* 60 (1974): 333–372.

"The Polyphony of St. Martial." *Journal of the American Musicological Society* 17 (1964): 29–42.

Vinsauf, Geoffrey of. *Poetria nova: Revised Edition.* Translated by Margaret F. Nims and Martin Camargo. Medieval Sources in Translation 49. Pontifical Institute of Medieval Studies, 2010.

Vitz, Evelyn Birge. "The Apocryphal and the Biblical, the Oral and the Written, in Medieval Legends of Christ's Childhood: The Old French *Evangile de L'Enfance*." In *Satura: Studies in Medieval Literature in Honour of Robert R. Raymo*, edited by Nancy M. Reale and Ruth Esther Sternglantz, 124–149. Shaun Tyas, 2001.

Vitz, Evelyn Birge, Nancy Freeman Regalado, and Marilyn Lawrence, eds. *Performing Medieval Narrative.* D. S. Brewer, 2005.

Voogt, Ronald Edwin. "Repetition and Structure in the Three- and Four-Part Conductus of the Notre Dame School." PhD diss., The Ohio State University, 1982.

Voragine, Jacobus de. *The Golden Legend: Readings on the Saints.* Translated by William Granger Ryan. Princeton University Press, 2012 [1993].

Ware, R. Dean. "Medieval Chronology: Theory and Practice." In *Medieval Studies: An Introduction*, edited by James M. Powell, 252–277. Syracuse University Press, 1992.

Weller, Philip. "*Vox – littera – cantus*: Aspects of Voice and Vocality in Medieval Song." In *Music in Medieval Europe: Studies in Honour of Bryan Gillingham*, edited by Terence Bailey and Alma Santosuosso, 239–262. Ashgate, 2007.

Wenzel, Siegfried. "A New Occurrence of an English Poem from the Red Book of Ossory." *Notes and Queries* 228 (1983): 105–108.

Wilkins, Nigel, ed. *The Works of Jehan de Lescurel: Edited from the MS. Paris, B. N., f. fr. 146*. Corpus mensurabilis musicae 30. American Institute of Musicology, 1966.

Williams, Kalian. "The Magnus Liber Organi: An Annotated Bibliography." *Music Reference Services Quarterly* 11 (2008): 37–65.

Woods, Marjorie Curry. "The Teaching of Poetic Composition in the Later Middle Ages." In *A Short History of Writing Instruction: From Ancient Greece to Modern America*, edited by James J. Murphy, 123–143. Erlbaum, 2001.

Woodward, Rebekah E. "'Blinded by the Desire of Riches': Corruption, Anger and Resolution in the Two-Part Notre Dame Conductus Repertory." *Music Analysis* 38 (2019): 109–154.

Wright, Arthur R., and Thomas E. Lones. *British Calendar Customs: England*. 3 vols. Glaisher, Ltd., 1936–1940.

Wright, Craig. *The Maze and the Warrior: Symbols in Architecture, Theology, and Music*. Harvard University Press, 2001.

Music and Ceremony at Notre Dame of Paris, 500–1550. Cambridge University Press, 1989.

Wulstan, David. "Contrafaction and Centonization in the *Cantigas de Santa Maria*." *Cantigueiros: Bulletin of the Cantigueiros de Santa Maria* 10 (1998): 85–109.

The Emperor's Old Clothes: The Rhythm of Mediaeval Song. Institute of Mediaeval Music, 2001.

Wyss, Arthur, ed. *Die Limburger Chronik des Tilemann Elhen von Wolfhagen*, Monumenta Germaniae Historica 4, part 1. 1980 [1883].

Yudkin, Jeremy, ed. *The Music Treatise of Anonymous IV: A New Translation*. Musicological Studies and Documents 41. American Institute of Musicology and Hänssler-Verlag, 1985.

Zaerr, Linda Marie. *Performance and the Middle English Romance*. D. S. Brewer, 2012.

Zumthor, Paul. "On the Circularity of Song (with Reference to the Twelfth- and Thirteenth-Century *Trouvères*)." Translated by R. Carter. In *French Literary Theory Today: A Reader*, edited by Tzvetan Todorov, 179–191. Cambridge University Press and Editions de la Maison des sciences de l'homme, 1982.

"Un problème d'esthétique médiévale: l'utilisation poétique du bilinguisme." *Le Moyen Âge* 15 (1960): 301–336 and 561–594.

Index of Works

General Index